CW01096109

A HISTORY OF SPAIN

Published

Iberia in Prehistory*
María Cruz Fernández Castro

The Romans in Spain[†]
John S. Richardson

Visigothic Spain 409–711
Roger Collins

The Arab Conquest of Spain, 710–797
Roger Collins

The Contest of Christian and Muslim Spain, 1031–1157[†]
Bernard F. Reilly

Spain, 1157–1300: A Partible Inheritance
Peter Linehan

Spain's Centuries of Crisis: 1300–1474
Teofilo F. Ruiz

The Spain of the Catholic Monarchs 1474–1520
John Edwards

Spain 1516–1598: From Nation State to World Empire*
John Lynch

The Hispanic World in Crisis and Change, 1598–1700*
John Lynch

Bourbon Spain, 1700–1808*
John Lynch

Spain in the Liberal Age: From Constitution to Civil War, 1808–1939
Charles J. Esdaile

Spain: From Dictatorship to Democracy. 1939 to the Present
Javier Tusell

Forthcoming

Caliphs and Kings 798–1033
Roger Collins

* Out of print
[†] Print on demand

Spain, 1157–1300
A Partible Inheritance

Peter Linehan

A John Wiley & Sons, Ltd., Publication

This paperback edition first published 2011
© 2011 Peter Linehan

Edition history: Blackwell Publishing Ltd (hardback, 2008)

Blackwell Publishing was acquired by John Wiley & Sons in February 2007. Blackwell's
publishing program has been merged with Wiley's global Scientific, Technical, and Medical
business to form Wiley-Blackwell.

Registered Office
John Wiley & Sons Ltd, The Atrium, Southern Gate, Chichester, West Sussex, PO19 8SQ,
United Kingdom

Editorial Offices
350 Main Street, Malden, MA 02148-5020, USA
9600 Garsington Road, Oxford, OX4 2DQ, UK
The Atrium, Southern Gate, Chichester, West Sussex, PO19 8SQ, UK

For details of our global editorial offices, for customer services, and for information about how
to apply for permission to reuse the copyright material in this book please see our website at
www.wiley.com/wiley-blackwell.

The right of Peter Linehan to be identified as the author of this work has been asserted in
accordance with the UK Copyright, Designs and Patents Act 1988.

All rights reserved. No part of this publication may be reproduced, stored in a retrieval system,
or transmitted, in any form or by any means, electronic, mechanical, photocopying, recording
or otherwise, except as permitted by the UK Copyright, Designs and Patents Act 1988, without
the prior permission of the publisher.

Wiley also publishes its books in a variety of electronic formats. Some content that appears in
print may not be available in electronic books.

Designations used by companies to distinguish their products are often claimed as trademarks.
All brand names and product names used in this book are trade names, service marks,
trademarks or registered trademarks of their respective owners. The publisher is not associated
with any product or vendor mentioned in this book. This publication is designed to provide
accurate and authoritative information in regard to the subject matter covered. It is sold
on the understanding that the publisher is not engaged in rendering professional services.
If professional advice or other expert assistance is required, the services of a competent
professional should be sought.

Library of Congress Cataloging-in-Publication Data
Linehan, Peter.
    Spain, 1157–1300 : a partible inheritance / Peter Linehan.
       p. cm. — (A history of Spain)
    Includes bibliographical references and index.
    ISBN 978-0-631-17284-0 (hardcover : alk. paper) ISBN 978-1-444-33975-8
(paperback : alk. paper)   1. Spain—History—711–1516.   I. Title.
    DP99.L66 2007
    946'.02—dc22

                                                                    2007026883

A catalogue record for this book is available from the British Library.

This book is published in the following electronic formats: ePDFs [ISBN 9780470695784];
Wiley Online Library [ISBN 9780470696538]

Set in 10.5/12.5pt Minion by Graphicraft Limited, Hong Kong

1   2011

MIX
Paper from
responsible sources
FSC   FSC® C013604
www.fsc.org

To all my Spanish friends,
but to some more than others

A strange period this, in which the most brutal of realities
went together with the most mannered and delicate
literary culture! (L. P. Harvey, *Islamic Spain*, 170)

Contents

Preface

Spain between 1157 and 1300 was a large land of mostly small places. The *domus municipalis* of Bragança, a place within our area until shortly before the beginning of our period, and an example of the sort of democratic gathering place distributed along the frontier where the clergy of Sepúlveda came together to harry their bishop up hill and down dale,[1] measures just seventeen paces across from corner to corner.

As the enigmatic land of three religions whose Christian kings were neither anointed nor crowned, Spain tended to be thought of by northerners in vertical terms. But how the Greek geographer Strabo had done so was as 'an ox-hide extending in length from west to east, its fore-parts towards the east, and in breadth from north to south'.[2] And that was the basis of the description of the boundary of a property sold by Domingos Martins in 1220 as lying along 'the road that goes from Coimbra to Málaga',[3] that is, along an Atlantic to Mediterranean axis. To that extent, the peninsula continued to think of itself horizontally, in accordance with a Visigothic orientation.

But *only* to that extent. For reasons to be explained I have refrained from treating the histories of the kingdoms of Castile and Aragón either as uncoupled parts of a Visigothic whole suspended in 711 or as anticipating the union of the two thrones in 1469. That strategy, by contrast with the procedure of Castile's own thirteenth-century historians for whom all lordships other than Castile-León's were illicit and therefore to be relegated to appendices,[4] has determined the arrangement of the chapters of this

---

[1] Below, 23.
[2] *The Geography of Strabo*, 3.1.3, Loeb transl., II. 5.
[3] '. . . de strata que vadit de Colimbria ad Malaga': Lisbon, Instituto dos Arquivos Nacionais Torre do Tombo, S. Cruz de Coimbra (Antiga C. E.), docs. partic. mc. 16, no. 13.
[4] Below, 5, 163.

volume. The same goes for Navarre and al-Andalus, whose incorporation into the story presents particular problems, as do the inter-relationships of its intersecting ethnic-religious and political planes.

One problem about the Crown of Aragón, as the battle of Muret demonstrated, is that the natural affinities of part of it were not with Spain at all but, despite the failure of all previous attempts to establish a regime straddling the Pyrenees, with Languedoc. Connoisseurs of the counter-factual may wish to reflect that it was only on account of a couple of chance deaths that Catalonia remained associated with Spain at all.[5]

On the face of it there is no better reason for running the histories of thirteenth-century Aragón and Castile together than for treating thirteenth-century Aragón and France likewise. An all-Iberia treatment in this period begs various questions, the artificiality of which will be referred to at various points in what follows.[6]

A different type of problem is the partiality of the chroniclers, which I hope I have had an eye for.

These days it is probably necessary to explain that the author of this book is a Christian. If a Muslim or a Jew had written it, it might have been a different book. But so might it have been if another Christian had done so. And all three of those hypothetical volumes would have been about the same place as this one.

I had not intended to crawl all over the political and diplomatic particulars of the Spanish kingdoms between 1150 and 1300 or to revisit facts of the matter already rehearsed in my contributions to three volumes of the *New Cambridge Medieval History*. But somehow narrative kept breaking in, with the consequence that the story sometimes gets chronologically ahead of itself.

The development (I had almost written the progress) of historical studies in Spain during the forty years since the death of Franco is probably already a subject for historical study. Scanning the shelves – and the tables and the floors – of Cambridge's incomparable University Library in search of grain amongst the chaff, I observe the inexorable development (or progress) spreading fungus-like week by week. Blackwell's ration of words might have been exhausted on the bibliography alone. In an exercise such as this the

---

[5]   Below, 84.

[6]   Examples of twelfth-century battles being refought into the twentieth include the Aragonese Ubieto Arteta's accusation of 'pancatalanismo' against M. Coll i Alentorn for laying claim to Huesca and other places which had always belonged to Aragón (*Hist. de Aragón*, 184 n. 14) and the Catalan Soldevila's lament in 1962 at the 'still disastrous consequences' of Alfonso II's cession of Murcia to Castile in 1179 (*Hist. de Catalunya*, 314; below, 35).

urge for completeness – for the latest monograph, the latest opened archive, the latest article – would be fatal. The cautionary tale of Lord Acton should remind us that history can only be done by cutting corners. So all sorts of interesting aspects of the period, all sorts of subjects – Berceo, Ramon de Penyafort, space (*espacio, espace*), Ramon Lull, pilgrimage, street-smells, castles and cathedrals, Military Orders, Vidal de Canellas, 'Society' itself[7] – will be found either to have been neglected or to be missing altogether. For what is not missing – and some will think the coverage of Alfonso X disproportionate; plainly I do not – I wish to thank friends and colleagues in Spain and elsewhere for keeping me in the picture by sending me copies of their works. For that and numerous other kindnesses I am indebted to Paco Bautista, Maria João Branco, Inés Fernández-Ordóñez, Raphael Loewe, Avi Shivtiel and Juan Miguel Valero. The late John Crook, Francisco Hernández, Magnus Ryan and Teo Ruiz all read drafts of part or all of the thing. None of what is wrong with it is down to them. As well as John Lynch, successive History editors at Blackwell, for whose departure from the firm I may be partly responsible, have been heroically patient with my dilatoriness.

The society organized for war, as it has so often been described, was also a society disorganized by war. Whether it was also a society in crisis I do not say, though since societies everywhere have always been in crisis I have avoided using the word in the pages that follow.

Biblical quotations are from the King James Version. Unless otherwise indicated, all other translations are my own.

PAL
1 April 2007

---

[7] Over the previous thirty years historiographical fashions had changed, Beryl Smalley remarked in 1983. At the earlier date it had not been 'thought desirable to add "and Society" to one's title': *Study of the Bible*, vii.

Chronology

1209–47	Archbishop Rodrigo Jiménez de Rada of Toledo
1210	study of Aristotle's works on natural philosophy banned at Paris
1212	July: battle of Las Navas de Tolosa
1213	September: battle of Muret; death of Pedro II of Aragón; succession of Jaime I
1214	September: death of Alfonso VIII
1215	Fourth Lateran Council
1216–17	papal confirmation of Order of Preachers
1217	June: death of Enrique I of Castile; succession of Fernando III
1224	Castilian Great Leap Forward commences
1229	December: reconquest of Mallorca
1230	combination of León and Castile
1231	reunion of Aragón and Navarre considered
1234	Ramon de Penyafort compiles Gregorian decretals; Fernando III's imperial ambitions revealed; death of Sanç VII of Navarre; succession of Count Thibaut IV of Champagne as Teobaldo I
1236	June: reconquest of Córdoba
1238	September: reconquest of Valencia
1247	rebellion of al-Azraq
1248	August: establishment of Aigues-Mortes; November: reconquest of Seville
1250	translation of *Lapidario*
1252	May: Alfonso X succeeds Fernando III
1254	Alfonsine law-code, *Fuero real*
1255	Alfonsine law-code, *Espéculo*
1256–8	translation of *Picatrix*
1256–65	first version of *Siete Partidas*
1257	Alfonso X elected German emperor
1258	May: treaty of Corbeil
1259	February: translation of *Libro de las Cruces*
1260	summer: African crusade (capture and loss of Salé)
1262	mid-June: marriage of Infant Pedro of Aragón and Constanza of Hohenstaufen
1262–72	Alfonsine Astronomical Tables constructed
1263	July: Jewish–Christian debate at Barcelona
1264–6	Mudéjar revolt in Murcia and Andalusia
?1265–74	Alfonsine *Cántigas de Santa María*
1270	work on Alfonsine histories begins
1272–3	rebellion of Castilian nobility

1274	work on Alfonsine national history interrupted
1275	May: Gregory X rejects imperial claim of Alfonso X; death of Fernando de la Cerda
1276	July: abdication and death of Jaime I; succession of Pedro II
1276–9	intensive period of Alfonsine translations
1277	Alfonso X does to death Infante Fadrique and Simón Ruíz de los Cameros
1278	Infante Sancho co-rules with Alfonso X
1282	March: Sicilian Vespers; April: 'Cortes' of Valladolid'; rising of Infante Sancho; work on Alfonsine national history resumed
1283	October: General Privilege of Union of Aragón conceded
1284	April: death of Alfonso X; succession of Sancho IV
1285	spring: French crusade invades Corona de Aragón; November: death of Pedro III of Aragón; accession of Alfonso III
1287	January: conquest of Menorca; August: Privileges of the Union
1291	May: death of Alfonso III; Jaume II succeeds to thrones of Aragón and Sicily
1295	April: death of Sancho IV; accession of bastard child Fernando IV
1295	summer: Cortes of Valladolid; Castilian *coup d'état*
1301	legitimization of Fernando IV
1302	treaty of Caltabellotta

Abbreviations

AC	Archivo de la catedral
ACA	Archivo de la Corona de Aragón, Barcelona
AEM	*Anuario de Estudios Medievales*
AHDE	*Anuario de Historia de Derecho Español*
AHN	Archivo Histórico Nacional, Madrid
BAE	*Biblioteca de Autores Españoles*
BC	Biblioteca del Cabildo
BEC	*Bibliothèque de l'École des Chartes*
BFW	Böhmer
BHS	*Bulletin of Hispanic Studies*
Book of Deeds	Jaume I of Aragón, *Llibre dels Fets*
BRABL	*Boletín de la Real Academia de Buenas Letras de Barcelona*
BRAH	*Boletín de la Real Academia de la Historia*
CAI	*Chronica Adefonsi Imperatoris*
CAX	*Crónica de Alfonso X*
CAXI	*Crónica de Alfonso XI*
CCCM	Corpus Christianorum Continuatio Mediaevalis (Turnhout)
CFIV	*Crónica de Fernando IV*
CHE	*Cuadernos de Historia de España*
CIC	*Corpus iuris canonici*: see Friedberg
CLC	*Cortes de los antiguos reinos de León y de Castilla*
CLHM	*Cahiers de linguistique hispanique médiévale*
CLCHM	*Cahiers de linguistique et de civilisation hispaniques médiévales*
CM	Lucas of Tuy, *Chronicon mundi*
CSIV	*Crónica de Sancho IV*

CSM	*Cantigas de Santa María*
Docs.JI	*Documentos de Jaime I de Aragón*
DrH	Rodrigo of Toledo, *Historia de rebus Hispanie*
EE	Alfonso X, *Estoria de España*
EEM	*En la España medieval*
EEMCA	*Estudios de la Edad Media de la Corona de Aragón*
ES	*España Sagrada*
e-spania	http://www.e-spania.paris-sorbonne.fr
F.	Fuero
GE	Alfonso X, *General estoria*
HS	*Hispania Sacra*
JEH	*Journal of Ecclesiastical History*
Ldf	*Llibre dels fets* (orig. of *Book of Deeds*, ed. Smith & Buffery)
Lucas of Tuy	*Chronicon Mundi*
MGH, SS	Monumenta Germaniae Historica, Scriptores
MHE	*Memorial Histórico Español*
MiöG	*Mitteilungen des Instituts für österreichische Geschichtsforschung*
NCMH	*The New Cambridge Medieval History*
Part.	Alfonso X, *Siete Partidas*
PCG	*Primera Crónica General*
RABM	*Revista de Archivos, Bibliotecas y Museos*
RdLA	Rodríguez de Lama, *Alejandro IV*
RdLU	Rodríguez de Lama, *Urbano IV*
REDC	*Revista Español de Derecho Canónico*
RFE	*Revista de Filología Española*
RIS	Rerum Italicarum Scriptores
SDSCl	Domínguez Sánchez, *Clemente IV*
X	*Liber Extra*
Zurita	*Anales de la Corona de Aragón* (cit. by book and chapter)

Tree showing some of those mentioned in these pages

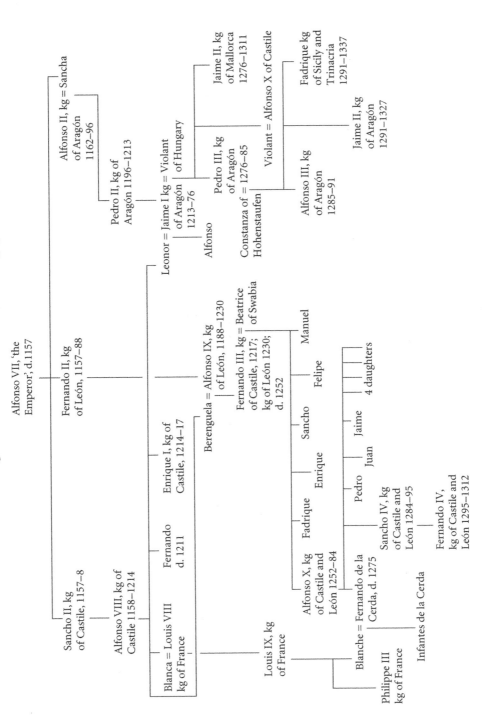

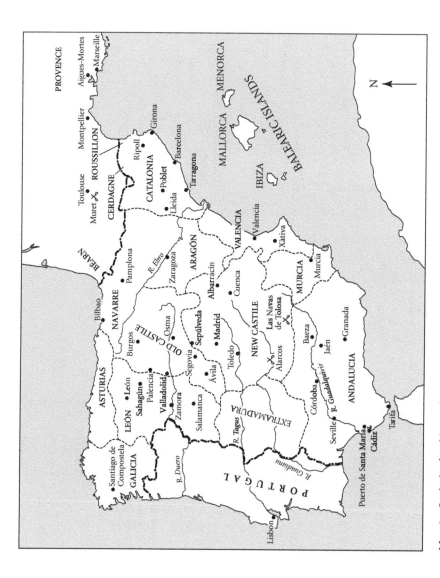

Map 1 Spain in the thirteenth century.
Source: based on J. Edwards, *The Monarchies of Ferdinand and Isabella* (Historical Association pamphlet), p. 4.

1

1157–79

Past and Present

In its description of the four major routes from France to Santiago de Compostela, the French author of the twelfth-century Pilgrim's Guide contained in the so-called *Liber Sancti Jacobi* proceeded on the *Guide Michelin* basis that a country is what it eats and drinks. Accordingly, travellers through Navarre were warned against quenching their thirst from its rivers. Rivers in Navarre were poisonous. Further west the water was safer. There, though, fish and meat were both best avoided. Bread was another matter. Estella, for example, had excellent bread, wine, meat and fish. (But since Estella was more French than Spanish, that was not to be wondered at.)

The inhabitants of the regions through which travellers were condemned to pass were also evaluated. With their alarming grunts that passed for language, those of the bosky Basque country (apples and milk tolerable; high mountains; fine views of France from the top) were barbarians. The Navarrese were worse. Like the Basques, the Navarrese would kill a Frenchman for a penny. Like the Scots (to whom they were thought to be related), they went naked below the knees. A bestial people, they lived and ate like pigs, scooping up food from the common trough. Being more prone to bestiality than to theft, when they secured their mules they padlocked their haunches together rather than attaching their legs to a gatepost. Their very name betrayed the malignity of their origins (*Navarrus: non verus*: not straight; in a word, brigands). Once out of Navarre, matters improved, but only somewhat. For the Castilians were prone to viciousness, and even in Galicia (the region of this troglodytic peninsula which most nearly approximated to polite, that was to say to French, society), even there, the inhabitants were liable to fly off the handle.[1]

---

[1] *Liber S. Jacobi*, 502–23. On the evidential value of the *Liber* and the circumstances of its composition: Hohler, 'A Note on Jacobus'; Díaz y Díaz, 58–60, 67–9.

Most of which had been said before:

> Northern Iberia, in addition to its ruggedness, not only is extremely cold, but lies next to the ocean, and thus has acquired its characteristic of inhospitality and aversion to intercourse with other countries; consequently, it is an exceedingly wretched place to live in.[2]

Observed from without, Spain was therefore an easy enough country to characterize. If Gervase of Tilbury, writing in the early years of the thirteenth century, was to be believed, what distinguished Spaniards was the tightness of their trousers (not a good sign in a land opposed to restrictions to procreation).[3] And fifty years later or thereabouts, another Englishman, the monastic chronicler Matthew Paris, voiced the opinion (which he attributed to King Henry III) that, in addition to being the scum of mankind, Spaniards were deformed in appearance, despicable as to social graces, and detestable in their moral behaviour.[4]

From the opposite point of view the wider world was characterizable too. Indeed, to the high-ranking Castilian civil servant, Diego García, the opportunity proved irresistible. In 1217 he delivered himself of a virtuoso performance on the subject. It was not people's moral behaviour that interested the chancellor of the king of Castile. In the case of the Scots, it was not even their dress. Rather than short-skirted, for Diego García Scots were, by definition, studious, just as Poles were serene, Normans amiable, Englishmen smart, Sicilians grave, Ethiopians pious, Hungarians bandits, and Irish dealers in tall stories. And so on, and so on, some of which may have borne a passing resemblance to early thirteenth-century reality, just as the author's estimation of the inhabitants of the peninsula itself may have done, of Galicians as chatty, Leonese as eloquent, rural *campesinos* as great trenchermen, Castilians as warriors, *serranos* as hard, Aragonese as constant, and Catalans as cheerful.[5]

All of which is illuminating, so far as it goes (particularly the ethnic emphasis to which we will return at the end of Chapter 8). But it does not go far enough. It does not take into account Spain's image of itself at the time of its 'loss' to the Muslim, as recorded in Alfonso X's national history in the 1270s, as a place enclosed with its inhabitants wrestling Miltonically

---

[2]   *The Geography of Strabo*, 3.1.2, Loeb transl., II. 3.
[3]   *Otia imperialia*, 299. The loose dress of Muslims was recommended by Ramon Lull on grounds of both comfort and hygiene: Hillgarth, *Spanish Kingdoms*, 168.
[4]   *Chronica Majora*, V, 450.
[5]   *Planeta*, 178.

to redeem themselves from the original sin of its last Visigothic king.[6] Nor, instructive though they are, do the Pilgrim's Guide and *Planeta* provide a substitute for the chronicle of the age which students of the history of twelfth-century León and Castile so singularly lack. For the period between 1147, when the chronicler of Alfonso VII laid down his pen, and the date in the 1220s when the author of the so-called 'Anonymous Latin Chronicle' seems to have begun work, we possess no account at all of contemporary events in the central peninsular kingdoms. Nor evidently did the thirteenth-century historians. When they reached this stage of their story they turned to epic material. Bitty and episodic annals apart, our knowledge of these years has to be pieced together from surviving documentary material, which, in a land whose central records were lost in the fourteenth century, means only that fraction of the documentation that students have had the energy to seek out in the archives of beneficiaries. Only for the 1280s and 1290s – and even then only patchily – do we possess for the kingdom of Castile fiscal records of the quantity and calibre that historians of medieval England and France take for granted.

The causes of this long spell of historiographical amnesia in the west of the peninsula, contrasting as it does so strikingly with the activity of the first half of the twelfth century, remain to be identified.[7] In Catalonia it was a different story. There, not only has the region's ample documentation been preserved in a central repository, but also, at the beginning of our period, in about 1162, monks of the monastery of Ripoll compiled the primitive version of the *Gesta comitum Barcinonensium* ('Deeds of the Counts of Barcelona'), that 'spinal column of Catalan historiography' which traced the county's independence to Count Wifred the Hairy's prowess in protecting it from the Saracen thraldom which the Carolingian ruler had proved incapable of doing. The confection of the *Gesta* was timely for more than one reason. Count Wifred (so called, the Chronicle reports, because he was 'hairy in places where hair doesn't usually grow') had died in about 897. Catalan independence was therefore a good half-century more advanced than the Castilian variety, wrested by the counts of Castile from the kings of León. Moreover, since Wifred's descendant, Count Ramon Berenguer IV of Barcelona, had inherited his mother's rights to the county of Provence, the interest in the Midi that the king of France was beginning to exhibit in 1154 may have seemed unhealthy. When he and Louis VII had met in that year, in the course of the Capetian's high-profile pilgrimage to Santiago, the count would have been aware of

---

[6]   *PCG*, c. 558 (p. 311a$_{38}$): '. . . cerrada toda en derredor: dell un cabo de los montes Pirineos que llegan fasta la mar, de la otra parte del mar Occeano, de la otra del mar Tirineo'.
[7]   Reilly, 252; Linehan, *History*, 246–7.

the other's earlier scheme to invade the peninsula. On that occasion, having made such a poor job of harrying Islam in the East during the Second Crusade, he had contemplated trying again in the West, all without so much as the by-your-leave of Spain's Christian rulers. With the 'Song of Roland' twelfth-century Europe's collective refrain, this was all too typical.[8]

To Spaniards the French were intolerable. By the account of some of them, rather than suffering defeat at Roncesvalles, Charlemagne had reconquered Spain from the Moors 'as far as Córdoba', whereupon the locals had then lost it again.[9] One of the recurrent themes of this book will be the strength of the Spanish response that such vaingloriousness elicited. As our story begins, the figure of Bernardo de Carpio, the fictitious nephew of Alfonso II of Oviedo, was beginning to develop. This was the man who saw Charlemagne off when, in the words of the so-called *Historia Silense* (probably written between 1108 and 1119), 'as is the way with the French, corrupted by gold and without a bead of sweat on him raised in saving Holy Church from the barbarians, Charlemagne went home'.[10]

To return to Catalonia. Historiography provided Catalonia with some compensation for the comparative disadvantage associated with its remoteness from the pilgrim road, for the lack of those hooligans and subversives from northern Europe who in certain circumstances might become the heroes of Christendom's southern frontier. It provided its count with the sort of ideological underpinning that the king of Castile would be seen to be seeking in the 1180s.

In the absence of such evidence as that with which their colleagues to the north are so generously provided – the writings of Walter Map and Robert of Torigni, the Pipe Rolls – historians of twelfth-century Spain have become accustomed to concentrating their attention instead on such issues as the direction in which rivers run, the topography of mountains and plains, and the shock to the system of butter-tolerant northerners at the heights of the Despeñaperros pass as they encountered the blinding light of al-Andalus and entered an olive-based economy. The contrasts were extreme; the mountainous region between Toledo and Ávila was appropriately described by the papal chancery in 1216 as 'alpine'.[11] In this connexion the reach-me-down

---

[8]   Coll i Alentorn, 187–91; *Gesta comitum Barcinonensium*, 5; Bisson, 'Essor de la Catalogne', 459–62; *Gesta comitum Barcinonensium*, 4; Miret i Sans; Linehan, *History*, 276–7.

[9]   Defourneaux, *Les Français en Espagne*, 273. As late as the 1270s the (French) Master-General of the Dominicans, Humbert de Romans, was repeating the *canard: Opusculum tripartitum*, 193, 206.

[10]   Defourneaux, *Les Français en Espagne*, 258–316.

[11]   AC Toledo, I.4.N.1.12 (Mansilla, *Honorio III*, no. 19). Similarly in 1188: Rassow, 6.

categories of modern French historical scholarship have proved useful and the experience of those Frenchmen who came to Castile in 1212 to fight for the Cross can be prayed in aid: the former for insights which have helped to liberate the subject somewhat from the costive limitations of documentary minutiae; the latter for the warriors' disappointment on being denied the booty they sought, which, combined with their capitulation to heat and diarrhoea, caused them to return home even before battle had been joined.[12]

Armies also marched on their stomachs. The author of the Pilgrim Guide had a point: if bread mattered, so did gastric fluxes. Whatever other perils it may have had in store for twelfth-century pilgrims, at least the journey westward towards Santiago was through terrain recognizable as familiar, adorned with such features as trees and grass, sheep and rivers. The rivers may have been poisonous, but at least they were wet. By contrast, such foreigners as crossed the Tagus in the years after 1212 found themselves in a desert. In those same years Castilian historians were engaged in putting the peninsular past in order and perfecting an account of it that has remained in place ever since. In the very structuring of their presentation of the period with which this volume will be concerned, Castile's thirteenth-century historians betrayed their conviction that within the Spanish peninsula Castile alone enjoyed political legitimacy. By the archiepiscopal author of the first general history of Spain since the beginning of history itself and the compilers of the earliest exercise in royal historiography alike, the kings of Navarre, Aragón and Portugal were treated as interlopers, faring even worse than the rulers of al-Andalus. Whereas both in Archbishop Rodrigo of Toledo's *De rebus Hispanie* and Alfonso X's *Estoria de España* the history of the Muslim south was integrated with that of the Castilian north, the rulers of the other Christian kingdoms were treated as peripheral figures and accorded only walk-on parts. It was only when, and only in so far as, particulars of their past were required in order to make sense of the story of the modern descendants of the paladins of Spain's Gothic period, when they made either love or war with them for example, that their very existence was so much as acknowledged.[13]

It is a version of that hierarchical arrangement that will be adopted in this attempt to convey to an English-speaking readership some sense of this multi-dimensional complex. The alternative would have been two or three (or twenty or thirty) self-standing chapters to be fitted together by the reader as best he or she might. It will be for others to judge whether

[12]   Vicens Vives, *Manual*, 143–53; Barrios García, *Estructuras agrarias*, 81–109; below, 54.
[13]   Fernández-Ordóñez, *Las* Estorias *de Alfonso el Sabio*, 23–4.

for that readership a Crown of Aragon-centred or an al-Andalus-centred, or even a Navarre-centred, approach to the history of a century and a half, during which in territorial terms the kingdoms of León and Castile, first independently and then combined, loomed largest on the peninsular scene, might have made better (as opposed to more politically correct) sense. However, there could be no justification for anything more than a version of such an arrangement. For reasons to be explained, strict adherence to it as an organizational principle would be perverse and anachronistic. In the course of the 1180s, as Catalan scribes were being instructed to refrain from dating documents by the French regnal year, the king of Castile had abandoned his Gothic credentials, by the 1230s the Castilian chronicler (and chancellor) had written the Goths out of the story, and in the 1280s the official history followed suit, drawing a line at the year 711 and crediting the recovery of the peninsula from Islam not to the descendants of that discredited clique but to subsequent generations of its indigenous inhabitants.[14]

According to the fourteenth-century statutes of the Spanish College at Bologna, the term 'Spain' was to be understood 'in the large sense of the word', as meaning 'all the kingdoms beyond the Pyrenees'. But that was not an agreed definition. Provençal troubadours tended to distinguish 'Espanha' from Aragón and to reserve the term 'espahnol' for the inhabitants of the kingdoms of Castile and León. In the *Liber provincialis* of the Roman Church the dioceses of Calahorra and Pamplona were identified as being 'on the way into Spain and Castile', in 1258 a visiting Norwegian delegation treated 'Castile' and 'Spain' as interchangeable terms, and in 1282 a German political theorist remarked that, although Spain had many kings, only one of its kingdoms was actually called 'the kingdom of the Spaniards'.[15]

That is why there is no better justification for combining the thirteenth-century histories of Aragón and Castile than for combining those of Aragón and France. Despite occasional posturing by both parties, the diplomatic record provides nothing adequate. In Martínez Ferrando's catalogue of more than two thousand documents in the Aragonese registers relating to the kingdom of Valencia, only one entry concerns Alfonso X of Castile.[16]

The refusal of the custodians of medieval Spain's historiographical tradition to admit the existence of the kingdoms which had sprung up since 711

[14]   Below, 38, 233–4; Catalán, *De Alfonso X al Conde de Barcelos*, 153; Martin, 'Contribution de Jean d'Osma'.
[15]   Marti, 132; Alvar, *La poesía trovadoresca*, 292–301; Cambridge, St John's College, MS. G.9. fo. 6ra; Guzmán y Gallo, 49–51; Alexander of Roes, *Memoriale*, 115 ('tamen unum dicitur regnum Hispanorum').
[16]   Madrid, 1934 (noted Burns, 'Warrior neighbors', 151).

has vitiated all subsequent attempts to tell the story that follows. Now more than ever of course, and of course rightly, that view of the past is rejected. Yet its influence lingers on, further complicating the task every modem historian of the period confronts as he or she embarks upon the history of a land in which a malign fate ensured that from time to time all its rulers simultaneously bore the same name. In the bemused words of one recent observer of the Iberian scene, 'the mid-1150s saw three kingdoms established in Christian Spain, with an Alfonso growing old in Castile, an Alfonso in the prime of his life in Portugal, and a small Alfonso growing up to be heir of Aragon, all dedicated to spread moderate confusion among the Muslims of their own day, and extreme confusion among historians until the end of the world'.[17]

After the Emperor

In fact, when our story begins in the mid-1150s Christian Spain was home to not three but five kingdoms. In 1134 an illegitimate member of the Navarrese royal house had resuscitated the kingdom of Navarre by having himself acclaimed king at Pamplona. Garcia Ramírez IV, 'the Emperor's dear son-in-law', had been conspicuous at the siege of Almería in 1147, the last significant feat of Christian arms for which 'the Emperor' himself, as he was forever known after his 'imperial coronation of 1135, Alfonso VII of Castile-León, had been principally responsible.[18] Although over the next century and a half Castile and Aragón would both strive to expunge it, when the emperor died in 1157 the kingdom of Navarre persisted in remaining on the peninsular map, resistant to each of its intermittently powerful neighbours and backing on to the southern extremities of the recently established Angevin Empire.

This made four, and the division of Castile-León on Alfonso VII's death in 1157 made five. Eighty years on, after the two kingdoms had been reunited, an anonymous chronicler (in all likelihood Juan de Soria, royal chancellor and bishop) ascribed the 'unhappy' division of the kingdoms to the 'sins of men'. But this was wisdom after the event. It was not the view of either of the chronicler's episcopal contemporaries, Lucas of Tuy and Rodrigo of Toledo, for both of whom the division of the kingdom was simply in accordance with customary practice. In 1157 division of the 'empire' into

---

[17]   Brooke, 319.
[18]   Reilly, 184; 'Prefatio de Almaria', ed. Gil, lines 286–8 (trans. Barton and Fletcher, 260). For the imperial coronation: Linehan, *History*, 235–7.

its constituent kingdoms had been allowed for in political calculation for almost a decade. In 1148 Alfonso VII addressed both his sons as kings, before the end of his reign the Infantes Sancho and Fernando, the future rulers of Castile and León, were both issuing royal charters in their own names, according to the troubadour Peire d'Alvernha, some of those who bewailed the emperor's death were only simulating grief. By the 1280s when the Alfonsine History was being improved, subversive sentiments such as these had been suppressed. But although that History's imaginative compilers conjured up an affecting account of the deathbed scene, replete with tales of the great and the good swooning at the prospect of the emperor's demise, and with Archbishop Jean de Castellmorum of Toledo, described as the king's inseparable companion 'both on the frontier and at home', very much to the fore, not even then was it suggested that there had been anything unnatural about León and Castile going their separate ways in 1157.[19]

Whether the division was also for the best would be for later generations to debate and determine, according to the then prevailing wisdom. To *Spanish* nationalists down the ages, for example, the separation of Castile and León between 1157 and 1230 has appeared a catastrophe because for them the principal item on the cosmic agenda has always been the annihilation of Spanish Islam. Equally imbued as they were with the confessional programme embodied in historiography ever since the ninth-century *Chronicle of Alfonso III*, to nationalist writers of the ages of Fernando III and General Franco alike, any deviation from the road to peninsular unification was by definition an 'absurd' step in the wrong direction.[20] To Castilian and Leonese nationalists of the present generation, the generation of the *autonomías*, by contrast, the question is rather whether the line that Alfonso VII drew between the two kingdoms before his death in August 1157 was drawn in the right place.

That was the question that exercised Alfonso's two sons, Sancho III of Castile and Fernando II of León, when they met at Sahagún in May 1158. According to the 'Castilian' Rodrigo of Toledo, Fernando at once offered to do homage for his kingdom, only to be rebuffed by Sancho on the grounds that it would be unbecoming for any son of so great a father to do homage to anyone. This was symptomatic of the hypersensitive obsession with hierarchy that was to characterize the dealings of all Spain's kings, their heirs and their heirs' siblings throughout this period and beyond. It was also a put-down. So too was the archbishop's report that the king of León

---

[19]   *Crón. latina*, c. 7; Lacarra, 'Lento predominio'; Escalona, 531; González, *Alfonso VIII*, I, 664–5; Reilly, 229; Alvar, *Poesía trovadoresca*, 39–40; *CM*, IV. 77; *DrH*, VII. 11; *PCG*, 662ab.
[20]   Thus González Jiménez, 'Fernando III legislador', 114.

arrived at Sahagún smelling of the farmyard, causing his elder brother to insist on his taking a bath before they sat down to dinner together. What D. Rodrigo's authority was for this story we do not know. But, unless it was his own invention, it reflected Castilian disdain of uncouth provincials such as is recited to this day by smart *madrileños*. Fernando may not have forgotten the slight when in August 1158 his fastidious brother died, leaving him master of the field. According to the Leonese Lucas of Tuy, Fernando II was all things to all men, energetic, very pious, a king everyone preferred to love than to fear, and (if that has a sinister ring to it) at least not notorious as his son Alfonso IX would be for his treatment of those who crossed him. Even so, the possibility has to be allowed for that, like his son after him, he harboured memories of the insult and that it remained with him and influenced his actions in the years to come.[21]

The agenda that Sancho and the deodorized Fernando settled down to at Sahagún in May 1158 (which Rodrigo of Toledo, incidentally, fails to mention) concerned the institutionalization of the division of their father's empire. But for one particular, the treaty of Sahagún might have exercised an influence equivalent to that of the treaty of Tudején of January 1151. Then Alfonso VII and Ramón Berenguer IV had combined to partition the kingdom of Navarre and agreed their respective zones of future reconquering activity in the south and south-east. Having sworn eternal collaboration against all-comers (other than their uncle Ramón Berenguer) and eternal enmity against the king of Portugal, at Sahagún the brothers planned the partition of the 'land of the Saracens' in the south and south-west. Portugal was to be expunged and Seville shared between them. Fernando was to have the territory towards the Atlantic as far as Lisbon; Sancho everything as far as Granada.[22] In 1158, therefore, it was already the consensus that Seville was the terrestrial meridian of Christian ambition.

The treaty of Sahagún completed the pragmatic division of the peninsula that had been initiated at Tudején. At Nájima three months earlier Sancho had surrendered the kingdom of Zaragoza to Ramón Berenguer and his successors in return for homage and Aragonese recognition of Castile's primacy of honour. The new king of Castile was perhaps contemplating a crown-wearing in the style of his father's of 1135, with the Aragonese ruler of Zaragoza in an appropriately servile ceremonial role.[23] Now, in the same rationalizing spirit, he sought to bring order to the Tierra de Campos, the untidiest stretch of the border between Castile and León. With

[21]   *DrH*, VII. 13 (cf. González, *Fernando II*, 30–1); *CM*, IV. 79; below, 39–40.
[22]   Miquel Rosell, nos. 29, 44; González, *Alfonso VIII*, I, 775–6; Reilly, 219.
[23]   Miquel Rosell, no. 36.

its pre-existing mosaic of jurisdictions and loyalties, this region was to remain a trouble spot until the end of the century and beyond. In 1158 Fernando had recently evicted the Catalan counts, Ponce de Minerva and Ponce de Cabrera, and Osorio Martínez, from areas he deemed to be part of his kingdom. By the treaty of Sahagún Sancho acknowledged his brother's claim in return for the latter's undertaking to allow the Castilians to retain their holdings within the disputed area as 'temporary fees', and in May 1158 there was no reason why this arrangement should not have held.

There was even some prospect of making headway in the 'land of the Saracens' itself. As Juan de Soria remarked in the next century, Alfonso VII had been 'fortunate in taking places, less so in keeping them'.[24] Easy come, easy go. Similar things would be said after Seville was reconquered a century later. The chronicle of Alfonso's own reign reveals why this was so. His reign had been marked by a series of spectacular sorties south and sieges successfully completed. But he was overstretched, his lines of communication were over-extended. Places quickly taken were as soon lost. Almería, whose capture in 1147 had been the toast of Europe, was recovered by the Almohads in the month of the Emperor's death.

Hence the significance of the only other event of Sancho III's reign mentioned by the chroniclers. The emperor had entrusted the Templars with custody of Calatrava, the fortress at the gateway to Andalusia that he had conquered in 1147. But ten years later, with an Almohad counter-attack believed to be imminent and the Templars unable to provide for its defence, the place was returned to Sancho III. Whereupon Raimundo, the Cistercian abbot of the Navarrese monastery of Fitero, brought a party of volunteers there from Toledo to oppose the enemy and, when the enemy did not materialize, constituted them as a religious confraternity which in 1164 was affiliated to the Cistercian order and provided with a version of the Cistercian rule dedicating them to warfare both defensive and offensive. Thus was founded the Order of Calatrava, the first of the Spanish Military Orders, to be followed in 1170 by Fernando II of León's establishment of the Order of Santiago, an order dedicated to the same purpose but differing from the other to the extent that its knights were lay-brothers and therefore allowed to marry. The two rules were approved by Pope Alexander III in 1164 and 1175 respectively. Whereas in Aragón the Templars and Hospitallers remained dominant, the kingdoms of Castile and León were now provided with indigenous military orders charged, in the words of the pope's commission to the Order of Santiago, with the task of 'fighting always against the enemies of Christ's cross for the defence of Christendom'. Here were

---

[24]   *Crón. latina*, c. 5.

professional warriors destined to supplement if not supersede the make-shift urban militias whose seasonal forays south of the Tagus had advanced the Christian reconquest since 1085.[25]

Many tasks lay ahead when (the particular that relegated the treaty of Sahagún to the footnotes of history) in August 1158 Sancho III died after a reign of a year and twelve days – on this occasion, according to Lucas of Tuy, 'not because of the people's sins' – and the chief of these was the survival of Sancho's three-year-old heir, Alfonso VIII. The 1150s saw new kings established in England, Germany and Sicily. In 1158 Louis VII of France was Christendom's senior monarch and Alfonso VIII its tyro. Indeed, for foreign chroniclers he would always be Alfonso the Small. According to Alberic of Trois Fontaines writing in the 1230s he was 'le Petit' because he had been small at the time of his accession and the name stuck, even in his glory days – though Alberic could not refrain from adding that all Alfonso's Spanish predecessors had been called small in order 'to distinguish them from the great king Charles'.[26] Like Estella, Alberic was French.

In 1158, however, Alfonso was indeed not only small, he was also hemmed in at home by experienced operators from the previous generation: by Afonso Henriques of Portugal and Fernando II of León to the west, and to the north and east by Sanç VI of Navarre and Ramón Berenguer IV, count of Barcelona, prince of Aragón and the 'bond of their friendship', as his nephews Sancho and Fernando had described him at Sahagún.[27]

Despite his Provençal preoccupations, Ramón Berenguer's mastery of affairs made him the peninsula's most effective ruler. The *Usatici* of Barcelona (Catalan *Usatges*), the regalian code issued by him and purporting to epitomize customary practices dating from the time of Ramón Berenguer I, not only vested ultimate judicial authority in the count-prince but also stated his right to the service of all men within his jurisdiction whenever necessity demanded. These claims were matched by his survey (1151–2) of peasant tenures and obligations in the county of Barcelona and the regions surrounding it, 'virtually a "Domesday" for Catalonia'.[28] True, he did not exercise such authority in Aragón, where he ruled by right of his wife Peronella, the heiress to the kingdom to whom he had been betrothed in 1137 when she was an infant. But that was not a source of weakness.

[25] Forey, 23–32; Powers, *Society*, 112–35.
[26] *CM*, IV. 78; Alberic, *Chronica*, 895; likewise, Ralph of Coggeshall, 14; Matthew Paris, *Chron. Majora*, II, 41.
[27] González, *Alfonso VIII*, no. 40.
[28] *Usatges de Barcelona*, c. 64; Soldevila, *Hist. de Catalunya*, 170–97; Bisson, *Fiscal Accounts*, I, 25; II, 3–29.

As the thirteenth-century chronicler Desclot imagined him saying as he accepted Peronella but refused the royal title: 'I am one of the greatest counts on earth and if haply I were to be called king, then I would not be amongst the greatest but rather the least of them.'[29]

When in the following century Alfonso X sought to impose a code alike in inspiration to the *Usatici* (albeit on a much larger scale) the attempt cost him his throne. As elsewhere in twelfth-century Europe, small was relatively effective. What the varying fortunes of the rulers of the 'Angevin Empire' and the self-contained Capetian kingdom demonstrated, the varying fortunes of the king-emperor of Castile and the count-prince of Catalonia amply confirmed.

Unlike the places reconquered by Alfonso VII, those reconquered by Ramón Berenguer IV remained reconquered. Moreover, the security of his successors was assured. Although at Tudején he had promised eventually to do homage to Alfonso VII for the kingdom of Valencia and the greater part of that of Murcia, by 1151 the basis of the claim to peninsular hegemony which justified the demand for such an undertaking – the claim founded on the alleged descent of the rulers of León from the kings of Visigothic Spain – had long been unsustainable. Only in the very different circumstances obtaining between 1580 and 1640 was peninsular unity in that rarefied sense achieved. Twelfth-century reality comprised a plurality of Christian kingdoms. And in Castile an alternative myth capable of accounting for it was in gestation. Already a substitute genealogy was being formulated, a genealogy which traced the ancestry of the king of Castile not to his Leonese forebears but to Nuño Rasura, the champion of tenth-century Castilian independence from León.[30] Such had been the real significance of the treaty of Tudején.

In January 1151 the principle of peninsular partition had been conceded, the principle that legitimized not only Portugal and Navarre but also the lordship of Albarracín, situated between Castile and Aragón. Calling himself 'the vassal of Holy Mary', and of no other, Pedro Ruiz de Azagra ruled over a vast area which drove a territorial wedge through the south-east right down to the Valencian coast. When the rulers of Castile and Aragón were at war, as they so frequently were, each strove for his alliance, and when they were not, he astutely allied himself with the Christian king of Navarre and the Muslim ibn Mardanīsh (King Lob, 'the Wolf-king'), the peninsula's most consistently anti-Almohad warrior throughout the 1160s, until such time as normal bad relations were resumed between his neighbours. With its

---

[29]   *Llibre del rei*, c. 3 (Critchlow, I, 18).
[30]   Catalán & de Andrés, I, liii–lv.

episcopal see attached to Castilian Toledo (and, as will be seen, constituting something of an ecclesiastical Trojan horse), the lord of Albarracín was an anomaly. But he was no less significant a political force, and the marriage in the 1260s of his descendant, Teresa Álvarez, to a scion of the Lara clan suggests that towards the end of our period the notion of peninsular formation, the corollary of that of peninsular partition, was still in its infancy. In the 1290s there was little reason for regarding the pendulum principality of Albarracín as a more transient feature of peninsular geopolitics than the kingdom of Portugal or (certainly) that of Navarre.[31]

The history of the nascent Crown of Aragón further demonstrates how far from 1492 we are in the year of Tudején. In a charter granted in August 1151 Ramon Berenguer IV described himself as 'count of Barcelona, prince of Aragón and Tarragona, marquess of Tortosa and Lleida'. And even this description begged a question, indeed the largest question of all, for it was only in his capacity as count of Barcelona that Ramon Berenguer was the Fourth. As king of Aragón, he was Ramón Berenguer the First. And despite Maravall's description of the kings of medieval Spain as rulers 'not of a kingdom but of a space', and in this case while functioning as king though entitled count, the distinction was one almost always scrupulously observed by Aragonese and Catalans alike. Thus, in 1157 a diploma of the previous century describing Ramon Berenguer I as 'count and king of Barcelona' was rejected as apocryphal on the grounds that Barcelona was 'not a royal place'.[32] For the next century and a half the divisive forces within the Corona de Aragón were more formidable than those at work between Castile and León either before or after 1230. With Jaime (Jaume) I dividing his realms between his sons and Pedro III (Pere II of Catalonia) accustomed to match a Catalan with an Aragonese on important diplomatic missions, not until 1319 was it decreed that 'whoever may be king of Aragón shall also be king of Valencia and count of Barcelona', with his year equally divided between his three realms.[33]

Of the other three lordships laid claim to by Ramón Berenguer in 1151, Tortosa and Lleida (1148, 1149) were both recent conquests from Islam, 'and came to define New Catalonia and its boundary with Aragon, while securing a vast frontier for Catalonian expansion'.[34] But not for the land-locked Aragonese whose exclusion from the consolations of crusading paralleled

[31] Zurita, II. 29, 32, 41; Ayala Martínez, *Directrices*, 219–22, 325; Doubleday, 76–7; below, 215–16.
[32] Altisent, *Diplomatari de Poblet*, I, nos. 140–1; Maravall, *Concepto*, 359, 373–4.
[33] Hillgarth, 'Problem', 3.
[34] Bisson, *Crown of Aragon*, 33.

the interruption of the regime of annual razzias into Castilian Extremadura recorded by the *Chronicle of Alfonso VII*. Although the inspiration of the *reconquista*, the secular determination to reverse a process of territorial trespass, both preceded and outlasted the religious motivation of the papal Crusade movement, by 1150 the one had come to encompass and exploit the other, with Spain happy to be regarded by Rome as a second crusading front dedicated to 'the defence of Christianity and the repression of Saracen malice'. Another generation would elapse before peninsular ideology returned the compliment. Meanwhile, as the bargains struck between the Jerusalem-bound northerners and the ruler of Portugal at the siege of Lisbon in 1147 demonstrated, crusade-mindedness did not exclude business-mindedness.[35] There was land for the taking, land meant wealth, and the possession of wealth provided this opportunity-society with its contours and its postulates. The *Poem of Almería*, recording events of the same year on the other side of the peninsula, told the same story. The reward of the Spaniards who came to the siege was 'all the gold that the Moors possess . . . a share of the silver, a share of the gold'. Contrary to the interpretation sometimes given to this passage of the *Poem*, it was these men's crimes that their bishops forgave, not their sins.[36] The generous terms of surrender enjoyed by Tortosa's defeated inhabitants – including guaranteed commercial status – a procedure hallowed by custom and justified by necessity – the granting of a third of the place to the Genoese who had been active at the siege (as they and the Pisans had been at the siege of Almería), and the Mediterranean dimension that that participation implied, combined to stoke the fires of frustration lit by exclusion from the spoils of conquest.[37]

For the ancient settlement of Tarragona, hitherto the limit of Catalan expansion down the Mediterranean coast, the year 1151 was made memorable by an attempt to evict the Norman Robert Burdet to whom in 1128 Archbishop Olleguer had 'given' the then abandoned 'capital of the churches of all of nearer Spain'. According to the chronicler Orderic Vitalis, in 1141 Burdet was seeking to have his principality declared independent of all secular authority and subject only to the papacy, just as the county of Portugal was in the process of doing. But twenty-three years later, when Burdet had served his purpose in the dialectic of peninsular reconquest and resettlement, the count-prince combined with Olleguer's successor, Bernat Torts,

[35]   Erdmann, 55 (Council of Valladolid, Jan. 1155). Cf. Fletcher, 'Reconquest and crusade', 42–3; González Jiménez, '¿Re-conquista?', 167–73; Linehan, *History*, 245–6, 264.
[36]   'Prefatio de Almaria', lines 38–63 (cf. Fletcher and Barton, 251, for this as 'a clear indication of the crusading nature of the Almería campaign').
[37]   Zurita, II. 15; Bisson, *Crown of Aragon*, 27, 32.

to dispose of him (and his formidable wife), though by the time that had been achieved, mid-April 1171, the archbishop had been murdered in his cathedral, and his killer, Burdet's son, had defected to the Moorish king of Mallorca.[38] Students of the period over time have remarked on the apparent parallel with the case of Thomas Becket, just four months earlier.[39] 'It was for the same reason', observed Zurita. Sadly, though, the parallel did not prove exact. In 1194 Catalonia went one better and Archbishop Bernat's successor but one met a similar end.[40]

While all this was coming to a head, in 1154 Pope Anastasius IV re-established the ancient ecclesiastical province of Tarraconenesis, thereby providing the count of Barcelona with a coherent ecclesiastical definition of the assemblage of territories over which he held sway – as the churches of Toledo, Compostela and Braga were for the kingdoms of Castile, León and Portugal respectively – and giving the whole complex a local habitation and a name by detaching the region south of the Pyrenees from the Narbonensis and endowing the church of Tarragona with a province of eleven sees. 'Thus the Papacy contributed in the most pronounced manner yet to the formation of the Corona de Aragón',[41] and by including the church of Pamplona, capital of Navarre, in the restored province facilitated the process of absorbing the neighbouring kingdom.

But Ramon Berenguer was not confined to the peninsular theatre of operations. His father had also been count of Provence by right of his wife Dolça, and in the same year, 1154, the magnates and free men of Béarn elected him as their lord and as tutor to the under-age Gaston V. This was one of many engagements in Languedoc and Provence, an area in which earlier counts of Barcelona had been active for as long as that county had existed. Ramon Berenguer and his successors would retain an interest in that region, the Midi and points east, as well as incurring the wrath of successive counts of Toulouse throughout the following century. Although lack of space precludes investigation of the history of the area and its dynastic ramifications, one consequence of the continuing connexion with Provence must be mentioned, namely the access it provided to the burgeoning school

[38]   Villanueva, XIX, 212–14, 280–83; Defourneaux, *Les Français en Espagne*, 224–30; Fried, 99–101 (sceptical).

[39]   Zurita, II. 31.

[40]   The victim was Archbishop Berenguer de Vilademuls and the perpetrator his niece's husband, Guillem Ramon I de Montcada. Though this incident had no connexion with the foregoing, being more of a family affair, it had the consequence of keeping successive archbishops of Tarragona on the qui vive: Villanueva, XIX, 163–71, 304–8; Shideler, *Montcadas*, 124–7.

[41]   Kehr, *Papsturkunden*, no. 65; idem, *Papsttum*, 50.

of Roman Law at Montpellier, and beyond that with Italy. Both in Catalonia and further west, civilian jurists had been influencing the language of government since the 1120s, with the formula 'What pleases the most excellent majesty of the lord emperor' being employed by the draftsmen of the Treaty of Tudején in 1151 and 'What pleases the prince has the force of law' occurring in the *Usatici* thereafter. Thirty years on, civilian arguments would be employed against the men of Vic's attempt to challenge the temporal lordship of their bishop. It was with Vic that the family of Pere de Cardona – teacher at Montpellier, chancellor to the king of Castile, archbishop of Toledo, and cardinal – was associated.[42]

Although the implications for government of Roman law notions were not unidirectional, in combination with the exertions of the bureaucrats responsible for laying the fiscal foundations of government they could be made to serve the dynasty's purposes. So too could the manipulation both of custom – as practised by the codifiers of the *Usatici* in persuading the political heavyweights of the 1150s that their predecessors had accepted the compilation almost a century before, making it appear 'less a legal text than a work of comital propaganda' – and of the dynasty's own past, in which the monks of Ripoll were currently creatively engaged, and in whose house Ramon Berenguer IV was buried in 1162. In 1131 Berenguer Ramon I de Montcada had reportedly told the count-king's father that 'for all I hold from you I would not thank you with a single fart'. It was a measure of the transformation in the relationship between the count-kings and their principal barons that by the mid-1220s the great-great-grandson of the one (Guillem de Montcada III) conceded to the great-grandson of the other (Jaime I) that 'your line has made ours what it is' – or so the latter claimed.[43]

A crucial part in that process was played by Guillem Ramon II, the Great Seneschal. Already a considerable force in the land during the lifetime of Ramon Berenguer IV, when the count encouraged his wife, the Montcada heiress, to separate from him the Seneschal had retaliated by cutting off Barcelona's water-supply. During the minority of Alfonso II (Alfonso I of Catalonia), who succeeded his father at the age of five or thereabouts, he achieved a role in public affairs secure enough for his family to survive the consequences of the actions of his tumultuous and then murderous

---

[42]   Reilly, 48–9; Bisson, *Crown of Aragon*, 33ff; Linehan, *History*, 270–1, 305–8; Miquel Rosell, *Liber Feudorum Maior*, no. 29; *Usatges de Barcelona*, c. 65; Kagay, 19–21; Freedman, *Diocese of Vic*, 84–7; idem, 'Another look', 180.

[43]   Below, 38; Gouron, 277–9; Bensch, 80–2; Bonnassie, 711–28; Kagay, 51–7; Kosto, 278–9; Shideler, *Montcadas*, 38 n. 128, 155–6; *Book of Deeds*, c. 33.

descendants. Alfonso II's early years are shrouded in mystery, with his Aragonese mother calling him by the Aragonese name Alfonso and his Catalan father referring to him in his will as another Catalan 'Ramon', and, as Reilly has suggested, much of the relevant documentation is either suspect or spurious.[44]

Had Castile itself not been in disarray in 1162, no doubt it would have seized the initiative not taken in 1137 when it failed to wed the infanta Peronella to the future Sancho III. As it was, at Agreda in the September of that year Fernando II of León, attended by the archbishop of Toledo and sundry other Castilian prelates, and calling himself 'king of the Spains' and 'king of the Spaniards' (*Ispaniarum rex*; *rex Hispanorum*), occupied the void by having the boy-king betrothed to his sister, Sancha of Castile, and declaring himself 'tutor' of the lad's 'body and honour' as well as defender of his interests against all-comers, 'particularly the king of Navarre'.[45] But that said, and despite the diplomatic pleasantries exchanged at Agreda by the child and the effective ruler of both León and Castile, it is reasonable to suppose that all manner of opposing forces were raging, Aragonese against the Catalans, Catalans against the Aragonese, and both against the Leonese. Since it was part of the king of León's strategy to trump a matrimonial proposal involving the ruler of Aragón and the Infanta Mafalda of Portugal, entered into when the happy couple were months rather than years old (and itself a response to the Castilian–Leonese intention declared at Sahagún to ostracize Portugal's ruler Afonso Henriques),[46] all five of the peninsular kingdoms may be said to have been striving for advantage, or at least involved, in the aftermath of the death of Ramón Berenguer IV. In short, it was a proper family funeral.

In the event, in his will the dead count was found to have declared Henry II of England the boy's guardian – or at least that was what his will was made to say. This was doubtless designed to keep papal influence at bay and forestall the raising of awkward questions regarding the monastic vows and episcopal status of Alfonso's maternal grandfather. Later the count of Provence (yet another Ramon Berenguer) became involved. He and Henry were both more or less distant threats; 'a smokescreen', Ubieto calls the former of them. Until 1174 when Alfonso came of age and married Sancha of Castile, the real ruler of Aragón-Catalonia was the Great Seneschal. Acting in concert with his co-regent and fellow Catalan, Guillem de Torroja, bishop of Barcelona, Guillem Ramon demonstrated all the dedication that in the

[44] Reilly, 226.
[45] Villanueva, XVII, 326–8.
[46] Ubieto Arteta, 'Un frustrado matrimonio'.

next century the Lara clan was to display on behalf of the Castilian Infantes de la Cerda.[47]

We shall leave the young king of Aragón here, but not before remarking that, although his alliance with Sancha of Castile hardly confirms the trend, in matrimonial terms Spain was looking outwards. Sancha, for example, was the daughter of Alfonso VII's second wife Rica, daughter of the Piast prince Wladyslaw of Poland. And for some that remained an achievement. For one or other of them the marriage, in the same year as the Alfonso–Sancha alliance, of Dolça, the king of Aragón's sister, to the future Sancho I of Portugal, may have turned out to be something to be thankful for. For centuries Spanish kings had married within the peninsula, and for reasons of policy *pro pace* marriages with neighbouring and closely related ladies would continue to be arranged. But as the twelfth century advanced a change of attitude becomes apparent. Already in 1145–6 Afonso Henriques of Portugal had looked to Savoy for a consort. Part of the reason for this new departure was an enhanced awareness of the possible consequences of marrying within the forbidden degrees and of breaching the canonical rules that made valid marriages a virtual impossibility for prince and peasant alike. A 'sin very great before the Lord' was how the Chronicler of Alfonso VII described the process of extracting Ramiro the Monk from the cloister in 1135 and having him couple with Agnes of Poitou for dynastic purposes, rather than out of any stirring of the flesh.[48] Stricter observance of the rules, something which for the Castilian chronicler Juan de Soria in the 1230s amounted almost to an obsession, came to be seen to serve dynasties well, but only by marrying outside the clan. And in both fiction and fact marriage outside the clan meant marriage outside the peninsula. While in the story of the origins of Catalan independence the woman whom Wifred the Hairy seduces and then marries is a daughter of the count of Flanders, real-life kings of Aragón begin to seek matrimonial alliances in Byzantium and Jerusalem and other peninsular royal houses.[49]

Many of these developments, material as well as spiritual, were associated with the Cistercian Order. In addition to providing the Order of Calatrava with personnel, the White Monks played a crucial role in the process of peninsular colonization. By infilling the hinterland in Galicia they made themselves 'a social force of the first order'. In Catalonia likewise their strategies of piety materially assisted the settlement of the area behind

---

[47] Idem, *Hist. de Aragón*, 196; Soldevila, *Hist. de Catalunya*, 199, 201 n. 10; Villanueva, XVII, 190–7; Shideler, *Montcadas*, 87–113; below, 175ff.

[48] *CAI*, I. 62.

[49] Vajay, 737, 740–1; Linehan, *History*, 252, 254; *Gesta comitum Barcinonensium*, 4–5; Aurell, 427–66.

the front line. While Robert Burdet and his like were being eradicated from Tarragona, monastic Frenchmen were making an indispensable contribution on the frontier of New Catalonia. Under the aegis of Ramon Berenguer IV Poblet was established in 1153 with thirteen monks from Fontfroide near Narbonne. Three years earlier Santes Creus, mausoleum of the Montcada family, had been founded.[50] Alfonso's choice of burial place, not with his father at Ripoll, the spiritual centre of Old Catalonia for two centuries or more, but at Poblet, registered the shift. In 1176 he indicated the possibility of further displacement – to Poblet's dependency of 'Cepolla' (now Puig de Santa Maria) in the kingdom of Valencia, 'should I be able to capture Valencia'.[51] In 1213 his son, Pedro II, would be laid to rest at Sigena, his Castilian mother's establishment and the third burial place in as many generations of a dynasty whose unfinished territorial agenda denied it the luxury of a permanent ceremonial capital.

It was the function of the land-hungry grandees of Aragón and Old Catalonia to urge the priority of that agenda and to hanker after the good old reconquering days of Alfonso the Battler. The impostor claiming to be that very king who appeared on the scene more than thirty years after his death at the battle of Fraga may be regarded as the incarnation of such sentiments. The late 1170s seem to have been rather a good time for pretenders: a pseudo-Sancho III of Castile is recorded, and also remembered as meeting a sticky end. For the Aragonese recidivists, Alfonso's involvement in Provence and the conflict with the counts of Toulouse unleashed after the death of his cousin the count in 1166 offered little prospect of enrichment through booty or a safety valve for the dispersal of the forces accumulating in peninsular society. The destructive effects of such pressure were everywhere apparent. The troubadour Bertran de Born dismissed Alfonso as of poor stock, mud from a muddy spring, while in the vitriolic verses of Giraut del Luc he was a 'false king' who, as well as disposing of the impostor, was credited *inter alia* with impregnating three nuns of Vallbona during the hours of compline and nones. (The epithet 'the Chaste' which came to be attached to him arose from a fourteenth-century chronicler's 'piquant' confusion with the ninth-century king of Oviedo of the same name and number.)[52]

---

[50]   Ibid., 261; Santacana Tort, 301–70; Altisent, *Hist. de Poblet*, 25–34, 51–99; Udina Martorell, *El 'Llibre Blanch' de Santes Creus*, no. 49 (Dec. 1150); Carreras i Casanovas, I, 15–251; McCrank, items V–VIII.

[51]   Altisent, *Diplomatari de Poblet*, no. 549; Guichard, 398. The claim that because his father's choice had been made *in extremis* Ripoll deserved compensation, though accepted by Alfonso's son after his death (Pujol y Tubau, 88), must therefore be rejected.

[52]   Defourneaux, 'Louis VII', 658–9; Ubieto Arteta, 'Aparición', 36–7; *Crónica latina*, c. 4; Riquer, *Trovadores*, 711 ('vengutz de paubra generacion'); idem, 'El trovador Giraut del Luc', 214; Ventura, *Alfons 'el Cast'*, 145–6, 150.

On another level, the monastic community of Sant Cugat del Vallès suffered persistent persecution at the hands of Guillem II de Montcada, son of the Great Seneschal, with his myrmidons threatening amputation of limbs and eye-gouging, smashing the place up, and demanding hospitality for as many as seventy of them – though it should be remembered that this account gives the monks' side of the story and that bishops if not monks were perfectly capable of replying in kind, amputation and the gouging of Christian eyes by Saracen hands being included in the repertoire of sanctions used by the bishop of Vic for the discouragement of sacrilege and the enforcement of law and order in his episcopal city. Even the king acknowledged that.[53]

One of the Sant Cugat incidents concerned a fish. The fish in question had been intended by the bailiff of Sant Cugat as a Christmas gift for the abbot and monks but had been seized by one of the ruffians. In the resulting mayhem widespread damage was done and seven hams stolen.[54] Another fishy story, from the other side of the peninsula, concerned an altercation that occurred in the city of Zamora in the first year of the reign of Alfonso VIII. A fisherman, whose name history does not record, was on the point of selling to a shoemaker of his acquaintance a trout just taken from the Duero when he was put upon by a servant of the *regidor* who claimed the treat for his master. As is the way on such occasions, voices were raised and, as was to be expected in a Leonese city in which there was not much else going on, a crowd gathered, and sides were taken. One thing led to another. The *regidor*'s man summoned reinforcements, and took them to the church of Santa María to consider his next move. The shoemaker's friends set light to the church. That is the first point of the story: the wholesale carnage. Amongst the many casualties was the eldest son of Count Ponce de Cabrera, a Catalan who had made a career for himself in León after coming there in 1127 in the entourage of Berenguela of Barcelona, the bride of Alfonso VII.

That the story had lost nothing in the telling by the time it took the form in which it has survived, the aftermath confirms. The arsonists, so the story goes, decamped in the direction of the Portuguese frontier, halting *en route* only in order to communicate with Fernando II and demand that he dismiss the count. Otherwise they would cross into Portugal. The king dismissed the count. That is the second point. The human presence,

---

[53] Benito i Monclús, 879, 883; Bisson, *Tormented Voices*; Shideler, 'Les tactiques politiques', 338. In 1222 Jaime I would recognize that except with the bishop's permission he 'neither could nor should' establish exchange facilities at Vic: *Docs.JI*, no. 35.
[54] Benito i Monclús, 881.

such as it was, had to be maintained. In the late 1150s respect for the remnants of the Catalan grandees brought in in the previous generation took second place to the continuing need to conserve human stock at a lower level. As between the claims of such horizontal alliances and those of the lowlier sort, the lowlier sort would always prevail, because it was they who would be needed when the time came for vertical activity, when the time came to take the battle to the enemy, and because meanwhile they had the task of keeping the enemy out.[55]

Of course, keeping the enemy out had been the Christian rulers' priority ever since it had ceased to be their policy to keep the enemy *in*, in order to milk it dry. The balance had shifted in 1085 when Alfonso VI had occupied or (as he thought of it) *re*occupied Toledo and the Christian north's informal empire over the petty kingdoms of al-Andalus had been brought to an end. After 1150 the demographic imperative remained the priority.

While most if not all of the towns established along the pilgrim road to Compostela were mercantile in character, those beyond the Duero ('Extremadura') and further south beyond the mountain range of the *cordillera central* ('Transierra') were principally military. Toledo on the Tagus marked the southernmost extent of an area stretching from the Atlantic to the Mediterranean, from Lisbon to Tortosa, an area dominated by fighting families organized by national groupings occupying strategically situated walled cities to each of which was attached an area of open land running down to the Tagus. The example of Ávila, with its massive fortified cathedral, or Zamora where churches provided sections of the city wall itself, demonstrated the ability of these groupings to retain their own identity while collaborating in the common task. The Arab geographer al-Idrīsī describes the city of Segovia as a cluster of small villages. Around such places live-stock was kept, to be moved inside at the approach of the enemy. At such times the countryside was evacuated, obliging the raiders from the south either to remain for only a single day or to bring all necessary provisions with them. The effective limit of the Christian reconquest at any time was determined by the furthest point south at which sheep might safely graze. The clearest indication of the confidence of the abbot of Fitero and his friends when they assumed responsibility for Calatrava in 1158 was that they took twenty thousand sheep with them. There could be no question of agriculture: standing crops were a standing invitation to enemy arsonists. Animals can

---

[55]   Fernández-Xesta y Vázquez, 261–83; Barton, 'Two Catalan magnates', 256–7; idem, *Aristocracy*, 284–5.

be moved, vines not. Eternal vigilance was the rule. When fire broke out at Plasencia the citizens' first duty was to secure the city walls.[56]

Those who undertook the task of manning Christendom's southern frontier might be prompted to do so by spiritual inducements such as those offered by the archbishop of Toledo, Jean de Castellmorum, to the saviours of Calatrava in 1157. But it is evident from accounts of the sieges of Lisbon and Almería ten years earlier that spiritual inducements alone were not sufficient to satisfy the appetites of that 'unstable fringe of society', as it has been described, made up of younger sons whom society north of the Pyrenees could no longer accommodate.[57] When, around 1200, the vernacular name of the eventual beneficiaries of the process emerged, that name was *ricos homes*.

Whether they originated in high society, such as the princes of Burgundy who created the kingdom of Portugal, or belonged to its lower reaches, these *ricos homes* were as exclusive as they were acquisitive. A point particularly insisted upon in the revealing little chronicle written up in the mid-1250s concerning the exploits of a group of them based at Ávila was that they were warriors who had no truck with lesser breeds. This was understandable inasmuch as many of them were the descendants of lesser breeds themselves, of the likes of the lawless desperadoes who had been encouraged to come from afar by terms such as those of the *fuero* which Alfonso VI had granted to Sepúlveda in 1076, a code subsequently adopted as far as afield as Morella in Aragón (1233) and Segura de León to the south of Badajoz (1274). Sepúlveda provided immunity for all-comers. Once across the Duero, even murderers were guaranteed refuge: 'if any man of Sepúlveda kill another of Castile and flee as far as the Duero, let no man pursue him'. These were the blood-brothers of the Zamora shoemaker whom the king of León was unwilling to let go. For the time being, as well as defending their cities, their role was to engage in offensive warfare as *caballeros villanos*, members of the non-noble municipal militia. In their pursuit of that activity they regularly travelled prodigious distances, striking deep into Muslim territory.[58]

Such was their role. But it was not the limit of their quest. The torching of the Zamora church by the shoemaker's friends was not an isolated

---

[56]   Gautier Dalché, *Hist. urbana*, 74; Reilly, 64–7; Barrios García, *Estructuras agrarias*; Portela, 94–115; Powers, *Society*, 93–205; García de Cortázar, 55–121; *CAI*, II. 47, 84; *DrH*, VII. 14; Lourie, 59; Linehan, *History*, 262–7.

[57]   *DrH*, VII. 14; Duby, 'Les "jeunes" ', 221.

[58]   *Crón. de Ávila*, 23; Sáez, 46, 190, 200; *CAI*, II. 2, 18; Blöcker-Walter, 151; Linehan, 'Spain', 494–5; Powers, *Society*, 1.

incident. In 1166 the pope was informed of the incineration of some three hundred of the faithful who had taken refuge in the church of San Nicolas at Medina (Salamanca). Nor did the cloth provide immunity. Five or six years later the same pope received news from the same diocese concerning the death of a priest at Candavera whose eyes had been plucked out and genitals torn off by assailants who had previously secured papal absolution by claiming that their victim had been living in sin with a female relative. Such scrupulousness for the letter of canon law was strikingly at variance with reality, not least at Sepúlveda itself where, in very much the same spirit of self-help as the townsmen of Vic were currently demonstrating, so aggrieved were the local clergy by Bishop Giraldo of Segovia's attempt in the early 1200s to deprive them of their concubines that they met, mutinied, and solemnly bound themselves to take their case to Rome.[59]

A society in which a Christian ruler could be commended by one of his bishops for securing peace and justice by dropping his enemies from towers, and drowning, burning, cooking and skinning them alive, as well as by lavishing gifts upon monasteries, was a society of sharp contrasts, contrasts which were not defined by the division of Christian and Muslim. Nor was such savagery distinctively Spanish. While the bishop of Tuy was describing Alfonso IX of León in these terms – and Alfonso was not the only king who cooked people; in the same good cause so did his son the sanctified Fernando III, in pots[60] – in Portugal the bishop of Porto and celebrated canon lawyer, Pedro Salvadores, was being reported for selling Christian women and children 'as though they were Saracens.'[61] Nor indeed was there anything crudely racial, and even less crudely partisan, about such negotiations. The noblemen 'de Ispania' delated to the pope in 1223 for pledging their womenfolk into Muslim servitude as security for Muslim loans were Christian noblemen of the diocese of Zaragoza, a diocese which had been 'liberated' from the Muslim yoke more than a century before.

[59]   Martín Martín, *Documentos de Salamanca*, nos. 39, 51; Pastor de Togneri, 143–4; Linehan, 'Segovia'; Villar García, no. 245; Freedman, 'Another look', 180–1.

[60]   *CM*, IV. 86; 'some he threw from towers, some he drowned in the sea, some he hanged, others he burned to death, or cooked in pots, or had skinned alive, and by means of various sorts of torture ensured that the kingdom remained in peace and justice' (Fernando III at Toledo, 1225): *Anales Toledanos II*, 408. According to the *Crónica de Ávila*, 20, Alfonso 'the Battler' of Aragón (d. 1134) had also cooked people. The fact that the place in which he did so was renamed 'Fervençia' (the name for the process of cooking criminals in pots) may imply that such occasions were memorably rare.

[61]   Costa, *Mestre Silvestre*, 382. For the bishop's scholarly contributions and the allegation that while at Bologna he had struck a cleric: Pereira, 'O canonista Petrus Hispanus'; Linehan, 'Juan de Soria', 386.

Lucas of Tuy would report similar *pro pace* practices from the reign of Mauregato in the 780s.[62]

The prevalence of practices reminiscent of those of Christian Spain's lowest eighth-century ebb was an aspect of *convivencia* for which any account of the triumphant decades which followed the victory of Las Navas de Tolosa has to make due allowance. Now that papal decretals had so fiercely embargoed the provision of military material,[63] the Christian north's principal export to al-Andalus since the 1020s, other commodities not hitherto specified as forbidden had to be exploited.

To successive popes, reports such as those coming out of Zaragoza were of course incomprehensible. Popes had their own mind-set, one which bore striking resemblance to the idealized impression of the peninsular past preserved in amber in the Gothic myth, one in which a handful of Christians, Sarah's descendants, eventually decontaminated the land of the pollution of Hagar's menstruating spawn.[64] However, the sad truth (sad for the pope, that is) was that to the extent that the Spanish *reconquista* was part of the crusading movement, it was part of it on terms set by Spain's kings. And those terms were not negotiable.

Two Royal Minorities

Whether any of these considerations weighed much with those in whose hands control of Castilian fortunes came to rest at the outset of the reign of Alfonso VIII, we can only surmise. But that they weighed not at all with Alfonso VIII himself we can be sure. For in August 1158 the new king was not yet three years old, and between then and the mid-1160s the only question that mattered was that of who had possession of him. Yet that fact alone suggests that descent counted for much and that the principle of hereditary legitimacy counted for everything. It was of no consequence that Alfonso was never smeared with holy oil as the kings of France were smeared. His unsacral status was not lost on the Catalan troubadour Ramon Vidal de Besalú, who belonged to another tradition, when he remembered a visit he had made to the Castilian court shortly before Alfonso's death. Together with his English queen, Alfonso had been in his pomp. In his

---

[62] Canellas López, no. 918; *CM*, IV. 12.
[63] X 5. 6. 6, 12.
[64] Thus Clement IV in March 1265: *Reg. Clem. IV*, no. 15 (SDSCl, no. 5). Papal correspondence with Spain's kings was full of such language: Southern, *Western Views of Islam*, 16–19; Catlos, 282.

'fabliau' *Castia-gilos* the poet sang the king's praises for his generosity and valour, his courtesy and chivalry, despite the fact that he was 'neither anointed nor consecrated'. He was 'crowned by merit', the poet insisted, 'and by sentiment, loyalty, valour and power'. Sentiment, loyalty, valour and power, not smearing, were the qualities and attributes that by the end of his long reign had raised Alfonso VIII to the summit of the hierarchy of Europe's monarchs.[65]

But at its beginning the relaxation of royal authority which was the usual consequence of a royal minority had the effect of polarizing the political community and reopening fissures within it that the emperor had contrived to clamp shut. The fault lines were defined by ancient enmities of the principal families and clans whose hostilities were at least as venerable as any king's claim to the kingdom. There was 'greater disruption in Castile than there had been in many years', Bishop Juan of Osma observed seventy years on, while his contemporary Rodrigo of Toledo identified the 'cause of this sedition' as the instruction Sancho III gave to his magnates on his deathbed ('mandavit omnibus') that all that they held from him they should surrender to his successor when he reached his fifteenth birthday, that is to say in November 1169.[66] Students of English history may here be reminded of Henry I's dealings with his barons twenty-three years earlier in an equally problematic situation.[67] Different in many particulars though the circumstances of that event were, and ignorant as we are of the precise nature of the order given, the dying king's directive determined the course of events over the following twelve years, a period dominated by two grim realities: one the deeply embedded rivalries of the competing clans and their anxiety to realize their temporary advantage while the going was good; the other the king of León.

According to D. Rodrigo, with his last gasp Sancho III appointed Gutierre Fernández de Castro the toddler's tutor.[68] From this point on, the chronicle evidence and the documentary record, such as it is, rarely converge.[69] The course of events during the royal minority is obscure. When not merely sparse, the testimony of the chroniclers of the next century is demonstrably

---

[65] Appel, 27, lines 9–12. Cf. Menéndez Pidal, *Poesía juglaresca*, 121–2; Riquer, *Hist. de la literatura catalana*, 116–19.
[66] *DrH*, VII. 15, describing these as holdings 'pheudo temporali', a technical flourish onto which scholars who attach importance to the question of twelfth-century Castile's feudal condition have eagerly seized. The author of the Latin Chronicle reports the dying king's wish without this gloss (ed. pp. 41–2).
[67] Garnett, 201–13.
[68] *DrH*, VII. 15.
[69] Such as it is, it is summarized by González, *Alfonso VIII*, I, 150–74.

wrong. It was certainly not the case, for example, as the archbishop of Toledo twice reports, that Toledo was under Leonese control for as much as twelve years.[70] The fact that D. Rodrigo was so grossly misinformed about a matter so close to home should serve to raise questions about the credibility not only of his account but also of all those which depended on it thereafter, namely the Alfonsine History and its derivatives, regarding all twelfth-century particulars. Another odd feature about his chronicle is its failure to mention the condition of his predecessor, Archbishop Cerebrun of Toledo (1166–80), as godfather to the young king.[71] The extent of the obligations acquired by the *padrinus* at the baptismal font, analogous to those created by the ceremony of dubbing to knighthood, were far-reaching.[72]

In the late 1150s meanwhile it appears that, alongside and regardless of the appointment of Gutierre Fernández de Castro as tutor, Manrique Pérez de Lara assumed the regency. This set the scene for what followed. The enmity of the Castros and the Laras dated from the early years of the century.[73] Unaccountably, and before the year was out, Gutierre Fernández was prevailed upon to surrender the tutorship to García Garcés de Aza, a creature of the Laras. By March 1160 violence involving the two clans had erupted, and the Castros were engaged in conversations with Fernando II of León. In August 1162 Toledo was in Leonese hands with Fernando Rodríguez de Castro installed as governor – symbolically a highly significant turn of events – and the king of León had established a *de facto* tutorship over the young Alfonso just as he was to attempt to do in the following month over the also tender-aged ruler of Aragón.[74] Contrary to the report of Lucas of Tuy, however, Fernando II was unable to exercise control over all of Alfonso VII's empire. Nor did he retain the young king in his entourage, entrusting him instead to Manrique Pérez de Lara. Since he might well have done both things, there is no reason for supposing that he wished to do either. Far into Castile though his influence extended, as near to the confines of Aragón as Osma and Soria indeed, his practical ambitions seem to have been limited to a strategy of dynastic expansion, principally

---

DrH, VII. 16, 18.

[71]   The relationship is stated in a Sigüenza charter of Oct. 1166: Minguella y Arnedo, 1, 423. Cerebrun, a native of Poitiers, had been archdeacon of Toledo since at least 1139: Rivera, 199; Hernández, *Cartularios*, index.

[72]   Linehan, 'Alfonso XI', 130–2.

[73]   Doubleday, 22. The careers of many of the individuals mentioned in the following pages are traceable in Barton, *Aristocracy*, 225–302.

[74]   Documents of the Leonese chancery from 1162–3 refer to Alfonso as under his uncle's tutelage: González, *Fernando II*, 373–4; idem, *Alfonso VIII*, I, 162. Lucas of Tuy (*CM*, IV. 79) describes him as being in Fernando's care ('nutrierat').

by marrying his sister, doña Sancha, to the king of Aragón (September 1162). His involvement in the long-running dispute between the churches of Osma and Sigüenza, into which he allowed himself to be drawn, he soon repented of, to the extent of seeking to bribe the king of France with dogs and hawks to get him off the papal hook.[75] Then, in 1163 if the story is to be believed, his nephew gave him the slip.

The story is one of the minor cameos of Spanish history. In Rodrigo of Toledo's description it runs as follows. Sometime in the summer of 1163 Fernando II had Manrique Pérez de Lara bring Alfonso to him at Soria to exact what (again according to D. Rodrigo) Sancho III had refused to accept from Fernando himself five years before. The king of Castile was to do homage to him and become his vassal. Courtesy of the *concejo* of Soria, however, to whose safekeeping the boy-king had been entrusted, none of this happened. The king of León was foiled because his nephew was hungry. He wanted his supper and began to cry, was removed from the scene in the arms of Pedro Núñez de Fuente Armejil, and spirited out of Soria wrapped in the cloak of that 'brave and faithful knight', and then moved to safety by Manrique de Lara's brother, Count Nuño.[76]

On the face of it, both in general and as to particulars, the story as related by the archbishop may appear far-fetched, not least in respect of the supposed role of the *concejo* and the reportedly infantile behaviour of the now eight-year-old Alfonso. Yet the incident was to establish itself as a landmark in the popular memory: in an enquiry of 1215 concerning disputed jurisdiction two witnesses calculated their ages by reference to it. On the subject of vassalage contemporary records are wholly silent and the Latin Chronicle reports far less specifically that the ruler of León 'wanted to have control of the boy and care of the kingdom', an ambition frustrated 'by trickery (albeit laudable) as well as force'.[77] So the archbishop's story may have had more to do with the time in which he wrote it than with that in which it was set. Castile had survived its moment of peril. In describing the events of the 1160s in the 1240s perhaps the archbishop had in mind the 1180s, the decade in which the tables were turned and, to his eternal infamy as it proved, Fernando's son and successor submitted to the ruler of Castile.[78]

---

[75] Linehan, 'Royal influence', 37.

[76] *DrH*, VII. 17, whence *PCG*, c. 989.

[77] Fernández-Catón, *CD Catedral de León*, VI, no. 1849 (pp. 278, 279); González, *Alfonso VIII*, I, 160–6; *Crón. latina*, c. 9

[78] Uncle and nephew were indeed both at Soria in September 1163: González, *Fernando II*, 376; Doubleday, 36–7.

All of which left Castile's reputation intact, but Manrique de Lara exposed to the wrath of Fernando II. The count had first delivered the king to his wicked uncle and had then lost him. According to the archbishop, it was on the latter account that he was arraigned before the Leonese court on charges of faithlessness and perjury, charges to which he replied: 'Whether I am faithful or am a traitor and perfidious I know not, but since I am a native of his domain ("eius dominii naturalis") I have preserved my tender lord from undue servitude by whatever means I could.' Whereupon the count was acquitted 'by unanimous judgement'.[79]

A likely story and an implausible conclusion to a bald and generally unconvincing narrative. Although the archbishop may have had reasons of his own for wishing to represent D. Manrique as a model of Castilian rectitude and the Leonese as a nation of rumour-mongers and bearers of tittle-tattle,[80] again the invocation of bonds of *naturaleza* is the currency of the 1240s or later, not the 1160s. Comparison of his extended account of the episode with the two-line account in Lucas of Tuy with its conclusion, 'Then King Fernando reigned in all the empire of his father, whence he was called king of the Spains', provides a further example of the former's aristocratic, by contrast with Lucas's monarchical, interpretation of the Spanish past.[81] But despite the endorsement the expression of D. Manrique's sentiments reportedly received in León, when in 1166 an opportunity for employing such vocabulary arose in Castile itself, as will be seen it was not used.

On the death of Sancho III, followed in February 1159 by that of his aunt Sancha, the Infantazgo de Campos between Castile and León had been transformed from a buffer state into a war zone. Despite the combined interest of the Laras and Bishop Ramón II of Palencia, Alfonso VIII's Catalan great-uncle, in ensuring that the Castilian case did not go by default,[82] the provisions of the treaty of Sahagún were now a dead letter. With both Aragón and Portugal allied to León (an alliance that left Ramón Berenguer IV free to attend to his Provençal interests), and Sanç VI of Navarre making common cause with Fernando II in 1165 the better to pursue his own ambitions in the Rioja, Leonese colonization of the entire region appeared inevitable. By then, however, the king of León was otherwise engaged towards the south-east, where in 1161 his establishment of a stronghold at Ciudad

[79]   *DrH*, VII. 17.
[80]   Thus *DrH* VII. 13, 24.
[81]   *CM*, IV. 79. Cf. Martin, *Juges de Castille*, 260–70, 286–90.
[82]   *DrH*, VII. 13; González, *Alfonso VIII*, I, 72–3, 663–78. The Infantazgo had been entrusted to the Infanta Sancha (Alfonso VII's sister) by 1147.

Rodrigo (a measure intended both to counter Lara influence in that area of Extremadura and to isolate the Portuguese) had again demonstrated the critical effects of shortages of manpower. From Ávila 'most of the city's settlers and the best of them' migrated to Ciudad Rodrigo, the Ávila chronicler reported, while at Salamanca the prospect of similar losses occasioned an uprising, enabling the Portuguese to occupy the place in the first half of 1163. Meanwhile, at Lugo to the north the local community was in rebellion against the temporal lordship of the bishop. Not until April 1165 was peace with Portugal restored by the treaty of Pontevedra, a settlement sealed by Fernando of León's marriage to Urraca, the daughter of Afonso Enriques.[83]

In Castile meanwhile hostilities between the rival families and their private armies continued unabated, with as many as five hundred knights girded by Gutierre Fernández de Castro, and culminating in the confrontation at Huete in July 1164 of his kinsman Fernando Rodríguez, the governor of Toledo, and Manrique de Lara, the king's guardian, and the latter's violent death. At which point a new force moved into the political void thus created. In what amounted to a late manifestation of the Peace of God, the Castilian episcopate now exerted itself. Churchmen had been intermittently active since the beginning of the reign, in particular Ramón II of Palencia, the ruler of his see for thirty-six years, whose emergence as Sancho III's major chancellor at the time of the treaty of Sahagún provides the earliest evidence of that relationship between his native Catalonia, the Castilian chancery and the church of Palencia which was to bear rich fruit in the *studium* established there. 'Not only a pastor but also the saviour of the kingdom', the king's citation would later read, and in mid-March 1166, in the face of an emergency regarded by them as a *national* emergency, the bishops under the leadership of Jean de Castellmorum, archbishop of Toledo (1152–66) and royal chancellor since at least 1160 (another significant development), took collective action, and in so doing momentarily played a role in national affairs unparalleled since before 711.[84]

Indeed the very name 'synod' used to describe their assembly at Segovia had a seventh-century ring to it, though despite the antiquarian terminology its focus was the immediate present, a present in which the bishopric of Osma had been sold by the boy-king's tutors in order to finance the defence of the city of Calahorra against the army of Sanç VI of Navarre.[85]

---

[83]   Ibid., I, 676–85, 786–91; *Crón. Ávila*, 23; González, *Fernando II*, 45–73.

[84]   *DrH*, VII. 15; Lomax, 'Don Ramón, bishop of Palencia'; Linehan, *History*, 291; Hernández, 'Orígenes del español escrito', 136, 138; González, *Alfonso VIII*, no. 327 (Sept. 1179).

[85]   Linehan, 'Royal influence', 31.

Describing itself as a gathering of 'all the bishops of the kingdom of King Alfonso', the synod issued seventeen decrees. Thirteen of these reiterated measures with which the Western Church had long been familiar. It was the other four that gave the occasion its point. All those holding 'honours' of the king within the kingdom were required, upon pain of deprivation, excommunication and interdict, to do homage to him within six weeks. And the same spiritual penalties were threatened against all inhabitants, whether the king's vassals or not, who either failed to respond to the king's call to defend the kingdom against invasion by any invader whatsoever, or who made war within its confines. There is no evidence that the 'saviour of the kingdom' was present on this occasion and it is a measure of the inadequacy of the record available to Spain's thirteenth-century historians of these years that none of them so much as mention the event.[86]

As well as breaching the ancient principle, enunciated by Archbishop Rodrigo paraphrasing St Paul, that no Castilian warrior should be constrained to fight at his own expense, the measures taken at Segovia in 1166 assumed the existence of a nexus of obligations that hitherto only the *Usatici* of Barcelona had sought to exploit. But whereas in the case of those who, having no fief to lose, failed to hasten to their prince's aid ('since no man must fail the ruler in such a great matter and emergency'), the *Usatici* had had to resort to threats of deprivation of allodial property, the measures adopted by the Castilian bishops, as well as affecting 'everyone in the kingdom', were enforced by the sanction of excommunication. Thus the Peace of God reached central Spain. Moreover, as a territorial measure of universal application, the Segovia decree tended to undermine León's temporary ascendancy in peninsular affairs, which – as attested by the alternative forms *rex Hispanorum*, as used on his seal for the rest of his reign, and *rex Hispaniarum* – remained uncertain of its own identity and unclear whether the hegemony it claimed was over persons or over territory.[87]

When, five months after the Segovia assembly, Toledo was liberated from Leonese rule, the consequences for peninsular politics of the second reconquest of the place were critical. On the earlier occasion, in 1085, the ancient capital's Mozarabic community had played an important part in the process, only to receive little or no reward thereafter for their services. Since 1085 they had found themselves alienated in their own city, excluded from high office both civil and ecclesiastical, marginalized by the French churchmen brought in to man the cathedral chapter, and at risk of being

---

[86]   Idem, 'Synod of Segovia'; *History*, 280–3.
[87]   *DrH*, V. 3 (cf. I Cor. 9.7); *Usatges de Barcelona*, c. 64 ('Princeps namque'; transl. Kagay, 80). Cf. Cowdrey, 66; Linehan, *History*, 280, 289.

deprived under Christian rule of the liturgical rite that had provided them with a psychological lifeline during the centuries of Muslim domination. Yet they had survived, and during the pontificate of the third French archbishop since 1085, Jean de Castellmorum, they became increasingly involved in the activities of the translators arriving there from all over Europe.' The early 1160s saw the first signs of an improvement in their condition and by 1164 the archbishop had appointed one of their number as urban archpriest of the city. Possibly at about the same time, and in the same spirit of calculated conciliation, it was decreed in Alfonso VIII's name that the provisions of the Mozarabs' distinctive *fuero* should henceforth apply to all Toledo's citizens. At any event, in August 1166, under the leadership of their *alguacil* Esteban Illán, the Mozarabs again took the lead in recovering the city for the Castilian king.[88] Whereupon Fernando II's ousted governor, Fernando Rodríguez de Castro, fled to al-Andalus to sell his services there.

More than any other single act to date, the recovery of Toledo, where both his father and grandfather were buried, secured the young king's future. In August 1166 he was approaching his eleventh birthday, already engaged in pursuing Castros and besieging castles in the company of his Lara tutor and the bishop of Palencia. On 11 November 1169 he entered his fifteenth year and the minority ended. Some days earlier he had marked his passage to manhood at the monastery of San Zoilo de Carrión, conferring knighthood upon himself by arming himself with weapons taken from the altar of the church.[89] The unanointed king of Castile was ceremonially beholden to no man. But equally he had no ceremonial centre in which to perform the symbolical act. It was not too soon to give thought to the future of the dynasty.

In this regard, choice was more limited than it had been a century earlier. For reasons previously mentioned, the canonical requirements for valid marriage were now being more strictly observed. The decisive considerations were as much pragmatic as conscientious. As would be shown at the very end of the century, a breach of the rules could cause a determined pontiff to bring the conduct of national affairs to a standstill. However, in the late 1160s no conflict with the rules was necessary. The recent seizure of Castilian territory by Sanç VI of Navarre made a match with the Angevin ruler of Gascony the preferred course. The issue was probably considered

---

[88]   Idem, 'Synod of Segovia', 34–6; Hernández, 'Mozárabes', 79–82; Olstein, 100–9; González, *Alfonso VIII*, I, 174–6; d'Alverny, 445–6; García Gallo, 'Fueros de Toledo', 361–2, 438–45, 480; Linehan, *History*, chap. 9.

[89]   The act was presumably performed while *en route* from Valladolid where he had been nine days before: González, *Alfonso VIII*, nos. 123–4.

at the first curia of the reign, at Burgos in November 1169, and within the year Eleanor, the ten-year-old daughter of Henry II of England, was installed as Queen Leonor of Castile.[90]

Some of the consequences of the opening up of Castile, of which the Angevin marriage was both symptom and cause, will be considered in the following chapter. Meanwhile, an immediate result of Alfonso VIII's coming of age was the transformation of the peninsula's diplomatic alignments. In a reversal of the pre-1169 situation, it was now the king of León's turn to be isolated. The alliance concluded at Zaragoza in July 1170 by the two Alfonsos, the rulers of Castile and Aragón, paved the way for a resumption of a concerted anti-Navarrese campaign, the recovery of the territory recently appropriated by Sanç VI in Alava and Guipúzcoa, and in 1177 the referral of a dispute already more than a century old to the arbitration of Henry II of England. Imperfect though it was to prove, the settlement of these ancient scores in London (after negotiations in which the Castilian delegation was headed by the ubiquitous Ramón of Palencia) enabled Alfonso VIII to direct his attention to his western frontier. With the kings of Navarre and Portugal now his allies, in September 1178 for the first time in his reign he entered the Tierra de Campos.[91]

For the Latin chronicler of the 1230s (whose opinion of the Basques coincided with that of the author of the Pilgrim Guide: a sterile land, he observed, its inhabitants inconstant and faithless) Alfonso VIII's activity in the north was all a waste of time that diverted him from fighting the Almohads in the south. By obliging Angevin interests the king was endangering his own. With Sanç VII of Navarre the emir of Morocco's pensioner, Gascony threatened to prove Castile's graveyard. Striving to possess it was wasted effort, tantamount to ploughing the sea-shore, he protested, quoting Ovid. 'Happy day was it for Castile and one for eternal rejoicing', when in 1205–6 Castile's 'glorious king' freed himself from that obsession.[92] What view the bishop took of the ruler of León's decisive intervention at Badajoz in 1169 has to be left to the imagination, for he appears to have been unaware that it was as the ally of the Almohad caliph Yūsuf I that Fernando II hastened thither to relieve the Moorish garrison from the siege led by the so-called Portuguese Cid and Scarlet Pimpernel of his age, Gerald the Fearless. A principal casualty of the occasion was King Afonso Henriques of Portugal who had his leg broken in the mêlée and never rode again.[93]

[90]   Ibid., I, 185–90.
[91]   Ibid., I, 687–91, 792–811.
[92]   *Crón. latina*, c. 17: an opinion closely paralleling that of some Aragonese regarding Provence.
[93]   Ibid., c. 10. See below, 173 (Alfonso X).

Although by no means unique (as the history of his son Alfonso IX would demonstrate), the king of León's exploits at Badajoz may nevertheless be regarded as illustrative of the prevalence of territorial over confessional loyalties, a scale of values still intact in some quarters when the episcopal chroniclers wrote up the history of the 1160s seventy years after the event. For although in the eyes of the Castilian bishop-chronicler Christian disarray was a scandal and Castile Christendom's only hope, his Leonese colleague Lucas of Tuy, far from attempting to exculpate Fernando for his performance on this occasion, positively gloried in it, representing as an object lesson in royal magnanimity his treatment of the king who had 'sinned against God and himself' by encroaching on territory which the treaty of Sahagún had assigned to León.[94] Fernando had made his truce with the Almohads in order to facilitate his campaign against Nuño Pérez de Lara. Meanwhile his erstwhile governor of Toledo, Fernando Rodríguez de Castro, was negotiating with the enemies of the cross in Seville. 'It was to be noted', Lucas of Tuy commented of the assistance which the latter's son Pedro provided to the enemy at the battle of Alarcos in July 1195, 'that the Goths were virtually never defeated by the barbarians except when the barbarians had Goths assisting them'. By Goths he meant Christians of course. But he did not describe them as such. Like the Ávila contingents who, before setting off on campaign, as well as – or even instead of – confessing and communicating consulted the entrails of birds, the colouring of the bishop of Tuy's mind was not that of a Christian crusader.[95] Unequivocal black and white were not always present where they might have been most expected.

To Fernando II likewise the Almohads were potential auxiliaries capable of being recruited to assist in the contest that really counted, the struggle for ascendancy over his Christian neighbours and relations. Whereas a truce with Islam was (as it would remain until the reconquest of Granada) just a truce – a matter for report without comment[96] – a treaty with Islam was a constructive truce. When a papal legate was in the vicinity, the kings of Castile, León and Aragón were capable of discovering the resolve to collaborate.[97] But papal legates went as fast as they came. In 1157 al-Andalus

[94]   CM, IV. 81: 'Truly I have sinned against both God and you', Afonso Enriques is made to say before offering to surrender his kingdom in expiation (an offer declined by Fernando, 'yielding to his customary piety' according to Rodrigo of Toledo: DrH, VII. 23).
[95]   González, Alfonso VIII, I, 902–3; CM, IV. 83; Crón. de Ávila, 24, 27.
[96]   Thus the Crón. latina in 1197–8: 'Then a truce was made between the kings of Morocco and Castile' (c. 15).
[97]   As in 1172 on the occasion of the visit of Cardinal Hyacinth (later Pope Celestine III): González, Alfonso VIII, I, 686.

comprised a congeries of nominal kingdoms, the detritus of the Caliphate of Córdoba. Inactive in isolation, only when a charge was put through them from across the Straits of Gibraltar were they capable of effective conduct. But the Almoravid gale having spent itself, fresh blasts from Africa had yet to gather force.[98]

If Gerald the Fearless was the Portuguese Cid, ibn Mardanīsh was the Cid of the south-east. From his base in Valencia, and more often than not in alliance with the Christian rulers of Albarracín, the Wolf-king bestrode the affairs of al-Andalus with an absence of confessional conviction at least the equal of that of a king of León.[99] Throughout the 1160s he juggled Seville and Córdoba against Barcelona and wherever the kings of Castile and León happened to be at the time, and entered into and equally effortlessly resiled from agreements to pay the kings of Aragón quantities of gold such as had not been so much as mentioned since the 1030s. Above all, he survived. But on his deathbed in March 1172, after the caliph Yūsuf's brother the governor of Granada had cornered him in Murcia, he gave instructions that all that he controlled be deposited with the caliph.

The departure from the Spanish scene of the third and, for all his zigzagg-ing diplomacy, its most consistent force produced an effect even greater than the numerous Castilian casualties suffered in 1161 when the Almohad caliph, Abd al-Mu'min, had crossed from Africa in order to superintend the foundation of the city of Gibraltar: sufficient indication of the signific-ance of the caliph's ordinary absence. The effect of ibn Mardanīsh's death was no less galvanizing. Led by Abd al-Mu'min's son, Yūsuf, in June 1172 an Almohad army left Seville to set siege to the Castilian stronghold of Huete, mid-way between the Christian settlement at Madrid and the Muslim fortress of Cuenca. Prostrated by hunger and thirst, seven weeks later the caliph's army withdrew. Victory was credited to Alfonso VIII.

As recently as 1158 a *force de frappe* from Ávila, led by the veteran of twenty-six expeditions, the hunchbacked Sancho Jiménez, had succeeded in creating mayhem in Seville. But when Sancho Jiménez returned there in the spring of 1173 he was seen off with heavy losses. In future, such expedi-tions would be under royal command. A lesson had been learnt from the caliph who before returning to Africa in the autumn of 1173 blazed a trail of devastation through Extremadura to punish the king of León for break-ing with him.[100] Despite Alfonso VIII's capture of Cuenca in September 1177, a feat which considerably strengthened his control of La Mancha,

[98]   Le Tourneau, 3–47.
[99]   For his pre-1157 activities see Reilly, 217ff.
[100]   *Crón. de Avila*, 23–4; Powers, *Society*, 40–50; González, *Fernando II*, 107–9.

and which in the estimation of the bishop of Osma marked the arrival of royal manhood, the ruler of Castile remained just one Christian ruler amongst many. Events of the previous twenty years had undermined the system of hegemony envisaged by his father and grandfather. Despite the provisions of the treaties of Tudején and Sahagún, the kings of Aragón and Portugal continued to consolidate their power to east and west. Indeed, part of the Castilian's reason for besieging Cuenca when he did so was to pre-empt a possible Aragonese move in that direction. Moreover, the price of the assistance Alfonso of Aragón had provided at the siege had been release from the homage which since 1136 his Aragonese predecessors had owed for the kingdom of Zaragoza; and by the treaty of Cazola, as well as forming a pact of alliance and friendship against all other rulers, Moorish and Christian alike, 'but most particularly against the king of Navarre', in return for Alfonso VIII's relinquishment of all claims to fealty in respect of future Aragonese conquests, Alfonso II ceded the kingdom of Murcia to Castile.

In the opinion of the Catalan historian Ferrán Soldevila, writing in the 1930s, for Catalonia the deal done at Cazola in March 1179 sacrificed Aragonese rights in Murcia in return for the renunciation of a purely nominal overlordship, and was 'disastrous'. Scrupulous regard for feudal niceties had betrayed the interests of idealistic Catalonia to calculating Castile.[101] It is a view still taken in 2007. However, if only on that symbolic level, the final severing of the threads of allegiance, of which there had at least been formal acknowledgement at Tudején, was not without significance for Castile either. Just two months later the extent of the rupture was fully revealed when Alexander III's bull 'Manifestis probatum' ratified the royal title of Alfonso of Portugal and his successors.[102] The old order had indeed changed. It was time for a new dispensation.

[101]   *Hist. de Catalunya*, 208–11; Constable, 162–3 (text). The alternative view, advanced by Ventura (*Alfons 'el Cast'*, 193–4), that the separation would protect the Corona de Aragón from invasion by a heresy-hunting feudal suzerain, appears fanciful and anachronistic in equal measure.

[102]   Almeida, 83–6; Feige, 300–12.

2

The Age of Las Navas

Life, Law and Memory

In or about 1221 the monastery of San Zoilo de Carrión sent one of its monks, Pedro González, to collect evidence regarding the ownership of certain churches in the diocese of Palencia. The way in which that evidence was presented provides a rather different perspective on the period from that afforded by royal charters and the official mind of the age, as deployed in the previous chapter. What kings did was to rule, decide questions and enforce decisions because they possessed sufficient clout to do so. But that was not what sustained local societies and society at large; what did so was not dynasties but memories, collective memories. And such memories were often uncertain. For example, 'because he had attended school and learnt', the chaplain Fernandus at San Martín de Fromista believed he understood the concept of prescription. However, as to his own age it was a matter of pure guesswork that he was 'at least forty-five'.[1] Many others, some claiming to be centenarians, were similarly uncertain of their date of birth, though they claimed to remember back to 'fifteen years before Alarcos', to 'ten years before the eclipse of the sun when Jerusalem was captured', or to the siege of Huete.[2]

In a similar dispute a few years earlier, alongside the spry witnesses whose memory reached back seventy years ('and he was already riding a horse then'), or who 'did not know because he did not have it in writing', there were those who calculated their ages in terms of not having been born when the emperor died, of entering the world in the very week of that event, or even remembering men weeping on hearing the news. True, the evidential

[1]   Pérez Celada, 144.
[2]   Ibid., 145, 152–7.

value of such recollections was often dubious. As was observed in a case that came before Alfonso X in 1261, sometimes they seemed suspiciously consistent. Yet the fact that they were shared did not weaken their significance; on the contrary. Moreover, although the historical collective memory, as enunciated by the Castilian bishops a couple of years later, stretched back to before the Saracen occupation, the consensus of their short-term memory only dated from 1212. But as to that their memory was clear. At Las Navas de Tolosa 'when the lord Alfonso was placed in the most extreme necessity no one from outside Spain came to his assistance'.[3]

As to popular memory in the early 1220s, curiously it was not the euphoria generated by Las Navas that registered but anxiety: the anxiety associated with events of the years 1172, 1187 and 1195, the Almohad siege of Huete, the loss of Jerusalem, and the battle of Alarcos, with witnesses to the ownership of churches disputed between the bishop of Palencia and the Hospitallers c.1225 dating events to shortly before or shortly after that event.[4] It is with that twenty-five-year period that the following pages will be chiefly concerned and with what replaced the old dispensation referred to at the end of the last chapter. No longer was it from the rulers of Asturias and León that the monarch in the ascendant, Alfonso the Small of Castile, traced his descent. Now he did so from the Castilian champions of independence from those Leonese tyrants via his Navarrese ancestors. In the 1230s and 40s the historians Lucas of Tuy and Rodrigo of Toledo, representing Leonese and Castilian interests respectively, would provide markedly divergent accounts of that passage of tenth-century history.[5] In the 1170s, however, the significance of that break in Spain's once seamless historical past was unambiguous. It was bolstered and confirmed by documents emanating from the Castilian chancery that emphasized Alfonso's majestic character as well as by the Arabic legend incised on the gold *maravedís* issued to replace the interrupted supply of Almoravid dinars. 'Prince of the Catholics', it proclaimed.

Regretted though it has been by Catalonia's modern historians, at the time Cazola enabled Alfonso of Aragón to consolidate his kingdom. The postponement of the scramble for Murcia made possible the reinforcement of the Aragonese hinterland, with the ambitions of the rulers of Castile and Navarre ensuring that Aragón continued to hold the king's attention, and the organization and codification of the chancery archives enabling

[3]   Fernández-Catón, *CD Catedral de León*, VI, no. 1849 (pp. 274, 276, 304, 278, 299, 272, 280); Quintana Prieto, 451; Benito Ruano, 12.
[4]   H. Kennedy, 225–8 (Huete); AC Zamora, 16/II/42 (Lera Maíllo, no. 396).
[5]   Martin, *Juges de Castille*, 212–29, 270–95.

him and his successors to exert greater control over the Catalan baronage. This was a process directed by the dean of Barcelona, Ramon de Caldes, who entered the royal service in 1178, culminating in the compilation of the *Liber feudorum maior* (the Great Book of Fiefs) in 1192. It was at least symbolically significant that it was in 1180, the year after Cazola, that the directive of Tarragona was issued discontinuing the practice of dating comital-royal instruments by the regnal year of the king of France.[6]

As the proem to Justinian's *Institutes* proclaimed, 'Imperial majesty had to be armed by laws as well as served by arms'. The tone of the name given to Cuenca, 'Alfonsipolis', in the prologue of the *fuero* accorded to the place by Alfonso VIII (?1189×1193) was strongly civilian in character. In this development members of Toledo's cathedral chapter who staffed the royal chancery were perhaps involved, and probably more significantly so the bishop of Palencia, Ramón II – in a certain sense the Castilian counterpart of Ramon de Caldes – another Catalan and purveyor of the thriving Romanism of Catalonia and the *studium* of Montpellier.[7]

With the canons of Barcelona in possession by 1188 of a copy of the Digest (Justinian's collection of extracts from the great jurists of the first to third centuries), much has been made of what such influences may have meant for the evolution of royal ideology. But so also has their role regarding the development of representative institutions, to the extent indeed that the two effects might seem to have cancelled one another out. Also in 1188, the Catalan barons assembled at Girona cited the *Usatges* and their 'novel Romanist ideas' *against* Alfonso II. However, that did not make the growth of the various peninsular cortes dependent on the civilian maxim that 'what concerns all must be approved by all'.[8] The devil could quote scripture. The functional significance of Roman law in twelfth-century Spanish society ought not to be exaggerated.

'Roman Law provided a theoretical justification for the convocation of the municipalities and the practical means to bring such a convocation about', it has been claimed apropos of the report of Alfonso VIII's recruitment of learned men ('sapientes') in the Gauls and Italy to staff his Palencia *studium*.[9] But this emphasis either belittles the tradition and pre-history of self-help in a frontier society, or descends into a skirmish for precedence in that development (between the cortes, if that is what they were, of

---

[6]   Soldevila, *Hist. de Catalunya*, 199–200, 213; Bisson, *Fiscal Accounts*, I, 21, 91–7.
[7]   Powers, *Code of Cuenca*, 28; Linehan, *History*. 289–93; Hernández, 'Orígenes del español escrito', 142–3.
[8]   Kosto, 288, 279–80; Constable, 172 (no. 21); above, 16.
[9]   O'Callaghan, *Cortes*, 15; DrH, VII. 34.

Burgos in 1169 and León in 1188), or is diverted into controversy regarding the authenticity of the Leonese decrees of 1188 and into exchanges the very asperity of which raises questions about the deep-rootedness of the peninsula's 'democratic tendencies'.[10] For it was to that tradition, rather than to the example of the sapient civilians of Montpellier and Palencia, that the two assemblies of 1188, of Girona as well as León, belonged, just as did the arsonists of Medina, the mutilators of Candavera, the concubinary clergy of Sepúlveda, the foaming radical Pedro Negro, leader of the *concejo* of Cordobilla at war with the monks of Aguilar de Campóo in the 1220s, with his cry of '*We* are the kings', not to mention students of the subject still bickering long after the last historical congresses on the question have dispersed.[11] By comparison with this powerful stuff, the Romanist content of these gatherings strikes the reader as tepid and, for the time being, was to prove evanescent.

'Do you really think that the count will lose his county through the art of pleading you have learnt in Bologna?' the Catalan count of Urgell's opponent asked the count's advocate not long after Pedro Negro had given voice to a rhetorical question containing various layers of contempt for the learned law. Neither corporate nor procuratorial representation was yet at issue, even less the representation of estates. 'Rather, it was administrative representation of a kind wholly characteristic of the twelfth century and still too little recognized by historians: a representation by which a community tended to be identified with its leading men.'[12] Because, moreover, ever since the publication of Martínez Marina's *Teoría de las Cortes* analysis of the history of that institution has been cast in a conceptual framework forged in the white heat of early nineteenth-century liberalism, there has been a tendency to adhere to a taxonomic approach inimical to 'the cross-currents of politics in all their complexity'. This has skewed our understanding of the period. Thus, as the *fuero* of Cuenca indicates, in 1188 far more significant than questions of representation was Alfonso VIII's knighting of the new king of León at the Cortes of Carrión. For it was from the public humiliation occasioned by that ceremony, conducted 'in the presence of all, with the court full', as the chronicle would record, that Alfonso IX's lasting resentment towards his cousin derived: the resentment that would keep him from Las

---

[10]   González Díez, 'Curia y cortes', 133–7; Prieto Prieto; Estepa & Arvizu, 'Notas críticas'; Fernández-Catón, 'Curia Regia de León', 355 ('sentido democrático').

[11]   Constable, 164–7; above, 23; Linehan, *History*, 306; Bisson, 'General court of Aragon', 109–10; Linehan, 'History in a changing world', 21.

[12]   *Book of Deeds*, c. 637 (mid-1228); Bisson, 'General court of Aragon', 109–10; Post, *Studies*, 70–9.

Navas.[13] Meanwhile, in the same year the foundation by Alfonso of Aragón's Castilian queen of the Hospitaller priory of Sigena, with the magnificent Romanesque wall-paintings of its chapter house, provided evidence of traditions shared with the English creators of these masterpieces and testified to the strength by this date of cultural relationships with the wider world.[14]

Three Battles

At any event, by that date the briefly favoured Roman theme of 'majesty' had been set aside, and it was as the champion of 'Christianity' and Christianity's concerns that the Castilian chancery was presenting Alfonso VIII at home and abroad. In assuming this role the king of Castile was assisted, first by Saladin's recapture of Jerusalem in October 1187 and the modest, not to say inglorious, performance of the ensuing Third Crusade, then by Pope Celestine III (1191–8) who, as Cardinal Hyacinth, had twice visited Spain as papal legate as well as having a hand in the foundation of the Order of Santiago and in the relief of Huete, but chiefly (and paradoxically) by the crushing defeat inflicted upon the Castilians at Alarcos, south of Calatrava, in July 1195.

In Yorkshire Roger of Howden recorded that news of the victory of the Almohad caliph Ya'qūb sent shock waves through the whole of Christendom. Further south the chronicle attributed to the head of the small Cistercian abbey of Coggeshall in Essex reported an enemy army of six hundred thousand at Europe's gates, 'the unexpected arrival of which had shaken all Christianity to the core'. William of Newburgh suggested parallels with recent reverses in the Holy Land and drew attention to the moral malaise of the West that some contemporaries regarded as the fundamental cause of both calamities.[15] This was Christian Spain's gravest reverse since 1086. Huge figures of Christian casualties were bruited abroad, as many as one hundred and forty thousand against a mere five hundred of that tremendous army. Possibly Christian morale was affected by the defection of Pedro Fernández de Castro to Ya'qūb's army.[16] But the disaster was also at least in part attributable to

[13]   Linehan, *History*, 528–9, 595; idem, 'Ecclesiastics and the Cortes', 108–13; Powers, *Code of Cuenca*, 28; *PCG*, c. 997; Palacios Martín, 'Investidura de armas', 171.

[14]   Oakeshott, 9–73 (giving foundation date as 1183).

[15]   Roger of Howden, III. 302; Coggeshall, 67; Newburgh, 445–7. The English testimonies cited by Lomax, 'Conquista de Andalucía', 38, are either derived from these reports or are insubstantial. Cf. Flahiff, '*Deus non vult*.'

[16]   *CM*, IV. 83 (above, p. 33).

Alfonso's impetuosity in engaging the enemy in advance of the arrival of the kings of León and Navarre and with only token Portuguese support. Having narrowly escaped with his life, Alfonso VIII himself is said, mistakenly perhaps, to have forbidden Castilians to take baths on account of the enervating effect they were thought to have.[17]

In the estimation of the troubadours, or most of them, Alfonso of Castile, unlike his Aragonese namesake, was both 'sans peur et sans reproche'. Aimeric de Peguilhan spoke not only for himself in describing him as 'the best king anyone has ever seen or heard of'.[18] His court, and that of the lovely Queen Leonor, was synonymous with generosity and plenty.[19] But Spain's other kings let him down. The Provençal, Giraut de Bornelh, spoke of having left the court of 'good' King Alfonso mounted on the fine palfrey given him by the king and laden with gifts from the barons of his court, only to be robbed of everything *en route* by the ruler of Navarre.[20] Writing in the decade before Alarcos, Peire Vidal dissented. Coming from Toulouse he thought all four kings equally to blame. 'For all their great valour, for all their dexterity, generosity, courtesy and loyalty', they failed to make peace amongst themselves and combine against the common foe so as to return 'all Spain to a single faith'. Indeed, during these years virtually every conceivable division of the five kings (not four; Portugal was also involved) is found, though with Navarre invariably on the receiving end.[21] Gavaudan (*fl.* 1195/1211) took up the cry that was the cry of all Europe: 'Our sins increase Saracen power.'[22]

This was an analysis in the main unduly favourable to Alfonso VIII, since he it was who had driven the other peninsular kings into opposition by alienating his cousin Alfonso of León and failing to abide by the terms of the agreement with Aragón for the partition of Navarre.[23] A start to repairing the

---

[17] Lomax, *Reconquest*, 120, perhaps confusing the occasion with the prohibition said to have been imposed after Zalaca in 1086: *CM*, IV. 71. For particulars of the battle and the different accounts of the exorbitant casualties suffered according to Almohad sources: Huici Miranda, *Grandes batallas*, 137–216, esp. 157.

[18] Shepard & Chambers, 126, 138: 'All the world agrees with me that the rich and valiant don Alfonso is blessed with all virtues.'

[19] Peire Gilhem de Tolosa: Mahn, I, 248; Alvar, *Textos*, 233; above, 24–5.

[20] Presumably Sanç VI (d. 1196): Alvar, *Poesía trovadoresca*, 53–9.

[21] Avalle, 70, 325; Alvar, *Textos*, 236, 241 ('I'm fed up with kings of Spain who only want to fight each other'); Zurita, II. 53.

[22] '. . . Saladin has taken Jerusalem and it has not been recovered. This encourages the king of Morocco and his allies to take on the armies of Christ': Riquer, *Trovadores*, 1049; Alvar, *Textos*, 91–2.

[23] Soldevila, *Hist. de Catalunya*, 213.

damage was made by the pilgrimage of the Aragonese monarch to Santiago in 1195 and by the meeting in 1196 of the rulers of Aragón and Castile with the new king of Navarre, Sanç VII, at the junction of their three kingdoms, reportedly with each monarch seated in his own realm.[24]

However, recourse to alliances cemented by consanguineous marriages, the Christians' secret weapon against Saracen might, met with the granitic opposition of Innocent III, the pope whose reign began three years after Alarcos and who viewed the union entered into by Alfonso IX and his cousin's daughter, the Infanta Berenguela of Castile, as an egregious example of such liaisons – despite attempts by the bishops of both kingdoms to persuade him to turn a blind eye to the closeness of this one.[25] According to the well-connected chronicler, Roger of Howden, Innocent's predecessor Celestine III had approved the match 'for the sake of peace' ('pro pace'), and Alfonso IX offered Innocent and his cardinals twenty thousand marks of silver and two hundred men for a year 'for the defence of the Christians against the pagans' if only they would allow the couple to remain together for long enough to produce an heir. What he got instead was a withering denunciation of his 'incestuous coupling', the exclusion of any offspring from a share in the paternal inheritance, excommunication for himself and interdict for his kingdom.[26] Not until June 1204, by which time they had acquired five children in as many years, including three negotiable daughters, did the couple separate and were the papal sentences lifted. The version reported by Alberic of Trois Fontaines – that Innocent had at first allowed the marriage 'of necessity', then prohibited it when children started arriving, 'and that the queen's incontinence, of which there were many reports, may have been the cause' – was incorrect, at least as regards Innocent.[27] The truth was that the first male offspring was preceded by two if not three daughters. Although avoidance of another Alarcos was paramount, that was not to be secured by bending the rules of the Universal Church. For Innocent III, incest was worse than Saracens.

Not for Alfonso VIII though. For him nothing was worse than Saracens. In order to defeat them he was confident that God would excuse depredations on churches and monasteries that he and his predecessors had endowed.[28] By 1204 developments elsewhere in the peninsula were

[24]   Ventura, *Alfons 'el Cast'*, 260–5.
[25]   Innocent thought the king of León was Berenguela's grandfather (Mansilla, *Inocencio III*, nos. 138, 305). In fact the couple were the grandson and great-granddaughter of Alfonso VII.
[26]   Linehan, *History*, 255–8.
[27]   *Cronica*, 895.
[28]   González, *Alfonso VIII*, III, no. 749 (July 1203).

reminding the pope that heresy was worse than Saracens too. These concerned Aragón-Catalonia where in 1196 King Pedro II (the Catholic: Count Pere I) had succeeded his father and, although the county of Provence and adjacent territories had passed to his younger brother (yet another Alfonso), had also inherited the lordships around Toulouse. In 1200, reversing the policy of his father and grandfather, Pedro responded to an approach by the count of Toulouse, Raymond VI, and entered into alliance with him. What necessitated this compact for the count was the threat of Capetian intervention in this politically fragmented region spearheaded by armies of brigands under the leadership of Simon de Montfort, the blood-brothers of the Lisbon crusaders against Islam in 1147, now fortified by the papal decretal 'Vergentis'.[29]

To this volatile situation Pedro's matrimonial complications added a further explosive component. In combination with a principled commitment to his Occitanian allies and vassals, his discovery in 1205–6 of scruples requiring him to repudiate his wife, Marie de Montpellier, but not before he had transferred her inheritance to Raymond VII of Toulouse as their daughter's dowry, determined most of his future actions. In an open letter his wife protested that she was being 'crucified'. 'Why do you want to defraud me thus?', she demanded. Having played a far from inglorious part in the victory of Las Navas in July 1212, in the following January he was informed of the pontiff's unwillingness to acquiesce in such 'shocking opportunism' (as it has been described). At Muret eight months later, after a final night of passion which, according to his son's autobiography, left him too jaded to stand for the gospel at mass before battle, he perished at the hands of the Albigensian crusaders.[30] The end of a reign that had begun with plague and famine ended with the king's policies in pieces and his realms bankrupted. He had risked losing Montpellier, with all the commercial advantages that that implied, and in pursuit of a diplomatic solution to his difficulties had not hesitated to entrust his young son Jaime to the tender mercies of Montfort and the prospect of betrothal to Montfort's daughter. Change and decay were to be seen all around him, and ruin both at home and abroad.[31]

In 1204, at the beginning of the process, Pedro had chosen to renew the infeudation of the kingdom of Aragón to the Roman Church and to have

[29] Innocent III's decretal of 1199 that defined heresy as spiritual lèse-majesté and specified its secular consequence as the confiscation of all temporal property: Smith, 37.

[30] Soldevila, Hist. de Catalunya, 216–41; Mansilla, Inocencio III, nos. 497–8; Smith, 70–1; Aurell, 434–5; Book of Deeds, c. 9.

[31] Bisson, Fiscal Accounts, I, 123–4; Soldevila, Hist. de Catalunya, 242 ('Ruïna, doncs, a l'interior i a l'exterior').

himself anointed by a cardinal and crowned, with the imperial paraphernalia of orb, mitre etc., and then knighted by the pope. For this ceremonial innovation historians have suggested a number of motives. In the sixteenth century Gerónimo de Blancas represented the occasion as a brilliant coup, a triumph of Aragonese diplomacy, with Pedro foiling what was to have been a display of theocratic condescension by providing a crown of soft dough for the purpose. Such fantasies apart, however, motives of his own the king evidently did have, amongst which, in view of the condition of Languedoc, may have been the desire to wrap himself in the papal mantle, just as the count of Toulouse had wrapped himself in the royal one. Already perhaps, even in 1204, questions regarding his marriage may have played a part. What was certainly a subject of his discussions with the pope, and on the pope's motion, was another marriage, that of Pedro's sister, Constança, the widow of King Imre of Hungary, to Frederick of Hohenstaufen, the ten-year-old king of Sicily.[32] The possibility of Aragonese military intervention in Sicily was therefore one object of the exercise. Another was the king's request for papal support in the shape of crusading indulgences as well as the assistance of the Genoese and Pisan fleets in order to deliver Mallorca from the clutches of Muḥammad al-Naṣr, the Almohad caliph of Morocco.

Though these particular initiatives proved of limited effect (in the first case owing to the king's reluctance, not the pope's, and to the plague that carried off most of the contingent of knights who accompanied Constanza to Palermo in 1209),[33] their tendency coincided with the direction of Barcelona's mercantile and colonial aspirations. The sea, the sea; it was inevitable. Every count-king to date made plans for the reconquest of the Balearic islands, most recently Alfonso II in 1177 with the aid of the Sicilian fleet indeed,[34] and periodically one or other of them had also expressed interest in Sardinia. The trouble was, none of them lasted long enough to proceed far beyond the business of absorbing the vestiges of the old Carolingian counties of the region whose earlier independence was so memorably evoked by R. W. Southern.[35] Ramon Berenguer III died at forty-eight, Ramon Berenguer IV at forty-seven, and Alfonso II at forty-two. Alfonso VIII of Castile (1158–1214) outlived two and a half Aragonese rulers.

---

[32]   Mansilla, *Inocencio III*, no. 307; Soldevila, *Hist. de Catalunya*, 222–7 (corrected by Palacios Martín, *Coronación*, 21–58, esp. 53–6); Linehan, *History*, 389, 622; Smith, 43–70.

[33]   Pedro appears to have regarded Frederick as beneath his sister. But the boy had enjoyed the royal title while still in the womb, the pontiff protested: Mansilla, *Inocencio III*, no. 382 (Feb. 1208); Zurita, II. 58.

[34]   Ibid., II. 36.

[35]   Southern, *Making of the Middle Ages*, 22–4, 118–24.

The twelfth century was Castile's century. If the thirteenth was Aragón's, one of the reasons was longevity. Jaime I of Aragón (1213–74) overlapped four kings of Castile. Royal survival was not everything, but it was a lot. Just how much it was Castile would discover in 1295 and 1312 when one minority was followed by another.

Though only thirty-six when he was cut down at Muret, and despite having to cope with heresy, Pedro II did find time to advance the Corona de Aragón's Mediterranean agenda. Maria de Montferrat, the lady he had taken into his bed in anticipation of the divorce that never came, was queen of Jerusalem.[36] In that capacity and that sphere of activity Maria anticipated something else, developments at the other end of the century, and, in particular, colonization of the area of Cyprus and beyond by Pedro's great-grandson Jaime II.

The Jerusalem connexion brings us back to Castile. In 1224 Berenguela, by now queen-mother of Castile, would marry off one of the products of her 'incestuous coupling' to the titular king of Jerusalem, the elderly Jean de Brienne, in order to prevent him from attaching himself to the girl's half-sister (one of Alfonso IX's daughters by his first unlawful wife, Teresa of Portugal), thereby frustrating Fernando III's prospects of becoming king of León.[37] In June 1204, however, just three months before the Fourth Crusade had reached its ignoble conclusion at Constantinople, Jerusalem possessed all sorts of other connotations. For Innocent the delivery of a decisive strike against Islam was the highest priority. Yet Alfonso of Castile was reluctant to seize the peninsular initiative. Indeed towards the end of that year his thoughts were focused elsewhere. ' "Clear in mind but weak in body", in December he made a will, salving his conscience by granting the church of Osma possession of the city in which it stood and ordering "all his silver" to be turned into chalices for the churches of his kingdom.' Whatever influences within the king's entourage may have been respons-ible for his doing so, Alfonso appears to have been the first king of Castile to have treated the royal fisc as though it were private property.[38] And when in February 1210 Innocent urged him to emulate the ardent king of Aragón, he proved battle-shy. At this stage it was his son and heir the Infante Fernando who was burning to take the fight to the enemy. According to the recently appointed archbishop of Toledo, Rodrigo Jiménez de Rada, when in September 1211 the fortress of Salvatierra was lost to the Almohad caliph

---

[36] Smith, 72–4.
[37] Crón. latina, c. 42; below, 58.
[38] González, Alfonso VIII, III, no. 769, failing to notice the novelty of the procedure. For the reasons for his bad conscience regarding Osma: Linehan, 'Royal influence', 33–43.

it was the infante who urged Alfonso to retaliate without delay. Mindful of Alarcos no doubt, the old king remained unmoved.[39]

Then, a month later, the infante died, carried off by fever at Madrid. 'And on hearing this, his mother the queen wanted to die too. She got into the bed in which he was lying and, linking fingers with him, gave him the kiss of life. She wanted either to give him life or die with him. Never had there been such grief, those who were there and witnessed the scene said.' Queen Leonor had already lost four sons in infancy or early childhood. The troubadours were inconsolable, Guiraut de Calanson remembering Fernando as 'handsome, good, agreeable in every deed, liberal, generous, valiant and lovable'. Epithets that had once defined his father were repeated in Archbishop Rodrigo's account of the infante's death and burial.[40]

D. Rodrigo, it has been plausibly suggested, had also been responsible for the pope's attempt to galvanize Alfonso in 1210 and for ensuring that the coming struggle would have the character of an international crusade against the enemies not just of Castile but – and here we may see a reversion to the spirit of the 1180s – of the whole of Christendom.[41] However, the associated suggestion that the Infante Fernando's 'zeal for battle may have been more a device for encouraging recruitment than the real impetus behind the new offensive' seems to harbour a false dichotomy.'[42] If only the infante had lived one year longer, Guiraut de Calanson reflected, he would have shown his worth as a 'wall against the Arabs'. Indeed, had he lived that further year he would have shared in the victory of July 1212 when, again by Archbishop Rodrigo's account, the Christians more than proportionately turned the tables of Alarcos by inflicting losses of twenty thousand at a cost of just twenty-five casualties. According to one Welsh source, three thousand Saracen *women* also perished. Las Navas de Tolosa, a battle won with the Almohad caliph himself in command, redefined Alarcos as Africa's last great victory in Spain.[43]

Implications of the Vernacular

But, as it was, and before that, the beleaguered Castilians had had to have recourse to an alternative, home-grown hero, namely Rodrigo Díaz del Vivar,

[39]   Mansilla, *Inocencio III*, nos. 416, 442; Linehan, *History*, 319; *DrH*, VII. 35.
[40]   *Crón. latina*, c. 20; Ernst, 331–2; Riquer, *Trovadores*, 1085–6; *DrH*, VII. 36.
[41]   Pick, *Conflict*, 36–43, 209–10.
[42]   Ibid., 41.
[43]   *Brut y Tywysogyon*, 195; H. Kennedy, 243–56.

as represented in the *Cantar de Mio Cid*, the vernacular epic 'written down' by Pedro Abbat in May 1207, which served as 'a sort of recruiting-poster' for the Las Navas campaign, designed to appeal to every social group capable of drawing inspiration from its hero's achievements. Perhaps it was even commissioned and paid for by the king, as has been suggested.[44] But alluring though such interpretations are, they have to contend with a number of problems concerning an epic work of provincial genius which transformed the mercenary who had sold his sword for Muslim gold into a crusading paladin of all Christian virtues, problems that have exercised scholars ever since the publication of Menéndez Pidal's canonical account of the matter a century ago. However, into the intricacies of the debate – and in particular the debate as to the stage when the *Cantar* achieved coherent shape, whether before 1140 or later in the century, and just what the 'writing down' of May 1207 signified – it is not necessary to enter here, if only for the reason that in 1207 Alfonso VIII seems not to have been much interested in recruiting-posters.[45]

When in the previous year Alfonso VIII had made a truce with his Leonese cousin there had been no suggestion that either party was actuated by the need for a common Christian front, and in blatant defiance of Innocent III's prohibition the massed episcopates of both kingdoms had gone surety for the provision that the Infante Fernando, the offspring of the Leonese monarch's 'incestuous coupling', would succeed his father as king of León. With its undertaking to provide mutual assistance against 'everyone in the world', Christians (other than the kings of Aragón and France) as well as Moors, the treaty of Cabreros was a classic frontier treaty between Christian kings regulating the custody of castles and strongholds.[46] What distinguished it from earlier such treaties, and from other public instruments prior to the 1230s, was its ratification in Castilian and Leonese forms of Romance rather than Latin. And ten months later, in January 1207, the sumptuary legislation of Alfonso VIII's Toledo Cortes was also recorded in the vernacular: another first (the language of the laws of the León Cortes of 1208 was Latin), as well as the end of the beginning of what was to be a forty-year process.[47]

[44] Lacarra, *Poema*, 182; Fradejas Lebrero, 56.

[45] Further to the discussion in Linehan, *History*, 319–27: on the date question, Russell, 'Problems'; Lapesa, *Estudios*, 11–42; Deyermond *et al.*, Mio Cid *Studies*; Catalán, *Épica española*, 491–2; on the transformation issue, Linehan, 'The Cid of history'; Fletcher, *Quest for El Cid*, esp. 192–5; for a contrary view, Lomax, *Reconquest of Spain*, 102–3.

[46] Fernandez Catón, *CD Catedral de León*, VI, 166–74.

[47] Wright, *Tratado de Cabreros*, esp. 34–78; Hernández, 'Cortes de Toledo de 1207'; *CLC*, 46–8; Hernández, 'Orígenes del español escrito', 144–53.

Historians of the period have naturally been intrigued by this cluster of vernacular indications concentrated around the years 1206–7 and have striven to discover the direction the current was flowing along the wires between the language of the scribes at Cabreros, the legislators of the Toledo Cortes, and Pedro Abbat's writing down of the *Cantar de Mio Cid* with its culmination a meeting of . . . the cortes of the kingdom at Toledo, and whether it was to that same circuit that the vernacular translation made at about this time of the history of the feats of another hero belonged, that of the by no means Christian but exemplarily martial King Alexander, echoes of whose career may have been audible to some in that of Alfonso VIII.[48] In this pantheon Guiraut de Calanson would have found room for the dead Infante Fernando's British exemplar 'in whom all the needy found counsel'.[49]

Some of them have traced the source to Palencia. In 1207 indeed, rather than in recruiting-posters Alfonso VIII may have been interested in recruiting faculty from France and Italy for his new university there 'so that', in the words of the archbishop of Toledo, 'the discipline of knowledge should never be absent from his kingdom': a campaign in which he was in competition with Alfonso IX with his similar and, as will be seen, better founded schemes for Salamanca. Perhaps it has not been previously appreciated that the two Spanish kings were the earliest to enter this particular race. For though other *studia* – Bologna and Paris in particular – were ahead of Palencia, these had been organic developments, thrusting up from below, not acts of state imposed from above. It was Palencia sometime before 1214, not Naples in 1224, that was 'the first university of all to be erected by a definite act'.[50]

What then was Alfonso VIII's purpose in bringing scholars to Palencia? Not, we may surmise, to provide cloistered calm for the anonymous translator of the verse *Libro de Alexandre* or even a quiet haven for the perfection of Per Abbat's syllables. Rather it was to provide the king himself with expertise in the business of government. In the 1180s Pere de Cardona had combined his responsibilities in the Castilian chancery with teaching Roman Law at the University of Montpellier. Henceforth Castile was to be a net importer of talent, talent such as that of Ugolino da Sesso, another Romanist, in this case an authority on procedural law, whose *curriculum vitae* had included spells at Cremona as well as Montpellier. But it was not just in order to school his court in Roman law, thereby providing it with governmental

[48] Arizaleta, esp. 240–59.
[49] 'For in him all the virtues of King Artus have been restored': Ernst, 331. For Arthur as 'Artus': Hook, 2–3.
[50] *DrH*, VII. 34; Cobban, 25.

yeast, that Alfonso recruited foreign scholars to teach at Palencia. The husband of an Angevin queen did not need his wife to inform him of the value of the staple education provided at Paris, Oxford and Northampton, and of the *trivium* – grammar, rhetoric and logic – in particular.[51] Correct accentuation, which was of such interest to the author of the *Alexandre*, was of no less concern to the king's chancery clerks charged with reciting texts written in a Romance dialect with which they were unfamiliar. And to judge by a surviving formulary of model letters associated with a group of Zamora students resident there at this time, so also was correct latinity and acquaintance with the history and literature of classical antiquity.[52]

How far either students or king were also motivated by the pastoral considerations which had given prominence to the issue of clerical education at the Third Lateran Council of 1179, and which were to weigh even more heavily at the Fourth in 1215,[53] was another matter. To judge by the scalding criticism of the Spanish Church contained in *Planeta*, the embittered treatise of Diego García dated 1218, the need for reform was widespread, especially amongst the episcopate whom the author's prologue describes as beyond redemption. 'By its prelates, for shame, the Church is being destroyed . . . Honesty and knowledge, in both of which they are themselves deficient, they persecute to the limit in others.'[54] So too was it the finding of Cardinal John of Abbeville, papal legate to the peninsula in 1228–9, 'that for lack of universities and learning souls were suffering great and intolerable harm'.[55] Yet, as Diego (who has been identified, wholly implausibly, as the author of *Alexandre*)[56] himself observed, disapprovingly of course, the age was one of social mobility.[57] Society might be rotten from top to bottom,[58] but it was also on the move, and, for the time being at least, Palencia was

[51] Above, 16; Linehan, *History*, 305–6; Maffei, esp. 12–21; Fleisch, 174–8.

[52] Rico, 'Clerecía del mester', 10, 17–18, 20–1; Hernández, 'Orígenes del español escrito', 144–6; Barrero García, 700–1.

[53] Morris, 489–96.

[54] ed. Alonso, 195 ('usque in ypotomiam': an unknown word; perhaps 'epotomiam': the dregs), 405.

[55] Council of Lleida (1229), c. 5 (*ES*, XLVIII, 308); Linehan, *Spanish Church*, 20–34; idem, 'Papal legation'.

[56] Hernando Pérez, 105–322. This is far from being the most outlandish of the author's suggestions regarding his subject's career. Cf. Arizaleta, 18–19.

[57] *Planeta*, 183: 'I am writing at a time when – oh calamity! – no one is content with his own place in society.' Although the following phrase ('et quisque statum quem desideraverat non prescribit' (?'nunc proscribit') is meaningless, the gist of it is tolerably clear. The quality of the unique contemporary manuscript of the work may be thought to confirm the author's strictures on the illiteracy of his age.

[58] Ibid., 195: '. . . when almost the whole world is running down'.

at the centre of that process, with French masters flocking thither and local men moving on in order to shed sweetness and light in areas even more morally depraved. Thus, Peter of Blois (albeit not *the* Peter of Blois) came there sometime between 1215 and 1220 and dedicated his *Verbiginale*, another verse treatise (this time on verbal morphology), to Bishop Tello,[59] and in 1234 the treasurer of Palencia, Tiburcius (who with that name perhaps was a foreigner himself), was sent by Pope Gregory IX to the see of Coimbra in the hope of bringing King Sancho II of Portugal to his senses.[60]

This was itself in return for an earlier transfer that might have been to Castile's advantage. In 1210 the Portuguese canonist Melendus abandoned a thriving legal practice at Rome where, according to the Englishman Thomas of Marlborough he 'was regarded as second to none in both laws' (that is, both civil and canon), to become bishop of Osma. Perhaps he came at Alfonso VIII's suggestion. Indeed, the fact that in the following year he sold his property in Palencia to its bishop-elect may indicate that he had hitherto been keeping his options open and contemplating returning to Castile, and to Palencia in particular, in a different capacity. In the event, his years at Osma were scarred by the refusal of Alfonso's daughter, doña Berenguela, and doña Berenguela's son, Fernando III, to honour the provision of her father's will and make the lordship of the city over to him. And, regardless of the imposition of extreme ecclesiastical sanctions, doña Berenguela had her way.[61] After all, Alfonso IX's incestuous consort had prior experience of ignoring ecclesiastical sanctions.

It was probably not by chance that Melendus had chosen to exchange the centre of Christendom for that relatively insignificant corner of Castile. For there are signs that other canonists were making their way to Osma at this time, and it is certain – and the two developments will not have been unconnected – that at Soria within that diocese during these years the next generation of chancery clerks was being trained for the royal bureaucracy.[62]

In the event, Osma did not develop as Castile's *studium* to replace Palencia, which by the 1230s was deprived of funds and in terminal decline. 'It is still standing' was as much as D. Rodrigo felt able to report.[63] Nor did Zamora prevail over Salamanca as the Leonese *studium*, despite the far greater level of legal activity there during the 1220s. Its failure to do so was partly due,

[59]   ed. Pérez Rodríguez, 38, 167.
[60]   *Reg. Greg. IX*, 2075. Cf. Fleisch, 226–7.
[61]   Linehan, *Spanish Church*, 10–11; idem, 'Juan de Osma', 387. The bishop's borrowing of materials from the monastery of S. Salvador de Oña for use in his litigation was still remembered there in 1239: Castell Maiques, 375.
[62]   Linehan, 'Juan de Soria', 386–7.
[63]   Cf. Hernández & Linehan, 57, 95–6.

no doubt, to fears for the safety of its students engendered by its proximity to León's frontier with Portugal, partly to Palencia's superior drawing-power in these years. The principal reason though was that it was at Salamanca that the kings of León wanted the Leonese *studium* established.[64] As Alfonso VI had declared when prohibiting the Hispanic rite despite its having survived trial by fire: 'Laws go where the king chooses.'[65]

Moreover, by the 1220s another variable had entered the equation. Osma and Palencia were the cities in which, before his foundation of the Order of Preachers, Domingo de Guzmán had spent his early years, as canon of the one and student at the other. For the entire peninsula, the impact of the friars was both sudden and profound, and for the peninsular Church in particular, economically hard-pressed as it was by its kings to provide support for the ongoing reconquest, the arrival of the Dominicans and Franciscans further damaged the already fragile social and ecclesiastical ecology. But the king 'loved them and held them dear'.[66] Diego García had recently inveighed against the morals of an age in which black monks transformed themselves into regular canons, regular canons into secular priests, secular priests into knights, and knights into minstrels.[67] It may be imagined what he would have thought of the activities of these professional vagabonds, neither one thing nor the other, who, because their numbers included so many of the intellectually most able and pastorally most charismatic members of their generation, were nevertheless everywhere received with open arms by the laity. Would not the friars have confirmed his conviction that the times were out of joint? Would not his sympathies have been with those canons of Burgos whose determined attempts throughout the century to frustrate the building operations of the local Dominicans were regularly but wholly ineffectually reported to Rome, and with those members of the ecclesiastical establishment who in the 1250s would be delated for touring the country whitewashing the stigmata from statues of St Francis? In face of the famine affecting Castile after Alarcos, the student Dominic had sold his books for the relief of the poor, not wishing to study on dead skins while men died of hunger. But as his Order developed, and concentrated its activity in the cities and in university cities in particular, such saintly self-effacement was less and less in evidence.[68]

[64]   Linehan, 'Impugned chirograph', 472–3.
[65]   'Quo uolunt reges uadunt leges': *DrH*, VI. 25.
[66]   González, *Fernando III*, no. 152 (requiring 'all men of his kingdom' to receive the Dominicans well, Jan. 1222; earlier probably than any other king).
[67]   *Planeta*, 183. Diego uses the word 'ioculator'.
[68]   Linehan, 'Tale of Two Cities'; Vauchez, 603; Manning, lines 1007–12; Linehan, *Ladies of Zamora*, 8–10.

Some idea of the material the friars were studying and the doctrines they were disseminating – and all this within a decade of the composition of *Planeta* – is provided by the list of books borrowed by local convents of both orders from the library of Archbishop Bernardo of Compostela. Aristotelian and pseudo-Aristotelian works of ethics and natural philosophy, together with various treatises of astronomy, astrology and mathematics were just some of the items outwith the traditional curriculum.[69] Half a century later a copy of Avicenna would be available to all in the choir of Orense cathedral.[70] Meanwhile, in the place ranked second after Rome as a goal of Christian pilgrimage in the West, and amongst the first generation of friars, the spirit of the twelfth-century Renaissance continued to flourish, animated and sustained by the influence of Aristotelian ethics, logic and natural philosophy mediated by disciples of Andalusia's two principal intellectual luminaries.

Ibn Rushd and Moses ben Maimon, better known as Averroes and Maimonides, both natives of Córdoba, to whom Islam and Judaism as well as their beneficiaries in the Christian area of the peninsula and beyond were chiefly indebted, died in 1198 and 1205 respectively. (The year 1210 saw the first ban on the study of Aristotle's works on natural philosophy at Paris.)[71] Both were also distinguished jurists and physicians; both had to contend with Almohad fundamentalism, with Averroes accused of heresy, having his books burnt, and in his last years being sent in exile. For him, the *shari'ah* required the study of philosophy and philosophy contained nothing alien to the *shari'ah*; philosophy and religion were 'friends and milk-sisters'.[72] So also were they for Maimonides. Taking reason to its limits while recognizing that human intellect had limits too, and originally written in Judeo-Arabic, the latter's *Guide of the Perplexed* and *Mishneh Torah* (*Book of Knowledge*) in particular sought to demonstrate the conformity of Scripture and the Talmud with Aristotelian teaching both metaphysical and ethical. Its influence within Judaism was to be both decisive and divisive; that of the Muslim sage would be felt less within Islam than within Judaism and Christianity, ultimately throughout Europe but in the first instance in Toledo.

[69]   García-Ballester, 'Nature and science'.
[70]   Linehan, *Spanish Church*, 237.
[71]   Rashdall, I, 356–7.
[72]   All the more did it grieve him therefore that religions should have suffered 'at the hands of people who claim an affinity with philosophy': Hourani, 70.

Castile Victorious

There the translation of Arabic texts and commentaries into Latin had been a principal activity since the 1150s. With Arabic-speaking Jews and Christian Mozarabs acting as intermediaries, Toledo, amongst other peninsular locations, had attracted from abroad men of the calibre of Gerard of Cremona, to whom no fewer than eighty-seven translations are attributed, and, in the 1210s and beyond, Michael Scot and Herman the German, as well as recruiting Mozarabs from al-Andalus (Juan de Sevilla/Limia) and Toledo itself (Domingo Gundisalvo and the Jewish scholar, Avendauth), all intent on recovering the 'wisdom of the Greeks', notably Aristotle, from the Averroistic commentaries in which it was encased, as well as that of the Arabs, notably Avicenna.[73] Indeed, in view of such cosmopolitanism, not to mention both the intimate links between the cathedral chapter and the royal chancery towards the end of the twelfth century and the evidence of courtly patronage of the translators, it has naturally been asked why it was Palencia rather than Toledo that was chosen to be Castile's *studium*.[74] Such indeed was the implication of the account of the place provided by the pseudo-Virgil of Córdoba in the 1290s.[75] But the prerequisites for that development were lacking. It was not for study of the liberal arts and law that foreigners flocked to Toledo. The place was more of an institute for advanced study, or think tank, than a potential *studium*. Moreover, as was the case of Zamora in relation to Portugal, until 1212 Toledo was exposed to the dangers of the frontier, in this case the frontier with the south, and, as well as an ethnic mix which facilitated the process of translation, it contained within its Christian community acute tensions between locals and outsiders.

Over the following century these tensions would be increased by the arrival of groups of newcomers from both within the peninsula and beyond. The first of these were the Navarrese compatriots of Rodrigo Jiménez de Rada, named as archbishop in 1209, whose monopoly of capitular appointments so incensed the locals that by 1245 both they and the archbishop had been

---

[73]   d'Alverny, 444–57; Burnett, 95–116; Gil, *Escuela*, 29–56.

[74]   Gonzálvez, 'Escuela de Toledo', 207. For the book (or books) on geomancy 'which Master Gerard of Cremona, the great doctor of physic, translated from Arabic into Latin, having his expenses from the king of Castile [Alfonso VIII]', and for the chancellor Juan de Soria's patronage of Hermann the German at Toledo in the 1240s: Burnett, 128 n. 144; Hernández & Linehan, 37.

[75]   Below, 227.

driven into exile at Alcalá de Henares.[76] In 1212 D. Rodrigo acted as the impresario of Las Navas, striving to ensure that the Christians who came to fight qualified for the benefits of the crusade indulgence and travelling to the French court and throughout France to recruit warriors, by his own account with notable success. Not, however, according to Juan of Soria, who by the time he wrote his chronicle was royal chancellor. According to Juan, from Philip Augustus D. Rodrigo received 'not so much as a word of encouragement'.[77] Moreover, if Pick is right in representing Las Navas 'in terms of a cosmic struggle between good and evil' and as a pan-peninsular operation, that was not how Castilians saw it. Having as recently as February 1212 urged the king to maintain his truce with the enemy 'until a more opportune time may come', Innocent III now insisted that the victory was God's.[78] But so far as the Castilians were concerned, it was theirs. Alfonso gleefully informed the pontiff of the defection of all but one hundred and fifty of the French before battle commenced, 'whereas we chose to die for the faith of Christ'. Admittedly, it had been 'rather hot', he explained, and the French had been dissatisfied with their share of the loot when Calatrava surrendered.[79] Here was revenge for a century or more of French cultural condescension, in particular for the claim that after Charlemagne had reconquered territory from the Moors the feckless Spaniards lost it again. Nor was that all. For if D. Rodrigo was at pains to stress Christian Spain's united front in 1212, with Alfonso the 'first among equals', that was not Alfonso's view either. In his report to the pope, the kings of Aragón and Navarre feature as very much the junior partners at Las Navas, bringing 'only a small number of noble knights' and 'hardly more than two hundred men' respectively, while the kings of Portugal and León had not been there at all.[80]

How very prescient of God it had been, the royal chancellor reflected, to have disposed of the French, ensuring thereby that the honour of victory would belong exclusively to Spaniards ('Yspanis') 'and particularly to the

---

[76]   Hernández & Linehan, 44–7.

[77]   Pick, *Conflict*, 41–2; *Crón. latina*, c. 21, noted Hernández, 'Corte de Fernando III', 108–9. As the chronicler remarks, such Frenchmen as did come were mainly from the south, the area visited by the king's medic, Master Arnaldo.

[78]   Pick, *Conflict*, 40; Mansilla, *Inocencio III*, 501, 521. Cf. *Crón. latina*, c. 25, remembering 'the few' who had been present 'from various parts of the world', and lauding the 'glorious king of Navarre' who had come, 'though with only a few'.

[79]   Mansilla, *Inocencio III*, 511–12; Linehan, *History*, 295–6.

[80]   Pick, *Conflict*, 44–5; Mansilla, *Inocencio III*, 512. Did a sense that the rewards enjoyed by the local Navarrese were disproportionate to their countrymen's contribution in 1212 fuel Mozarabic resentment within the chapter of Toledo?

kingdom of Castile'. And as the wider world sighed in relief before again losing interest in Spain and developments south of the Pyrenees, in Spain itself that sentiment was echoed. For all the attempts of the French chronicler to salvage French morale by claiming that until the French had withdrawn the Saracens had been afraid to fight, and attributing victory to the miraculous appearance at Las Navas of the banner of the Virgin of Rocamadour,[81] the consensus was as stated by Bishop Sicard of Cremona, that 'not only its own salvation but also that of Rome and indeed of the whole of Europe' was due to Spain – 'and in particular to the kingdom of Castile'.[82] Castile was a kingdom whose king enjoyed an authority uncompromised, whereas the authority of three of his four peninsular neighbours was in a certain sense diminished, in the case of Aragón and Portugal by their status as feudatories of the Roman Church, and in that of Navarre's rulers by Rome's refusal to acknowledge that status until the mid-1190s.[83] Despite the notable absence from the battlefield in July 1212 of the fifth peninsular monarch, the Leonese king, the Leonese chronicler felt able to insist that it was the kings of *Hispania* who fought for the faith. Praising the exploits of the 'Hyspani', the canonist Vincentius Hispanus (chancellor of the Portuguese king and bishop of the Portuguese see of Guarda) agreed. In his gloss to Innocent III's decretal 'Venerabilem', which had acknowledged the king of France's *de facto* independence of the German emperor, he referred to Charlemagne's defeat at Roncesvalles. If France had defeated the empire, Spain had defeated France, *ergo* Spain was supreme 'because if I beat someone who beats you, then I beat you', Vincentius claimed – in somewhat parochial tones, it has been suggested.[84]

In fact, anything but. With his aphorism that Spaniards were renowned for deeds and Frenchmen for words, Vincentius was in expansive mood.[85] Amongst the chattering classes euphoria was widespread. 'Do not Spaniards

[81] *Crón. latina*, c. 22. By Alberic's count there were 185,000 Saracen soldiers present, 925,000 cavalry and innumerable foot soldiers. Prior to the arrival of the banner 100,000 of the enemy had perished and rather more Christians. Thereafter the latter suffered hardly thirty further casualties: *Chronica*, 894–5.

[82] *Chronica*, 180.

[83] Kehr, *Papsturkunden*, nos. 228, 230. Cf. the beguiling observation that D. Rodrigo's presented the three warrior kings of Las Navas – those of Castile, Aragón, and Navarre – as counterparts of the biblical Magi, and the Almohad caliph as King Herod; the suggestion that that presentation echoes the content of the *Auto de los Reyes Magos*, the earliest vernacular version of the Three Kings story; and the proposal that 'at the very least Rodrigo commissioned the *Auto* and dictated its form and content': Pick, *Conflict*, 195–203.

[84] *CM*, IV. 94; Linehan, *History*, 296–7; Cortese, 23.

[85] Post, 485.

rule in France, England, Germany, and Constantinople?', he asked, writing probably in 1243. (Well actually, no they didn't.) 'Blessed are they', he continued, 'those Spanish ladies who obtain dominion and in their domination expand it by virtue of their valour and probity.'[86] The theme had been developed by Lucas of Tuy three or four years earlier. 'The kings of *Yspania* are everywhere victorious. Bishops, abbots and the clergy are engaged in building churches and monasteries, and husbandmen work their fields without fear, feed their animals and enjoy peace with no disturbance from anyone.'[87] An idyllic scene, in short. But far from the truth, alas. For the autumn of 1212 found Castile in a state of prostration, with the 'almost unbearable expenses' of the recent campaign being followed by widespread illness of every description, in particular what sounds like a diarrhoea epidemic ('fluxus ventrium') which carried off the greater part of the elderly, and with the fruits of victory widely dispersed amongst its king's recent allies.[88] In the chapters that follow those harsh realities will be further explored.

[86] Ibid., 489, emended as follows: 'Nonne in francia et in anglia et in theotonica [*sic?*] et in constantinopoli Yspani dominantur? Beate domine Yspane que dominium pariunt et dominantes audacie et probitatis virtutibus expandunt!' As well as seeking to make sense of Post's syntactically incoherent reading, this recognizes that J. Gil's interpretation of the words 'beate domine Yspane' as referring to Alfonso VIII's four daughters ruling on France etc. (rather than to Post's enigmatic 'Blessed Lady Spain') unfortunately fails to correspond to reality either in the 1240s or earlier: 'A apropriação', 18.
[87] *CM*, IV. 94.
[88] Mansilla, *Inocencio III*, 510; *Crón. latina*, c. 25; González, *Alfonso VIII*, no. 898.

3

1214–48

Doña Berenguela and Son

Having reigned for fifty-six of his fifty-nine years Alfonso VIII of Castile died on 22 September 1214. Ten years earlier he had made a will; rumours would soon be circulating of another. For his victory at Las Navas he was remembered, at the end of the process Las Navas had begun, as another David 'but even stronger'.[1] His queen, doña Leonor, the toast of the troubadours, followed him to the grave in the same month, leaving as his successor their eleventh and last child, the ten-year-old Enrique. With three of his surviving sisters the queens of Portugal and Aragón and queen-in-waiting of France and the fourth immured as a nun of Las Huelgas de Burgos, it was clear who would control events in the immediate future. The reins of power passed to the hands of Alfonso's experienced eldest daughter, the former consort of Alfonso IX of León and a lady *d'un certain âge*, some forty-three summers in fact.

In the event, the immediate future was a brief one. For child-kings will do childish things and have accidents. In June 1217, while in the custody of Count Álvaro Núñez de Lara, Enrique suffered an accident when something hit him on the head while he was playing. Was it a tile, or was it a stone? Did it fall, or was it thrown? Thrown, it has been suggested, and with traces of doña Berenguela's fingerprints all over the missile, after her earlier foiled attempt to dispose of the young king by means of poison in order to prevent a marriage that would have made him heir to the throne of León.[2] Others

---

[1] 'G. Petri Rithmi', line 154.

[2] Doubleday, 55–6, though the author misreports D. Rodrigo's account of the fate of the queen's messenger found with her incriminating but allegedly forged letter and ignores Juan of Soria's more circumstantial description of the incident on which D. Rodrigo's is evidently based: *DrH*, IX. 3; *Crón. latina*, c. 32. Further detail in Jaime of Aragón, *Book of Deeds*, c. 17.

too thought that he had been done away with, and not only in order to satisfy the requirements of poetical metre: in 1250 Guillermo Pérez de la Calzada would openly refer to Berenguela's acquisition of 'the kingdom of her murdered brother'.[3]

Be that as it may, if you had managed to survive that long as a member of the royal family in thirteenth-century Castile, forty-three was king-making age, and doña Berenguela's strategy was now clear. It was to secure the throne of Castile for her eldest son, the thirteen-year-old Fernando, by relinquishing her rights to him, and to secure his Leonese interests by frustrating the schemes of Alfonso IX and his other children. To this the king of León countered by declaring his daughters by his first wife, Teresa of Portugal, to be his heirs, the effect of which would be to debar Fernando from the Leonese inheritance as well as serving his own ends, since, according to D. Rodrigo, he 'coveted the empire'. By this the archbishop can only have meant the empire that had perished with Alfonso VII.[4]

It was perhaps at this stage that the further spoiling tactic designed to put paid also to Fernando's Castilian prospects was devised. This was the assertion that Berenguela had nothing to relinquish because it was not she but her sister Blanca (Blanche of Castile) who was Alfonso VIII's eldest surviving child; a demonstrably absurd claim though one the chroniclers felt the need to refute and one which continued to enjoy credence for centuries to come in interested circles, and particularly interested French circles down to Jean Bodin and beyond.[5] Associated with this *canard* was the offer of the crown of Castile to the future Louis IX of France, a proposal made in letters (probably of 1224) from the rebel nobles Rodrigo Díaz de los Cameros and Gonzalo Pérez de Molina to Blanche, her husband (Louis VIII) and children. This, they asserted, was in accordance with the king's deathbed wishes in the event of his son Enrique dying without issue, and was, one of them stated, the king's 'last will'.[6]

In the event, both these obstructions were overcome. The death of Louis VIII in 1226 and the succession of a king thirteen years younger than his Castilian cousin deprived the Castilian malcontents of any hope of French intervention, and on the death of Alfonso IX in 1230 his daughters preferred hard cash to whatever rights they may have had to his kingdom. Then, as in 1217, Berenguela achieved her objective by shrewd political management

[3]   'Que Regnum optinuit tunc occisi fratris': 'G. Petri Rithmi', line 183.
[4]   Shadis, 343–5; *Crón. latina*, c. 36 (whence *DrH*, IX. 5).
[5]   *Crón. latina*, c. 33 (whence *DrH*, IX. 5); Linehan, 'Accession', esp. pp. 71–3.
[6]   Rodríguez López, '*Quod alienus regnet*', 113–15; Hernández, 'Corte', 110–18, 141–3. Berenguela had been born in 1171, Blanca in 1188.

and, as Juan de Soria's account of events makes clear, control of an effective clientage network within the cities and the political high command. Except to the extent that all thirteenth-century bishops were mitred grandees, the decisive character of the role Rodrigo of Toledo attributed to the Leonese episcopate, 'for whom it matters to keep Church and State under close scrutiny', is less easy to discern. Indeed the bishops' collective resoluteness is no more conspicuous than the resolve of Honorius III who, as soon as Fernando had secured the Castilian throne, 'on account of evident utility and urgent necessity' gave his apostolic blessing to the offspring of the 'incestuous copulation' his predecessor had declared forever excluded from the paternal inheritance. 'Evident utility and urgent necessity' were the grounds on which the Fourth Lateran Council had modified the existing forbidden degrees while declaring the new limitations to be 'perpetual'. *How* perpetual was now revealed, just two years later.[7] At Burgos in November 1219 the king knighted himself and married Beatrice of Swabia, cousin of the Emperor Frederick II, thereby securing that *entrée* into the world beyond the Pyrenees that the cancellation of his mother's match with Conrad of Hohenstaufen, the son of Frederick Barbarossa, had frustrated in 1188.[8] Two years later the queen produced their first child, the future Alfonso X.

According to Lucas of Tuy, Fernando III was the first king of his line not to have indulged in extra-marital affairs, though whether his abstinence may have been a consequence of doña Berenguela's iron rule or a reaction against her alleged lasciviousness, the chronicler does not speculate. The chronicler also describes him as a king dominated by his mother – 'queen of Toledo' as the papal chancery addressed her – and permanently under her 'iron rule'. In violation of all the rules of chivalry the 'noble queen' participated in his knighting ceremonial by ungirding her eighteen-year-old son.[9] Her protectiveness (if it was that) resembled her sister Blanca's reluctance to allow her son, the king of France, to sleep with his wife. In his plaint in memory of the patron of troubadours, Blacatz d'Alms, the Mantuan poet Sordello da Goito imagined Europe's rulers feasting off the deceased's heart in order to acquire those qualities they lacked themselves. As the ruler of two

---

[7]   X 4. 14. 8. The pontiff was optimistic. So is the implication of Duby's judgement (*Medieval Marriage*, p. 80) that the concession of the 'ecclesiastical' to the 'lay' model of marriage, as acknowledged in the Council's changes to the law, excluded those intent on marrying within the new limits. Spanish kings had an appetite for more. So did others, and would find popes sympathetic: below, 175. Cf. Linehan, *History*, 258–9, 393–4.

[8]   *DrH*, IX. 10; Mansilla, *Honorio III*, no. 179 (July 1218); Rassow, *Der Prinzgemahl*.

[9]   *CM*, IV. 93; Alberic, *Cronica*, 895 ('incontinentia, de qua multa dicebantur'), *Reg. Greg. IX*, 2370; *DrH*, IX. 10 (the chancellor could not bring himself to mention her involvement: *Crón. latina*, c. 40). Cf. *Part*. 2. 21. 11, cit. Linehan, *History*, 597.

kingdoms the king of Castile required two helpings. 'But if he does dine twice', the poet observes, 'he will have to do so secretly because if his mother finds out she will beat him with her stick.'[10] Sordello's contemptuous squib, datable to 1236 or early 1237 (a high point of Fernando's reign), was based not only on rumour but also on his own observation, as was his matching swipe at the expense of that other mother's boy, Louis IX of France, who, he says, lacked the appetite to be king of Castile himself.[11]

Indeed, it may be that Sordello's derogatory remarks were inspired by the unfavourable reception he and his colleagues experienced at Fernando's court and his knowledge that the puritanism of the place and its lack of *joglares*, by comparison with that of Alfonso VIII, was due not to the king, as has been suggested, but rather to his formidable mother.[12] May it have been another indication of a grandmother's claustrophobic concern that the *Libro de los doze sabios*, with its account of the unhappy ends to which their wantonness had brought the likes of David, Solomon, Aristotle, Virgil and the last king of the Visigoths, was addressed to Fernando's sons, the infantes of Castile?[13]

'The Gate is Open and the Way is Clear'

The picture of Fernando III painted by the poet whom Dante commemorated for his knowledge of the valley of negligent rulers[14] was not that of the masterful monarch of tradition. Nor for that matter is the piety of *San* Fernando any more credible. It was not principally historical accuracy that occupied the promoters of the cause of his canonization between 1627 and 1671. It is not from them that we learn of his wholesale appropriation of the *tercias* in 1228,[15] or the persecution of the bishop and church of Calahorra that in 1231 caused the pope to issue so withering a

[10] Boni, 158–65; Riquer, *Trovadores*, 1464–7.
[11] Whose meal would encourage him to recover Castile, lost by his own stupidity, though only if his mother allowed him to eat since he did nothing without her permission: Boni, 160; Menéndez Pidal, *Poesía juglaresca*, 141–2. For Sordello's exile in Spain and France: Boni, pp. xlvii–liii.
[12] Cf. Alvar, 'Poesía y política', 6–7.
[13] ed. Walsh, 80–1.
[14] *Purgatorio*, canto 7.
[15] AC Toledo, Z.3.D.1.5; AHN, Clero, carp. 3019/5 (Domínguez Sánchez, *Gregorio IX*, no. 50). The *tercias* of Madrid were reportedly being used for repairs to the town walls: AC Toledo, I.4.N.1.7 (Domínguez Sánchez, no. 51).

denunciation,[16] or the contempt for the precepts of canon law displayed by his permission to the clergy of Guadalajara in 1238 to bequeath property to their offspring.[17] Sixty years ago a Redemptorist panegyrist held Diego López de Haro responsible for the enormities reported in the second of these cases, pleading strategic considerations in a frontier area between Christian kingdoms, castigating 'irreverent authors and unscrupulous peddlers of historical anachronisms' for 'fustigating Fernando's memory', and, as to the third, offering the helpful suggestion, so characteristic of its time and place, that the clergy in question may have been laymen in disguise. But such are the 'mysteries of History', Fr. Retana reflected consolingly as he pondered the exemplary biography of that 'faithful son of the Church', the very 'antithesis of Frederick II'.[18] 'Until such time as historical criticism clarify these points, San Fernando is not to be accused of mistreating the Church, above all when the Church was so enormously enriched by him and the religious orders favoured in a thousand ways', Fr. Retana continued, regardless of the fact that in 1234 the pope himself had clarified them.[19]

That year 1234 was also the year of issue of the Gregorian decretals, the compilation of canon law organized by Ramon de Penyafort, the Catalan Dominican and Master General of the Order. The Dominicans were already diversifying their pastoral role, notably within the Aragonese episcopate,[20] canonists of all colours were active throughout Europe, and Spaniards were at the forefront of that activity, little as their kings appear to have been influenced by the principles they espoused. Also in 1234 Alberic of Trois Fontaines reported that Fernando III had informed the Roman curia that he 'wished to be granted the imperial title and blessing, as had certain of his ancestors'. The king was doubtless looking forward to the imminent centenary of Alfonso VII's imperial coronation at León as well as to Seville, where, as his son Alfonso X would later contend, Spanish emperors had once been crowned.[21] The force of the request was

---

[16] *Reg. Greg. IX*, 594 (Domínguez Sánchez, *Gregorio IX*, no. 173); Linehan, *Spanish Church*, 26; Díaz Bodegas, 39–42; Rodríguez López, *Consolidación*, 209–18.

[17] González, *Fernando III*, no. 623. The evil effects of the custom had been complained of at Palencia in 1228: Abajo, no. 178.

[18] Retana, 173, 176.

[19] When Diego López de Haro declared that all his actions had been undertaken on Fernando's instructions and Fernando confirmed as much: Lecuona, 138.

[20] Linehan, *Spanish Church*, 69–80. For the contribution of the long-lived bishop of Valencia Andreu de Albalat (†1276), brother of Pere, the reforming metropolitan of Tarragona, and his commitment to breaking the Jewish monopoly of medical practice: ibid., 71–2, 311; García-Ballester, *Hist. social de la medicina*, 18–23.

[21] *Cronica*, 936; Linehan, *History*, 235–7, 434.

augmented by his exertions over the previous decade that had brought Seville into focus.

Juan of Soria, by now the king's chancellor, describes the beginnings of the process. 'One day' in 1224, when the court was at Muñó near Burgos, 'suddenly' the king (now a man of twenty-four) rose and, addressing his mother, recalled that Berenguela had abdicated in his favour and 'by her efforts and industry' had provided him with a wife. Was it not now time for him to exert himself and do battle with the Moors, he asked her ('to whom after God I owe everything I possess'). The barons present were amazed by this,[22] but, after the queen-mother had seized the opportunity of providing a display of constitutional rectitude by inviting the barons to utter, utter they did and war was declared. By this account, despite his filial sentiments the initiative was Fernando's. The archbishop of Toledo, by contrast, gives the queen-mother the credit.[23]

The victory of Las Navas and the destruction of Almohad power had left al-Andalus at the mercy of the Christians. The fertile lands beyond the desert of La Mancha south of Toledo beckoned. 'The gate is open and the way is clear', the king is reported as saying at Muñó. 'Our kingdom' – in historical mode, be it noted, Juan de Soria uses the singular form; as chancellor he would itemize the component kingdoms – 'is at peace and our enemies in disarray.' Of this the last part at least was true. For Las Navas had prompted no response from the Almohads. Contact with Spain had proved ultimately fatal to the successive Berber movements that had emerged from the North African desert and intervened in Spain's affairs. In the next century Ibn Khaldūn would describe the recurrent process whereby the tribes derived cohesion from the rigour of their nomadic existence and the loss of it due to meat-eating and other delights of the cities of the plain.[24] It was the death of al-Nāsir's successor, al-Mustansir, at the beginning of 1224, reportedly impaled on the horns of a cow, that prompted the Christian North to embark upon the Great Leap Forward into Andalusia.

Towards Valencia

But for all that, not least because in 1224 Castile remained such a hungry place, the response of the Castilian barons to their king's call for action

[22]   *Crón. latina*, c. 43. 'Obstupuerunt', the word used here was the word the chronicler had used to describe the shock caused by the death of the Infante Fernando in 1211 (ibid., c. 20).
[23]   *DrH*, IX. 12; Linehan, 'Chancellor as chronicler', 9.
[24]   *Crón. latina*, loc. cit.; Le Tourneau, 89–92; Arié, 49–54; Brett, 625–6; Crone, 321–2.

was remarkable. There could be no sharper contrast than that of the Aragonese nobility when, as recorded in the autobiography of Jaime I, two years later he summoned them because 'we wished to enter the kingdom of Valencia to attack the Moors'. When the day arrived for Jaime's barons to join him, just three of them did so. In its unglossed state, the *Book of Deeds* sheds more light on the fraction of Jaime's reign it covers (just twenty-nine of his sixty-three years) than all the exegesis that modern scholarship has lavished upon it (which is not to say that as much as half of its contents is credible). Apart from its account of his father's reluctance to allow him to be conceived at all ('since our father and mother did not care greatly for each other, it was rather by the will of God that we were born into this world': a revelation later chroniclers would improve on by suggesting that it had been only achieved because Pedro II, the Catholic, thought he was sleeping with a girl friend) and of his near-starvation as a child, the king's account of his youth, and indeed of his entire reign, is principally memorable for its combination of bracing draughts of political nous and unremitting vigour. It was a precept of the king that 'great matters are better treated in the morning . . . than at any other hour of the day', and a suggestion of early-morning mist hovering above it is one of the two most noticeable characteristics of his *Llibre del Fets*. The other is its Catalan bias. Catalan is the language in which the *Llibre* is written and, if the work has a hero other than the king himself, that hero is Catalonia personified, vigorous, outward-looking, not easily caricatured, and, in its author's own words, 'the most noble land in Spain'.[25]

The Aragonese meanwhile – whose relationship with the Catalans was as unstable as that of the king's parents – and the Aragonese nobility in particular, were landlocked, blinkered, wedded to the past and intent on keeping the king in leading strings, the author wished it to be understood. 'If you kings were to achieve everything you wanted all the land would be yours', Blasco de Alagón is recorded as saying at the siege of Burriana in 1233. After associating himself during Jaime's minority with the king's ambitious uncle, the Infant Ferran abbot of Montearagón, and then leading a shadowy existence at the court of the Muslim ruler of Valencia, Blasco de Alagón was well qualified to express the Aragonese version of sentiments Alfonso X was to inveigh against in his letter to his son forty years later.[26]

[25] *Book of Deeds*, cc. 5, 11 25, 48, 145, 392; Soldevila, *Els primers temps*, 1–9; Burns, 'Spiritual life'.
[26] *Book of Deeds*, c. 166; Arroyo, 'Blasco de Alagón'; below, 166–7. The fullest account of the first fifteen years of the reign is that of Soldevila, *Els primers temps de Jaume I*.

Rather than with their Castilian cousins, however, these 'evil men' (as Jaime described them when rejecting their advice)[27] were to be compared with the French who had shirked battle in 1212 on being denied the opportunity to plunder Calatrava. For whereas it was clear to the king that storming a town was bound to cause 'great disputes' between the Catalans and the Aragonese, the surrender on terms of enemy strongholds was the last thing they wanted. Anything was preferable to that, the options being either no change of proprietor (and therefore continuing tribute) or sack and booty.[28] For reasons such as these, in 1232 Jaime was advised that it would be preferable for the Moors to continue to occupy Morella than for D. Blasco to have it. Six years later, with Valencia itself in sight, so damnable were the 'machinations' of these noblemen that Gregory IX was prevailed upon to require them on pain of excommunication to dissolve their 'societies' since their 'pacts' were obstructing the business of the faith.[29]

Another consideration was the state of the kingdom of Valencia, both inviting and inhibiting intervention according to which course of action seemed likely to prove more profitable for both king and nobility. With the *sayyid* Abū Zayd, *wālī* of the region, hard pressed in his struggle for survival against Zayyān, the grand-nephew of King Lob, its last *pre*-Almohad (Banū Mardanīsh) ruler, when in 1228 Ibn Hūd seized control of Murcia and proclaimed himself emir in the interest of the Abbasid caliph of Baghdad, in order to survive he was obliged to combine alliance with Castile (a recurrent element in the politics of the area) with surrender of castles and revenue to Aragón before taking collaboration to its logical conclusion and seeking refuge in conversion to Christianity. Together with the king's divorce, it was the last of these ploys (eventually realized when he was baptized with the name Vincent and, with a view to controlling his promiscuous tendencies, married off by the bishop of Zaragoza to a lady of that city) that brought the papal legate, Cardinal John of Abbeville, to the kingdom of Aragón at this time.[30]

But in 1224, with Valencia still far distant, (almost) 'all the cities of Aragon' against its king, 'not more than four knights' with him, the king himself in hand-to-hand combat with the leader of the baronial opposition, Pedro de Ahones, and Pedro's brother Sancho, the bishop of Zaragoza, rewarding his troops for fighting by allowing them to eat meat during Lent, the

---

27   *Book of Deeds*, c. 169.
28   Ibid., cc. 178, 278, 281, 283; Burns, *Islam*, 138–42.
29   *Book of Deeds*, c. 135; *Reg. Greg. IX*, 4070 (Domínguez Sánchez, *Gregorio IX*, no. 727).
30   Above, 12; *Book of Deeds*, c. 25; Burns, *Islam*, 30–37; Fernández-Armesto, *Before Columbus*, 72–3; Zurita, III. 25; *Crón. latina*, c. 54; Catalán & Jerez, 75–6.

sixteen-year old decided to 'invoke his lordship'. 'Early one morning' he ordered his vassals to present themselves with their weapons the next day (also 'first thing in the morning') or otherwise 'lose all the possessions they held in our lands': a brave, if risky, undertaking. With three of the kingdom's twelve great barons appearing, together with seventy or eighty knights, the result was not bad, though Jaime does not say so. The principal significance of the occasion, though, was not that. It was the national scope of the sanctions invoked, precisely those sanctions Ramon Berenguer's Catalan subjects had been threatened with seventy years before. It will not have failed to register with the Aragonese 'richs homens' that they were being subjected to the brisk discipline of the Catalan *Usatici*.[31]

There were two rites of passage for the young king to endure before he returned to the charge and the advance into the kingdom of Valencia. First, in the late summer of 1228, the lady Aurembiaix who had been dispossessed of the county of Urgell approached the king for justice. Having recently had his marriage to one infanta dissolved on grounds of consanguinity and being already engaged in the process of binding himself to another related to him in precisely the same degree,[32] Jaime responded to her pleas by taking possession of both the city of Lleida and the lady herself, their contract of concubinage providing for all possible eventualities, including future control of the county.[33] Vigorous as he was, Jaime may have been reflecting on the need to develop other less strenuous procedures for bringing the remaining ex-Carolingian counties under his control when in the following November the opportunity arose of extending that control beyond the Spanish mainland.

The Mallorca campaign marked the coming of age both of the king, who owed it his epithet of 'Conqueror', and of his capital city in the affairs of the Mediterranean. The enthusiasm with which the proposal was greeted, when Pere Martell first mooted it at a dinner party he was hosting at Tarragona, could not have contrasted more sharply with the truculent reaction of the Aragonese four years earlier. Martell is described as a merchant of Barcelona, Jaime's mercantilist commitment to which had already been revealed, as

[31]   *Book of Deeds*, cc. 25–9; Zurita, II. 80; Soldevila, *Primers temps*, 240–72 (based almost exclusively on Jaime's own account); González Antón, 'Revuelta de la nobleza aragonesa'; above, 30.

[32]   Leonor, daughter of Alfonso VIII of Castile, and Sancha, daughter of Alfonso IX of León (a union frustrated by the latter's death): *Book of Deeds*, c. 107; Tourtoulon, I, 249–50, 311–12; Sagarra, 286–7. Both shared the same great-grandfather with the king of Aragón.

[33]   *Book of Deeds*, cc. 34–46. The contract provided *inter alia* for the king's eventual marriage to a lady worth more than the county of Urgell and for the countess's entry into religion (but not into the married state): Soldevila, *Primers temps*, 273–300.

was Pere Grony at what has been called 'the planning committee for Catalan colonialism', though in fact Tarragona and Marseilles both made a greater contribution than Barcelona to the expedition. Amidst the general euphoria Grony is remembered (misremembered actually) as volunteering all the city's men and ships for the expedition, an expedition that was undertaken not in the grudging spirit of limited liability characteristic of the king's Aragonese subjects but with the entrepreneurial commitment of the venture capitalists within the urban patriciate which in these years was coming to dominate Barcelona's governing *Consell de Cent*.[34]

The fiscal administration perfected during the reign of Jaime's grand-father was fully capable of supervising the territorial division of the island amongst the conquerors, and when Mallorca fell on the last day of 1229 it was the inhabitants of the Catalan coast who reaped the richest rewards in the form of privileged status (though not monopolistic access) to trade with Ḥafṣīd Tunisia and points west. They were even enabled to extort *parias* again and thereby gain access to supplies of gold denied them since the 1080s. According to the chronicler Desclot, writing in the 1280s, it had been the determination of the Catalans to rid the waters around the Balearics of Muslim pirates that had fuelled the enterprise, while for the historian Soldevila in the 1930s the isthmus that had once connected Mallorca and Catalonia was now symbolically re-established: Mallorca was Catalan in blood, language and culture.[35] For the Catalans the capture of Mallorca was what the victory of Las Navas de Tolosa had been for the Castilians. According to Muntaner, its capital was entirely inhabited by them.[36] Because of it their king now enjoyed an international reputation – even if the Englishman Matthew Paris credited his achievements to the king of Castile.[37] Small wonder therefore that the view expressed more recently by another English writer, concerning the 'large Provençal and Montpelliérain contingent' involved in the conquest and the 'Occitan character of the settlement of the islands', should have produced a storm of protest from Catalan historians[38] – not least on account of something the troubadours regularly complained about, namely Jaime's consistent neglect of the Occitan part of his inheritance.

---

[34]   *Docs.JI*, no. 96 (Oct. 1227); *Book of Deeds*, cc. 47–55; Bensch, 176–8 (showing the ascend-ancy of the Grony family amongst the city's *consellers*), 277; O'Callaghan, *Reconquest*, 126 (further details).

[35]   Ibid., 99, 287–304; Soldevila, *Hist. de Catalunya*, 273–7. Lively accounts of the campaign in ibid. cc. 55–125; Fernández-Armesto, 13–22.

[36]   *Crònica*, c. 8.

[37]   *Chronica Majora*, III, 639; V, 193.

[38]   Abulafia, *Mediterranean Emporium*, 41. Cf. Ferrer Mallol, 454–5, charging the author with having misrepresented A. R. Lewis.

Jaime certainly let slip the opportunity of acquiring Navarre when in 1231 the childless Sanç VII, nearly eighty and too fat to show himself in public, proposed a compact of mutual adoption, an arrangement evidently wholly to Jaime's advantage, analogous to the *compadrazgo* relationship that bound together members of the Nasrid and Ashqilūla dynasties in contemporary Granada, and one to which, mercifully, no historian has yet attributed homoerotic motives.[39] The failure of the scheme, alleged by Jaime to be due to its 'unprofitability' to both parties and to his having to 'go to the land of the Moors', was in fact on account of undertakings regarding the succession of his half-Castilian heir, the Infante Alfonso, given at the Cortes of Daroca of 1228.[40] In 1234 the conviction of the Navarrese establishment that there was an option even worse than rule by an unknown Frenchman resulted in the installation of Thibaut IV of Champagne, Sanç's nephew, as Teobaldo I of Navarre.[41]

While the new king of Navarre occupied himself anywhere but in his kingdom, the new-model king of Aragón went to the land of the Moors but not before persuading the pope to exclude the faithful of the Navarrese dioceses of Pamplona and Calahorra from the spiritual benefits of the crusade indulgence extended to the remainder of the province of Tarragona.[42] Still impecunious and contemplating reconquest on the never-never, still lacking galleys, but now with the smell of success about him and a fecund wife, the Hungarian princess Violant, Jaime was ready for action. The beginnings of this, as described by himself, are reminiscent of the *longueurs* of an Edwardian house-party:

> Now, we were hunting small game in our own kingdom (. . .) relaxing and at leisure. We were at Alcañiz, and with us were the master of the Hospital and Don Blasco de Alagón. Both came to us, on the roof of the building. While we were sunning ourselves and chatting, [the Master] began to speak, and said: 'Lord, since God has guided you so well in the conquest of Majorca and those islands, might you and we not begin something over here, in this kingdom of Valencia . . . ?'

---

[39] *Docs.JI*, no. 147; Harvey, *Islamic Spain*, 31–2.

[40] Jaime's counsellors had replied on his behalf: '[The king] has ordered Aragón and Lleida to swear to that son. (. . .) And this is the greatest difficulty that the king has. He cannot take away his son's rights while he may live': *Book of Deeds*, c. 140; Bisson, 'General court of Aragon'.

[41] *Book of Deeds*, cc. 138–53; Lacarra, *Hist. política de Navarra*, 109–16, 121–7.

[42] *Reg. Greg. IX*, 3486 (Domínguez Sánchez, *Gregorio IX*, no. 639). Cf. the effect of papal *inclusion* of Pamplona in the province in the 1150s: above, 15.

So off they went. They might as well have been going off to hunt hares.[43]

One of the kingdom of Valencia's chief merits was its physical delight-fulness. Accordingly, from Burriana to the capital a scorched earth policy was adopted. For, the king asked, 'How can we leave these beautiful wheat-fields before us without laying waste to them?'[44] The process consisted of sieges, truces and surrender on terms, in order both to keep the Catalans and the Aragonese from one another's throats and to leave the economic infrastructure and the workforce in place. For if the Christians had to fight in order to defend and to feed themselves, the kings of Castile and Aragón combined could not hold Burriana, D. Jaime was warned. In the area between Islam's home-land and the territory of the infidel (dār al-'ahd: Realm of the Pact) the generosity of the terms allowed could be absolute. At Xàtiva, for example, ceded in 1244, the city's qā'id Abū Bakr became Jaime's vassal and his Mudéjar subjects retained their mosques and muezzins, their social organization, and, for two years, the more impregnable and precipitous of its castles, 'the best castle in all al-Andalus' in the qā'id's estimation. And once one place fell the others followed: after Peñiscola surrendered with-out a blow being struck, or Almenara fell, a domino effect ensued.[45]

The particulars of what followed, the succession of sieges and truces within both the Aragonese and the Castilian spheres of al-Andalus down to the surrender of Valencia in 1238, and that of Seville ten years later, will not be recorded here. In the words of King Jaime himself and of the History of the period commissioned by his son-in-law half a century later, to do so 'would greatly extend the story'.[46] Suffice it to say that in view of the failure of the Almohad caliph in Marrakesh to provide assistance, as Ibn Khaldūn would report, al-Andalus came to contain 'as many kings as there were castellated towns' and 'every qā'id and man of influence who could command a few score of followers, or possessed a castle to retire to in case of need, styled himself sultan and assumed the insignia of royalty', or otherwise placed themselves under one or other of the contending native leaders, Ibn Hūd or Muḥammad ibn Yūsuf, founder in 1237 of the Nasrid dynasty which for the remainder of century would periodically contend with the Banū 'Ashqilūlah for control of the kingdom of Granada.[47] Since both displayed a ready aptitude for changing sides and making peace with

---

[43] Book of Deeds, cc. 127, 164 (unless indicated, trans. here and elsewhere by Smith & Buffery); Hillgarth, 'Problem', 8–9; Soldevila, Hist. de Catalunya, 283.

[44] Book of Deeds, cc. 128, 156.

[45] Ibid., c. 180, 184–5, 249; Crone, 359; Burns & Chevedden, 131–42, 164–7, 197 (Epalza).

[46] Book of Deeds, c. 376; PCG, c. 1069. What follows summarizes my account in NCMH, V, 673–8; also González, Fernando III, I, 287–394. Further detail in Guichard, 397–407.

[47] Ibn Khaldūn, trans. P. de Gayangos, in Forster, Chronicle, II. 696; Arié, 55–60; H. Kennedy, 273–6; Harvey, Islamic Spain, 31–7.

Fernando III for substantial profit, with *parias* being paid and Christians fighting for Muslims in the manner of the unreconstructed Cid, the situation closely resembled that of two centuries before. In 1236 Ibn Hūd had almost two hundred Christians to assist him in the defence of Córdoba, twice the number of those attacking the place. Muslim resistance resulted in wholesale massacre of the defenders; surrender in the exaction of huge payments.

Even so, Christian progress was not uninterrupted. Quesada, captured in 1224, was lost again until 1231. Only after three sieges was Jaén taken in 1246. By then though Ibn Hūd's son, al-Wāthiq, had become Fernando's vassal for the kingdom of Murcia (Treaty of Alcaraz, 1243) and the Infante Alfonso had captured Cartagena. Though, as would soon be discovered, the acquisition of Murcia was a process too superficial to merit the name 'reconquest', it did give the king of Aragón notice of Castilian ambitions in the southeast and towards the Mediterranean. The next step was Seville, which would provide access to the Atlantic. With no prospect of aid from Africa, by 1248 Seville's fate was sealed. To Ibn Khaldūn it seemed that the Christians had erected a human wall around al-Andalus. After a siege of seventeen months during which its blockaded inhabitants had endured appalling privation, being reduced to a diet of roots, leather and human excrement ('and even this was in short supply'), the city surrendered its *alcázar* on 23 November. Its inhabitants asked for and were granted one month in which to sell such of their possessions as they could dispose of and were then expelled, one hundred thousand of them to Ceuta and, according to the Alfonsine History, three times that number to Jerez. On 22 December, with his vassal Ibn Hūd in his entourage, Fernando III took possession of the place.[48]

Conquest and Colonization

> Ask Valencia what became of Murcia,
> And where is Játiva and where is Jaén?
> Where is Córdoba, the seat of great learning,
> And how many scholars of high repute remain there?
> And where is Seville, the home of mirthful gatherings
> On its great river, cooling and brimful of water?
> These centers were the pillars of the country:
> Can a building remain when the pillars are missing?[49]

[48] 'Histoire des Benou l'Ahmar, rois de Grenade', 324–5; González, *Fernando III*, I, 384, 387 (suggesting that these figures are inflated tenfold); *PCG*, cc. 1124–5; García Fitz, 'Cerco de Sevilla'.

[49] Nykl, *Hispano-Arabic Poetry*, 338.

Written nineteen years after the event, al-Rundī's elegiac lament on the loss of a place at one with Nineveh and Tyre marks a line across the history of Spain. But that does not justify the statement that, with the subsequent capture of the Sevillan hinterland from Arcos to Cádiz on the Atlantic coast, 'in one sense the Reconquest had ended'.[50] Not in the sense that most mattered it hadn't, despite all the poetic threnodies of exile.[51] The military reconquest was only one thing. The process of colonization was another altogether. How, in the terminology of Jaume Vicens Vives, was the 'reconquista militar' to be translated into the 'reconquista lenta'? By that historian's reckoning, between 1212 and the Mudéjar revolt of 1263 the area under Christian control of a sort almost doubled, with most of this expansion concentrated in the period 1224–48.[52] But without a Christian human presence, without a workforce to secure the area and keep it economically viable, what price all that exertion? González calculates the area 'liberated' from Islam as at least one hundred and nine thousand square kilometres less thirty thousand occupied after 1252 by now subject Muslims.[53] Where, for example, were the human resources to be found to replace those four hundred (or forty) thousand expelled from Seville? Far fewer warriors were needed to secure the surrender of a place than to ensure its maintenance thereafter. The crucial seizure of Córdoba from Ibn Hūd in 1236 had been achieved by a force of not more than one or two hundred troops, after the king had raced southwards through torrential rain to capitalize on a chance opportunity exploited by the city's Mozarabs – though of course not without first checking with his mother that she would pay his soldiers.[54] It was the same story in the kingdom of Valencia, with the Christians attacked by a force of just one hundred and seventy at Burriana and detained by floods at Tortosa.[55]

Fernando III's strategy needs to be set within a historical context. In the words of two historians of nineteenth-century British imperialism, 'Refusals to annex are no proof of reluctance to control.' The situation of

[50]   Lomax, *Reconquest*, 159.
[51]   For those of Ibn 'Idhārī ('O Paradise, from whose flowing streams our sins have snatched us') and Ibn Saʿīd al-Maghribi ('This is Egypt, but where is my fatherland? . . . It was madness to leave you, o lovely Andalusia . . . Where is my Seville?'): respectively, Melville & Ubaydli, 147–9; Sánchez Albornoz. II, 430–2.
[52]   Vicens Vives, *Manual*, 144, 223.
[53]   *Fernando III*, I, 398.
[54]   *Crón. latina*, cc. 70–1: 'From a distance he sent greetings to his mother by messenger, who gave her a faithful account of what had happened but told her that on no account was her son to be dissuaded from what he had undertaken to do.'
[55]   *Book of Deeds*, c. 174, 239.

the 1240s was the mirror-image of what had obtained five hundred or more years earlier when a relatively small Berber army had swept across the country but had been obliged by lack of manpower to adopt 'a series of local arrangements, which barely troubled the existing local order of the peninsula'. 'In a civil war' (and what else was the history of the medieval *reconquista* but that of a society intermittently disorganized by civil war?), as the *caudillo* of another *reconquista* reflected rather less than seven hundred years later, 'a systematic occupation of territory accompanied by the necessary purge is preferable to a rapid rout of the enemy armies which leaves the country still infected with enemies.'[56] As in 1936–9, both parties depended to a degree on the assistance of outsiders. By 1236, however, there was little or no prospect of material assistance from Christian Europe either. It was in order to prevent the remnants of the defeated redressing the balance by bringing in zealots from North Africa, and to forestall the dangers associated with 'a country still infected with enemies', that Fernando III expelled Córdoba's Muslims, 'starving, groaning, weeping and protesting'. Likewise, although at the siege of Valencia two years later 'even in the cannon's mouth' a joust with the opposition was thinkable, when some of the opposition's sharpshooters made a nuisance of themselves in the tower of the Boatella gate, and the tower caught fire, Jaime I had no hesitation in leaving them to burn to death. If surrender treaties were made light of, an iron hand intervened.[57]

When the weeping Muslims left Córdoba, D. Rodrigo reports, Christian settlers flocked to the place 'as to a king's wedding', in such numbers that there were not enough dwellings to house them all. The mass celebrated by the royal chancellor, Juan de Soria, in the purified mosque provided the cue for great outpourings of Christian piety.[58] Yet with the militias of the Leonese *concejos* refusing to serve beyond the end of their three-month obligation during the battle for the place, and the situation only being saved by Fernando's alliance with the Moorish king of Jaén,[59] in reality there is as little evidence of confessional commitment to the cause as there is of the availability of demographic resources sufficient to press home the military advantage.

---

[56]   Gallagher & Robinson, 3; Collins, 41; General Franco in 1937, cit. Linehan, 'At the Spanish frontier', 49.

[57]   *Crón. latina*, c. 73; *Book of Deeds*, cc. 266–8, 273.

[58]   *DrH*, IX. 17.

[59]   *Crón. latina*, c. 72, a detail neglected by Powers, *Society*, 60. Juan de Soria's authoritative testimony is to be preferred to D. Rodrigo's assurance that reinforcements poured in from both Castile and Leon (as reported by him, in that order) on a daily basis: *DrH*, IX. 16.

The Castilians had been here before. D. Rodrigo himself provides the revealing vignette of Alfonso VII capturing Córdoba almost a hundred years earlier and the archbishop of the day celebrating mass in the decommissioned mosque. But, as it turned out, only temporarily decommissioned. Because the city was heavily populated ('nimium populosa') and the emperor could not afford to commit sufficient warriors to its defence against the locals should they turn ugly ('si uellent forsitan malignari'), he was obliged to install the Almoravid governor of Andalusia, Ibn Ghāniyah, as protector of the place and to receive homage from him sworn on the Qur'an.[60] In the 1150s it had been the Almohads who had swept away the Emperor and the remnants of Almoravid rule. In the 1230s, with the Almohads now a spent force, the currently preponderant Castilians had to be on the lookout for whatever new movement might be gathering strength across the Straits of Gibraltar. Some drew their historical analogies from elsewhere. After Seville had followed Córdoba in surrendering to Fernando III, the ex-abbot of Sahagún, Guillermo Pérez de la Calzada, cited both peninsular and recent overseas experience:

> Gaining it's a struggle but keeping it is tougher;
> Worse by far to let go where winning made you suffer
> Than forfeit what you've never either had or wanted.
> Weeping you could lose today what yesterday was granted.
> Note then what I say and stay vigilant and chary;
> Watch for Moorish artfulness, people, be ye wary.
> Take the case of Córdoba; mark it to the letter,
> Or consult the chronicle under Damietta.[61]

Juan de Soria put it rather more crisply.[62] In short, the situation was precarious. In particular, the prospect of the Muslim locals 'turning ugly' would haunt Spain's Christian rulers until at last they confronted the problem and, having done so, at once repented of the remedies they had adopted.

---

[60]   *DrH*, VII. 8.
[61]   'Minus est acquirere forte quam tueri;
Turpius amititur quod solet haberi
Quam quod non acquiritur uel quod nequit queri;
Dolens perdis hodie quod habebas heri.
Propter hoc satagite, uigiles estote;
Maurorum insidias, o plebs, cauetote:
Quid egerit Corduba olim mementote;
Damiate insuper cronicam scitote':
'G. Petri Rithmi', lines 357–64. Captured by Louis IX in June 1249, Damietta was surrendered eleven months later.
[62]   Above, 10.

In 1248 the effects of this dilemma were apparent in the absence of clear-cut solutions either ethnic or confessional. The process of *repartimiento* required the intervention of Arabic speakers capable of establishing where boundaries had run before 1248 as well as of translating title deeds. It is evident that Mozarabs from Toledo were active in this role (in 1251 Seville received Toledo's *fuero*). But so too were Toledo's Jews. For example, when in the following year Alfonso X endowed its church with properties including the mosques there had been in the city 'in the time of the Moors', the terms of the conveyance excluded three in the Jewish quarter that had already become synagogues. It was not for this, not for the re-establishment of the community the Almohads had driven from the city a century before, and in clear breach of the canonical prohibition on the establishment of new synagogues, that five years earlier Innocent IV had given his blessing to a long-standing abuse by granting Fernando half of the *tercias* (the third part of the tithe) of the Castilian Church for three years.[63]

The portrayal of Islamic Andalusia as 'a kind of paradise, consisting of an immense orchard sustained by irrigation agriculture and characterized by an egalitarian sharing out of the land among its fortunate Muslim inhabitants' has been represented as a myth of modern propagandists intent on contrasting the idyllic condition of the kingdom of Seville before 1248 with its sorry situation thereafter, carved up into *latifundios* that survived until recent times. And, inasmuch as some conceptually confused and politically interested modern commentators have made it their business to represent the reconquest of Seville as ushering in a period of Andalusi servitude with those expelled from Seville in 1248 'not Muslims but Andalusians', the critique is welcome.[64] But it is also the case that it was precisely as a 'paradise on earth' where 'all is sweet and nothing bitter', and as a 'land of milk and honey' with bread and wine in abundance as well as access to the seas, both the greater 'which circles all the world' and the lesser 'which they call the Mediterranean', that the kingdom of Seville was promoted both by Guillermo Pérez de la Calzada in the set of acrostic verses dedicated to the future Alfonso X and by Alfonso himself in his *Setenario*. Writing in May 1250, the poet describes a host of settlers flooding in from all over the peninsula, beginning with the 'agile Basques'.[65] Agile the Basques

---

[63]   Hernández & Linehan, 68; Ecker, 825–7; González Jiménez, *Diplomatario andaluz*, no. 4; Montes Romero-Camacho, 483–5; X 5. 6. 3&7; Linehan, *Spanish Church*, 111–12 (cf. Hernández, *Rentas*, I, cix–cxvii). In addition, the king had retained 4,000 marks sterling of *census* due to the papal camera: sums still outstanding in 1263: ibid., 123. Cf. González Jiménez, *Fernando III*, 230.

[64]   Cabrera, 465–6; González Jiménez, *Andalucía a debate*, 13–25.

[65]   'G. Petri Rithmi', lines 13–16, 29–36, 40–60, 301–24; *Setenario*, 19–20.

may have been, but they were not stayers. Indeed, the development of the *latifundios* was due to the fact that nor were many of the others who arrived in the first wave. Why they left is not clear; perhaps they were young men quick to sell up, making a profit while the going was good, and get back home. At the very least, that was one of the features of the Andalusian situation that makes facile comparison with England after 1066 so unprofitable.[66] The aftermath of 1248 was not Anglo-Norman; it was Balkan. According to a story that entered into the historical canon a generation or more later, it took a court jester to alert the king to the consequences. On learning that Fernando was intent on returning to Castile, the minstrel Paja took him to the top of the city's highest tower, showed him that the place was barely one-third settled, and warned him that if he left it in that condition he would never see it again. 'At which the king said: "Now I promise to God that for the rest of my life I will not go to Castile but will remain and be buried here."'[67] And remain he did, either there or thereabouts.[68]

It was on the return north of those earliest settlers that the process of the creation of the *latifundios* began, after the second *repartimiento* early in the reign of Alfonso X. In the case of Seville, the Muslim population was replaced by fewer than twenty thousand settlers from the north and Catalonia, whereas in that other paradise, Valencia (a region far richer than Catalonia, Innocent IV was informed), initially there was not enough land to satisfy all the promises the king had made – although by his own account the canny conqueror as usual succeeded in shifting responsibility for this to others. The answer to the sometimes-debated question whether the north might not have been capable of doing more for the south depends there-fore on the condition of the areas of the north under consideration. While there are signs to suggest that the Burgos region and the Rioja remained well populated, even before 1248 the economy of rural Segovia was said to be blighted by 'sterility of holdings and a lack of inhabitants'.[69] The exten-sion of Christian rule into al-Andalus only served to increase the extremes of regional variation within the kingdom.

---

[66]   Cf. Glick, *From Muslim Fortress*, 127–30; Marín & Ecker, 'Archaeology', 344: 'The obvious crux of the matter lies here. The obligation to repopulate, so blithely affirmed by Glick, was a result of the expulsion or flight of the Muslim population in the conquered territories, a phenomenon which did not occur after the Norman conquest of England.'

[67]   'Historia hasta 1288 dialogada', 6–9; *PCG*, c. 1131; Menéndez Pidal, 'Relatos poéticos', 363–72. For the date of this: Hijano Villegas, 127.

[68]   González, *Fernando III*, III, nos. 769–848.

[69]   González Jiménez, *En torno*, 55–6; *Reg. Inn. IV*, 5315 (March 1251); *Book of Deeds*, cc. 128 (testimony of Blasco de Alagón), 285–9; García de Cortázar, 198; Linehan, *Spanish Church*, 178; Ruiz, *Crisis*, 29–174, 291–313.

Toledo and Seville

Whereas the initial intention of the *repartidores* was to promote small-scale settlement within the old kingdom of Seville, from the outset the desert area of La Mancha northwards towards Toledo was a region of large estates, exposed and inhospitable, dominated and contested by the Military Orders of Santiago and Calatrava and the archbishop of Toledo. The archbishop of Toledo who ruled the see from 1209 until 1247, Rodrigo Jiménez de Rada, represented the church militant in a quite particular sense. Leading his own troops he conquered the area bordering the kingdom of Granada, the *adelantamiento* of Cazorla with its stronghold of Quesada gifted to his church by the king, and defended it until his death. With five of his suffragans in tow, he had been in the thick of things at Las Navas. The militant ethos suffused the Castilian Church. The pope's reminder of St Paul's injunction that 'a bishop must be no striker', issued to Bishop Rodrigo of Sigüenza for flooring a member of his flock in his cathedral with his pastoral staff, was as necessary as it was widely ignored. It was for the sake of his soul that in 1239 Master Juan, the archbishop's personal physician, canon of Toledo and translator, bequeathed his weapons to the defenders of Quesada.[70]

All of which was in flagrant defiance of canon law, as Bishop Melendus of Osma, one of those mentioned in dispatches in 1212, knew better than most. (He also discovered the fragility of episcopal solidarity when the king had to be challenged. In his attempts to secure Alfonso VIII's bequest to his church no help did he receive from his metropolitan.)[71] When in 1215 the Fourth Lateran Council had granted clerics three years' paid leave to enable them to go on crusade to the Holy Land it had been stipulated that they were to restrict themselves to prayer and exhortation. However, it had not been by prayer and exhortation that D. Rodrigo had distinguished himself at Las Navas. Nor is it to be supposed that, when in October 1225 he secured papal leave of absence on the same terms for the canons of Toledo, that was all he had in mind. But D. Rodrigo was not a details man. Just six weeks before, three years after the papal curia had ceased to do so, he had been describing himself as papal legate, and when distributing a crusade indulgence issued by Honorius III at about the same time was continuing to use the title that the pope's letter so conspicuously withheld.[72]

[70] González Jiménez, *En torno*, 115–40; Cabrera, 474–81; Lomax, 'D. Rodrigo'; Mansilla, *Inocencio III*, no. 412; Gonzálvez, 'Maestro Juan de Toledo', 188–9.
[71] Linehan, *History*, 299; above, 50.
[72] Tanner, 267 (can. 71); Hernández & Linehan, 22–3; AHN, Órdenes Militares, Uclés, carp. 58, no. 23; Mansilla, *Honorio III*, nos. 148, 390, 575; Barrios García, *Documentación*, no. 61.

This was sharp practice, or worse, and not a first offence. In 1220 the archbishop had been caught out in the commission of 'many enormities and abuses' relating to the diocese of Segovia and deprived of responsibility for collecting the crusading tax prescribed by the recent Lateran council. This latest lapse was not unconnected with the expenses of another of the archbishop's projects, the transformation of Toledo's former mosque into a Gothic cathedral, the first stone of which was laid by Fernando III in 1226, not without some further defalcation at Rome's expense.[73]

Though by the time of his death the soaring edifice was hardly begun, the building he had in mind was a material expression of Toledo's past, a past in part imaginary but one with definite contours, one wherein almost since the beginning of Christian history the primacy of the church of Toledo had provided the key to an understanding of the dynamic of peninsular development. Accordingly it dominated the archbishop's History, the *De rebus Hispanie*, ostensibly a national history commissioned by Fernando III, in reality a celebration of his church's ascendancy.[74] Bricks and mortar; and pen and ink: all media served the same purpose, a purpose that found its inspiration in Toledo's Visigothic past and in particular its governance by Toledo's seventh-century councils, the standard to which every modern system of government should conform and the model to which it should aspire. It was on account of Seville's impressive role in national affairs during that period that the prospect of Seville's reconquest was a matter of such concern to D. Rodrigo, impelling him, as almost a compensatory measure, to engage in litigation to wrest jurisdiction over the church of Valencia from the province of Tarragona.

But the hegemonic antiquarianism of D. Rodrigo and his research department between 1239 and 1246 flew in the face of all the realities of the modern world. Though he claimed (incorrectly) to be Aragón's fourteenth king, in his exchange with Zayyān, Valencia's last Muslim ruler, Jaime I made no mention of Visigothic Valencia. All that concerned him was the amount of tribute owed. The Aragonese were ambivalent in their attitude to the past. The papal bull dated eight years before Valencia's reconquest, now in the archive of Valencia cathedral, must have been brought there as a sort of talisman. Yet when on the eve of entering the city Jaime rebuked Zayyān for a series of diplomatic offences there was no reference to the prior fact, insisted upon at Lisbon in 1147, that his very presence in Valencia was an act of trespass.[75]

---

[73]   Hernández & Linehan, 8–9.

[74]   Linehan, *History*, 313–56; Pick, *Conflict*, esp. 63–9.

[75]   Domínguez Sánchez, *Gregorio IX*, no. 148 (confirming certain measures in defence of the clergy decreed by the Corts of Lleida, 1210); *Book of Deeds*, cc. 31, 275.

Meanwhile, the methods of the Toledo party were nothing if not thorough. Evidence was adduced from Pliny the Younger, Isidore of Seville and the 'Division of Wamba' (a purportedly seventh-century but in fact recent and spurious diocesan partition of the peninsula) as well as a total lack of scruple evinced regarding more recent events. Thus, when accused of pluralism and of having incurred automatic excommunication on account of John of Abbeville's legatine decree, the Toledo judge was prepared to argue that no such decree existed.[76] Monastic libraries were scoured for codices of the seventh-century councils, their texts collated and the most trivial of variants recorded. As usual, the memory of scores of witnesses was consulted, with one helpfully remembering that a certain opinion had been shared by 'between three and a hundred' individuals and another dating his reminiscences from 'the battle of Úbeda' (i.e. Las Navas). The Toledan *ordinatio* paralleled the failed attempt of the *sayyid* Abū Zayd to surrender the kingdom of Valencia to Fernando III in 1229, an attempt fostered by the same John of Abbeville.[77]

Had Toledo prevailed, a dagger would have been thrust through the entrails of the Crown of Aragón. For that reason Toledo did not prevail, though had it done so the king of Aragón would have intervened, in accordance with the familiar adage regarding kings and laws.[78] And there were other considerations of course, as voiced by Vidal de Canellas, the Bologna-trained bishop of Huesca. Where had the archbishop of Toledo been during the siege of Valencia? With whose blood and money had the place been conquered? In the event of a Mudéjar uprising there, what could the archbishop of Toledo at eight days' distance do – since Castilians would not come to the assistance of Catalans and Aragonese, even if the king of Castile allowed them to, which he wouldn't? The archbishop of Tarragona, by contrast, could be on the spot in a day and a night (note the expectation that prelates would be in the front line). And how, even in times of peace with Castile, was it supposed that Catalans and Aragonese would transact their legal, matrimonial and spiritual business across national frontiers?[79] Pragmatism ruled.

Toledo's anxieties regarding Seville and her reverse over Valencia were matched by its archbishop's loss of the royal chancery. From the beginning of Fernando III's reign Juan de Soria (abbot of Santander at the time, later bishop of Osma, then of Burgos) was his chancellor, and after the reunion

---

[76]   Castell Maiques, 431, 433.
[77]   Linehan, *History*, 356–84; Castell Maiques, 266–76, 310–12, 337, 358–425 (362, 382); Burns, *Crusader Kingdom*, 253–81; Catalán & Jerez, 74–5.
[78]   Above, 51.
[79]   Castell Maiques, 479.

of the two kingdoms in 1231 control of the chanceries of Castile and León was transferred to him from their respective archbishops. Formally, the conveyance was made with the concurrence of both prelates, with the abbot acknowledging D. Rodrigo's possession of the office and his entitlement to the reversion of it after the abbot's death or appointment to 'pontifical honour' outside the province. Historians have therefore treated it as mere formality. But it was more than that. It was a significant blow to archiepiscopal prestige. Since as bishop of Osma the chancellor was Toledo's suffragan, when in 1236 he presided at the first mass in Córdoba's former mosque the archbishop was at pains to record that he did so as his deputy. Moreover, at the time of Juan de Soria's first appointment in 1218 and again on his nomination to the chancellorship of Castile in 1231 D. Rodrigo sought to compensate for the loss first by means of a papal grant and then a papal confirmation of Toledo's primatial jurisdiction in the province of Seville.[80]

Associated with the transfer of custody of the chancery was a further development of what has been termed 'scripturistic modernism', that is the combined chancery's use for all domestic purposes of Romance, a language accessible to Fernando's diminishing numbers of 'French' subjects as well as Toledo's Navarrese and the kingdom's Jewish populations.[81] But regardless of Diego García's firm adherence to Latin, the mechanical identification of D. Rodrigo and Juan de Soria with the old language and the new is not tenable. Both wrote their chronicles in Latin (with the archbishop more or less filching the other's account of contemporary affairs), while after 1223 the archbishop's own chancery continued to issue charters and *fueros* in Romance.[82] Yet, despite the linguistic expertise which, according to a Toledo-inspired account, put his Fourth Lateran Council audience in mind of Pentecost, and according to Diego García made almost every language known to men seem to be his mother-tongue, the archbishop himself was not altogether at ease with the consequences of the destruction of the tower of Babel. The 'variety of tongues' at the muster before Las Navas, he observed, provided the 'enemy of the human race' with an opportunity for mischief-making.[83]

Everywhere there was mischief. Exiled by capitular bickering from his episcopal city, when the ex-chancellor, ex-legate and historian died in June

---

[80]   González, *Fernando III*, I. 506; Linehan, 'D. Rodrigo', 88–9, 99; *DrH*, IX. 17; Linehan, 'Juan de Soria'.
[81]   Above, 47–9; Lapesa, *Hist. de la lengua española*, 237.
[82]   Wright, 'Latin and Romance', 122–4; Hernández, 'Corte de Fernando III', 112.
[83]   Gil, 'Historiografía', 104 (cf. Fita, 'Santiago de Galicia', 40–1, 183–4); *Planeta*, 172–3; Linehan, *History*, 328; *DrH*, VIII. 1.

1247 either on or in the river Rhône, the direction affairs were taking for the church of Toledo was ominous. In grooming his sons the Infantes Sancho and Felipe for the archbishoprics of Toledo and Seville, Fernando III appeared set on privatizing the entire Castilian Church.[84] By his own lights therefore, with the recovery of Seville imminent D. Rodrigo's pontificate ended in failure. And when the dread day arrived eighteen months later, confirmation was provided by the royal chronicle's dating of the king's entry into the city to the feast-day of St Isidore of León – for centuries prior to 1248, Seville's *chargé d'affaires* in the Christian North.[85]

By his conquest of the southern city Fernando had staked his claim to be Spain's saviour. And that was how posterity would remember him.[86] But he was not the only claimant. As a rule, Diego García had not much time for bishops. However, D. Rodrigo was an exception, and in the prologue to *Planeta* in 1218 he had borrowed a conceit recently applied to the poetic Cid, and declared the title the archbishop's. It was Archbishop Rodrigo who had redeemed what centuries before King Rodrigo had so shamefully lost. In 711 the kingdom had run red with the blood of slain Catholics; now, thanks to the archbishop's exertions at Las Navas, it gloried in the gore of the gentiles.[87] It was in 1218 that D. Rodrigo so conspicuously failed to assist his suffragan, Melendus of Osma, against king and queen-mother. Could not someone else be made to bell the cat, he asked? As Sancho of Zaragoza sententiously observed from the safety of the kingdom of Aragón, if bishops were always to be browbeaten by kings justice would sleep forever.[88] But, for the chancery and other reasons, since 1218 king and archbishop had grown apart. The latter may well have failed again in his metropolitan duty when in 1234 Gregory IX ordered him to require the other to desist from his 'molestation' of the bishop of Calahorra. Whether or not, the language of the papal reproof will not have surprised him. He had used it himself as early as 1221 when he had secured for his vassal, Gonzalo Pérez de Lara, the apostolic see's protection against 'every molestor'. This can only have meant the king.[89]

Since the resumption of the reconquest in 1224 the king and his mother, the archbishop's ally, had been growing apart too. By 1236, despite Sordello's

[84] Hernández & Linehan, 52–6. Cf. Rodríguez López, for whom the reign saw no change in ecclesiastical policy: 'Política eclesiástica', 48.
[85] *PGC*, c. 1125.
[86] Milhou, 369–73.
[87] *DrH*, VIII. 3, 10; IX. 16; *Planeta*, 181; Linehan, *History*, 318, 322.
[88] Idem, *Spanish Church*, 10–11.
[89] *Reg. Greg. IX*, 2104 (Domínguez Sánchez, no. 400); above, 60–1; Rodríguez López, '*Quod alienus regnet*', 121–3.

taunts, Fernando was beginning to master the excessive deference to doña Berenguela that had characterized the first half of his reign. The cord seems to have been cut when he let her know as he hastened to the siege of Córdoba that he would not be stopped by anything she might say.[90] The success of that venture seems to have given him a new confidence, sufficient at least for him to suggest to Gregory IX that as reward he be granted a papal token exchangeable for one prohibited marriage, of himself or one of his sons.[91] By then, the year in which all three episcopal chroniclers closed their accounts,[92] the king's prime minister was his chancellor, who viewed his historiographical task more matter-of-factly than either Lucas or Rodrigo, with their monarchical or aristocratic presuppositions. For Juan de Soria more or less all history was more or less unvarnished and more or less contemporary. His absence of interest in the Goths and the Gothic myth made him the perfect foil for Alfonso VIII.[93]

After Valencia

In 1247 the pragmatism that had recently foiled Toledo's designs on Valencia was evident in the kingdom of Valencia itself when al-Azraq, lord of the mountainous region of Alcalá between Xàtiva and the Mediterranean, resentful at the encroachment on his sphere of influence, tore through the Christian cover which over the previous decade had been stretched paper-thin across the entire kingdom. al-Azraq's rebellion spread like wildfire, demonstrating both the precariousness of Aragonese control and what a Mudéjar more resolute than the *sayyid* Abū Zayd was capable of if he had the support of the king of Castile and put his mind to it. It took all of a decade to extinguish.[94]

It also badly rattled King Jaime, and in his own account of it that showed. Either his response was disproportionate or he was playing to the gallery. As described by him, the conclusion of the conversations he had with a

[90] *Crón. latina*, c. 70 (a notice omitted by D. Rodrigo: *DrH* IX. 16). See also Hernández, 'Corte de Fernando III', 116–17, Martin, 'Régner sans régner'; Linehan, 'Juan de Soria'.
[91] Fransen & García, 149 (Domínguez Sánchez, *Gregorio IX*, no. 606). The pontiff demurred. (Queen Beatrice had died in 1234.)
[92] Notwithstanding the final chapter of D. Rodrigo's History (*DrH*, IX. 18), devoted to the king's second marriage in 1237, arranged by the queen-mother 'lest the king's chastity be damaged by alien commerce', and dated March 1243.
[93] Martin, *Juges de Castille, passim*; Fernández-Ordóñez, 'De la historiografía fernandina a la alfonsí', 106–8, 112.
[94] Burns, *Islam*, 323–32.

group of intimates after learning that the rebels had seized 'two or three of our castles (. . .) even though we allowed them to stay in our land and live alongside us and our lineage' was that their perfidy gave him 'good reason to settle the land with Christians'.

> And when the men of our kingdom and of other lands know and hear that we have this good proposal to serve God, so many people will come that it will not be necessary to call for the army or a raid (. . .). But let us keep this in mind: that those who have not come against me, and have not seized my castles, shall receive no evil from me or from mine, but rather they should be given a fixed day by which to prepare themselves to leave the kingdom of Valencia with their wives and their children . . .[95]

The punishment of exile was therefore to be visited not only on the rebels, or on rebel communities, but on the entire Mudéjar community and the entire Mudéjar workforce, which when Valencia had fallen to him the king had taken under his protection, allowing them to leave the city 'safe and sound' together with their arms and all their movables, and when terms of capitulation had been conceded to the *aljamas* of the sierra of Eslida in May 1242 had again been left 'safe and sound' in possession of all their property, with their customs as they had been 'in the time of the pagans', their mosques in which to preach and teach the Qur'an under royal protection, and with Christian settlers and those 'of any other law' debarred from entering their territory.[96]

The bishop of Valencia declared that the pope would be cheered when he learned of the king's resolve. And if he ever did doubtless he was; at any rate more so than by recent news from Aragón concerning Christianity's champion taking slices out of Berenguer of Girona's tongue for allegedly making free with royal secrets of the confessional.[97] So a fifteen-mile queue of a hundred thousand refugees formed at Villena, the border post with Castilian Murcia where the Infante Fadrique was on duty to provide a welcome to Castile by charging every immigrant for the privilege. No such gathering had been seen since the battle of Las Navas, it was said.[98]

The Banū 'Īsā were ejected from Xàtiva. Having incurred the king's displeasure by failing to hasten to his aid as a good vassal should, and having had his offer of (also) a hundred thousand bezants refused, Abū Bakr was deprived of custody of the finest castle in al-Andalus and Xàtiva's Mudéjars

---

[95]   *Book of Deeds*, cc. 377, 364–5.
[96]   *Docs.JI*, nos. 273, 354.
[97]   Ibid., nos. 432–3, 443–4; Villanueva, IV, 324–32; XIII, 174–7.
[98]   *Book of Deeds*, cc. 366, 369.

were transferred beyond the city walls, and further still if the royal account of the mass expulsion is to be believed.[99]

In the reduced circumstances provided by the castle of Montesa to the west Xàtiva's Banū ʿĪsā survived another generation, in what has been described as a state of 'sullen apartheid', until in 1277 the same Abū Bakr played the Castilian card again, this time fatally. Whether the Christians necessary to replace Xàtiva's Mudéjars ever materialized is another question. But in 1248 the Mudéjar exodus from the kingdom of Valencia joined that from Seville, and thereafter the situation of the urban refugees in their rural *aljamas* was increasingly precarious, as the very language used to describe their presence there indicates. The grudging acquiescence implied by the verb 'commorari', rather than 'habitare', connoting the temporary journeyman rather than the fixed resident, reflects the king's attitude to his Muslim subjects for the remainder of his reign. Having declared six years before his death that the kingdom of Valencia needed a hundred thousand Christian settlers and contained less than a third that number, in the last pages of his autobiography he instructed his successor to do what he had never brought himself to do, to expel all Muslims: an instruction repeated in a codicil to his final will of July 1276 when the Valencian Mudéjars were again in revolt. Yet less than four months earlier he had made it clear that he had only rebels in his sights. By contrast with his Castilian contemporaries, Jaime I was haunted by subversives.[100] When their time came for famous last words, neither of the kings of Castile who were Jaime's contemporaries, Fernando III and Alfonso X, so much as mentioned the matter.[101]

The chronicler Muntaner, writing in the 1320s or later, provided a richly embroidered account of Jaime's deathbed calculated to enhance the reputation of his heir. In this the sick old man has himself carried to the battle front, is there reassured by the Infant Pedro that he has defeated the 'damned Sarracens' (*malvats sarraïns*), and expires praising God and blessing his son.[102] Fernando III in similar circumstances, though no less legendary, is less proactive. What he passed to his son, according to an also posthumous description, was conditional on his fulfilment of the obligation of continuing the struggle against the old enemy:

[99]   Above, 68; Burns & Chevedden, 106–14. with observations on the king's obsession with hundreds of thousands (p. 109).
[100] Fernández-Armesto, 89; Burns, *Islam*, 337–52; Burns & Chevedden, 110; Torró, 1006; Capmany, 35; below, 151.
[101] *PCG*, cc. 1132–3; Solalinde, *Antología*, 224–42.
[102] Muntaner, c. 27 (Goodenough, 67–8). Cf. Soldevila, *Pere el Gran*, 412–13.

Sir, I bequeath to you all the land from the sea to here which the Moors took from King Rodrigo of Spain, and whether conquered or held in tribute may it all remain in your lordship. If you manage to maintain it in the state in which I bequeath it to you then you will be my equal as king, and if you extend it you will be a better. But if any of it be lost by you then you will be the worse.[103]

In short, his future reputation depended on completion of the task to which the events of 1248 had brought him.

The Mediterranean Dimension

So 1248 was a significant year for the history of the peninsula. Not only did the capture of Seville increase Castile's options by re-establishing the passage between the Atlantic and the Mediterranean closed for more than five centuries and, to the extent that that was possible, restore navigation in the opposite direction too.[104] Three months earlier the new port of Aigues-Mortes had been brought into use by the crusading king of France – and not only for the embarkation of crusaders. Situated between imperial Marseille and Aragonese Montpellier, and providing a trading rival to both, Aigues-Mortes was also symbolic of the arrival of the Capetian dynasty on the Mediterranean. And this in the very year in which in his latest will the king of Aragón had partitioned his realms for the third time, thereby re-emphasizing the fundamental contrast between Castile and France on the one hand, where national considerations predominated, and on the other Aragón, where the interests of family continued to be given priority.[105]

This particular division was occasioned by the need to provide for the Infant Ferran, the king's short-lived third son. Here was yet another issue regarding which Jaime would have reason to repent towards the end of his life, one to which we shall return.[106] For the moment, however, let us consider a different aspect of the immediate circumstances and the longer-term consequences of the particular instance.

[103] *PCG*, c. 1132. Cf. Chamberlin, 402–8.
[104] By 1278, if not earlier, Genoese merchants had reopened the direct route between the Mediterranean and the North Sea: Lopez, 'Ugo Vento', 244. For problems about this: Pryor, 12–15.
[105] Le Goff, 109, 169; Soldevila, *Pere el Gran*, 26–7. In 1231 Jaime could grant the coastal region as far as Aigues-Mortes to the commune of Montpellier for a peppercorn rent: *Docs.JI*, no. 158.
[106] Soldevila, *Hist. de Catalunya*, 318.

Though they were a common enough feature of contemporary high society throughout the West, for the Aragonese dynasty matrimonial unions with cadet branches of the family were an essential corollary of the conjunction of kingdom and county and, in the case of their cousins of Provence and Toulouse in particular, one hallowed by tradition. Thus in his will of 1232 Jaime I had declared Count Ramon Berenguer V of Provence his second heir.[107] But in the 1240s, while the king of Aragón was begetting rather too many sons, thereby necessitating constant revision of the partition of his realms, his comital cousins failed to beget any male heirs at all. Accordingly, Soldevila's remark that the ties of blood linking the three dynasties paradoxically rendered impossible the forging of political links between their peoples rather overstates the case. Jaime's best efforts to prevent this outcome, by means of a new round of marriages within the wider family, were foiled by the failure of that family to be quite wide enough, and also by death, which in 1241 did for Pope Gregory IX just days before he was to have provided the count of Toulouse with the necessary dispensation and four years later for Ramon Berenguer, 'the last representative of the House of Barcelona in Provençal territory'. Because her elder sisters were already well provided for as queens of France and England, the count had declared his youngest daughter Beatrice his heir, and in 1245 Innocent IV, as arbiter of her suitors' canonical admissibility, not to say political suitability, awarded her to Charles of Anjou, the youngest son of Louis IX of France. As usual, the Catalan historian grumbled, when it mattered the Church obliged the French. The pair were married in the following year and on the death of Count Raymond VII in 1249 his son-in-law Alphonse of Poitiers, Charles's elder brother, succeeded to the county of Toulouse.[108]

Although the spectacle of death striking twice might be regarded as an example of the force of the contingent in history, the king of Aragón was not inclined to ignore the consequences of the Capetian breakthrough to the Mediterranean. By the treaty of Corbeil (May 1258) Jaime rationalized his frontier with Capetian France, surrendering all his rights in Languedoc other than Montpellier (his mother's bequest to him and his wedding gift to Yolanda, his queen) and the Carladès, and two months later his ancestral claims in Provence. Although understandably not even mentioned in Jaime's autobiography, in the history of peninsular development Corbeil deserves to stand with Cazola.[109] At Cazola the king of Aragón had slipped the Castilian leash, at a price. Now, in compensation for his surrender of territory he was

---

[107]   *Docs.JI*, no. 168.
[108]   Ibid., no. 330; Soldevila, *Hist. de Catalunya*, 295–300.
[109]   Ibid., 300–1; *Docs.JI*, nos. 224, 1003, 1018.

released from the vassalage to the king of France he had inherited as count of Barcelona. Much has been made by Catalan historians of the potential danger of the status, partly by analogy with the later case of English rulers of Gascony, partly perhaps by the contemporary phenomenon of the king of Aragón doing homage to the archbishop of Tarragona for what 'he had and held' there and to the bishop of Maguelonne for the town of Montpellier.[110] In the Catalan counties as in Gascony, though, such potential was never more than . . . potential. Thus in 1246 and for long after, Charles of Anjou withheld the homage due to the emperor for the county of Provence because imperial authority in those parts was nugatory.[111]

More immediately relevant in 1258, just twenty-six years after Jaime had nominated the count of Provence as his relief heir, was his abandonment of the county of Béarn, because the heiress of Béarn, Constance de Montcada, was the wife of his alienated son, the half-Castilian Infant Alfonso, and by Jaime's current will heir apparent to the kingdoms of Aragón and Valencia. The effect of the Infant Alfonso's death early in 1260 was therefore instantaneous.[112] The removal from Aragonese affairs of the detritus of the diplomacy of a remote decade and (no less significant since it spared the Aragonese realms a succession question of the sort soon to overtake Castile) the failure of the lady of Béarn to produce an heir, transformed the peninsular scene. Six months later, the deceased's half-brother Pedro, now Jaime's undisputed mainland heir, was betrothed to the lady described by the chronicler Muntaner as 'the most beautiful creature to have been born since the Virgin Mary, and the wisest and the purest'; not to mention one of the wealthiest.[113] And more besides, for Constanza was also the granddaughter of the Emperor Frederick II and the heiress of the Hohenstaufen. Of Pedro a near contemporary wrote that 'from his earliest years he had hated the French'. The feeling was mutual. For Guillaume de Nangis the lovely Constanza was that 'detestable woman'.[114] The conflict of sentiments would dominate almost every aspect of Spanish affairs for the rest of the century and beyond.

[110]   Ibid., nos. 55 (May 1224), 241 (Dec. 1236).
[111]   Dunbabin, 44.
[112]   Soldevila, *Pere el Gran*, 85–6.
[113]   That September Jaime acknowledged receipt of fifty thousand ounces of gold from Manfred of Hohenstaufen, the lady's father: *Docs.JI*, no. 1203.
[114]   Muntaner, c. 11 (Goodenough, 30); *Gesta comitum Barcinonensium*, 85; *Gesta Philippi III*, 516.

4

Some Permanent Features

Figure 1 The sweat-stained dalmatic of woven silk, in which the reconquering archbishop of Toledo, Rodrigo Jiménez de Rada, was buried in the Cistercian abbey of S. María de Huerta (Soria) in 1247. Akin to products of Almoravid Almería, in the golden thread of its decorated borders the Arabic words for 'clement', 'felicity' and 'blessing' are incorporated in kufic characters. Patrimonio Nacional. Reproduced by permission.

Abadia Cisterciense de Santa Maria de Huerta, Soria.

The year 1248 provides a high-water mark from which to observe some of the peninsula's non-narrative features during our period, and the recent death of D. Rodrigo serves as a focus for the most significant of these, *convivencia*, the term used to describe the coexistence of Spain's three great religions. The signs of this are everywhere, in the melding processes evident in the languages, literatures and verse forms of Judaism, Christianity and Islam, which I do not attempt to summarize, in the Mudéjar architecture of Aragón's cathedrals and the synagogues which the law both canon and civil forbad to be built (but not to be repaired),[1] in the hesitant Latin signature of the Toledo Mozarab, Sibibib Micael, appended to an Arabic document of 1231.[2] As is testified by the Arabic words for 'clement', 'felicity' and 'blessing' in kufic characters sewn into the richly embroidered sweat-stained silk dalmatic in which D. Rodrigo was buried, influences operated in both directions.[3] Not even the archbishop whose own cathedral was to be more French than its French Gothic models was immune from them.[4]

Jews

In his History D. Rodrigo made no mention of the Fourth Lateran Council of 1215 and in real life he studiously ignored its legislation regarding the Jews. Though disaffected members of his chapter declared themselves scandalized by the spectacle of Hebrew usurers entering the chapter house, taking short-cuts through the cathedral, and receiving tithes and *tercias* there, all regardless of the requirement that in the presence of the eucharist non-Christians either genuflected or made themselves scarce, the employment of Jews as his business agents was essential to the prosperity of the archbishop's affairs.[5] As author of the *Dialogus libri vite*, a work in dialogue form between the champions of Christianity and Judaism, he was, it has been suggested, far from advocating their wholesale conversion.[6]

In his exhaustive manual instructing confessors in the art of questioning penitents, the cleric Martín Pérez listed the besetting sins of every profession

---

[1]   Borrás Gualis, *Arte mudéjar aragonés*; Cerro Malagón, 369–81 (Toledo synagogue, now S. María la Blanca, rebuilt after 1250). Cf. X 5. 6. 3; Part. 7. 24. 4.
[2]   Hernández & Linehan, 13 and plate 4. Cf. Olstein, 135–7.
[3]   *Vestiduras ricas*, 194. The burial garb of Fernando de la Cerda at Las Huelgas de Burgos likewise: ibid., 157–67. See also *Vestiduras pontificales*, fig. 114 and p. 107.
[4]   Cómez Ramos, 157; Hernández & Linehan, 11.
[5]   Grassotti, 291; Pick, 'Jiménez de Rada and the Jews', 214–19; Argüello, 33 (Cortes of Seville, 1252).
[6]   Pick, *Conflict*, 141.

of early fourteenth-century Castilian society, and, in a genre pioneered by Ramon de Penyafort in the 1230s with his taxonomic approach to the subject in terms of the particular failings of butchers, and bakers and candlestick-makers, provided a sort of *catalogue raisonné* of a *demi-monde* of bakers' *wives* (notorious for their racy stories), sacristans and subversives of every description.[7] Amongst these were Jews and Muslims, included on account of the dealings Christians had with them by serving them, raising their children, bathing or eating with them, or accepting medicine from them.[8]

The law on these matters was not new law. It had been in place for as long as the Church had been concerned about 'the other', in some cases since the seventh century. However, on the grounds that he relied on Jews for the 'great part' of his revenues, in 1219 Fernando III prevailed upon the pope to dispense the Jews of his kingdom from the recent Council's requirement to wear distinctive dress.[9] (The legislation, which also applied to Spain's Mudéjars, was justified by the scarcely plausible reason that for lack of a dress code mixed marriages were occurring 'by error'.) Albeit Honorius III revoked the exception two years later, non-compliance remained widespread, with the clergy of Córdoba and Baeza complaining in 1239 that Jews, pretending to be Christians, were infiltrating their dioceses, capturing Christian children and selling them to the enemy, 'not to mention many other enormities'. Some of these enormities would have been those specified in other complaints sent by churchmen to Rome: the withholding of tithes, excessive usury, attacks on the clergy, and the siting of Jewish cemeteries alongside those of Christians.[10]

Complaints such as these continued throughout the century, and remained unanswered because to Castile's rulers the Jews remained indispensable, in particular as farmers of the royal revenues; Çag de la Maleha for Alfonso X, and his successor in the following reign Abrahem el Barchilón, a Catalan whose receipts were written in Hebrew, whom the Count promoted to a position of unprecedented authority, and who survived the Count's downfall.[11]

---

[7]   *Libro de Confesiones*, 355, 470–90; Teetaert, 'Doctrine pénitentielle'; Linehan, *Spanish Church*, 76–7 (for Penyafort's influence in Aragón via Pere d'Albalat, archbishop of Tarragona (his *Summa septem sacramentorum*, promulgated in 1241)).

[8]   *Libro de Confesiones*, 468–9 (and 185).

[9]   Linehan, *Spanish Church*, 18; Pick, *Conflict*, 172–3.

[10]   X 5. 6. 15 (Tanner, 266); Mansilla, *Honorio III*, no. 212; Linehan, *Spanish Church*, 18; BC Córdoba, cajón P, no. 71; Domínguez Sánchez, *Gregorio IX*, nos. 97, 303, 866. Gregory had previously prayed in aid c. 65 of IV Toledo (633) as well as the Lateran decree: ibid., no. 304.

[11]   Below, 181; Gaibrois, *Sancho IV*, I, 143–88; Baer, 132–3. In January 1281 Alfonso repaired his finances by arresting all the Jews in their synagogues and demanding a payment of 4.3 million gold *maravedis*, twice the annual tribute of the Castilian *aljamas*: Baer, 124–30.

But significant numbers within the Spanish *aljamas* were hostile to the occupation of such positions at court by Jews, not only because the likes of Çag de la Maleha bred resentment amongst Christians but also for fear of contamination by Gentiles and the risk of apostasy. Such was the viewpoint of the cabbalist author, Isḥāq ibn Sahula.[12] 'Men in the royal service have been permitted to study Greek science, to learn the art of healing and the science of measurement, and all the other sciences and their application, so that they may earn their livelihood in the courts and palaces of kings.' So spoke Rabbi Moses ben Naḥman (Naḥmanides) of Girona in the context of the division created within the Jewish community by the writings of Maimonides. The hostility of the anti-Maimunists (Naḥmanides amongst them) ensured that his works were delated to the Church and, with schism threatening,[13] in 1236 Nicholas Donin, a French Jew-turned-friar, extended the polemic in contending that by their adherence to the Talmud his former co-religionists had forfeited the entitlement to the toleration allowed them by Christians as the upholders of Mosaic law. (The Alfonsine texts would be hot on this.)[14] In June 1239 Gregory IX directed the rulers of France, England and Spain to investigate the Talmud as an anti-Christian libel and obstacle to conversion and ordered the surrender of all copies to the friars. In Blanche of Castile's Paris these were burnt, in accordance with the opinion later enunciated by the canonist Sinibaldus (Innocent IV) that when Jewish 'prelates' failed to punish transgression of Old Testament legislation the pope was empowered to act.[15] But neither that doctrine nor the canonists' insistence that Christ's injunction to Peter to 'feed his sheep' justified similar chastisement for the failure of 'pagans and Jews' to punish violation of the natural law sufficed to induce Blanche of Castile's nephew, Fernando III, or Spain's other kings to comply with pontifical instructions.[16]

Whether anti-Talmudism was cause or symptom of the anti-Jewish climate of these years, the development was certainly associated with mendicant friars linguistically competent to scrutinize Hebrew texts with or without the assistance of apostates such as Donin.[17] But, despite manifesting itself

---

[12]   For whose allegories concerning the Castilian court see below, 184–5.

[13]   Baer, 96ff, esp. 104, 245–6; Septimus, 61–74.

[14]   *F. Real*, 406 (Jews not to read books that 'speak of their law or are against it to undo it'; they may possess such books 'as were given them by Moses and the other prophets'); *Part*. 7. 24. 1 (Jews suffered to live in captivity within society in memory of their responsibility for the Crucifixion and as upholders 'to the letter' of the law of Moses).

[15]   Baer, 147–51; Kedar, 'Canon law', 80–1; Cohen, 55–60, 97–8; Rembaum, 'Talmud'.

[16]   Muldoon, 6–12; Zacour, 64–5; Domínguez Sánchez, *Gregorio IX*, no. 850.

[17]   Smalley, xv, 329–55, Monneret de Villard, 35–40; Cohen, 60–78.

in the Barcelona debate of 1263 between Nahmanides and another ex-Jew, Pablo Christiani O.P. on the messianic question, with the latter arguing that his adversary's case was disproved by his own rabbinic texts and the other triumphantly vindicated by the *esprit d'escalier* that suffuses his version of the contest, it was a development to which Spain was only imperfectly attuned. Although it was the king of Aragón who was responsible for staging the event and allowing the Dominicans to compel Jews to attend their sermons, for fear of civil commotion he would later forbid the friars to pressurize their hearers.[18]

This was because the services of the likes of Benveniste de Saporta, a man of such substance and pan-peninsular consequence that a Catalan translation of his Hebrew will came to rest in the archive of Toledo cathedral, were essential to the king of Aragón and his Castilian son-in-law.[19] The effect of this was to neutralize the efforts of anti-Jewish theologians and rabble-rousers. Of the first group, the chief orchestrator was Ramon de Penyafort, in whose opinion, because they were thought to have relinquished the privileged role St Augustine had assigned to them of preserving scripture, Jews were heretics and therefore accountable to the Inquisition: a view shared by his fellow Catalans, Ramon Martí O.P., author of *Pugio fidei* (*Dagger of the Faith*), and Ramon Lull. Inasmuch as the principal coercive tool of the so-called persecuting society was law, it is altogether appropriate that it should have been the codifier of canon law who initiated this development, another aspect of which was mendicant opposition to Jewish medical practitioners.[20]

At least in its inception, however, the argument from scripture was an elitist argument and the preserve of the intelligentsia, as indeed *convivencia* itself usually was. At less sophisticated levels of society more direct methods dominated. But the spectrum of possibilities remained wide. One expression of social mores was provided by bath-house legislation. In twelfth-century Cuenca Jews but not Moors were permitted to use the Christian bath-houses twice a week, while at Teruel and Albarracín both Jews and Muslims were allowed to do so on Fridays, and at Valencia and Tortosa also, though here without restriction as to days.[21] While these provisions varied, all bathers used the same water: a metaphor of a sort for *convivencia*. In Castile this continued.[22]

[18]   Ibid., 83–4, 103–28, Finke, *Acta Aragonensia*, 1, xcviii n. 3; Chazan, 17–141; Régné, nos. 386–99. For other disputations, Ceuta in 1179, Mallorca 1286: Limor, 2–30; Hillgarth, 'Disputation'.
[19]   Bensch, 323–4, Hernández, 'Testamento'.
[20]   Cohen, 44–50, 126–69, 199–225; Tolan, 234–45; Moore, 109.
[21]   Powers, 'Frontier baths', 661–2; Catlos, 297.
[22]   It was mixed bathing that Alfonso X forbad, not, as stated by Hillgarth (*Spanish Kingdoms*, 211), the sharing of premises: *Part*. 7. 24. 8.

So too though did religious animosities, especially after the establishment of the feast of Corpus Christi in the year following the Barcelona debates, with processions of the host and the Good Friday celebrations providing occasions for stone-throwing and a good deal of ritualized violence (at Girona for example) wherein students of the subject have been able to discern comforting signs of routine, of 'idioms that provided stability'. It is not altogether clear how well this description would fit the sentence of degrading death prescribed by Alfonso X for those of them rumoured to have ridiculed the Crucifixion.[23]

Forced conversion, forbidden by both laws, was less of problem than the prevention of conversion, since Jews and Muslims might be slaves, and slaves were property, to be bought, sold and donated, but not surrendered. In July 1177 Alfonso VIII confirmed in perpetuity the church of Palencia's possession of its Jews and Saracens and their offspring.[24] Hence the report from Ávila eight years later of Christian refusal of baptism to Muslims (the spiritual equivalent of the Aragonese nobility's reluctance to allow the enemy the luxury of surrender) and the complaint of the chapter of the place in 1199 about loss of tithes when Christian lands were conveyed to them.[25] Since only Christian slaves could be freed, baptism was a necessary condition for manumission. But it was not a sufficient condition, so at least in theory Christians ought not to have worried about being stripped of their human assets. Practice and principle were often at variance however. In the case of Jews (but not Muslims) freedom could be obtained for a modest payment, while both groups had Jaime of Aragón's reassurance that conversion would not cost them their property.[26]

To return to Castile. When Castile's kings employed Jews to exercise public office and lord it over Christians, they were in breach of another of the Lateran decrees. In confirming the legislation of III Toledo (589), the 1215 measure had demonstrated that Spain's Jewish problem preceded its Muslim presence, while by subjecting those suspected of non-compliance with its terms to the censure of a provincial council it had virtually guaranteed their impunity, since Castile's thirteenth-century kings had rather little patience with provincial councils. The Visigothic context was crucial. It is from the decree of IV Toledo (633) excluding from office not only Jews but also those descended from Jews that the *converso* problem dates, and

---

[23]   Nirenberg, 200–30; *Part.* 7. 24. 2 (also requiring them to remain locked up in the *judería* until the morning of Holy Saturday).

[24]   Abajo, no. 80; *Part.* 7. 24. 6; 7. 25. 2.

[25]   Barrios García, *Documentación*, 22, 24; Mansilla, *Inocencio III*, no. 193.

[26]   Verlinden, 291–2, 300–4; *Docs.JI*, no. 369 (March 1243). For Christian opposition to the baptism of Muslim slaves in the Holy Land, where manumission was automatic: Kedar, *Crusade*, 146–52.

with it all the ambiguous signals transmitted thereafter: on the one hand, the employment of Jewish advisers by kings and archbishops alike and the episcopal representation of Alfonso X in 1279 as a species of crowned rabbi under whom 'Jews are preferred to Christians, from which many evils flow, the chief of them being that many Christians hoping to gain the favour of the Jews subject themselves to them and are corrupted by their rites and traditions';[27] on the other, the laws of titles 24 and 25 of the last of the Seven *Partidas* and their insistence that converted Jews and Moors must never have their 'lineage' held against them.[28]

According to the *Partida*'s title 'Concerning the Jews', with extraordinarily none of its just eleven laws having to do with usury, Jews were to proceed 'quietly and make no noise' so that Christians would hardly know they were there (which was precisely what Christians all too soon would be complaining of), and, in conformity with the Lateran decrees, as well as wearing a 'certain sign' on their heads, having forfeited the right to do so on the first Good Friday, were never to hold office over Christians. All of this of course was also fantasy, other than the measure that in strict accordance with canon law forbad the construction of new synagogues, but then went on to add: 'other than with our permission'. That was the point. In the words of the Infante Sancho in March 1283, the Jews had 'no *fuero* other than royal favour'.[29]

The Lateran decrees had been issued in a crusading context. Christmas 1292 was another such time. Eighteen months earlier the Latin kingdom of Jerusalem had been expunged from the map and Nicholas IV had called on the West to retaliate. Yet Sancho IV spent that Christmas Day in a Jewish household in Córdoba, presumably sharing food and drink with his host, a practice strictly forbidden time out of mind. And two years later Jews were present at his deathbed, again in defiance of the law. The demands of the *procuradores* at the Valladolid Cortes in the following May that tax-farming to Jews cease, money-lending by them be strictly limited and their ownership of real estate be outlawed, showed that while there was little popular sympathy for royal permissiveness, only when royal government was incapable of preventing it could disagreement with such sentiments be aired.[30]

---

[27] X 5. 6. 16 (Tanner, 266); Linehan, *History*, 64–5; idem, 'Spanish Church revisited', 146 (below, 179).

[28] Part. 7. 24. 6; 7. 25. 3.

[29] Romano, 'Los judíos y Alfonso X', 210; *Part.* 7. 24. 2, 3, 11; Carpenter, *Alfonso X and the Jews*; AC Zamora, 16.II/39.

[30] Gaibrois, *Sancho IV*, II, 189; Juan Manuel, *Libro de las Armas*, lines 494, 501 (ed. Blecua, I, 136); *CLC*, I, 111–12, 127–9; Baer, 135–6.

With income from the ecclesiastical *tercias* and funds extorted from the Jewish *aljamas* the only safety valve available,[31] the anti-Jewish explosion that followed Sancho IV's death was the result of constitutional constipation caused by the closure of the frontier. Latent hostility was evident in the royal entourage itself, dependent though it was on Jews for the work of translation. In the Alfonsine *Cantigas de Santa María* the only good Jew is a converted Jew; in the illustrations to the work the stereotypes are all negative: crooked noses and crafty sidelong looks. In seeking exemption from the Lateran requirements, Fernando III informed the pope that if it were not granted, his Jews would defect to the Moors, thus evoking memories of the year 711 when, according to Lucas of Tuy, they had delivered the city of Toledo to the enemy. And when in 1211, on the fifth centenary of that event, the universally admired Infante Fernando of Castile was struck down, it came naturally to Lucas to revert to that incident, reporting that the infante's knowledge of it had filled him with such hatred that he was determined to 'delete' the Jews and that, 'as it was rumoured', they had anticipated his move by poisoning him.[32]

The chronicler in this vein was faithfully representing the prejudices of his hero, Santo Martino de León, the inspissated anti-semitism of whose sermons was widely disseminated across the peninsula.[33] A century later, when royal authority failed, the kingdom's Jewish communities were targeted. The year 1311 was the sixth centenary of the 'loss of Spain', and the bishops who met at Zamora in the July of that year were evidently aware of the fact. The kingdom's dire situation made it vulnerable to the enemies of the faith, they stated openly: 'For reasons such as these it was lost in the past.'[34] If encouragement to press an analogy fatal to the Jews were needed, the ecumenical council that opened at Vienne in the following October provided it, by playing upon their collective angst and tarring the Jews with the same brush, or soiling them in the same eschatological emulsion as the Templars whose destruction the council had been summoned to ratify. The loss of the kingdom of Jerusalem had raised old questions about the guilt of the Jews and new ones about the function of the Templars. Now

---

[31]   For the first of these, Hernández, I, 88–113, 304–15. The 'tribute of the Jews', charged at a daily rate of 7,000 *maravedís* (2.55 million *per annum*) in 1286, actually represented an annual *reduction* of 1.8 million on the fine imposed by Alfonso X in 1280: Hernández, *Rentas*, I, cxxxiv–cxliv.
[32]   Bagby, 674–88; Mansilla, *Honorio III*, no. 212; *CM*, III. 63; IV. 88; above, 46. It is to be noted that although Rodrigo of Toledo rejected both stories the Alfonsine *Estoria* reported the first of them: *PCG*, cap. 561 (p. 316a).
[33]   Mandianes Castro, 'Personalidad del judío' (a robotic account).
[34]   Fita, *Actas inéditas*, 118.

Jews and Templars alike found themselves accused of reviling Christ and desecrating Christ's crucifix.[35] At Vienne, moreover, the Spanish bishops had heard Castile described by ecumenical hard-liners as the Christian kingdom in which Jews were most highly exalted in public office, and, on returning to a country now ruled by an infant king, at a provincial council celebrated at Zamora in January 1313 the archbishop of Compostela not only promulgated the recent conciliar decree cancelling Jewish privileges of indemnity from legal action but also epitomized the relevant title of the Gregorian Decretals in its entirety, together for good measure with material on the subject drawn up from the dregs of the legislation of the Visigothic councils.[36]

The language of that legislation, the language of ingratitude, rodents and serpents, rang all the old bells. But this was all from the Gregorian Decretals. None of it was specific to Spain.[37] What was, was the confirmation of these measures that the Cortes of Palencia provided later that year, or rather the *two* Cortes of Palencia held between April and June 1313.[38] For history had repeated itself. Just as in the early years of Fernando IV, the Infantes Enrique and Juan, the king's great-uncle and uncle, had vied for ascendancy, so now did Alfonso XI's great-uncle and uncle, the Infantes Pedro and (the same) Juan. And it was that division of authority, rather than any difference between the anti-Jewish measures of one faction and the other, that set the seal on the century that was just beginning. The double Cortes of Palencia of 1313, meeting initially in the city's Dominican and Franciscan churches, indicated two things: one how far the mendicant orders had come in the previous century; the other how far Castile had not. In the seventy-eight years after 1313 Castile was to enjoy periods of firm government and to suffer periods of no government at all. At the end of the process lay the pogroms of the year 1391.

Wrong though it would be to read history backwards from 1300, the question must nevertheless arise how, if at all, the celebrated *convivencia* of the past can be reconciled with the agonies that lay ahead. It is a question one answer to which has already been suggested here: that *convivencia* is largely a thing in the mind of modern scholars and, so far as the twelfth

---

[35] Significantly, before the bishops went to Vienne there had been no verification of these outlandish practices other than hearsay (e.g. Alfonso X's alleged attempts to discover 'the secrets of the Templars' by means of a youth planted in the Order): ibid., 97–8; Sans i Travé, 243, 249–64.

[36] Linehan, *History*, 549–52; Baer, 310.

[37] Fita, *Actas inéditas*, 141. Cf. X 5.6.13 (Friedberg, I, 776).

[38] *CLC*, I, 227–31, 240–1, 144; Gaibrois, *María de Molina*, 199–200.

and thirteenth centuries were concerned, largely one of the best minds of the age, largely an elitist thing. The answer may therefore be thought to lie somewhere between Márquez Villanueva, with his talk of truce or disarmament between the three religions 'at a collective level', and Tolan and his insistence on the 'key role (...) played by the affirmation of the superiority of Christianity and the denigration of Judaism and Islam'.[39] Historians ought not to be surprised when ruffians behave badly.

Moors

As a glance at the Alfonsine legislation shows, questions regarding the country's Muslims were the same as those concerning the Jews but were also different. Both non-Christian religions were of course by definition wrong. However, there were degrees of wrongness and Jews were held to reside closer to the light, principally because 'the works and deeds that Mohammed made and did do not show him to have been of sufficient sanctity to have raised him to so sacred a state', which looks pretty much like a light tap on the Prophet's wrist. Accordingly, the Castilian 'official mind' devoted seven of its ten Muslim laws to questions of conversion (by contrast with two out of eleven in the case of Jews) and, while banning the mosque because 'the Moors do not have a good law', allowed the synagogue 'because it was the place where the name of God was praised'.[40]

All of which was in full accord with Aquinas's conclusion that whereas 'against the Jews we are able to argue by means of the Old Testament', 'the Mohammedans and the pagans accept neither one nor the other'.[41] If they occurred at all, debates with Muslims were rare, especially in Castile, because, by contrast with Jews, there was no hope of their ultimate conversion and therefore nothing to debate with them.[42] Moreover, even if it had ever been thought profitable to proceed on the basis that religion was a rational business, with Malikite theologians supplanting the Almohads and Sufi mystics jostling with Jewish Cabbalists in the flight from reason, the very possibility of debate seemed now to have withered.[43] Anyway, for all that the king of Aragón referred to the Mudéjars as 'his treasure' and Alfonso X concurred, the fact was that in Castile it was the Jews that counted,

[39]   Márquez Villanueva, *Concepto*, 104; Tolan, 192–3.
[40]   *Part.* 7. 24. 4; 7. 25. proem., 1.
[41]   *Liber de veritate*, cit. Cohen, 106.
[42]   Humbert de Romanis, 195. A possible exception: van Koningsveld & Wiegers, 179–83.
[43]   Septimus, 75–115; Urvoy, esp. 281–2, 291–2; Burns, *Muslims*, 105–8.

with those of Seville in 1294 contributing twenty times as much to the royal coffers as the Mudéjars pattering away at their homely crafts.[44]

On the other hand, Muslims did accept Christ, just as they revered His Mother, which the Qur'an chided the Jews for not doing. They also shared the shrines of Christian saints, of S. Ginés (believed by some to be a relation of the Prophet) at La Jara near Cartagena, for example.[45] Thus it was that, although after the revolt of 1264 Murcia's urban Muslims were sent into the suburb of Arrixaca and a wall built to separate them from the city-centre, in deference to the conviction of the Moorish ruler of the place that 'only harm comes to those whom Mary does not love', the church dedicated to the Virgin in the outskirts was allowed to remain.[46] But again, only the most sophisticated members of the Christian elite were privy to such information.

For Mudéjars and Christians alike the cumulative consequences of coexistence were considerable in essence but circumstantial as to particulars. Thus, the Nasrid ruler of Granada sent his grandees to carry lighted candles in Seville cathedral at the anniversary of Fernando III's death and in 1273 was himself dubbed to knighthood by Alfonso X. But the effects of *convivencia* for Granada's Christians would be differently estimated in the king of Aragón's report to the General Council of Vienne. Of the capital's two hundred thousand 'Saracens', Jaime II reported, fewer than five hundred were so 'by nature', the rest having converted from Christianity over the previous two or three generations 'on account either of association or cohabitation'.[47] Evidences of this process were to be found everywhere. In the year 1300 the archbishop of Seville's name was Almoravid. Meanwhile, trading across the line in prohibited commodities (including Christian noblewomen) continued, and in the 1350s the king of Aragón is found granting passports to his Navarrese neighbour's Mudéjar subjects in order to enable them to perform the *ḥajj*, in defiance of the solemn duty imposed on Christian princes by the same general council to prevent the pilgrimage to 'that place where was once buried a certain Saracen whom other Saracens hold to be a saint'.[48]

The same legislation had banned the muezzin's call. But Spain's kings ignored that too, unless there was any risk of their being disturbed by the

[44]   Boswell, *Royal Treasure*, 30; O'Callaghan, 'Mudéjars', 26; Hernández, *Rentas*, I, cxxxv, whose information supersedes that of Harvey, *Islamic Spain*, 68–9; also ibid., 138–45.
[45]   Epalza, 170–86; Nirenberg, 193–6; Torres Fontes, 'S. Ginés de la Jara', 45–6.
[46]   *CSM*, 169.
[47]   *CAX*, cc. 9, 58; Finke, *Papsttum*, 236 ('propter adherenciam et commixtionem').
[48]   Linehan, 'At the Spanish frontier', 39–40; Catlos, 285.

noise themselves.[49] Attitudes varied. It was not on account of religion that Christians waged war on Muslims, D. Juan Manuel insisted in the 1330s. It was because they were trespassers. Accordingly, Jaime I acknowledged that the military contribution to the Aragonese reconquest made by the Catalan bishops was neither confessional nor obligatory but wholly gratuitous.[50] Yet in his *consilium* 'Whether a war against the Saracens of Spain is licit', the Italian jurist Oldradus, D. Juan Manuel's contemporary, made light of Innocent IV's proposition that 'those wishing to live in peace and quiet ought not to be disturbed', taking the view that, even if they appeared peaceful, sooner or later the Saracens would attack, 'for this seems to be in their nature'. So pre-emptive retaliation was acceptable. And there was another justification available, short of having to have recourse to conversion by force: the compulsion warranted by hostility to Christian missionaries in order, in the formulation of Aquinas, to prevent 'hindrance of the faith of Christ'.[51] This was one of the strategies adopted by Lull. Alternatively, there were the instructions given by Pedro II of Aragón to Bishop Raymundo of Zaragoza in 1202 when granting him territory 'on the Saracen frontier': 'to people it, to construct and build for the increase of Christianity, for the defence of my kingdom and for the confusion of the Saracens'.[52]

The confusion of the Saracens: that was always an objective in a society in which their presence was so unnervingly ubiquitous. Jaime I regretted that Huesca cathedral (like Toledo) was a derelict mosque and not a 'proper' church.[53] But when building work was undertaken, the need to align with Jerusalem rather than Mecca might involve wholesale structural modifications. That consideration was closely analogous to the translators' attitude to the 'Arabs' whose wisdom they wanted but whose religion they disparaged: witness the preface to Mark of Toledo's translation of the Qur'an, done on the eve of Las Navas, with its 'martial resonances' and depreciation of the Prophet signalizing its time and place.[54] 'Cultures can come into contact', Harvey comments, 'but only with the utmost difficulty can they communicate. I would speculate', he continues, 'that to be successful, cultural communication demands contact *on equal terms*.'[55] The sandwiching

[49] Tanner, 380; Burns, 'Muslims', 95; *Book of Deeds*, c. 445.
[50] *Libro de los Estados*, I, 30 (ed. Blecua, I, 248); *Docs.JI*, nos. 110, 123, 194.
[51] Zacour, 47–53; Kedar, 159–71.
[52] Ibid., 183–99; Sénac, 565–6.
[53] Cit. Burns, 'Parish', 250; Epalza, 'Mutaciones', 508–10.
[54] Tolan, 183–4; Pick, 117. The translator regarded Islam as a combination of the other two religions, the Prophet having found the evangelical precepts of Christianity too demanding: d'Alverny & Vajda, 262–3.
[55] 'Alfonsine school of translators', 117.

of the laws on Jews and Moors in the Seventh *Partida* between those regarding augurs, pimps and prostitutes on the one hand and heretics on the other
speaks volumes. The establishment at Murcia of Dominican schools of Arabic
and Hebrew and the spectacle of the local Franciscan bishop, the king's
confessor, engaged in translating Arabic works of astronomy may seem consistent with the climate of openness characteristic of Alfonso X's youthful
years there. But that was not how one Muslim intellectual viewed it. 'I was
in the city of Murcia (may Allah restore it to Islam)', he wrote,

> during the time when its inhabitants were suffering the trials of the tribute.
> There had come to the city, sent by the king of the Christians, a group of
> priests and monks dedicated, according to their lights, to a devout life and
> the study of the sciences, but above all intent on translating the science of
> the Muslim into their own language in order to fault it (may Allah frustrate
> their schemes).[56]

To this observer at least ('May God annihilate them to the last man', he
concluded) the process was less one of acculturation than of cultural asset-
stripping. It was not the first time the observation had been made.[57]

With its physical landscape transformed by ghettoization and Gothic
churches, this was a slave society and one offering huge and sometimes
deplored opportunities for sexual exploitation. Because they subverted all
society's categories, treatment of the apostate and the renegade was exemplary.
After the uprising of 1264–6 few Mudéjars remained in Andalucia, and by
1305 the same went for Murcia. The wealthy had emigrated, leaving behind
the rural proletariat and an urban riff-raff.[58] Soon after, when Fernando IV
captured Gibraltar in 1309, an old man who had been harried from pillar
to post could bear it no longer. 'Señor', he protested:

> What are you doing driving me out of here? Your great-grandfather,
> Fernando III, when he took Seville, drove me out of there, so I went to live
> at Jerez. And when your grandfather, Alfonso X, took Jerez he drove me out
> of there, so I went to live at Tarifa. And when your father King Sancho took
> Tarifa he drove me out of there, so I went to live at Gibraltar, thinking that
> nowhere in the land of the Moors would I be safer. But now I see that there
> is nowhere here for me to stay, and that I must go beyond the sea . . .[59]

[56]   *Part.* 7. tit. 23–6; Coll, 132–4. For Bishop Pedro Gallego, see Martínez Gázquez,
'*Summa de Astronomía*'; Cortabarría Beitia, 206; Burnett, 118–19; Granja, 67.
[57]   Cf. the warning issued by Ibn 'Abdūn in the late eleventh century, cit. d'Alverny, 440.
[58]   Assis, 36–50; *Part.* 7. 24. 7; 25. 4–8; Catlos, 221–38, 286–9, 305–12; Ladero Quesada,
'Mudéjares', 271–3, 275–7; González Jiménez, *En torno*, 72–3; Menjot, 158–85.
[59]   *CFIV*, c. 17 (p. 163b).

In Castile, St Dominic's own land, the conversion campaign failed to compare with the Aragonese. The writings attributed to Bishop Pedro Pascual of Jaén, martyred in Granada in 1300, once celebrated for their 'very notable contribution' to the understanding of Islam, have been shown to have been foisted on its supposititious author in the seventeenth century.[60]

Foreign accounts of peninsular events revealed similar suspicions of dealings with Islam. When in the late 1190s Sanç VII of Navarre, in danger of having his kingdom partitioned between Castile and Aragón, took refuge with and received subventions from the Almohad king of Morocco, Roger of Howden imagined a love story involving Sanç and the sultan's daughter of his exile, well larded with quotations from Ovid and ending with the former's detention by the girl's brother. According to another English chronicler, Muslim treachery almost cost Fernando III his life before the surrender of Seville.[61]

'The Muslim, whether Mudéjar or not, after conversion to Christianity, still seemed alien.' In areas where they constituted a majority of the population – in the kingdom of Valencia, for example, they may have outnumbered Christians by as many as four or five to one – even after baptism many of them continued to wear the same clothes, eat the same food and speak Arabic.[62] Their blackness had always been an issue. It was this that D. Rodrigo insisted on in his account of the invaders of 711, 'their faces as black as pitch, the finest of them as black as a cooking pot, and their eyes shining like candles'. Las Navas provided Christian contemporaries with an opportunity to contrast the inherent viciousness of the Moorish leader with the innate nobility of Alfonso VIII.[63] Blackness and the possibility of enslavement, as occurred on Menorca in 1287, remained distinguishing marks of shame.[64] Although Sancho IV may have been better informed than some of his predecessors regarding the main tenets of Islam, he was nevertheless of opinion that, because (whatever Innocent IV may have thought) 'they do not belong to the flock of God's sheep', Muslims were destined for hell and the 'Moor was simply a dog and his woman a bitch'.[65] No matter that just two years before this was written the Templars of Tortosa were drawing revenue from the town's Muslim prostitutes. Here was 'yet another

---

[60]   Burns, *Muslims*, 80–108; Catlos, 246–60; Monneret de Villard, 57–8; Riera i Sans, 56.
[61]   Howden, III, 90–2, Matthew Paris, III, 639–40.
[62]   Burns, 'Muslims', 76, 79; idem, *Muslims*; Roca Traver, 121–79.
[63]   *DrH*, III. 22 (whence *PCG*, 312b$_{1-3}$); also IV. 16 (*PCG*, 379a$_{48}$–b$_5$: etymology of Zamora: *moras* being the name for *black* cows); Márquez Villanueva, *Concepto*, 101–2; Catlos, 281; Alvira Cabrer, 'Imagen del Miramolín'.
[64]   Verlinden, 253–8.
[65]   Bizzarri, '*Castigos*', 87, 90, 201–6.

of the apparent ironies of the Church's posture vis-à-vis mudéjares in the thirteenth-century Ebro'.[66] The situation of the Mudéjars was one of institutionalized ambiguity.

Hunger, Kings and Capitals

The Mudéjar presence and the predominance of Jews were specific to Spain. Hunger was not. Hunger was everywhere. In the too little studied case of Spain it could raise a siege against Aragón's Muslims sooner than fire-power and be prayed in aid in Castilian negotiations with France even ahead of the 'infinite number of Muslims' said to be entering the kingdom.[67] In 1258 reports were received of crowds descending upon Burgos begging for water, spring frosts destroying the vines, and bread not to be had for love nor money. Four years later an appeal went to Rome from Alfonso X's bishops begging to be excused from subsidizing the beleaguered Latin Empire of Constantinople. Charity began at home where they were in the throes of a subsistence crisis of biblical proportions. 'Spain', they reported, 'has been beset by an affliction so serious and severe and by such unremitting famine over the past seven years that parents have been unable to succour their children, children their parents, friends their friends, and neighbours their neighbours. And those who were once rich are now poor and those who once were poor are now dead.' Admittedly, Castile had long been a hungry place, and Spanish bishops had long been adept at parading their bleeding stumps at Rome when seeking exemption from contributing to the common pool. In the present case, however, the evidence is too compelling to dismiss their lamentations as special pleading. In 1257 Alfonso X was firmly warned against invading Navarre on the grounds that 'in the army of the king of Aragón there were such stores of bread and wine and meat and corn that they counted these almost as naught, by reason of their abundance, whereas in that of the king of Castile there was so great dearth of all things that soldiers and horses were dying of hunger'.[68]

So there was as much simulation of abundance as there was real hunger. And, as to Spain's two kings, equally there were as many superficial

[66]   Catlos, 311.
[67]   *Book of Deeds*, c. 166; Daumet, 210.
[68]   Benito Ruano, 14; Desclot, *Crònica*, c. 50 (Critchlow, I, 147). Sancho IV similarly tormented his Aragonese opposite number in 1289: *CSIV*, cap. 6 (p. 81b). For some of this evidence, relating to Castile as well as elsewhere, Linehan, 'Gravamina'; *Spanish Church*, 162–3 (whence Aguadé Nieto).

similarities as there were profound differences. According to Martín Pérez, the confessor was to interrogate 'kings, princes, knights and secular lords' as to whether they had acquired their lordship 'by deceit or force', whether they had levied taxes unauthorized by *fuero*, and if so whether they had been motivated by the need to protect the land, finance loose living or, equally reprehensible, purchase paradise.[69] But this was the identikit monarch of the confession manual. In reality, there were huge differences between one peninsular king and another. The spectacle of Jaime I doing homage to one of his bishops, or deferring to another in a matter of municipal government, would have been as unimaginable in Castile as it would have been in France.[70]

In 1229 Jaime had expressed a desire to be crowned by the pope, as his father had been, but Gregory IX was too preoccupied at the time to give the matter the attention it deserved. That some advantage could be derived from coronation, or at least from papal coronation, was evident eight years later when he got the pontiff to revoke alienations made by his father – although whether that was because he was crowned or because the kingdom was a fief of the Holy See is unclear. When on raising the matter again at the Council of Lyons forty-five years later Gregory X demanded payment of arrears of tribute, he decided to manage without.[71] His son and grandson, who were both crowned, were at pains to resist the consuetudinary and constitutive implications of coronation at Zaragoza, both ecclesiastical and unionist.[72]

The unsacral condition of the kings of Spain and Portugal was noticed by contemporaries. Rather than viewing unction as 'subsidiary', 'secondary', 'dispensable' or even 'irrelevant', Ramon Vidal de Besalú, Gerald of Wales, John of Paris considered its omission worthy of remark but, not, as a distinguished Scotsman was to observe in 1292, charged with fatal consequences.[73] Coming from France in 1257, Teobaldo II of Navarre wanted to be anointed and crowned 'like other Catholic kings', as he informed the pope, and was horrified to learn that the Navarrese nobility expected him to be raised on the shield like his predecessors and were having none of these new-fangled foreign rituals. But the papal chancery clerks responsible for the *Liber provincialis* calmly bracketed the peninsular monarchs

---

[69] *Libro de Confesiones*, 416–26. For the purchase of paradise elsewhere in Castilian society: Ruiz, *Heaven to Earth*, 12–53.
[70] *Docs.JI*, no. 242; above, 85; Fawtier, 81–2.
[71] Domínguez Sánchez, *Gregorio IX*, nos. 101, 666; *LdF*, cc. 536–7; Zurita, III. 87.
[72] Palacios Martín, *Coronación*, 93–105, 116–26.
[73] Nieto Soria, 'Origen divino', 74–5; above, 24; Linehan, *History*, 389, 443.

together with almost all Europe's other kings while noting that only those of them who were crowned and 'enjoyed the privilege of old' could be anointed.[74] The device of 'invisible anointing', consoling though it has proved to some modern historians, was unknown both at Rome and to kings themselves, for whom the divine origins of their rule were non-negotiable and anyway another matter altogether.[75] It was the mediation of that rule that was of concern to kings intent on ensuring that no particular combination of location and officiating minister came to monopolize the process of kingmaking. Thus, although in the 1280s, uniquely in our period, the thrones of both Castile and Aragón were occupied by crowned kings, and although Sancho IV and Alfonso III had been crowned in Toledo and Zaragoza respectively, the cities hallowed by tradition ancient and modern, no part in either ceremonial had been played by the prelates of those cities.[76]

It was cities that counted, and the plurality or absence of capital cities, ceremonial or administrative, that distinguished the Spanish kingdoms from England and France. It was not that the concept was unfamiliar to the land which in seventh-century Toledo may be said to have patented the institution: León thus described slipped easily enough from the pen of the versifying ex-abbot of Sahagún.[77] In fact, by 1250 Aragón had two capitals (or was it three?). But Castile had none. And that was because, whereas by that date the king of Aragón, like the king of Portugal, had completed his reconquering stint, so far at least as lines on the map went, the king of Castile had not.

Meanwhile a range of starkly contrasting concepts – concepts as much as locations – confronted one another. To the west, Toledo and newly enfranchised Seville vied for supremacy, fighting a thirteenth-century battle with seventh-century precedents, while, sustained by the human traffic of the pilgrim road and fed by the flocks of the Mesta and the profits of trade through Bilbao and other Cantabrian ports, Burgos brought contemporary resources to the contest, with its dominant clan of non-noble knights (the *caballeria villana*) constituting a standing invitation to any ruler intent on redistributing the political balance. To the east, Barcelona's patricians, entrepreneurs in slaves and spices, served much the same purpose, in this

---

[74]   Linehan, *History*, 392; idem, 'Utrum reges Portugalie coronabantur', 394–5; Rousset de Missy, 343a, 377a.

[75]   As acknowledged by Nieto Soria, whose authoritative exegesis of his earlier treatment of the subject disposes of the existence of its material version: 'Origen divino', 77n., 78. Cf. Linehan, *History*, 587–8; Ruiz, *Heaven to Earth*, 136–8.

[76]   In 1286 Alfonso was consecrated by the bishop of Huesca, Jaime Sarroca, who may have been his illegitimate uncle: Palacios Martín, *Coronación*, 120–1; *LdF*, c. 563.

[77]   'Regni caput Legio': 'G. Petri Rithmi', line 305.

case for the benefit of a succession of rulers intent on shaking off the restraints imposed by Aragón's land-locked feudatories.[78]

Black pudding or fish? The culinary alternatives expressed the Atlantic–Mediterranean options the acquisition of Seville had opened up. As a new reign began in Castile there were other, larger, options too. But their resolution would continue to require strict regard to the indispensable need for the ruler to keep his word and by remaining credible retain the trust of his suffering subjects.[79]

[78] Linehan, *History*, 313–412; Vicens Vives, *Manual*, 232–4, 241–4; below, 127–8; Bensch, 289–93.
[79] *Libro de los doze sabios*, 113.

5

1252–9

Alfonso X: Promising Beginnings

Perhaps because, unlike his younger brothers, the future King Alfonso X never attended university, his adolescence passed without incident or anything to report other than his interest in learning in general, translations from the Arabic, the study of history, and young women. He may also already have been dabbling in the law and was certainly anxious to investigate the entitlement he had inherited from his Hohenstaufen mother.[1] Whatever Fernando III may have had in mind in 1234 when he spoke of the imperial title and blessing, when he and his German queen sent their younger son D. Fadrique to the court of Frederick II six years later their purpose was the same as when they had had him baptized with the Spanish form of a German name. That purpose was to lay claim to the duchy of Swabia, and although by May 1246 the baton had passed to the Infante Alfonso and Innocent IV was promising support, in 1252, as Alfonso's reign began, William of Holland was in possession of both empire and duchy.[2] To the extent that the matter of his German entitlement dominated the reign of Alfonso X it will influence the shape and development of this and the next chapter, though it will not dominate them. But there is no possibility of preventing that interest of his 'in everything' from interrupting progress.

As to the young women, neither his father nor his German mother would have approved of his youthful interest, which seems to have been

---

[1] By 1252 he had already had vernacular translations made of *Calila e Dimna*, the earliest collection of oriental tales done into Castilian, as well as of the *Lapidario*: González Jiménez, *Alfonso X*, 17–23, 424–5.

[2] Above, 61; *Reg. Inn. IV*, 1816; González, *Fernando III*, I, 269–71; Rodríguez López, 'Reino de Castilla', 622–30.

as wide-ranging as it was in virtually the whole of creation. In 1243, at the age of twenty-one and with negotiations in train for his marriage to the seven-year-old Infanta Violant of Aragón, he made Mayor Guillén de Guzmán pregnant. But Mayor Guillén was not the only close companion of these years. In January 1249, the pope was prevailed upon by Violant's father to provide a dispensation from the canonical consequences of the sexual relations he had enjoyed since his betrothal with 'various women', all of them related to his future wife, a subject with which Jaime of Aragón could claim intimate knowledge. In the following year the verses on the subject of the conquest of Seville addressed the Infante Alfonso as if he were already on the throne, celebrating him as 'proven, upright father of the fatherland' and mentioning erudition 'in all things' and sobriety 'as though made of salt', but not stamina, amongst his many qualities.[3]

The poetaster intended his effusions to be incorporated in the chronicles, the chronicles wherein all the achievements of the recent past were recorded and kept safe for posterity.[4] Now although Fernando III had commissioned D. Rodrigo's History, history was as of little interest to that king as venery. Even so, to judge by the tenor of his deathbed speech, he was clear about his own place in it.[5] Fernando's reign had been a success story from beginning to end, and was the pattern according to which his successor's would be measured. This we know because it is how the tale was told in the *Estoria de Espana* account of the scene compiled after Alfonso X's own death, with the kingdom and Alfonso's reputation both much diminished, and evidently in order to point a moral and adorn a tale. It was Alfonso X's misfortune to be judged by a version of the History that he himself had created.

There can be no denying that Alfonso's historical interests constituted a central element of his complex personality. But if we wish to approximate to an understanding of that complexity we must avoid compartmentalizing the man or dealing serially with his interests. To treat him vertically, in sections devoted in turn to his imperial activities, his interest in history, law, natural philosophy and the rest, as historians of the reign have generally done, is to sacrifice the connecting tissue wherein his genius or defects lay and to admit the possibility that his 'metaphysical and cosmological pre-suppositions had no influence whatsoever on his choice of a political ideology'.[6] In what follows therefore, a horizontal, chronological account

[3]   *Reg. Inn. IV*, 4308, 4325; Kinkade, 'Violante of Aragon', 2; Hernández & Linehan, 25–6; *CAX*, c. 3; 'G. Petri Rithmi', lines 283–4, 389–96.
[4]   Ibid., Preface, lines 169–72.
[5]   Above, 83.
[6]   B. Tierney, *JEH*, 22 (1971), 264 (review of A. J. Black, *Monarchy and Community*).

of the man is attempted within which, so far as possible, separate aspects of his activity may resonate with one another. True, this is an untidier approach than is customary. However, although a simple, single commanding principle may be seen to have underlain all his schemes, his was not a tidy life. It left many ends trailing, especially at its end. As has been written of his contemporary, Henry III of England, 'the various projects entertained by [him] were interdependent to such a degree that their motivation is often obscured when they are studied separately'.[7]

Later in the Renaissance of which the Learned King may be said to have been a leading light, the historian Alfonso de Palencia would write of one whose reputation and distinction 'in all the good arts' had earned him election as emperor, but whose prodigality had cost him his kingdom.[8] A shrewd observer at the time saw matters differently. Though the 'enormous sums' disbursed and the 'almost incredible expenses' incurred in purchasing support for the imperial candidature had indeed weighed heavily on his subjects, the flood of foreigners attracted to his court by his largesse, affability and 'those other virtues which are the mark of a king' had raised him above all other rulers of his age. The level of expenditure involved in his schemes, in his dealings with Charles of Anjou in 1269 for example, indicates the extent of that largesse and confirms the correctness of the nugget of political wisdom which Henry III caused to have inscribed on his palace walls and chess board: 'He who does not give what he has will not get what he wants.' To get what you want you must risk what you have. Another observer of the reign, Gil de Zamora, a mendicant friar, and therefore no less calculating, concurred. If his liberality verged on the prodigal, that was just one of the sterling qualities displayed during the manhood of one whose adolescence had been distinguished by 'sharpness of intellect, penetration in study and excellence of memory'.[9] Coming from contemporaries both of whom for different reasons were out of sympathy with his designs, these were not unfavourable testimonials.

Since (as true wisdom, wisdom after the event, has decreed) what Castile needed in 1252 was more of the same, more of his father's dogged determination, the eventual outcome of Alfonso X's flirtation with Europe was therefore more or less inevitable from the outset. Succeeding his father at a disturbed moment in Europe's affairs, the new king of Castile fully appreciated the opportunities created by the Emperor Frederick II's death

---

[7] Bayley, 458 n. 1.

[8] *Gesta Hispaniensia*, I. 307.

[9] Jofré de Loaisa, *Crónica*, 80; Southern, *Western Society and the Church*, 112; below, 160; Fita, 'Biografías', 319.

two years earlier. The calamity that ensued stemmed from his determination
to exploit those opportunities. 'El rey Sabio' was cleverer than he was wise,
it has as easily as it has often been said, though it will hardly do to insist
that his imperial candidature was 'neither impolitic nor chimerical'[10]
without demonstrating that he was wiser in his generation than the children of light. Much as Germany's nineteenth-century historians attributed
German nationalism's 'failure to develop' during the Middle Ages to the
imperial preoccupations of that country's rulers, so have Alfonso X's modern
critics taken him to task for not staying at home, consolidating his father's
achievements by putting paid to Spanish Islam, and only when time allowed
busying himself with his books. But the one verdict is as unrealistic as
the other. In the decade after the death of Frederick II the marriage of
Ferdinand and Isabella and the conquest of Granada were no more to be
anticipated than Bismarck was to be conjured out of the Saxon mists.

It was not as if there was no alternative. At the Toledo Cortes of 1259
Muḥammad I, the Nasrid king of Granada, undertook to help him secure
a 'greater and better empire still' if the German scheme came to nothing.
This prospectus can only have meant Africa, and the access that such a
foothold would have provided to supplies of gold dust (*paiola* gold) and
quantities of minted dinars brought to the Maghreb from Mali and Upper
Senegal. A similar report reached the ears of Gil de Zamora. Such was
Alfonso's fame and glory that the Gascons had offered him Gascony and
the Africans part of Africa – thereby providing credibility for the view that
'the Empire of Germany and the Empire of Africa were interchangeable,
as both could serve equally well to achieve [his] real goal' and that that goal,
'the Spanish Empire', was the 'prize . . . that he pursued all his life'. By this
reckoning, far from falling victim to *folie de grandeur* of imperial magnitude,
his pursuit of a 'more positive empire' cast Alfonso X as the arch-pragmatist
of his age, the arch-empiricist even, and far in advance of his father and
his father's ambitions for some species of peninsular imperial title.[11]

Though in fact the king of Granada's alternative was not an alternative
at all. African and Italian shores were both washed by the same water;
everything was inter-related and contingent. Provision of assistance off
the Moroccan coast was one of the promises Alfonso extracted from the
communes of Pisa and Marseilles in 1256 in return for accepting their

[10]   Thus Márquez Villanueva in his estimate of Alfonso's achievements: *Concepto cultural*,
214–15.
[11]   González Jiménez, *Diplomatario andaluz*, 313–14; Dufourcq, *Espagne catalane*, 136–8;
Insoll, 471–5; Fita, 'Biografías', 321; Maravall, 'Pensamiento político', 65, whence the sentiments of Socarras cited here: *Alfonso X*, 129.

invitation to make a bid for empire. Although prompted by the ruler of Granada, Alfonso was opposed by the Hafṣīd king of Tunisia whose cross-cultural allies and confederates included Jaime of Aragón as well as Alfonso's own brother, the permanently turbulent Infante Enrique.[12] Then there was the Treaty of Toledo, the agreement concluded with Henry III of England in April 1254 whereby, as well as agreeing to have his heir Prince Edward knighted by Alfonso – a significant act of condescension in an hierarchical age – and accompany him on campaign against Navarre, the English king undertook to combine with the Castilian in a joint crusade into Africa, a venture of unlimited liability with any gains made to be equally divided between them: a project which, had it eventuated, might have given English imperial history a different direction.[13]

But of course it did not eventuate, and not only because Henry III and Alfonso X were in joint charge of the undertaking. Although later in 1254 Prince Edward became Alfonso's brother-in-law, after 1257 the latter was in competition with the prince's uncle, Richard of Cornwall, for the German throne. Then there was the issue of the kingdom of Sicily where Frederick II's son Manfred held sway and Henry had committed himself to the candidature of his second son Edmund. So insistent was the new pope, Alexander IV, on vigorous pursuit of the Sicilian claim that in the autumn of 1255 Henry felt obliged to postpone the African enterprise for six years, regardless of the fact that one of the main reasons for the Pisans' promotion of Alfonso's imperial cause was the prospect of securing com-mercial privileges in Sicily.[14] Meanwhile, feeding and firing all this in the Castilian's mind were the historical imperatives which underlay all his schemes, in this case the conviction that the Visigothic rulers from whom he believed himself descended had once held sway across the straits of Gibraltar.[15]

With that proviso in mind, despite the fact that Germany was a land in which Alfonso never set foot, there is some justification for making the

[12]   On account of the 'amor maximus' linking him and Alfonso, in April 1260 Jaime forbad his subject Bernardo de Santa Eugenia from travelling to Tunis with Enrique on presumably shady business. But that affection was insufficient to induce Jaime to join the Castilian's proposed expedition against the Hafṣīd ruler: *MHE*, I, no. 74; *Docs.JI*, no. 1183. For Catalan commercial interests in the area and Jaime's alliances there and at Ceuta: Dufourcq, *Espagne catalane*, 97–168.
[13]   Rymer, 299–300. In c. 18 of the *Crónica de Alfonso X*, all this is confused with the marri-age of Fernando de la Cerda and Blanche of France and attributed to the year 1269.
[14]   Weiler, 'Image and reality'; Rymer, 331; Bayley, 475; Socarras, 153.
[15]   Cf. 'G. Petri Rithmi' (lines 375–6), urging the 'great pontiff of the city' to decree the return of 'Tingitania' (Tangier) to 'our king' since ('as it is written') it belongs to the kingdom.

imperial theme the spine of the narrative. For not only was the quest for *the* empire his 'greatest good' (as he was to describe it shortly before the chase was called off), also it was awaiting him when his reign began. And, for the king of a loosely strung kingdom exhausted by extended exertions, it began promisingly enough. A state of war interrupted by peace was the natural condition of the mid-thirteenth century peninsula, with its progress marked by the expiry and renewal of truces underwritten by marriage pacts, and during his first four years Alfonso, as Ayala Martínez has characterized him, was more a man of treaties than battles maintaining and exploiting the initiative bequeathed him by his father.

In 1253 it was agreed with Portugal that Afonso III would marry young Beatriz (Alfonso's daughter by the Guzmán lady) and Castile retain control over the Algarve and other strongholds to the east of the Guadiana until a son of that match reached the age of seven. Thereupon sovereignty would pass to the Portuguese: a diplomatic solution admirable in every respect other than that the Portuguese ruler had a wife already, the Countess Mathilde of Boulogne, alive and well and living in France, and young Beatriz was very young, just eight at the time. Here then was another example of that time-honoured device, the fudge achieved by means of a flagrant breach of canon law resulting inevitably in the imposition of papal sentences of excommunication and interdict. However, not for the first time at that level of peninsular society the ploy succeeded. In 1263, on the death of the wronged woman, Urban IV lifted the penalties and legitimized the couple's offspring, the future King Dinis, who five years later duly reached the specified age.[16] Also in the south, the first year of the reign was marked by another development which drew the pope's vigorous protest: the renewal of the vassalage of the Nasrid king of Granada (apparently at the same exorbitant rate as under Fernando III, three hundred thousand *maravedís* annually, half the revenues of his kingdom), as well as by the conquest of Tejada, Jerez, Arcos and Lebrija, and the transfer of those places from the Infante Enrique to the Order of Calatrava, and the strengthening of the frontier defences thereabouts.[17]

Meanwhile, also in 1253, in the month of July Teobaldo I of Navarre inconveniently died, and in continuation of his previous policy Jaime of

---

[16]   *Directrices*, 105; Linehan, 'Castile, Portugal and Navarre', 686; González Jiménez, *Alfonso X*, 52–8, 68; *Reg. Alex IV*, 494 (RdLA, no. 63); *Reg. Urb. IV*, 375–6 (RdLU, nos. 74, 77).

[17]   Linehan, *Spanish Church*, 155–6; Ayala Martínez, *Directrices*, 30–41; idem, *Órdenes militares*, 441–2; González Jiménez, *Alfonso X*, 82, 85–6. The statement in *CAX*, c. 1, that the Granada *parias* were reduced appears mistaken and, like much else (but not all) in the *Crónica*, calculated to diminish Alfonso's reputation: González Jiménez, *CAX*, p. 7.

Aragón entered into a series of offensive/defensive alliances with the government of his successor, Teobaldo II, a fourteen-year-old from Champagne
with as little sympathy as his father for the curious customs of the place
to which fate had condemned him (Pact of Tudela, August 1253; Treaty of
Monteagudo, April 1254). In the peninsular political chess game in which,
by reason of Castile's central position on the board, Alfonso was *the* king,[18]
however, the really important players were off the board altogether. Moreover, in his handling of these – and of England and the papacy too – Alfonso
proved altogether more adept than his Aragonese senior. By flirting with
disaffected elements in English Gascony, thereby threatening to destabilize
that region at a time when Henry III had other problems to deal with, he
acquired sufficient diplomatic leverage to secure in that same month the
terms of the Treaty of Toledo, including a marriage settlement between
the future Edward I of England and Alfonso's sister Leonor (since there
was 'no better means [than a marriage settlement] of securing friendship
between princes').[19] As well as being in accordance with the rules for once,
this union established one of the most harmonious royal partnerships of
the age, reminiscent of that of Alfonso VIII and his Plantagenet wife.

Also on Alfonso's payroll was the Infante Alfonso of Aragón, King Jaime's
disaffected heir, matching whom were various Castilian malcontents, notably
the Infante Enrique, chafing at the aforementioned confiscations as well as
having it rumoured about him that he had been enjoying an affair with his
stepmother (Fernando III's charming young widow, Jeanne de Ponthieu),[20]
and Diego López de Haro, lord of Vizcaya and *alférez real* of Castile no less,
who in August 1254 adopted the drastic Hispanic expedient of denatural-
ization, shifting his allegiance to Jaime I.[21] Haro's 'desnaturamiento' has been
attributed to the favour the king had shown to the rival Lara clan. If so, it
was not sufficient to retain the Lara either.[22]

Oaths entered into were a serious matter, society's cement and the only
currency worth anything, especially once the king of Castile began tinkering
with the coinage (though despite the report in chapter 1 of the Chronicle

---

[18]   Ayala Martínez, *Directrices*, 41–141, on which the present paragraph is chiefly based, rightly
describes the peninsular policy inherited by Alfonso as hegemonic and Castile-León as a
peninsular colossus predatory upon its neighbours (pp. 52–3). For summary of a recent scholarship see articles by Ayala Martínez and González Jiménez in *Alcanate* 4 (2004–5).
[19]   Rymer, 290 (Henry III to Alfonso X, May 1253).
[20]   Kinkade, 'Royal scandal'.
[21]   *Docs.JI*, 657. The procedure is described in *Part.* 4. 24. 5: 'In the language of Spain
desnaturar means for a man to abandon the natural bond (*naturaleza*) he has with his lord
or the land where he lives . . .'
[22]   Ayala Martínez, *Directrices*, 95–7; below, 166.

this was not yet). It was in part oaths given in favour of the succession of that disaffected heir that had prevented King Jaime from reaching a settlement capable of incorporating Navarre to Aragón.[23] Yet when in April 1254 Alfonso reported to the pope solemn undertakings entered into by his subjects that were to his detriment, Innocent IV had them declared null and void. As the truce with Aragón neared its end later that year, therefore, and Jaime had recourse to ever more desperate expedients, the Castilian monarch could afford to remain untroubled while entertaining his future English son-in-law at Burgos. When in March–May 1256 that truce was renewed at Soria, Jaime figured rather as the junior partner to the agreement.[24]

The king of Aragón was not the only petitioner at Soria. William of Holland, king of the Romans, had died in distant Frisia on 28 January. As early as 18 March Baldino Lancia, ambassador of the maritime republic of Pisa, was in central Castile acknowledging Alfonso as William's successor and emperor by hereditary right. He did so both in the mistaken belief that, in addition to being the son of his Swabian mother, Alfonso was descended from Manuel Comnenus, the emperor of Constantinople (so that in him 'the empires divided by abuse might by divine intervention be reunited') and in the more practical expectation of securing significant commercial advantage over Pisa's Guelf enemies, Florence and Genoa, from a king who was potentially master of the Mediterranean as well as of African waters because his kingdom included Seville, a city with numerous strategic and mercantile advantages, and perhaps ideological ones too, as Europe's principal Africa-facing port viewed within the 'universal grandeur of the Roman empire'.[25] Roberto Lopez's remark on the economic consequences of the Castilian capture of Seville has already been noted.[26] The Pisan emissary of 1256 was the first acknowledgement of its political implications.

Similarly motivated by anti-Genoese sentiment, and in this case also by the desire to escape the severe tutelage of Charles of Anjou, Marseilles now followed suit and allowed itself to be drawn into Alfonso's diplomatic net, a net 'which rejected few fish, however unlikely'. Indeed, the commune of Marseilles had also been negotiating with Castilian diplomats months before William of Holland's death, albeit neither they nor the Pisans were entitled to offer the empire to anyone, and by June 1257 both had received

[23]   Above, 67.
[24]   *Reg. Inn. IV*, 7497 (QP, no. 952); Ayala Martínez, *Directrices* , 100–1, 140–1.
[25]   Thus Engels, 35–6, citing *PCG* in support of the assertion that Caesar's imperial authority had been augmented by taking Seville: apparently a strained interpretation of *PGC*, c. 5 ($8b_{30-31}$); 'G. Petri Rithmi', lines 1–20.
[26]   Above, 83.

their come-uppance at the hands of their respective adversaries, with the king of Castile ominously proving incapable of rendering either of them any form of assistance whatsoever.[27]

All this though was no more than prologue to the swelling act of what had ensued at Frankfurt between January and April of that same year, 1257, when the seven German electors, functioning as an electoral college for the first time, proceeded to choose as king of the Romans both the earl of Cornwall *and* the king of Castile, to the enormous enrichment of everyone except the candidates, but especially of Ottokar II of Bohemia, one of Alfonso's two cousins amongst the electors, who played a key role by selling his vote to both sides, thereby securing the result of a three-and-a-half-all draw and serving his own purpose of crippling German power.[28] At Burgos in mid-August Alfonso formally accepted the crown and undertook to travel to Germany to receive it; this he never did. Since March 1256 the question of coronation – *imperial* coronation – had been very much in the uncrowned king's mind, his letter accepting the Pisan 'invitation' mentioning it on three occasions. He had already assumed the trappings of empire, styling himself more than a year ahead of the Frankfurt election 'by the grace of God king of the Romans elect and emperor elect, king of Castile, Toledo' etc. Now, as 'Romanorum rex semper augustus' he entered into his inheritance with a vengeance, establishing an imperial court and chancery, and regaling his imperial courtiers with German castles in the sky and tangible Spanish gold. The prospects looked good. According to Bishop Eberhard of Constance, who was present at Burgos, endorsement had been received from 'many princes', with the nuncios of the kings of Bohemia, Hungary, France and Navarre by letter, and the rulers of Aragón and Portugal in person all rallying to the cause.[29]

To most commentators since 1275 of course the entire spectacle has seemed preposterous. What chance did either of these peripheral Europeans have against the imperial old guard? Yet to many Castilians during the years after 1257, and particularly at the beginning of that period, a gilded Castilian of distinguished descent may well have seemed as little improbable a successor to the dismal and clerically infested William as a younger brother of the king of England reputed to be a complete incompetent.[30] Moreover,

---

[27]   Bayley, 476; Mondéjar, 132–4; Scheffer-Boichorst, 241–8; Socarras, 154–6.

[28]   Fanta, 97–100 (the submission of Master Ridolfo of Poggibonsi, Alfonso's proctor at the papal curia in 1267); Bayley, 478–82; Socarras, 165–9.

[29]   BFW, 5488c, 5485 (Mondéjar, 138), 5489–90; Schwab, 'Kanzlei und Urkundenwesen'; Mondéjar, 158–9, 162–5; Redlich, 661.

[30]   Weiler, 1137–41.

if only because it was papal policy to keep the king of England committed to the cause of destaufenizing Sicily, Alexander IV, with whom judicial review of the matter rested, seemed likely to be not unsympathetic to Alfonso's case and to his 'decaffeinated', or 'domesticated', or 'circumstantial', brand of Ghibellinism. When on the death of Conrad of Hohenstaufen in May 1254 Alfonso had resurrected his claim to the duchy of Swabia, Alexander had lent him his support and, if the bishop of Constance is to be believed, in the autumn of 1257 he did so again. Nor had it been by chance that, even before the process was derailed at Frankfurt, the papal legate and Franciscan friar Fr Lorenzo had been present at the Soria colloquium of 1256 and also, earlier and later in that year, at Marseilles and Segovia.[31] Likewise, Louis IX of France had no desire to see Englishmen enthroned at both Aachen and Palermo and every reason in the world for stretching the Anglo-Castilian *entente* to breaking-point. Moreover, to Alfonso's six royal supporters in 1258 there was a seventh to be added. A Norwegian emissary had been present at Soria and in 1257 King Håkon Håkonsson's nubile daughter, Kristina, was fetched by a Castilian delegation which included 'Sir Ferant', a seasoned diplomat whose sea-sickness became the stuff of sagas. 'And men think that never has an expedition been made from Norway which has been as worthily received as this by foreign princes since king Sigurd Jewry-farer set out.' On arrival, Kristina was offered the choice of Alfonso's two most eligible brothers as husband. Rather than the elder D. Fadrique, with his cleft lip received in a hunting accident, she opted for D. Felipe, the archbishop of Seville *manqué*.[32]

One – perhaps the chief – reason why the king of Norway was prepared to sacrifice his daughter to the fate from which death delivered her four years later[33] seems to have been the expectation that, in return for assisting Alfonso in his African venture, the future emperor would cede to him control of the imperial city of Lübeck. And thereby hangs a tale, because Håkon's principal interest in Lübeck was the access it provided to Baltic grain at a time when Europe's granaries were fast emptying. With the seasons behaving unseasonably and famine threatening, in the summer of 1258 fifteen

[31] Ayala Martínez, *Directrices*, 173; idem, 'Alfonso X', 52; Iturmendi Morales, 129–39; Bayley, 474; *Reg. Alex. IV*, 139 (RdLA, no. 23); Redlich, 661; Scheffer-Boichorst, 246–7; Linehan, *Spanish Church*, 203.

[32] Winkelmann, I, no. 579; Dasent, 298, 300, 302–3, 311–15 (the version publ. Guzmán y Gallo, 45–51, has no authority, being a Latin translation of the nineteenth century). ('Sir Ferant' must have been Fernán Rodríguez de Cabañas, abbot of Covarrubias, later Alfonso X's candidate for the see of Toledo: Hernández & Linehan, 151.)

[33] The date of birth of Fernán Alfonso, the bastard fathered by her husband, is unknown: Moxó, 'Descendencia', 81.

thousand Londoners died of starvation, according to the chronicler Matthew Paris, and more would have gone the same way had not the authorities imported grain from . . . the Baltic.[34]

A Command Economy

For the majority these were hungry times. Throughout the peninsula the times were out of joint, with earthquakes as background to political disruption.[35] But five years into the reign here was a king all too susceptible to the siren songs of the troubadours for whom the new dispensation promised far richer pickings than the meagre offerings available at his parents' court. In one of his *sirventeses* Bonifaci Calvo, recently arrived from Genoa, warned that if Alfonso failed to take up arms against Aragón and Navarre his reputation would be blasted. He had started well, but men would soon have cause to revise their favourable opinion of him and conclude that he was more concerned with the chase than warfare. Some were already murmuring. In another composition Calvo lambasted those vile and idle subjects who were more interested in browsing and sluicing than in laying siege to castles, cities and kingdoms and derring-do in general.[36] Chivalry's hour was striking. The arrival of the Norwegian princess confirmed as much. Her coming would have flattered the king. For when since Alfonso VII's marriage to his Polish wife had anyone travelled so far to marry a Spanish king? Yet the Castilian nobility, those vile and idle drones, threatened chivalry's future. 'King of Castile, the empire awaits you', proclaimed Guilhem de Montanhagol, another member of the glory brigade, probably somewhat later.[37] For the likes of Guilhem, a native of Toulouse who at an earlier stage of his career had haunted the Aragonese court and profited from the reconquest of the kingdom of Valencia, new adventures were the ozone of existence.

Even before the charade of Frankfurt, then, the guns-or-butter alternative was under discussion. As international statesmen Alfonso X and Henry III appeared well matched. With the one seemingly as detached from

<hr/>

[34]   Gelsinger, 56–7, 60–63; *Chronica majora*, V, 690, 693–4, 701–2, 746–7; Linehan, *Spanish Church*, 163.
[35]   Quakes were reported near Xàtiva in March and at Segovia in August: Burns, 'Earthquake', 236–7; Fita, 'Biografías', 322–3.
[36]   Riquer, *Trovadores*, 1419–23. Cf. the same writer's 'Tant auta dompna·m fai amar' with its eulogy of Alfonso 'whose valour will protect me' and in the enjoyment of whose patronage he need seek no other: Branciforti, 85.
[37]   'Reys castellas, l'emperis vos aten': Ricketts, 135.

reality as the other, it was in the same period that each experienced the first serious jolt to his rule. In both cases the costs of foreign entanglements, and the burden of imperial expenses in particular, played their part, aggravated by the effects of nation-wide penury, exhaustion and hunger. There were differences between them, of course. In 1257 Henry had ruled for forty years and England's political high command had had occasion to square up to him before. By contrast, the Castilian nobility was not yet ready for a confrontation. Of all improbable constituencies, in 1257–8 it was Castilian churchmen who gave earliest notice of exasperation with Alfonso's conduct of affairs.

Although this volume is only incidentally concerned with questions of Church and State, mention has to be made of the action of the Castilian bishops on this occasion in emulating their English, and indeed their Aragonese, colleagues and observing the instructions of the Fourth Lateran Council for collective conciliar action.[38] In Castilian terms collective conciliar action was tantamount to sedition. At the first cortes of the reign, at Seville in 1252, Alfonso had branded *cofradías* (brotherhoods) and their proceedings as 'evil' and banned all assemblies other than those organized for such charitable purposes as burying the dead. Such legislation was not novel. It merely repeated a prohibition included in Fernando III's *fuero* for Salamanca in 1231 and issued to the entire kingdom at the Seville Cortes of November 1250.[39] What was novel was the response it elicited, not immediately but significantly in January 1257, when with the imperial venture under way six bishops of the province of Toledo, including some of Alfonso's principal curial prelates, met at Alcalá de Henares under the presidency of Alfonso's brother, Archbishop Sancho, and undertook to repeat the exercise twice a year or even more frequently thereafter if the archbishop judged the Church to be in 'great danger'. It was perhaps no coincidence that the king was far away in the south-east at the time. For when, following suit, the Leonese bishops met at Madrid in December 1258, with the presence of Braga's Spanish suffragans but not Compostela's Portuguese brethren indicating a non-ecclesiastical agenda, and the king in the vicinity, no such record of their deliberations has survived. The fact that nothing immediately came of either initiative – principally because the archbishop of Toledo had a political agenda of his own – does not diminish their significance, not least because it coincided with lower-level collective clerical action. Sedition in such quarters had precedents as

---

[38]   Linehan, *Spanish Church*, 54–82.
[39]   Gross, 103 (c. 14). Also Procter, *Curia and Cortes,* 273–84; González, *Fernando III,* II, 352; III, 389; González Jiménez, 'Fernando III legislador', 115, 120.

venerable as royal measures to prevent it. Not for nothing had Fernando III in 1250 denounced such gatherings in civil society as occasions for mischief and 'evil dealing'.[40] But in 1257–8 the spirit of Sepúlveda was abroad, with the clerical committees ('cabildos de curas'), which flexed their muscles at Ávila, Salamanca, Toledo, Talavera, Rodiellas and elsewhere, declaring that they had the king as well as the pope in their sights, providing early warning of the grievances of the clerical proletariat that was to reveal its full potential forty years later in the revolution of 1295.[41]

When, midway between the two episcopal *frondes*, the cortes met at Valladolid in January 1258, the king, acting in concert 'with my brothers the archbishops', again proscribed 'cofradías', in terms almost identical to those of six years before.[42] More of the 1252 legislation was repeated on that occasion, much of it *verbatim*.[43] But the tone and tenor of the 1258 decrees were significantly more severe. Although at the earlier date, a matter of months into the reign, Alfonso's absolutist tendencies were already apparent, he had not yet got the measure of his kingdom. Fussy though they are, and preoccupied with such questions as the colouring of blasons and the quality of horse trappings, his subjects' footwear, the welfare and market value of nesting hawks, falcons and sparrow-hawks and their eggs, and fair-play for partridges, leverets and baby rabbits when the snow was on the ground, the particulars of the 1252 legislation read rather as the lucubrations of a keen, green genealogist anxious to secure the approval of a provincial meeting for a set of local bye-laws.[44]

By 1258, by contrast, the community in question was an entire kingdom whose various stresses had necessitated a sumptuary code at the service of a command economy. In the opinion of one recent historian of the reign this was a system that would require another decade to achieve perfection.[45] Even so, the scale of the operation itself had already transformed the nature

---

[40]   González, *Fernando III*, III, 389.

[41]   Linehan, *Spanish Church*, 168–74; below, 229–30.

[42]   *CLC*, I, 55, 61 (proem., c. 36).

[43]   1258 c. 12/1252 cc. 19 (export of horses and livestock prohibited), 20; 1258 c. 13/1252 c. 12 (dietary restrictions); 1258 c. 27/1252 c. 40 (Mudéjar dress); 1258 c. 28/1252 c. 11 (observance of boundary-marks); 1258 c. 36/1252 c. 14 (banning non-caritative *cofradías*); 1258 c. 38/1252 c. 41 (rearing of non-Christian children by Christians and vice versa prohibited); 1258 c. 40/1252 c. 33 (maintenance of pasture land); 1258 c. 41/1252 c. 21 (birds of prey protected); 1258 c. 42/1252 c. 30 (mountain fires prohibited); 1258 c. 43/1252 c. 31 (pollution of rivers prohibited, salmon smelt protected); 1258. cc. 44–46/1252 c. 13 (limitation of wedding parties; gifts of leggings outlawed).

[44]   1252 cc. 1–3, 10, 21–9.

[45]   González Jiménez, *Alfonso X*, 213.

of the exercise, and the true inspiration of the measures that it is fashionable to ascribe to the king's 'precocious' commitment to best ecological practice had been laid bare in terms comprehensible without the assistance of twenty-first-century perceptions.[46] The reason why Alfonso X was so interested in birds' eggs was that they were needed to feed his subjects.

The successive stages of that transformation over the first six years of the reign are untraceable because the record of such meetings of the cortes as may have occurred is unknown to us.[47] However, every last corner of the kingdom was now under royal scrutiny, at least in principle. Now the obsession with detail was rampant, in particular in respect of food and dress. Everyone's plate was liable to inspection, even Alfonso's own, his and his queen's daily ration being limited to 150 maravedís-worth of victuals 'and not more', except when there were foreign guests at table – which perhaps afforded a measure of relief to the Norwegian sister-in-law-elect who reached the Castilian court while the Valladolid Cortes was in progress. For although one hundred and fifty maravedís was a considerable sum in 1258,[48] the tendency was Spartan. The king was on a healthy diet. As he explained in an ordinance destined to be broadcast throughout the kingdom, he was concerned 'for the good of his body' (c. 1). His subjects were to be likewise concerned and eat 'more sparingly': no more of those long lunches that had delayed the reconquest over the previous five hundred years, just two meat dishes a day (or one done in two different ways), no fish on meat days other than trout, and a limit of three fishes on fish days – though, for what the concession was worth in mid-thirteenth-century inland Castile, with no restriction on seafood (cc. 3, 13). As to clothing, only the king was allowed more than four new outfits a year. Ermine, otter-skin, silk stuffs and orphrey were all proscribed. Members of the royal household were forbidden white feathers, silks, gold or silver saddles and spurs, gilded sombreros, and scarlet (cc. 2, 4). Clergy of the royal chapel were to appear properly tonsured, with no bright colours or fancy footwear (c. 5); shield-bearers likewise (c. 22). Restrictions were placed on the number of joglares (troubadours) and the like at court (c. 6).[49] In society at large, numerous restrictions were placed

[46] Cf. Márquez Villanueva, Concepto cultural, 114, 200–1; Arranz Guzmán, in whose view the evidence of the Partidas as well as that of the cortes legislation is 'to a certain extent' to be understood by reference to 'what has been called "the history of sensibility"' (p. 135).
[47] Procter, Curia and Cortes, 125–8. In view of the gap in the records of the previous reign it must be allowed that Fernando III may have anticipated some of these measures.
[48] In Dec. 1255 being half the cost of an episcopal return ticket to Rome plus accommodation: Duro Peña, no. 280.
[49] Cf. Menéndez Pidal, Poesía juglaresca, 166.

on the size, conduct and duration of wedding parties, and the prohibition of the giving of leggings, or possibly shoes, as presents was solemnly reiterated (cc. 44–6).

In the conduct of wedding parties, which were regarded as seminaries of all types of mischief,[50] as well as in the welfare of nesting partridges, hawks etc. and the preservation of salmon smelt (cc. 34–5, 41, 43), the king of Castile had already been exhibiting a particular interest six years before. Since then, however, Alfonso X had changed. Since 1252 he had become what would now be described as a control-freak, a man obsessed, in the words of one student of his reign, 'by the imperialistic urge to order every aspect of life'.[51] Preoccupied to an unhealthy degree with matters of detail and aspects of majesty, as the ruler of a colour-coded society he alone wore scarlet while knights were prevented from breaking bread with their squires (c. 24). The description of all this as 'imperialistic' is hardly helpful. It smacks rather of Juan II's Castile,[52] if not of Ceausescu's Romania, or, to provide a comparison available at the time, of the court of Leovigild, king of the Visigoths. Six hundred years before, Isidore of Seville had marked the moment at which Leovigild had taken to sitting on a throne and wearing royal garments, thereby distancing himself from his subjects and hastening the end of the accessible régime over which he had presided.[53] Those who knew their Isidore in 1258 would have recognized a new Leovigild in the making.

How many of those most inconvenienced by Alfonso's way of thinking had heard of Isidore is another matter. So far as we know, those most at risk were no great readers, whether or not they were regaled at table with 'stories of great deeds of arms that others had performed before them', or read such tales to themselves as a cure for insomnia, as the king's *Partidas* reported had been done of old.[54] But if he could not control what members of the nobility had read to them as they ate, or what they discussed with their wives in bed, by 1258 virtually every other aspect of their existence was subject to restrictions of a most oppressive and intrusive nature. The food on their plates, the clothes on their backs, the harnessing of their

---

[50]   Fernando III had been similarly haunted by the spectre of nuptial feasts, and had restricted the bride and groom's guest-list to five each: González, *Fernando III*, III, 389. While modifying this rule to the extent of allowing members of the household, parents and godparents to count extra, Alfonso placed a limit of *two days* on the celebrations.

[51]   Socarras, 123.

[52]   Cf. the symbolism of colours and clothes associated with this period as described by Ruiz, 'Festivités', 536–40.

[53]   Linehan, *History*, 22.

[54]   *Part.* 2. 21. 20.

horses (c. 15), all this and much more was regulated by decree. A culture of control pervaded the kingdom, made none the less unpalatable to the nobility by the availability of dispensations courtesy of the king's Jewish minister, Çag de la Maleha, who, as reported in one of the poems of his co-religionist, the servile Todros ben Yehudah ha-Levi Abulafia, 'on the strength of letters from the king authorized many of them to wear the clothes they wanted to wear'.[55]

In any event their access to the king was strictly limited. Only when bidden or when they had a cause to plead were the nobility to come to court, and (though doubtless exceptions could also be made to this rule provided they knew whom to ask for them) after the pleading of it had been completed, a process which the king undertook would be completed within three days, they were to depart; bishops, masters of Military Orders and abbots too (c. 16). Leading figures – *ricos homes* with rents from the king of ten thousand *maravedís* who were entitled to eat the king's food – were to come accompanied by no more than ten knights. Lesser men were to fend for themselves and to have only two knights with them (c. 17). No one was to present himself at court without giving prior notice of the business he proposed to raise (c. 18). Alfonso was in the process of denying his principal subjects that freedom of access to their lord upon which the social system of the territorial aristocracy of thirteenth-century Europe was based.

While all this gave massive offence to the entire political establishment, it was its elite that was most gravely affected, to the extent that members of the royal family were distinguished only by being allowed pride of place within the excluded community.[56] In 1258 Alfonso had five full brothers still living: Fadrique, Enrique, Felipe, Sancho and Manuel, three of whom had been given names redolent of their mother's German descent. Sooner or later they would all cause the king trouble, but thus far only Enrique was in open opposition, lurking at the court of the king of Tunisia. None the less, the ostensible reason for his disaffection was rooted in the imminent malaise afflicting Castilian society at large which within little more than a decade was to tear its fabric asunder.

As well as allegedly engaging in pleasant dalliance with his stepmother, D. Enrique had been deprived by Alfonso of territories in the south-west, and although there had been respectable enough strategic reasons for the confiscation it had created huge resentment. And albeit in the last months

55 Yellin (ed.), *Gan ha-meshalim we-Haḥidoth*, I, no. 394; cit. Targarona, 204.
56 '(The Cortes) agree that no brother of the king . . . nor any other man . . . shall seek to have any plea approved by the king unless the king have notice of it in advance' (c. 18).

of 1255 Alfonso had got the better of his brother and of his confederate, Diego López de Haro, the lord of Vizcaya, he had done no more than scotch the snake of noble subversion.[57] He had set himself the task of straightening a carpet the size of his kingdom while leaving all or most of its pieces of animate furniture in place. If he obliged a member of one clan by preferring him in his counsels he alienated the constituency of another. 'When a lord takes more than two or three into his confidence', the king's nephew D. Juan Manuel was to observe in the 1330s, speaking through the mouth of his fictional King Moravan,

> perforce he has to take many more. For at all levels there are inter-connexions between men, so that when that lord calls in four or five to advise him those left out feel themselves . . . left out and have to be included.

And with that, all semblance of confidentiality was lost.[58] All of which perhaps amounted to no more than the commonplace that it was 'consonant with reason for a king to honour those who strove for his honour and that of his kingdom'.[59]

For some, though, that task is more problematic than for others. On this occasion D. Juan Manuel did not particularize. Later he did, stating what was no secret, that the Haros and the Laras were the two leading families of the kingdom. But as well as that they were at daggers-drawn, as also were the Laras and the Castros.[60] Indeed, the whole kingdom was rent asunder by such hereditary enmities, a circumstance that might have assisted Alfonso X in his carpet-straightening operations but for two circumstances: his own ineptness in exploiting these differences, and the determination (as he saw it) of these families to make common cause, despite their particular differences, deliberately in order to frustrate his schemes.

The *fueros* that, as he was to insist twenty years into the reign, he had no designs upon were a stumbling-block from its very beginning. Even before he was presented with the imperial option, Alfonso had been engaged in the task of giving juridical expression to the process of consolidation of the conjoint kingdoms in continuation of his father's earlier exertions at the administrative hub of central government. The essence of that task was control of the legislative process throughout his realms

[57] Above, 109; Ayala Martínez, *Directrices*, 129–33.
[58] *El Libro de los Estados*, c. 18 (ed. I, 229).
[59] Jaime I of Aragón to Bishop Vidal de Canellas of Huesca, June 1238: *Docs.JI*, no. 258.
[60] *Libro enfenido*, c. 7 (ed. I, 164); Doubleday, *passim*.

and the imposition of monarchical norms akin to those enshrined in the *Fuero juzgo*, as it was applied in the kingdom of León, at the expense of the kaleidoscopic system of local customary law based on the principle of self-determination which, in popular sentiment as well as actual practice, located its origins in the rebellion of the tenth-century counts of Castile against their Leonese monarchs: autarchy intent upon the elimination of autarky in short; the 'descending thesis' allowed free rein in something approaching laboratory conditions.[61]

In Alfonso's case, however, the task may be said to have been fuelled and driven by his missionary zeal in superintending every last detail of the everyday life of his subjects. One example of this mania for minutiae is provided by a letter he sent to the *concejo* of Burgos in April 1279. In the *fuero* he had earlier granted the city, penalties had been specified for calling one of its residents a bugger or catamite (*fududincul*). But what about '*fi de fududincul*'? What if, after an evening in a local hostelry, the term of abuse employed was that: *son* of one? The question was put to the king and, at a stage of his reign when the direction of national affairs was fast slipping from his grasp, he duly responded. Time was when the local trade in insults had been a matter for local communities to regulate. The contrast with the minimalism of the *fuero* of Sepúlveda has only to be invoked for the true scale of Alfonso X's intrusion into the affairs of those communities to be appreciated.[62]

The Law

To the extent that the ability to make his writ run and impose his will at a distance from the centre was the acid test of any medieval king's competence, the history of Alfonso X's reign may be said to be epitomized by its successive legislative initiatives. Though the course of that process has long since resisted elucidation, and continues to do, it is not lack of material that is the problem. No fewer than four testimonies to Alfonso's legislative endeavours and expressions of his legislative strategy have survived – *Fuero Real*, *Espéculo*, *Setenario* and *Siete Partidas*, as they eventually came to be known. But in Alfonso's lifetime, when none of these titles was yet established, the term 'el libro de fuero', which was frequently used, might

---

[61]   Below, 165; MacDonald, 'Law and politics', 169–71. Cf. Ullmann, *Principles of Government*.
[62]   González Díez, *CD Concejo de Burgos*, no. 83 (the law referred to was *Fuero Real*, 4.3.2); above, 23.

equally well have meant any of either two or three of them.[63] Moreover, only of the *Fuero Real* (itself an artificial identifier) does any manuscript witness contemporary with Alfonso's own reign survive. So despite the massive exegesis to which the products of the Learned King's juristic excogitations have been subjected, clarification of their controversial relationship is still awaited, with the simplest proposition obscured beneath a luxuriance of qualification, continuing disagreement over a question as fundamental as whether the *Setenario* was composed at the beginning of the reign or the end of it,[64] and scholarly discussion of the subject, often acrimonious, conducted on the margin of a Serbonian bog into which the curious are at risk of being fatally attracted. Nothing more closely resembles the hesitations and velleities, the vacillating and inconstant progress of Alfonso's legal programme than the conduct of that discussion by its modern expositors and the modifications and revisions to the theories proposed by them as they proceed.[65]

Here indeed is a case of art imitating what once was life. For in the 1250s reconsiderations and reformulations were very much the order of the day, and students of that decade of false starts should not wonder at the spectacle of its legal historians reliving those uncertainties. Yet for all that, despite occasioning heated exchanges more productive of smoke than illumination, it is beyond question that at Aguilar de Campóo at least the first stage of the process had been completed by mid-March 1255 when,

---

[63]   According to Iglesia Ferreirós ('Fuero Real y Espéculo', 169 n. 238), 'fuero del libro' in Alfonsine usage signifies the *Fuero Juzgo* (the vernacular form of the *Lex Visigothorum*) and 'libro del fuero' (as well as 'fuero de nuestro – *or* de mio – libro') the *Fuero Real*. However, 'libro del fuero' may also indicate the earliest version of the *Espéculo*: MacDonald, *Espéculo*, xviii. In which case, what was 'el libro de los fueros que fizo el rey', a copy of which was bequeathed by Master Pedro Pascual, archdeacon of Burgos, in 1277 (Pereda Llarena, 201): a copy of the *Fuero Real*, or of the developed form of the *Espéculo* known as the 'libro del fuero de las leyes' (i.e. the prototype of the work eventually to be entitled the First *Partida*)?

[64]   Below, 197. MacDonald, 'Law and politics', 176–86; idem, *Espéculo*, xix–li; Iglesia Ferreirós, 'Labor legislativa' (and Petit in *AHDE*, 56); Craddock 'Legislative works'.

[65]   Thus, by 1976 MacDonald was inclined to date the composition of the work that came to be known as *Espéculo* to 1254 and its completion to the spring of 1255 ('Law and Politics', 180), in 1986 he was of opinion that it was 'probably' put together between 1249 and 1253 ('El Espéculo atribuido a Alfonso X', 653), and in 1990 opted for 1253 as the year of its implementation (*Espéculo*, xxx–xxxi). Many other cases of changes of mind and direction might be cited, as well as various instances of other scholars in the field gleeful at their colleagues' apostasy – though of late they have been able to discover a measure of unanimity in dissociating themselves from the ultimate pronouncements of Alfonso García Gallo, the scholar whose 'El "Libro de las leyes" de Alfonso el Sabio' brought the study of the subject into the modern age. Although still useful, the account in van Kleffens, 153–214, requires considerable modification.

after recovering by purchase and exchange rights and properties alienated from the royal fisc by the religious orders and the nobility, Alfonso provided the place with 'the same *fuero* that they have in Cervatos', so that it 'should remain his forever' and its inhabitants live their lives there undisturbed.[66] It was this, the Cervatos-Aguilar *fuero*, that thereafter was to serve as the template from which municipalities throughout Castile, and in due course Extremadura, were supplied with copies.

The 'model municipal code' that came to be known as the *Fuero Real* was a *fuero* unlike any *fuero* issued by his predecessors, Alfonso VIII and Fernando III, whose work the king disingenuously claimed to be completing.[67] 'It was one thing to grant privileges to the *concejo* and inhabitants of a place or to concede liberties and exemptions to particular individuals or groups. It was another altogether to establish general norms and promulgate voluminous legal tomes. The difference is qualitative; the novelty revolutionary.'[68] For as well as being voluminous (in its most recent edition occupying more than three hundred printed pages), by abrogating the local codes that those predecessors and other kings had granted or confirmed the *Fuero Real* flung the gauntlet of central government at the traditions accumulated and enshrined in the so-called *Fuero Viejo de Castilla*, an apparently factitious though not uninformed compendium of pre-*Fuero Real* Castilian law which claimed to be a compilation of 'good *fueros*, customs and oral precedents' submitted to Alfonso VIII by his *ricos homes* and *fijosdalgos*[69] – though had such been the case Alfonso X would have found his work largely done for him. Indeed, nothing more surely belies the credibility of the *Fuero Viejo*'s alleged origins than the resemblance of its organization to that of the *Fuero Real* itself, with its cascading arrangement of books, titles and laws, which is in turn reminiscent, albeit a poor imitation, of that of the *Liber Extra*, the law of the Church recently systematized by Ramon of Penyafort.[70]

However, whereas in his letter introducing the *Liber Extra* to the wider world Gregory IX had contented himself with the usual pessimistic murmurings about man's unbridled cupidity and the law's role in bringing the

[66]   *MHE*, I, no. 27 (pp. 58–9).

[67]   'so as to finish what they began': ibid.; Craddock, 'Legislative works', 184; Iglesia Ferreirós, 'Labor legislativa', 309–10; idem, 'El privilegio general'; 'Fuero Real y Espéculo', 128–30 (list of known recipients).

[68]   González Alonso, 41.

[69]   Ibid., 79 (the prologue of the earliest known redaction of the work, dated 1356 and recording the ordering of its composition by Pedro I who doubtless found this testimony to royal–noble collaboration politically useful).

[70]   Above, 61.

human race back to better ways, the dissemination of the *Fuero Real* provided Alfonso X with his earliest opportunity to give notice of the legal principles to which he was committed in those parts of his realm within which it constituted a general law parallel to the Leonese *Fuero Juzgo*. These principles he enunciated in its proem where, while associating himself with the pontiff's Augustinian view of human nature, he located the source of society's malaise not only in original sin and man's natural tendency to division and strife but also in those structural defects which required the ruler to 'make laws' so that bad and good alike should receive their just deserts. The 'many ills and great harms suffered by men and *pueblos*' were for him the inevitable consequence of the *fuero*-lessness of the localities for which the *Fuero Real* was intended and of their rule by 'fazannas e por alvedrios departidos de los omnes et por usos desaguisados e sin derecho', a situation that would be regulated now that their inhabitants had sought from him a remedy which would enable them henceforth to enjoy a lawful existence.[71]

All the fatal symptoms listed here – *fazannas* (oral precedents), *alvedrios* (arbitrary decisions) and *usos desaguisados* (unjustifiable customs) – were features of Castilian customary law at its most disreputable. But it was not only Castilian localities such as Aguilar de Campóo, purging the contempt of their tenth-century ancestors, that the *Fuero Real* benefited. So also did it Cervatos and Sahagún, both places within the kingdom of León. If it was indeed its recipients who had petitioned the king to intervene (possibly at the Seville Cortes of 1252), the king whose role it was 'to make laws' had required little formal encouragement to do so.[72]

In the following century it would be recorded that in the year 1255 Alfonso delivered his *fuero* 'to the municipalities of Castile' – to *all* Castile's municipalities. In view of the extent of the text of the *Fuero Real* as well as of indications that in that same year work was already in train on the *Espéculo*, that report either presupposes resources scarcely imaginable in any thirteenth-century royal chancery or fatally undermines its author's credibility.[73] Moreover, the consensus that the two works were both at least in gestation by 1255 requires the question of the nature of their relationship to be addressed, as to both the date by which each of them was in some sense complete and the presumably distinguishable purposes they were

[71]   *CIC*, II, 2–3; Pérez Martín, 'El Fuero Real y Murcia', 89–90; *F.Real*, 184–5.
[72]   *MHE*, I, nos. 27, 43–4, 59, 83.
[73]   González Alonso, 79. Cf. O'Callaghan, *Learned King*, 34–5: 'To accommodate all the towns, anywhere from fifty to one hundred copies were probably needed, making the task of multiplication truly formidable.'

designed to serve. Central to the answering of the chronological question, upon which gallons of ink have been spilled, is the need to differentiate the date of promulgation either in the king's court (*corte*) or in the cortes of the kingdom (itself, in the nature of the evidence, a largely hypothetical exercise) from the earliest date on which a copy is known to have been issued (a test only applicable in the case of the *Fuero Real*).

Systematic examination of that evidence is not necessary here.[74] What may be – and in the case of a king whose career, if it demonstrates anything, reveals a degree of confidence in himself to do more than one thing at a time, the dating question need not constitute an impediment – is the sensible change of tone between the *Fuero Real* and the *Espéculo*, the shift of key from minor to major. For while both codes sought to restore that measure of central control fondly supposed to have been exercised by the Visigothic kings, in reality it would be 'hard to exaggerate the differences between' them, the latter being considered 'insistently didactic, frequently philosophical, [reflecting] a far more advanced jurisprudence', and having as its insistent theme 'juridical unification', whereas the objective of the *Fuero Real* is seen to be 'legislative monopoly'.[75] Another recent writer, by contrast, has described the *Espéculo* as a text kept at court from which engrossments of the *Fuero Real* were made for dispatch to particular localities, thereby effectively fusing the two works,[76] while a third has even been able to descry in the two works Alfonso X 'imitating' Justinian and, respectively, a preoccupation with the 'laws' with which the Code was concerned and with 'justice' as represented in the Digest, which, not least because the two texts

---

[74] According to Craddock ('Cronología', 367–86), the *Espéculo* was 'done' (if that is what the word 'fecho' means) at the *corte* at, or by the Cortes of, Palencia on 5 May 1255, and the *Fuero Real* completed on 25 August of that year, with copies of the latter distributed to individual municipalities from July 1256. But in that case, how is 'el fuero del libro aquel que estava en Cervatos' granted to Aguilar de Campóo in March 1255 to be accounted for, not to mention the prior concession to Cervatos? The question is of interest if only because it raises the possibility that the composition of the *Fuero Real* may have pre-dated Alfonso X's accession in 1252 and have been influenced by the (Italian?) jurist Jacobo de las Leyes. Cf. Iglesia Ferreirós, 'Fuero Real y Espéculo', 156–71; *Fuero Real*, ed. Martínez Díez, 91–103 (esp. 96–7); Pérez Martín. 'El Fuero Real y Murcia', 75–7. For alternative proposals – that the *Espéculo* (as well as the *Fuero Real*) was promulgated in May 1255; or at the Cortes of Toledo early in 1254: O'Callaghan, 'Sobre la promulgación', 176–9 (as to the 1255 date for *Espéculo* repudiated in his *Alfonso X, the Cortes*, Addenda; idem, *Learned King*, 34 n. 9) (*contra*, Craddock, 'Legislative works', 187 n. 8); MacDonald, *Espéculo*, xlix–l.

[75] Ibid., 188; Iglesia Ferreirós, 'Labor legislativa', 310; idem, 'Fuero Real y Espéculo', 178–9. The contents of the *Fuero Real* as well as of the *Fuero Juzgo* and the *Siete Partidas* are listed by van Kleffens, 285–373.

[76] O'Callaghan, 'Sobre la promulgación', 170; idem, *Learned King*, 33.

provide no support for the distinction, may be going rather far. What signified was that the *Espéculo* was intended for the use of the king's judges everywhere throughout the king's domains, and that the king was acting in accordance with the advice proffered by the sages his father had recruited in appointing officials capable of ensuring that justice was done because 'justice was the crown of a king's lordship',[77] and, in short, taking the law into his own hands.

If all this is heavy and strikes readers as an arid exercise, such also must its effect have been on the king's subjects just when he was committing the kingdom to extravagant adventures abroad at the expense of local communities which time out of mind had controlled their own affairs in accordance with rules developed by their forefathers for dealing with everyday incidents. Take accidents to animals, for example. When an animal fell into the water or over a cliff in the area covered by the *fuero* of Baeza, the procedure was well understood. There was a hue and cry and men came running to pull the creature out. And if they failed to come they were liable for a share of the cost of the loss suffered. With a cow in trouble, it would not have occurred to a native *baezano* to seek out a scribe in order to petition the king's judge. Now in 1255 Baeza still had its own *fuero*, the *fuero* that Fernando III had given it, based on the *fuero* of Cuenca. But the locals in 1255 may well have sensed that the days of that *fuero* of theirs were numbered.[78] And then where would they be, with their familiar keepers of the peace replaced by royal judges armed with new books of rules which legal historians centuries later would have difficulty in distinguishing between? News may have reached them about the 'king's law' that was coming in, divided into Books, Titles and so on, and which, beginning with a discourse on the Trinity and the Catholic Faith, dealt in succession with the honour due to the king and the rule of law (Book 1); the function of public officials, the administration of justice and its technicalities (Book 2); marriage, orphans, inheritance, debts, loans etc. (Book 3); Moors and Jews coupled with livestock issues, rural (including sexual) matters, sodomites, rapists, forgeries, robberies, surgeons, homicides, corpses and a whole 'hodgepodge of miscellaneous legislation'[79] (Book 4), but nothing about cows in ditches.

[77] Pérez Martín, 'Fuero Real y Murcia', 78–9 (cf. Gibert, 745–6, for whom the distinction is that between 'ius particulare' and 'ius commune' respectively); Iglesia Ferreirós, 'Fuero Real y Espéculo', 178–9; *Libro de los doze sabios*, 95.
[78] Roudil, § 836; Iglesia Ferreirós, 'Fuero Real y Espéculo', 145–6.
[79] The phrase is Craddock's: 'Legislative works', 186. For an innovative code, the *Fuero Real* left something to be desired in terms of organization.

Their own self-centred *fuero* began with alien poachers and, in accordance with a logic that made sense locally, ended 915 items later with a summary of standard fines and terms for the division between the officials (*juez* and *alcaldes*) of the place of monies mulcted on behalf of the municipality. It prescribed penalties for such incidents as the cutting off of a woman's breasts, procuring an abortion, thrusting one's own backside into a neighbour's face or a stick into his, assault by egg or cucumber, plucking a neighbour's beard or castrating him or interfering with other parts of his anatomy, and making a window in your house wider than a man's hand. But now none of these everyday contingencies was provided for.[80] The supersession of assurances such as these was no small matter. Viewed objectively, the case of Valladolid, which sometime between 1255 and 1258 was granted the *Fuero Real* because it was said to have no adequate *fuero* at all 'whereby justice might be done', was one thing.[81] That of places such as Baeza was another.

Not that such matters *were* viewed objectively. They were viewed from the particular perspective of each local community. The denizens of Valladolid, for example, one of the peninsula's most sophisticated urban centres, would certainly have failed to recognize a description of themselves as a community of troglodytes accustomed to settling their differences by means of heavy implements. The reason why Valladolid consented to exchange its established system based on *alvedrio* and *fazannas* for Alfonso's uniform *fuero* was that the granting of that uniform *fuero* was accompanied by the concession of various royal privileges to the city and because since the beginning of his reign Alfonso had been at pains to ingratiate himself with a social group within the city, as within the other cities of his kingdom, with whose support he hoped to be able to reduce the political influence of the *ricos homes*, the dynastic aristocracy.[82]

These were the *caballeros villanos*, members of the non-noble urban militias upon whose seasonal expeditions the military reconquest of the previous century had so largely depended. By 1256 the new king's courting of them had alerted the *ricos homes*, the old guard of Laras, Haros and royal

---

[80]   Roudil, §§ 256, 261, 305–6, 290, 292, 277–89, 329. Cf. Powers, *Code of Cuenca*, 84, 86–91. As noted by Craddock (loc. cit.), the only physical insult for which the *Fuero Real* prescribed penalties was the offence of burying an adversary's head in mud (IV.3.1). As for the term of verbal abuse later specified by the *concejo* of Burgos (above, 121), *F.Baeza* (§ 276) had previously provided what the king's new *Fuero* singularly lacked.

[81]   Craddock, 'Texto del *Espéculo*', 224–5, 241–3; *MHE*, I, no. 102 (p. 224). Cf. Iglesia Ferreirós, 'Fuero Real y Espéculo', 150–3.

[82]   Rucquoi, I, 86–90.

infantes, to the trouble that they were going to have with him.[83] Here then was one potential political flash-point, not least because military service brought fiscal exemption for the warriors – and correspondingly heavier fiscal burdens for the non-military 'good men' of the place – with possession of a horse and armour the qualification for membership, just as in England, which in 1256 was approaching a political flash-point of its own, where horse and armour had long been exempt from distraint for debt.[84]

Another sensitive issue was the recruitment amongst members of the king's favoured social elite of the judges charged with the task of enforcing the king's law, and of ensuring that that was the only law in place. Another still stemmed from the fact that in the kingdom's straitened economic circumstances it was not only the king who was intent on rationalizing his affairs. So too were the men upon whom the king depended for the realization of his schemes, the men advanced by him in Church and State. Formed in his image and likeness, they were as firmly committed as the king himself to business principles, no less dedicated than he to extracting full value from the estates in which, just as Alfonso had invested his resources at Aguilar de Campóo, they had invested theirs. Sooner or later the king was bound to clash with his own new-model judges, and because he had taught them language their profit on't was, they knew how to curse. One example of this process, one from amongst many of the king's model bureaucrats, was that of don Suero Pérez.

Emerging from obscurity at the beginning of the reign, Suero Pérez was soon appointed notary for León as part of a reorganization of the royal chancery. In 1255 the king put him into the see of Zamora. Here he proved more of an energetic landlord than a pastoral bishop and found no difficulty in combining diocesan duties with services at court, for example, as one of the *repartidores* of recently reconquered Cádiz. His will of 1285 and the memorandum he left of the improvements he had made in the see, buying back and rounding off property holdings, rationalizing, planting and replanting woodland and vines, damming the Duero, creating fishponds, putting in lavatories, and much more besides, show him operating at the diocesan level in precisely the manner of his royal master. In doing so he soon clashed with the local *concejo*, and sometime before 1275 with Gutier Pérez, the *concejo*'s and therefore the king's judge at Zamora, and Gutier Pérez had the bishop's judges hanged, declaring as he led them to their death (it was reported) that 'he would deal in the same way with any others who

[83]   Ruiz, *Crisis*, chap. 8; González Jiménez, 'Alfonso X y las oligarquías urbanas', 205–12; González Díez, *Regimen foral*, 62; Rodríguez Velasco, 57–77.
[84]   *Dialogue of the Exchequer* (*c.*1170), cit. Harvey, 'Knight's fee', 34–5.

called themselves judges in church territory'. Towards the end of Alfonso's reign don Suero Pérez would be one of the first of the king's bishops to abandon him.[85]

Implications of Empire

At the beginning of the reign, however, as one of the king's intimates he was closely involved in promoting the imperial business, which was the context of Alfonso's legal innovations of 1255–6. But what was the scope of that business and those innovations? Was not the 'matter of the empire', for which the cortes were summoned to Toledo in the spring of 1259, in reality a coded expression of Castile's peninsular ascendancy? True, Pope Alexander's cautious sympathy had cooled as result of the Alfonso's failure to assist him against Manfred and his association with that bane of the Roman Church, Ezzelino da Romano III.[86] Yet, great as was the love he bore his Castilian son-in-law, the king of Aragón was also sufficiently concerned to dispatch the bishop of Zaragoza to the papal curia in the following September in order to counter Alfonso's efforts to have himself declared 'emperor of Spain' and 'us and our kingdoms and territories placed under his subjection by reason of empire or any other reason'.[87]

Confirmation of the existence of that agenda is provided in the prologue to the *Libro de las Cruces*, translated from the Arabic in that year, and in the lapidary inscription at the great Sevillan shipyard of Las Ataranzas celebrating the ruler of Castile as king of 'Spain' and of 'the Spains'

---

[85]   Linehan, 'Economics of episcopal politics'.

[86]   Scheffer-Boichorst, 241, 248; BFW, 5484; *MHE*, I, no. 71; Jordan, *Origines*, 109–12, 218–22.

[87]   Barcelona, Archivo de la Corona de Aragón, Reg. 11, fo. 218r: '[C]onstituimus vos venerabilem et dilectum nostrum A. Dei gratia episcopum Cesaraugustanum certum et specialem procuratorem nostrum in curia d[omini] pape ad agendum, d[efendendum], [excipie]ndum et recipiendum et [ad] omnia alia faciendum [que licite] possit facere quilibet legitimus procurator contra nuncios regis Castelle, etsi [*or* etiam si] dicti nuncii voluerint obtinere ex parte dicti regis Castelle quod sit ymperator hispanie [*or* hispanus] vel quod nos sive regna et terras nostras ponerentur subiectione racione imperii vel qualibet alia racione, et quidquid per vos inde actum sive procuratum fuerit ratum habebimus atque firmum. Et ut hec procuracio maiorem gaudeat firmitatem presentem cartam cum sigillo nostro maiori fecimus sigillari. Datum apud Moram IX° kalendas octobris anno domini M° CC° L° nono' [23 Sept. 1259]. I am much obliged to Dr Alberto Torra and his ultra-violet lamp for assistance in reading a much damaged document, by the defective and incomplete account of which, printed in *MHE*, I, no. 69, students of the period have long been misled. See Ayala Martínez, *Directrices*, 254. My conjectural emendations are shown in square brackets. (The bishop of Zaragoza was Arnaldo de Peralta, one of Jaime's most trusted advisors.)

respectively.[88] The unfinished state of the *Espéculo* (itself a work addressed to a Spanish rather than just a Castilian constituency) and the survival of the only medieval manuscript of the work have both been accounted for by the possibility that in 1256 Alfonso's legal team was reassigned to the differently inspired project required by the imperial candidate's need for a law code 'worthy of his pretensions', the code that ultimately came to be known as the *Siete Partidas*, which according to the scholarly consensus was completed over the course of the next nine years.[89]

When asserting in the *Espéculo* his right to make and change laws, Alfonso had insisted that if emperors and kings who held office by election were entitled to do so, 'how much more' was he who ruled 'by hereditary right', citing in support Roman Law, the law of Holy Church and the 'laws of Spain that the Goths made' and, for his disquisition on the nature of kingship, 'wise men knowledgeable of the law'.[90] Now, in the first title of the Second *Partida* – with the 'ancient philosophers and in particular Aristotle in the book called the Politics' his guides (2. 1. 6), and in what one commentator has pronounced the earliest example of the genre of the neo-Aristotelian *De regimine principum* – the emperor has four laws to himself, the same as the king, and in another (2. 1. 9) it is explained that in certain circumstances the emperor can 'make' kings. By contrast with the king, who may grant hereditary possession of towns and castles to whomsoever he pleases, the emperor must never do so, for 'he is bound to increase (*acrecentar*) his empire, not to diminish it' (2. 1. 8). (Not that Alfonso X in royal mode was shy of 'increase'.)[91] Thus would imperial authority reflect back on the peninsular, or at least on the Castilian, scene, just as for the elected Hohenstaufen it had reflected back on Sicily (and arguably Germany), and the prospect of royal authority being thereby enhanced would ensure the opposition of the Castilian aristocracy to the imperial venture (*la ida al imperio*).[92] And

---

[88]   *Libro de las Cruces*, 1. For the inscription's leonine verses: Ortiz de Zúñiga, I, 140. Though doubtless the sentiments were Alfonso's, implausibly both Ballesteros ('Toma de Salé', 93) and Márquez Villanueva (*Concepto cultural*, 65–6) also regard the Latin as his.

[89]   *Espéculo*, e.g. 2. 7. 4. Cf. Iglesia Ferreirós, 'Fuero Real y Espéculo', 180–4; idem, 'Labor legislativa', 409–63 (esp. 455–6); Craddock, 'Cronología', 386–400; idem, 'Texto del *Espéculo*', remarking that by the date at which the unique manuscript of *Espéculo* was written (*c.*1390) the text was liable to contamination by interpolations from the *Partidas*.

[90]   *Espéculo*, e.g. 1. 1. 13; 2. 1. 1. There had been no such discussion in *Fuero Real*.

[91]   Martin, 'Alphonse X, roi et empereur', 54; (from a different perspective) Linehan, *History*, 430–5; below, 153.

[92]   In 'El "fecho de Imperio"', 204–5 Estepa Díaz identifies a need for such calculations and in 'La política imperial de Alfonso X', 214–15, believes he has found it. Cf. Abulafia's description of Frederick II's imperial rule within Germany as 'possessing an over-arching authority even where practical expression was lacking': *Frederick II*, 69.

though the kings of France and England might have been unconcerned by the emperor's four-fold agenda – to remove differences from amongst men, to make *fueros* and laws for their imperial subjects, to bring down the mighty from their seats, and to defend the faith of Our Lord Jesus Christ (2. 1. 1) – which was so little different from the traditional tripartite prescription of peninsular monarchs (in D. Juan Manuel's formula, law-making, conquest and colonization),[93] the requirements that 'all subjects of the empire must obey the emperor's commands' and that 'the emperor must have such power as to ensure that those of his *señorío* should be constrained to obey him' (2. 1. 1, 3) may have caused Jaime of Aragón to wonder just how far that *señorío* was thought to extend. Having only recently rid himself of French claims over Catalonia that had been rooted in the Carolingian empire, he is unlikely to have been altogether satisfied by the assurance that the sole purpose of Alfonso's imperial ambitions was 'to control his patrimonial kingdoms and exercise monarchical primacy over the peninsula'.[94]

To some historians for whom the purpose of Alfonso X's *fecho del imperio* was to provide an 'escape valve' for the disposal of his disruptive nobility, it does not seem remarkable that he should have thought it necessary to create a Turnerian frontier at the other end of Europe when suitable facilities were already available on his own doorstep. Others are sceptical about the proposition that it was the prospect of empire that spurred him to compile a law code 'worthy' of the occasion since his imperial rival felt no such need,[95] which is to disregard the very different contexts to which the king of Castile and the earl of Cornwall belonged as well as the very mind-set of the man whom Juan de Mariana famously described as having lost the earth beneath his feet while scanning the heavens above.[96] It may therefore be profitable to introduce Alfonso's intellectual omnivorousness into the equation, his insatiable appetite, as well as for law, for astrology, astronomy and translations from the Arabic about everything else, and, as will be attempted in a later chapter, for history.

Rather than with the vertical Thales, to Plato's tale of whose disappearance down the well Mariana was perhaps unconsciously indebted, Alfonso may deserve to be likened instead to Mr Casaubon with his search for that horizontal 'Key to all Mythologies' that would

---

[93]   *Libro del cauallero et del escudero*, c. 3 (ed. I, 43).
[94]   Ayala Martínez, *Directices*, 155; below, 146–7.
[95]   Calderón, 259; Petit, *AHDE*, 56 (1986), 1090.
[96]   Mariana, XIII. 20.

show (what indeed had been attempted before, but not with that thoroughness, justice of comparison, and effectiveness of arrangement at which
Mr Casaubon aimed) that all the mythical systems or erratic mythical frag-
ments in the world were corruptions of a tradition originally revealed.

There is certainly something recognizably Alfonsine about the conviction of
George Eliot's fictional creation that 'having once mastered the true position
and taken a firm footing there, the vast field of mythical constructions became
intelligible, nay, luminous with the reflected light of correspondences' (of
those between astrology and history, for example) within an ideal world
of perfect syncretism.[97]
But, for all that the king of Castile (by contrast with Mr Casaubon)
was fully apprised of the latest German authorities, 'to gather in this great
harvest of truth was no light or speedy work' for him either.[98] Gathered in
it all needed to be, though, for a simple, single commanding principle
underlay all his schemes. Just as all prices and the conduct of all wedding
breakfasts needed to be controlled, so too had all knowledge to be sub-
sumed into the Alfonsine system. Thus the correspondences latent in the
vast corpus of Arabic science and in the wisdom of the Greeks embedded
within that corpus inspired the learned monarch to commission a programme
of translation which, because in true Alfonsine style it was altogether com-
mensurate with its subject-matter, by the end of the reign had barely scratched
the surface. However, since work on it was already under way at court at
its very beginning, alongside everything else that was going on there in those
years, account will need to be taken of it in the next two chapters.

[97] Cf. Plato, *Theaetetus*, 174a, and for the identical fate of an astrologer at the court of
Alexander the Great, as recorded by al-Suyūṭī (†1505), Asín Palacios, 'El juicio de P. Mariana
sobre Alfonso el Sabio'; George Eliot, *Middlemarch*, chap. 3. Cf. Ménendez Pidal (though
referring to the 1270s): 'Alfonso (. . .) se empeña en una labor sincrética total': 'Como
trabajaron las escuelas alfonsíes', 369. For the alleged correspondences between astrology
and history: below, 140.
[98] Cf. *Middlemarch*, chap. 21.

6

1259–74

Toledo and Translations

It would have been not unlike Alfonso X to have chosen Toledo as the venue for his 'imperial' cortes of 1259 in order to prompt memories amongst those summoned of Spain's first Catholic century. For although the context of the *Espéculo*'s allusion (1. 1. 13) to 'the kings of Spain who were of old' (*antiguamente*) probably referred to a more recent period of the Spanish past, the adverb could also be thought to hark back to a time when the entire peninsula had been united under a single rule and its affairs directed, as was fondly believed, by the councils of Toledo.[1] It was also the case that it was above all at Toledo that the translation of Arabic works into Latin had been undertaken throughout the previous century. The reputation that the place had acquired thereby was evoked in the story told by the Italian Franciscan Salimbene of the young Lombard on the make who, thinking he might make it all the sooner if he mastered the black arts, had betaken himself there, only to be run over by demons, dogs, cats and pigs, and then sent packing by a curmudgeonly tutor with the words: 'You Lombards aren't cut out for this game. Leave this magic business to us Spaniards, boy. We can handle it because we're as mad as the demons themselves. You get off to Paris, my lad, and study theology. That's the place for you.'[2] And it was at Toledo that in 1243 the then Infante Alfonso

---

[1] As in *Setenario*, 19, where 'antiguamiente' evidently refers (imaginatively) to the Visigothic period: Linehan, *History*, 439.
[2] Which he did, and by 1251 was archbishop of Ravenna. A principal persecutor of Ezzelino da Romano, Alfonso's major Italian ally at the end of that decade, Archbishop Philip inspired scarcely less fear than that psychopath (*Cronica*, 594–5), so perhaps his Toledo apprenticeship had not been time wasted. On the reputation of the place: Burnett, 135–6.

acquired the work of Arabic astrology/astronomy that its Jewish owner, 'neither wanting to make use of it himself nor wishing that anyone else should', had kept hidden, and had it translated into Castilian with the title *Lapidario*.[3]

Completed in 1250, the *Lapidario*, a treatise on stones and their magical properties, was the earliest of the seven scientific (or pseudo-scientific) works translated from Arabic between then and the completion of the *Libro de las Cruces* in February 1259 by Yehudá ben Mošé ha-Kohén, a Jew who as well as being Alfonso's physician was 'learned in the art of astrology and knew and understood well both Arabic and Latin', assisted by the Christian, Garci Pérez. So much in accordance with Toledo practice was such collaboration between Jews and Christians that it has been suggested that it was partly in order to appease Jewish sensibilities at court that Castilian was preferred to Latin as the language of discourse.[4] During the 1250s, with Jews such as Yehudá ben Mošé establishing themselves as the dominant partners in the enterprise, the object was no longer the provision of Latin texts but rather of vernacular versions for the benefit of the Latin-less in order that 'men might better understand and profit the more from [them]':[5] *all* men. 'For Alfonso, the only realistic course was to detach, to a certain point, the idea of learning from the idea of Latin for the very first time in the Western Middle Ages': of all ideas 'one of the most unthinkable for a man of the thirteenth century'. With the objective of uncovering the mysteries of nature for the general good, central to the entire enterprise was a reverence for Aristotle, 'the most accomplished of all the philosophers', in the words of the opening of the prologue of the *Lapidario*, 'who most *naturally* revealed all things by right reason and made them fully comprehensible for what they are.'[6]

And more. For Aristotle was also conceived of as the author of the *Lapidario*, as the first and more imposing of the two miniatures in the manuscript that pre-dates Alfonso's imperial phase seems intended to suggest. Venerably bearded and elevated on his professor's chair, with the index finger of his right hand raised didactically towards the young Alexander, the

[3]   Solalinde, 197–8.

[4]   Above, 78.

[5]   *Lapidario* (prol.): Solalinde, 198; Hilty, 20–5; Romano, 'Opere scientifiche', 687–9, 710 (with the calculation that although of the twelve individuals known to have been associated with the work of translation or authorship only five were Jews, between them they were concerned with as many as 23 of the 31 works identified); Roth, 61–2; Procter, 'Scientific works', 22–3; Menéndez Pidal, 'Cómo trabajaron las escuelas alfonsíes', 364–8. For the wider context: Glick, 'Science in medieval Spain'.

[6]   Márquez Villanueva, 'Cultural concept', 79–80; Solalinde, 196.

illuminator's Aristotle is attended by recumbent ancients of oriental aspect encamped around him. The other illustration, showing the king receiving the translation from its two authors, is on a smaller scale. As the reign progressed, depictions of the authorial monarch accompanying the translations commissioned by him steadily magnified his contribution to the process, eventually rendering him indistinguishable from the Stagirite himself,[7] though Aristotle was not the only distinguished ancient with whom the learned king liked to identify. Albeit the philosopher *par excellence* preceded them he would still have to compete as exemplar with the likes of Jupiter and Alexander for Alfonso's favour.[8]

The prologue to the *Lapidario* dated Alfonso's acquisition of the Arabic original of the work to the year of the acquisition (rather than the conquest) of the kingdom of Murcia. The detail and the distinction are both important. Having been spared the destruction the Almohads had wrought in other regions of al-Andalus, in 1243 Murcia was transferred to Christian administration with minimum disruption, and its celebrated *madrasa* continued to thrive under the direction of the celebrated Muḥammad bīn Aḥmad bin Abī Bakr al-Riqūtī. Such was the reputation of 'El Ricotí', and so considerable the influence he reputedly exercised over the young Alfonso, that it may even be wondered whether when setting out to represent Aristotle the miniaturist of the *Lapidario* manuscript may not have had him in mind. At any event, after 1243 the Murcia *madrasa* continued to attract Christians as well as Muslims and Jews by providing instruction in the Romance which had been one of the languages spoken in Murcia over the previous two hundred years.[9]

Whereas Fernando III's Andalusian policy of dispossessing the Muslim population had dispersed the scholarly communities of both Córdoba and Seville, in the kingdom of Murcia Alfonso established what has been described as a 'protectorate that preserved intact all its Islamic structures'.[10] Thus, whilst his younger brothers were with more or less assiduity acquiring the typical education of Western princes by the banks of the Seine, Alfonso was engaged in fostering those intellectual traditions that in due course would provide him with the services of skilled translators. Also available to him as king for this purpose was the expertise associated with the Toledo school, one alumnus of which, Herman the German, had moved on from the Arabized

---

[7]   Domínguez Rodríguez, *Astrología y arte*, 9–12.

[8]   Despite Engels's assurance regarding Jupiter as legislator figure in the *Espéculo*: 'Idea imperial', 35.

[9]   Menjot, 117–28; Torres Fontes, *Cultura murciana*, 6–7; Martínez Ripoll, 36–7.

[10] Arjona Castro, 197–8; *MHE*, I, no. 25.

Aristotle to the Hebrew psalter, though rather than at Toledo itself, or in Apulia, it was probably principally at Palencia that Herman was based.[11]

The moribund university of Palencia was associated with the study of traditional Christian theology, which Alfonso chose not to promote. In his charter of privileges to the *studium* of Salamanca (May 1254) study of the subject was not provided for. Neither, so far as we know, was it at the *studium generale* 'of Latin and Arabic' founded by him at Seville in the December of that year, though six years later he was at pains to provide for the *fisicos* 'who had come there from over yonder' (*de allende*), requesting the local archbishop and chapter to provide them with former mosques in which to live and, in what sounds rather like the Murcia *madrasa*, 'to teach those to whom we have ordered them to impart their great learning'.[12] Whatever knowledge it was that these *fisicos* had been brought to Seville to communicate – whether natural philosophy in the Aristotelian mould or physics or medicine – it was only because Alfonso's father had expelled the local talent in 1248 that their services were required, and only by means of the likes of Yehudá ha-Kohén, the Jew 'who knew and understood well both Arabic and Latin' and Romance-speaking Christian assistants that Alfonso himself was able to supply the need.[13]

Knowledge counted. The king who depended upon another for his control of affairs made himself that man's servant, Alfonso would declare

---

[11]   Morreale, 470. Herman died as bishop of Astorga in 1272. According to Ferreiro Alemparte, 36–7, 43–50, he was at the court of Manfred of Hohenstaufen between 1256 and 1266 (whence Diego Lobejón, 38–9); this on the strength of Roger Bacon's list of translators from Arabic into Latin from Gerard of Cremona to 'Hermannus Alemannus, et translator Meinfredi nuper a domino rege Carolo [Charles of Anjou] devicti': 'Opus tertium', I. 91–2. For the more plausible interpretation, that the 'et' before 'translator . . .' in Bacon's report is disjunctive and refers to another person altogether, Bartholomew of Messina: Grabmann, 59, and for Herman at Toledo from 1263 and Palencia by 1265, Hernández, 'Fundación', 69–71; Hernández & Linehan, chap. 4.
[12]   Rashdall, II, 80–1, 91; Beltrán de Heredia, I, 210–16, 604–6; *MHE*, I, no. 25. Although there are those who continue to believe in it, the evidence of the so-called 'Libro del Candado', containing certain verses by Alfonso recording the outcome of his invitation to an Egyptian sage summoned to instruct him in the secrets of the philosopher's stone, may be discounted – unless its employment of the 'octava real' verse-form all of two centuries before its introduction to the peninsula be regarded as a further example of Alfonso's exceptional prescience: Ortiz de Zúñiga, II, 201–2, 289; Mondéjar, 461–2; Salvador Martínez, *Alfonso X*, 170 n. 26. Cf. Sánchez Pérez, 158–62.
[13]   Two 'maestros de fisica' had been provided for at Salamanca – 'of physic', according to Rashdall, II, 81; Beltrán de Heredia, I, 605. According to Amasuno (p. 179), the *Lapidario* should be regarded as 'the earliest Castilian treatise of medical literature', such is its wealth of *materia medica*, largely derived from the works of Ḥunayn ibn Isḥāq in ninth-century Baghdad.

in the Second *Partida*, citing not only David and Solomon but also Boethius ('who was a very wise *caballero* [gentleman]'). This was hackneyed stuff, however, scarcely less trite than the advice that a king 'needed to be wise and forewarned', as the *Libro de los doze sabios* had recommended. But the inadequacy of the mirror of princes commissioned by Fernando III had been demonstrated at the beginning of Alfonso's reign, allegedly causing the new king to seek fresh advice from the ten surviving sages (and two replacements) for dealing with the 'great discords' recently caused by his brothers and the grandees of the kingdom.[14] The prescriptions of the previous generation were evidently proving inadequate.

Knowledge was power. But how, and to what ends, was it to be exercised? The instructions in the *Libro de los doze sabios* for rendering infantes biddable having failed to prevent the escapades of D. Fadrique and D. Enrique, in due course Alfonso X would dedicate himself to the education of as many of his subjects as were capable of opening a book. This he indicated in his instructions to Rabi Çag, 'el de Toledo', translator of the *Libros de saber del astrologia*.[15] Writing in the 1330s, his nephew D. Juan Manuel recorded that programme of education in the following terms:

> Amongst the many accomplishments and virtues with which God endowed King Alfonso . . . the Almighty endowed him with a zeal for the increase of knowledge such as no king since Ptolemy nor any other man has been possessed of. So determined was he that the men of his kingdom should be very wise that he had the whole of theology, logic and the seven liberal arts, as well as what they call mechanics translated into Castilian. Also all the false teaching of the Moors, in order to reveal the errors into which their false prophet Mohammed had plunged them; . . . also the entire law of the Jews as well as their Talmud and another doctrine of theirs which they keep safely hidden and call *cabbala*. And this he did . . . so as to show that like the Moors they are in great error and in danger of losing their souls. Also he had all laws both ecclesiastical and secular turned into the vernacular. What more can I say?[16]

What more indeed? For some contemporaries it was already too much. In the account of Gil de Zamora, for example, there is no mention of translations from Arabic or Hebrew whatsoever. According to the Franciscan friar,

---

[14]   *Part.* 2. 5. 16; *Libro de los doze sabios*, 77, 117. Only their twelve alternative suggestions for inscriptions for Fernando III's tomb are specified (pp. 117–18), not the substance of the 'good and true counsels whereby the king felt himself very well served' on this occasion.

[15]   'thoroughly and intelligibly so that any man who examines the book will be able to work with it': cit. Cárdenas, 'Alfonso X and the *Studium generale*', 71. For Rabi Çag, 'el de Toledo' (Isḥāq ibn Sīd): Romano, 'Opere scientifiche', 689–91.

[16]   *Libro de la caza*, prol. (ed. Blecua, I, 519–20).

it was only the canonical texts of the Christian West, theological and legal, that Alfonso had had rendered into his 'mother tongue'. The Franciscan polymath, who as tutor to the Infante Sancho was in a position to know, could not bring himself to refer to a Christian king's translations of infidel writings. Partial though it is, however, his account of the matter is nevertheless instructive. The work had been done, he reported, in order to make intelligible all writings the meaning of which in their original Latin had remained hidden 'even from the professionals'.[17]

The admission from the heart of the establishment that that establishment was unable to understand its own official language goes some way towards providing a minimal definition of what has lately been identified as the 'Alfonsine cultural concept'. But only some way. For the purpose of that concept went far beyond a routine objective of servicing that establishment by providing reductionist versions of Petrus Comestor and the *Liber Extra*. Alfonso X was not interested in the set-books of the Western Church either for their own sake or for the Church's – even if in some of them he was for purposes of his own, purposes to which we shall return in connexion with his historical works.

Regarding what has survived, and what has been published and studied, the description of his initiative as 'one of the great personal undertakings known to the Middle Ages' and its purpose as that of establishing 'a new sociology of knowledge' within which the wisdom of the 'oriental other' confronted the intellectual traditions of the Christian West within 'peninsular space' may be to overstate the case. The 'purpose of instructing his kingdoms' is certainly a generous paraphrase of D. Juan Manuel's report of his ambition 'that the men of his kingdom should be very wise': 'que los de los sus regnos fuessen muy sabidores'.[18] How far he managed to proceed in this direction we shall never know because, of the translations mentioned by his nephew of 'all the false teaching of the Moors' and of 'the entire law of the Jews', for example, no trace remains, while whole tracts of the *General Estoria* still await publication. But whether or not the *Estoria de España* was correct in its inference from the story of the collapse of national morale at the end of the Visigothic period that 'all men everywhere are formed in the likeness of their king and resemble him',[19] King Alfonso was not intent

[17]   Fita, 'Biografías', 321. In litigation of the year 1251 one such professional, the abbot of S. Martín de Castañeda (dioc. Astorga), was described as 'a simple man, one who had known no Latin' ('homo simplex et qui Latinum [*sic*] non noverat'): Cavero Domínguez, 114.

[18]   Márquez Villanueva, *Concepto cultural*, 123, 138, 185; also 30–1.

[19]   PCG, c. 559 (p. 314a₇), paraphrasing the axiom cited by Rodrigo of Toledo: DrH, III. 22. Cf. Fernández-Ordóñez, 'Variación', 46–7: 'The translation of the causes for the loss of Spain [in the *Estoria de España*] reflects the importance that this idea had for Alfonso.'

upon a programme of universal education. The learned men by whom kings and lands were served, according to the Learned King in the Second *Partida*, were university men, and the opportunity society he envisaged was one peopled by graduates, law graduates in particular. From the prohibition on mass meetings in the cities and the kingdom wisely decreed by the ancients (as well as by Alfonso himself and his father on the grounds that such assemblies 'invariably did more harm than good'), they alone were exempted.[20] And the example that inspired the king to make an exception of them was not the meritocracy of the *madrasa*, as has been suggested, but the privileges in favour of the Roman law scholars of Bologna contained in the authentic *Habita* granted by Alfonso's ancestor Frederick Barbarossa, exorbitantly extended perhaps in deference to the opinion later reported by Baldus that such scholars were 'spiritual sons of the emperor'.[21]

To Vicente de Lafuente in 1884 it was 'very shocking' that the king should have recruited Arabs 'from over yonder' to staff his new university at Seville.[22] And so it seemed six hundred and more years before, six hundred years before *precisely*, everywhere other than in Alfonso's final refuge, Seville itself. It was shocking because it was novel, and it was novel because it breached all the conventions to which Europe's universities had ostensibly adhered over the previous century.[23] But it was not unprecedented. Courtesy of the Spanish entrepôt, for generations the Christian West had been spoiling the Egyptians. It was on the authority of Rodrigo of Toledo that Alfonso wrote of Mohammed as schooled in the natural sciences by a Jewish tutor. For Lucas of Tuy the Prophet had been a dealer in magic and spells and Aristotle a Spaniard.[24] Like the friars, Alfonso X was the testamentary legatee of the Twelfth Century Renaissance.[25]

In his summary of his uncle's achievements D. Juan Manuel listed 'all that art that they call mechanics'. Before 1260 at least, the king's purpose does

[20] *Part.* 2. 31. 6; above, 116–17.
[21] Márquez Villanueva, *Concepto cultural*, 169–71; *Part.* 2. 31, proem. and *leyes* 2, 7, 8, including the provision that masters of twenty years' standing in the schools of law should enjoy the rank of counts: Rashdall, I, 142–4; II, 79–80. Cf. Ullmann, 'Medieval interpretation', 112.
[22] *Hist. de las universidades*, I, 129.
[23] Márquez Villanueva, *Concepto cultural*, 174, with whose assertion (note 14) that Rashdall attempted to explain away the introduction of Muslims as a missionary initiative compare Rashdall's actual words (I, 91): 'A monarch so devoted to astronomical and mathematical studies was probably not uninfluenced by the desire to throw open to the learned of his realm all the wisdom of the Arabians.'
[24] *PCG*, c. 472 (p. 263a); *Historia arabum*, c. 2 (p. 89). Cf. *CM*, III. 5; Rico, 'Aristoteles Hispanus'.
[25] Above, 52.

seem to have been 'fundamentally pragmatic', concerned with metallurgy rather than metaphysics. Whereas Plato's Thales, like Mariana's Alfonso, displayed a propensity for putting his foot in it and falling down holes, according to Aristotle's account the Greek sage's study of the heavens enabled him to predict a bumper olive crop in time to corner the available supply of olive-presses.[26] Transferred into the world of Mediterranean power-politics in the late 1250s, this was not a worthless talent. Moreover, not only did the real-life Alfonso commission translations of treatises on agriculture from eleventh-century al-Andalus. He was also at pains to stress that the *Lapidario* possessed a value beyond its interest to connoisseurs of stones and what we would call astrologers. According to the prologue to the work, much of the mystery of the 'arte de fisica' was contained within the qualities of stones.[27] Nor was astrology a mere pastime for dilettantes. It was a science, studied particularly by those who because they had most to lose were particularly interested in 'knowing the things that were to come before they happened'.[28] History was also useful in this connexion. Indeed, *everything* was useful when properly understood.

Had Alfonso not lost his throne and been smeared by Mariana and Mariana's posterity, how far-sighted his encouragement of translations on the astrolabe etc. would now be accounted, with comparisons drawn with the legendary planting of oaks by his Portuguese grandson, D. Dinis, to be shaped into caravels in the time of Henry the Navigator, and (matching the 'romantic canard' of D. Enrique brooding over the ocean from his eyrie at Sagres)[29] the no less fanciful tableau of D. Alfonso scanning the Atlantic, either from the top of the Giralda, the tower in the city of Seville he alone had saved from destruction in 1248, or, rather more plausibly (since the other would have required a miracle of eyesight), from his shipyards on the Guadalquivir downstream.

[26]   Juan Manuel, *Libro de la caza*, 519; Márquez Villanueva, *Concepto cultural*, 35; Aristotle, *Politics*, I. 4, 1259a 6–19; above, 131.
[27]   García Gómez, 'Traducciones alfonsíes'; Solalinde, *Antología*, 198. Notwithstanding Alfonso's alleged lack of interest in the subject, as reported by Márquez Villanueva, *Concepto cultural*, 37, 'fisica' here must indicate medical science, as the author himself acknowledges (p. 176). Of the 56 occurrences of the word in the Alfonsine corpus, 43 appear to have this meaning and only two that of physics or natural philosophy: Cárdenas, 'Alfonso X and the *studium generale*', 73 n. 16.
[28]   Cit. Cárdenas, 'Toward an understanding', 84, *q. v.* also (pp. 85–8) for the connotations of 'astrology' and 'astronomy' in Alfonsine terminology. Cf. Márquez Villanueva, *Concepto cultural*, 198–209.
[29]   Cf. Russell, whose phrase this is: *Henry 'the Navigator'*, 7.

As to Alfonso's own role in the realization of his 'cultural concept', there is room for more than one opinion. Until the mid-1270s at least, contemporaries readily corroborated Gil de Zamora's report of the 'sharpness of intellect, penetration in study and excellence of memory' the king had evinced in his adolescence. Some went even further. In the judgement of his collaborator Egidius de Tebaldis, 'his intellect embraced everything'. 'He loves knowledge ("scientia") and honours those who profess it ("scientes"), searching them out from all ends of the earth and bringing them to him.' He had uncovered the hidden wisdom of the ancients for the enlightenment of posterity.[30]

Expressed rather more modestly, the opinion is one that has found some support amongst modern historians. Procter, for example, finds in the prologues of his astronomical and astrological works evidence that Alfonso was 'more than a mere patron'.[31] The contrast between this estimate of him and that of the 'mere patron' who, albeit illustrious, was entirely dependent on others for expertise in the subject matter of those works, is paralleled in differing appraisals of his authorial role. For while the king may have been qualified to intervene in favour of stylistic clarity, insisting that the translation of *Estrellas fixas* be rendered in 'correct Castilian',[32] and perhaps was even himself responsible for identifying the inadequacies of Fernando of Toledo's translation of the *Libro de la açafeha* (1255/6) and having the work done again,[33] it is another matter to declare a corpus of knowledge, legal and historical as well as scientific, not just something with which he tinkered interestedly from time to time but the distinctive creation of an encyclopaedic genius pervaded by a single style, as 'one of the great personal works of the Middle Ages', 'all legitimately his'.[34]

For those lacking such acute perception, Alfonso's own account in the *General Estoria* of what royal authorship amounted to deserves notice. The sense in which a king might be said to 'make' a book was the same as that in which he built a palace, not with his own hands but as the promoter and

[30]   Above, 106; Procter, 'Scientific works', 21–2. Egidius translated into Latin the (lost) Castilian version of Ptolemy's *Quadripartitum*.

[31]   Ibid., 22.

[32]   Romano, 'Opere scientifiche', 683, Márquez Villanueva's account of whose opinion misrepresents it as a commendation of the king's technical competence in the material: *Concepto cultural*, 195; Cárdenas, 'Alfonso el Sabio's "castellano drecho"', 3.

[33]   'And later he had them better and more fully "*trasladar*" at Burgos by Master Bernaldo the Arab and don Abraham his alfaquí', cit. K. Kennedy, 181, with the suggestion that 'trasladar' here means copying rather than translation. Cf. Procter, 'Scientific works', 16.

[34]   Márquez Villanueva, *Concepto cultural*, 44–6, 113–23, 126–8.

guiding intelligence of the operation, like the Almighty in the Book of Exodus using Moses as his agent on Mount Sinai.[35] The tinkering process, evidenced in the prologues to the translations and in the passages of the historical works to be considered later, might therefore be likened to miraculous interventions by the divinity in the affairs of the sub-lunary world.

Be that as it may, whether by design or *force majeure*, in the year 1260 that programme was interrupted. By now it was becoming apparent that the empire the king of Castile was obsessed with was not even a chimaera. It was a metaphor. Nor was it only on that 'greater and better empire still' envisaged by the ruler of Granada that his sights were set. In the zone to which Sicily was the key he had the Mediterranean in general in mind. But Sicily was firmly under the control of Manfred of Hohenstaufen, as after his crushing defeat of the Florentine Guelfs at Montaperti in September 1260 so also was the Italian mainland. Moreover, the death twelve months earlier of Ezzelino da Romano had deprived Alfonso of his only northern Italian ally, and since Ezzelino while alive had been the papacy's bitterest enemy, by the end of 1259, when the Cortes of Toledo assembled, papal sympathy for him had evaporated. After Manfred had had himself crowned king of Sicily in August 1258, and with rumours rife that Pope Alexander was about to crown Richard of Cornwall emperor, in May 1259 Alfonso informed Albert de la Tour-du-Pin, his seneschal for the kingdoms of Arles and Vienne, of his 'irrevocable' resolve to visit Italy for that purpose 'that same summer'. From this course of action he was firmly discouraged and made to settle for the humiliating alternative of the diplomatic mission headed by his brother D. Manuel that led to the referral of the dispute to papal arbitration. Hard as the sycophants might strive to promote the cause of the Alfonsine eagle by representing the earl of Cornwall as a kite (and therefore, presumably, toothless), the fact remained that the king of Castile had demanded his crown and had been granted a committee.[36]

Moreover – and this was even more damaging to Alfonso's credibility than recent reverses at the papal curia – by 1259 such domestic morale as there had been three years earlier was fast disintegrating. In part, this was due to the extreme behaviour of the Spanish climate. But the weather was only

---

[35]   *GE*, 1. 477; Solalinde, 'Intervención', 286. The authority for the theological analogy was the *Historia scholastica* of Petrus Comestor: Montoya, 'Concepto de "autor"', 460–1. Cf. MacDonald, *Espéculo*, xxxii.

[36]   Jordan, *L'Allemagne et l'Italie*, 336–44; Valbonnais, I, 194; Mondéjar, 168–72; Fanta, 102–3. Cf. the (excruciating) verses of Gutetus de Mixigia, notary of Milan, advising the earl to stay amongst smaller birds or lose his feathers, and likening him to black lead in comparison with shining gold, to a donkey with a stag, a tortoise taking wings with the bird of Jove, and a lark with a hawk: Hahn, 394–5.

an irritant; it was not the cause. The cause (if it be legitimate to identify a single cause of malaise) was the accumulated exhaustion of a society disorganized by war.

In circumstances such as these, those on the spot are often both blind and deaf to developments. It is newcomers who see and hear most, outsiders who observe deep interstitial cracks in the institutional cloisters. And in this case it is the rootless adventurers who were in and about the Castilian court with an eye to the main chance to whom we are chiefly indebted for an understanding of a sort of what was wrong. Bonifaci Calvo's complaint about the Castilian nobility's appetite for wine and snacks at home rather than glory abroad has already been mentioned. In 1259 another member of that restless confraternity, the Catalan Cerverí of Girona, issued his analysis of the peninsular scene, an analysis occasioned by recent political turmoil in his own part of the world. According to Cerverí society was rotten from top to bottom. But it was at the top that the rot started. Their vile behaviour the Aragonese counts had copied from their kings, from the counts it had passed to the barons, and from the barons to the 'little people and the townsfolk'. The whole world was corrupt. Let Castile learn the lesson, and the king of England too (in 1259 Henry III was also experiencing a little local difficulty) as well as (the location of another lost cause by that date) 'the place where God by dying won us life'.[37]

In 1259 (or thereabouts), however, it was for another reason that Juan d'Aspa thanked God. It was for having provided the age with a new Solomon, 'the seeker-out and lover of philosophy and of all other sciences, and this is the lord Alfonso . . . at whose command wise men render into the Castilian language the best and most perfect books of every art and science in whatever language they may have been composed.' Thus the prologue to the *Liber Razielis*, a cabbalistic work of astral magic translated by Juan from the Latin (as was customary) together with related treatises assembled by the king to make it 'more excellent', including one or more requiring translation from Greek, in which the means of controlling the celestial bodies by means of angels was described. Entrusted by the angel Raziel to Adam as consolation for his divorce from wisdom, it was inscribed by Noah on a talismanic sapphire and eventually fell into the hands of King Solomon who had it translated from Chaldee (i.e. Aramaic) into Hebrew.[38] And there was no denying its usefulness. The *Liber Razielis* itself remains inedited, but after identifying the names of the angels 'in the third encampment', the

[37]   Riquer, *Cerverí de Girona*, 106.
[38]   García Avilés, 29–31, 35. For the possible, though not undisputed, identification of 'Raziel' with Aly Aben Ragel, author of 'El Libro Conplido', ibid., 32.

Book of the Mysteries, a text of the Hellenistic period to which its sixth part, the 'Libro de los cielos' is closely related, recommends the following:

> If you wish to know and understand what will be in each and every year, take a hieratic papyrus and cut it into slips and write in hieratic with a mixture of ink and myrrh each and every possibility separately. Then take a new flask and put it in spikenard oil and throw in the written slips (as well); then stand facing the sun when he comes forth from his bridal chamber and say: 'I adjure you O sun that shines on the earth, in the name of the angels who make men of knowledge understand and comprehend wisdom and secrets, that you will do what I ask and make known to me what will be in this year – do not conceal a thing for me.' And you will adjure (the sun with) this adjuration for three days, three times and the third time you will scrutinize the oil. Notice everything brought up upon the face of the oil, that is what will happen in that year . . .[39]

Similarly there was provision for the protection of 'a man going forth to war', involving seven bay leaves and more spikenard oil, which may have served some useful purpose in the spring of 1260 when, with D. Manuel still at Anagni on the king's business, the king himself was finalizing preparations for his African crusade, and a fleet of thirty-seven ships was being assembled at Puerto de Santa María, no doubt provisioned, as the Second *Partida* would require, with (*inter alia*) cheese, onions and garlic, and ample supplies of lime to blind the enemy and soap to make them lose their footing.[40] That summer the order to set sail was issued when a disaffected member of the Marīnid ascendancy, Yaʿqūb bin ʿAbd Allāh, captured the town of Salé in the vicinity of Rabat and called upon Alfonso to provide him with reinforcements against the reigning sultan Abū Yūsuf. But though the Castilian fleet proceeded to seize the place they did not remain there for long. For the sultan was soon on the scene and on 22 September, after an occupation of just twelve days, the invaders were sent packing.

After all the build-up since the beginning of the reign this was an ignominious reverse.[41] Even if the expedition was at least in part designed

---

[39] Transl. Morgan, 29–30.

[40] Ibid., 55; *Reg. Alex. IV*, 3084 (RdLA, no. 464; 10 Apr. 1260); *Part*. 2. 24. 9. The papal letter of 9 April 1259, summarized in RdLA, no. 413, and cited in this connexion by Ayala Martínez (*Directrices*, 283 n. 271) had nothing to do with the matter, its purpose having been to restore relations between the king and his recently seditious brother Archbishop Sancho of Toledo: AC Toledo, A.7.C.2.6 (printed *MHE*, I, no. 67); above, 115.

[41] Huici Miranda, 'Toma de Salé', esp. 45, rightly rejecting Ballesteros's suggestion ('Toma de Salé', 105–6) that Alfonso was motivated by Innocent IV's cession of the place to the Order of Santiago in 1245 after its surrender to the pontiff by Saʿīd Aaron on the occasion of his conversion (*Reg. Inn. IV*, 1511); Dufourcq, 'Projet castillan', 37–41.

to impress the major players on the Mediterranean scene, which is possible, the outcome can hardly be described as a triumphant vindication of Castilian endeavour – least of all in the eyes of Alfonso himself whose recently appointed admiral Juan García de Villamayor was forced to seek refuge from the king's wrath in Portugal.[42]

However, the Salé campaign was more than just a failed propaganda display. There was another dimension to it of a more material nature, one that goes no small way towards accounting for the transformation of Genoa in the five years after 1256 from opponent of Alfonso's imperial aspirations to recipient of most favoured mercantile status in Alfonso's kingdom. This was the fact that in 1252 Genoa had begun to mint gold *genovinos*, and that Salé, where Genoese merchants had been trading for a century, was a principal entrepôt of the trans-Saharan gold trade. Alfonso too was in urgent need of supplies of the metal, and not only for the purpose of affixing impressive seals to the diplomas of his imperial chancery, authenticating privileges in favour of his beloved Seville, or meeting the 'almost incredible expenses' reported by Jofré de Loaisa.[43] He also needed it because by 1258 he had resumed the issue within Castile of the immobilized gold *maravedí alfonsí* (that is, of the *maravedí* typologically identical to the coin issued in the high days of the reign of Alfonso VIII).[44] In which case, it may be asked, why should Alfonso X willingly have admitted the Genoese to this precious source of supply?

The search for an answer to this question takes us into diplomatic waters even murkier than those of the Mediterranean.

International Complications

In 1256 Genoa had been ranged against the king of Castile because Pisa, Genoa's rival, was the main champion of his imperial cause. Yet in August 1261 the king of Castile both confirmed and enhanced the privileges that his father had granted the Genoese at Seville nine years earlier.[45] This was not because Castilians had suddenly come to think better of the Genoese; that would take longer to achieve.[46] It was because in the course of those

[42] Thus Ayala Martínez, *Directrices*, 277–9.
[43] Lopez, 'Back to gold', 221–5; Schwab, 613–14; López Gutiérrez, 'Sevilla'. For 'pre-imperial' gold seals attached to diplomas of 1254: Chaplais, nos. 271, 275.
[44] Todesca, 154, 162; Hernández, *Rentas*, I, clxiii.
[45] González Jiménez, *Diplomatario andaluz*, nos. 250–1.
[46] When besieging Algeciras in 1344 Alfonso XI would recall the help the Genoese had given to 'los Moros' there in the reign of Alfonso X (i.e. in 1278–9) *CAXI*, c. 323, cit. Dufourcq, 'Projet castillan', 40.

five years the geopolitics of the Mediterranean had been transformed. Castile and Genoa were operating within a single metallic zone, a Castilian fleet (of sorts) would soon be under the command of a Genoese admiral,[47] the Mongol army seized Baghdad and put paid to the last Abbasid caliph (February 1258), and the ruler of the Latin Empire of Constantinople, Baldwin II, woke up one fine morning in July 1261 to find that his empire had disappeared overnight, gathered up by Michael Palaeologus and *his* Genoese allies.

Five centuries earlier, the Abbasid overthrow of the Umayyad caliphate in Damascus had set in train a series of events whose consequences for Spain (not to mention Western Europe) had proved altogether more profound than would be acknowledged in the Alfonsine History of Spain (a work not yet in progress in 1258) in which all that would be mentioned regarding the Syrian *coup* would be the story of the Umayyad refugee 'Abd al-Raḥmān's arrival in Córdoba.[48] Now, by contrast, developments on every shore of the Mediterranean were of immediate concern to the whole of Christendom, and to the ruler of Córdoba and Seville in particular. The world within which Alfonso was operating was a larger one than it had been even five years before, and one ever more delicately sensitive in all its parts. Within just twelve months many horizons had been extended. In 1257 the inexhaustible king of Aragón had attempted to hijack the princess Kristina, whom Alfonso of Castile had sourced from Norway. By peninsular standards, that may have been regarded as fair play.[49] In 1260, by contrast, Alfonso X denounced the betrothal of Jaime's son to the heiress of Sicily as anything but fair. He declared himself wounded to the quick. Never before, he protested to his Aragonese father-in-law, never before, never, had anyone been so monstrously mistreated. The mainland implications of the marriage of Juan Núñez de Lara to the Azagra heiress of Albarracín will have afforded him scant consolation.[50]

Regardless of Castilian as well as of papal protests, though, in mid-June 1262 Pedro and Constanza were married at Montpellier, and, with his tumultuous half-Castilian son now dead and buried, two months later Jaime made the last partition of his territories, bequeathing (for the first time) all his peninsular realms (principally the kingdoms of Aragón and Valencia

---

[47]   Ugo Vento, successor of the discredited Juan García de Vilamayor, who by April 1264 was engaged at Genoa in commissioning for Alfonso the construction of six galleys each of 116 oars: Lopez, 'Ugo Vento', 244–5.

[48]   *PCG*, c. 596.

[49]   Dasent, 313. Cf. above, 18.

[50]   *MHE*, I, no. 80 (Sept. 1260); Almagro, III, 250–64.

and the county of Barcelona) to Pedro, and assigning to the Infante Jaime, the other's sibling, Mallorca and the other Balearic possessions, together with Montpellier and the congeries of Catalan territories which by the treaty of Corbeil (May 1258) the king of France had liberated from their Carolingian shackles.[51]

For those Catalan historians who then and since have regarded Jaime's policy of periodic partitions as unforgivable, the creation of a kingdom of Mallorca in 1262 is of course 'absurd' and the attachment to it of mainland possessions 'mad'.[52] It is indeed the case that Pedro himself objected to it as a gimcrack aberration and that, although his son would attempt to absorb it, it would continue to act as an irritant to successive kings of Aragón until its reincorporation in 1343. In 1262, however, with his frontier with Capetian France recently rationalized and his Castilian son-in-law engaged in testing his imperial muscle, by means of this compromise of family and what might be called national interests Jaime was able to put the Pyrenees behind him, face the Mediterranean and engage with Charles of Anjou.

In that quarter the strategic implications of dynastic issues had already been demonstrated. On account of Pedro's recent union, at the end of June 1262 Louis IX was expressing misgivings about the match arranged between his heir, the future Philippe III, and Pedro's sister Isabel, and when in the following November Marseilles rose up against its Angevin master Charles did not hesitate to enter Montpellier in pursuit of those citizens of the place providing aid and comfort as well as of the Aragonese *infants*. Moreover, when Charles was elected Senator of Rome in the following year votes were also cast for Pedro, around whose dinner table Ghibelline malcontents were regularly to be found throughout the remainder of the decade.[53]

Not that Alfonso was any stranger to those waters either. Having previously assisted in redeeming from pawn the son of the Latin emperor Baldwin, in 1263 he brought Baldwin himself to Castile and in the following year was sending Princess Kristina's widower, his brother D. Felipe, eastward, ever eastward, with a view to giving Michael Palaeologus a drubbing. In a secret communication of August 1264 the pontiff fulsomely thanked the infante for his willingness 'to go in person to Romania', on the king's instructions, 'to dispose of the Greek schismatics who to the shame of the Latin

---

[51]   *Docs.JI*, no. 1282; Soldevila, *Pere el Gran*, 100, 113–14. Abulafia's startling inclusion of Sardinia in the package presumably derives from a mistranslation of 'Ceritania' (Cerdagne in the Catalan Pyrenees): *Mediterranean Emporium*, 44.

[52]   Thus Soldevila, *Hist. de Catalunya*, 317–18. For contemporary opinion: Hillgarth, 'Problem', 22.

[53]   Cartellieri, 14–15; *Docs.JI*, nos. 1277, 1294–5; Soldevila, *Pere el Gran*, 103–4, 180–5, 208–9.

people occupy that empire'.[54] While Aragón was narrowing its horizons Castile was broadening hers. By now Arab historiography adopted the name 'Alfonso' as a synonym for *any* Castilian king.[55]

For further evidence of these wider horizons see the stuffed crocodile on display in Seville cathedral to this day.

Seville cathedral's stuffed crocodile serves to bring discussion of the early years of the reign of Alfonso X down to earth. According to the Chronicle of the reign, the crocodile was sent to Alfonso in 1260 by the 'king of Egypt', together with a giraffe, a zebra and other exotica.[56] For his part, Alfonso had every reason for entering into diplomatic relations with the Mamluk sultanate at about this time, especially after the Mamluk defeat of the Mongol army at 'Ayn Ŷālūt (the Pools of Goliath) in Galilee in September 1260, immediately followed by the *coup d'état* in Cairo which made Baybars the political master of Islam. By treating the latter as his Christian opposite number, not only did the Muslim's attention flatter Alfonso's imperial pretensions. Because another upshot of that battle, arguably one of the most decisive in history,[57] had been to extend Mamluk influence to Syria and beyond, and to set their sights on Iraq and the Yemen, the new geopolitical configuration provided a relatively safe corridor for the convenience of Muslim scholars in flight from Mongol persecution further east. So a further point of comparison with the peninsular past suggests itself, this time with the recruitment by the Umayyad caliphs of tenth-century Córdoba of talented émigrés from Abbasid Baghdad. Indeed, tradition has it that whereas it was rich fabrics, precious stones, 'muchas naturas' (drugs probably) and strange animals that Alfonso received from the sultan, what he was really interested in was a certain 'great astrologer that there was in Egypt'.[58] And whether or not he was successful in securing that particular luminary, there is no question but that his understanding with Baybars, as well as providing an outlet for Andalusian olive oil, enabled the king of Castile to establish contact between his translators and the Ismaili astronomers of divers origins established under Mamluk protection at the observatory at Marāgha to the south of Tabriz in modern Azerbaijan. Although inevitably the line of influence rather resembles a rope of sand, it is sometimes

[54]   Jordan, *Origines*, 343; Wolff, 64; Linehan, *Spanish Church*, 181–2; Geanakoplos, 252–4.

[55]   Martínez Montávez, 356, n. 35. Fernando III at Seville in 1248 had been so described by Ibn 'Idhārī in *Kitāb al-bayān al-Mughrib*: Melville & Ubaydli, 149.

[56]   The following year is more likely: *CAX*, c. 9, naming the 'king of Egypt' as 'Aluandexauer', possibly a corruption of 'al-Muẓaffar', the honorific title borne by the sultan Qutuz: Martínez Montávez, 346–55.

[57]   Thus Runciman, *Crusades*, III, 313. Cf. Ayala Martínez, *Directrices*, 261–2, 291–4.

[58]   Ortiz de Zúñiga I, 201.

possible to catch a glimpse of certain of those savants whose activity during the following decade was to make at least theoretically possible collaboration between observational astronomers at work in Toledo and Seville and their colleagues in Persia and Pekin.[59]

To some of the fruits of this activity we shall return in the next chapter. Meanwhile we may wonder whether it was with his new university at Seville in mind and in order to reinforce the contingent of *fisicos* 'from over yonder' that in 1260 (if that was when it was) Alfonso had his eye on the 'great astrologer that there was in Egypt'. And another question poses itself. When in the June of that same year he granted the king's new and distinctively personal establishment the title of *studium generale* and the privileges that went with it (though in the first instance only for thirty-six months), did Pope Alexander IV have any idea of the scope of Alfonso's academic programme?[60] Probably not. For the pontiff twenty years on it would be a different matter, as it would also be for the king, but for the king sooner because he was about to be brought up short and made to lower his sights from distant horizons both intellectual and political and focus on his own doorstep.

For a process of political disintegration was about to commence, marked by a succession of major setbacks: the Mudéjar uprising of 1264, the rebellion of the Castilian nobility in 1272–3, the disappointment of Alfonso's imperial schemes in 1275, and the Infante Sancho's declaration of civil war in 1282, with at each of its stages further restriction of the extent of Alfonso's political compass. But meanwhile, by contrast, the range of his intellectual initiatives was broadening, into historiography, extending back to Hercules and the beginnings of Spanish history and to the Book of Genesis and the beginning of everything, and deepening into the profundity revealed by the alternating modes of his *Cantigas*.

The Mudéjar Rising

But first things first. At the beginning of February 1264 Alfonso sought to reactivate his European foreign policy by sending agents to Italy to petition

---

[59]   Regarding trade with Egypt: Martínez Montávez, 374–5; for the use at Marāgha of a version of the Alfonsine *cuadrante sennero* and the presence there of the Hispano-Muslim mathematician and astronomer Muhyī al-Dīn al-Magribī al-Andalusī, his collaboration there with members of the school of Nāsir al-Dīn Tūsī, and the latter's acquisition of knowledge of the principles of Chinese astronomy from Fu-Mengji: Vernet, 'Alfonso X', 27–8; Seemann, 72–81; Needham, 16; Sayili, 204–7.

[60]   *MHE*, I, no. 78.

Urban IV for the 'crown of the empire that is due to Us'. In the following August he was ingratiating himself with the pope by threatening the 'Greek schismatics' (and at the same time ridding himself of one of his pestilential brothers).[61] As befitted an emperor-elect, the king of Castile was acting as the pontiff's sword-arm in defence of the Faith. And if only at arm's length, this was significantly more than any of Urban's pontifical predecessors had received by way of imperial service from Alfonso X's German forebears.

With the French in the Mediterranean, however, and Louis IX crowding in behind Charles of Anjou for crusading reasons of his own, by 1264 the old papal–imperial condominium was a thing of the past. There was also the fact that, despite Alfonso's being described as the '*almost* king of Granada',[62] in the course of the six months since the pontiff's confidential message his Mudéjar subjects had risen in a rebellion coordinated by Granada's actual ruler, Muḥammad I. Originating in Jerez in late spring, in no time it had spread east into the kingdom of Murcia, where Alfonso's earliest essay in the process of colonization, initiated in 1257, had only succeeded in provoking a Mudéjar reaction out of all proportion to its limited scope, and had engulfed the entire southern swathe of the kingdom of Castile.[63]

If the king of Aragón's account is to be believed, by the end of June Alfonso had lost control of no fewer than three hundred cities, great towns and castles, which in the judgement of Bishop Domingo of Huesca represented the most serious reversal of Christian fortunes ever, more than negating the benefits of the 'battle of Úbeda'.[64] Doubtless the episcopal hyperbole was calculated to emphasize the significance of Jaime's role in retrieving the situation for his Castilian son-in-law. But it was not entirely without foundation. Although the occasion of the rising was circumstantial, namely Muḥammad I's chagrin at Alfonso's insistence on his surrendering Tarifa and Gibraltar as prerequisite for the attack on Ceuta he had himself proposed, the rapid course of its development cruelly revealed the superficiality of Castilian settlement of the region over the previous twenty years.

By contrast with the 1050s when the Christian rulers of the north had kept the petty kingdoms of the south in thrall by means of a system of military protectionism, what was called for after the hectic succession of sieges and surrenders of the 1230s and 1240s was a human presence. In the wake of the warriors a supply of settlers was needed, all the more

---

[61] Weiland, 499.

[62] By At de Mons of Toulouse: 'reys apen / Granad' et Almaria / e l'autr'Andalucia': Alvar, *Textos*, 29. Cf. Le Goff, 727.

[63] Arié, 63–4; Menjot, 125–7.

[64] *Book of Deeds*, cc. 378. 380.

so because by contrast with the conquered Mudéjars who abandoned the vast, unprotected desert area south of Toledo after 1085, in many places their thirteenth-century co-religionists stayed put, either in urban ghettoes (*morerías*) or dispersed across the countryside. And they stayed put because, as the Christian rulers never tired of repeating, Andalusia was not a desert, it was a verdant paradise; the same could be said, and was, for the ~~fertile region~~ (*la huerta*) of Valencia.[65] The rulers repeated their prospectus in order to lure colonizers from the north. But settlers would not come from anywhere if there was no rural workforce available and no economic infrastructure. And what if the mood of that workforce was resentful and ready to assist the first stirrings of sedition from within or without the territory? That was the dilemma that Jaime of Aragón put (or wished it to be thought he had put) to his nobles at the time of al-Azraq's revolt.

orchards

As his autobiography reports the occasion, the king explained that he was minded to expel the Mudéjars from his realms:

> And we said to the nobles that they should speak; and those that had Saracens spoke reluctantly, since we did something that did not please them. (. . .) And we said to them: 'Why does this not please you and why do you not advise us to do it? (. . .) For even though your revenue will be reduced, because it will not be worth so much to you through Christians as through Saracens, mark well how great is the mercy that you and I will do there, since they have given me reason to expel them without breaking my word.
>
> The second reason, which is very powerful, is that if, by chance, and through the sin of Christians, some day the Saracens who are on this side of the sea and those who are beyond the sea should reach an accord, and the Saracen people from each of the towns should rise up, they would take so many castles from us and from the king of Castile, that everybody who hears of it would marvel at the great harm that would befall Christianity.'[66]

The balance to be struck between the expectation of profit and the risk of subversion would continue to haunt him until his deathbed. Meanwhile, he represented his nobles as carefully calculating the costs to them of expulsion and himself as a Christian ruler suffused with crusading zeal, intent on settling the land with Christians, confident that 'the men of our kingdom and of other lands' would flock to the kingdom of Valencia without further prompting.[67] Which, alas, was not the case.

[65] Molénat, *Campagnes et Monts de Tolède*, 27–42; *Book of Deeds*, c. 128 (above, 68).
[66] Ibid., c. 366.
[67] Above, 75, 84–5.

As already stated, the reconquest of Murcia in 1243 had been token in nature, involving at most the establishment of a protectorate which had left the city's Muslim elite in place. The events of 1264 revealed the full perilous extent of what so loose a protectorate implied.[68] Now the consequences were apparent of northern Europe's failure to supplement the peninsula's shortfall, as King Jaime of Aragón had cheerfully predicted it would readily do. When most they were needed, the human resources that had held the line throughout the previous century failed to materialize. And seven hundred years on, historians continue to wonder why. Why was it that, at a time when society beyond the Pyrenees was straining at its natural resources, and when population pressure was driving the fathers of northern European families to plough up pavements in order to feed their wives and children, so little interest was aroused in the opportunities offered by the fertile plains of the Guadalquivir and the *huerta* of Valencia? Why was it that thirteenth-century Europe's equivalent to the Irish potato famine failed to persuade people to uproot themselves, as their predecessors had done a hundred years before, thereby obliging Jaime I to leave the Muslims in possession of the larger of Xàtiva's two fortresses in 1244, and Alfonso X, as he would lament in his *Cantigas de Santa María*, when the Moors seized Jerez in 1264 to leave them in control of the entire city?[69]

Comparison with the twelfth century, when extruded elements of the comfortable society of northern Europe, especially its younger sons, had made their careers south of the Pyrenees, suggests that the failure of their thirteenth-century successors to do likewise may have had something to do with the more southerly end of the road after 1212, so far from the pilgrim route to humid Galicia. Was it a combination of climate and diet that deterred them? Scorching heat, blinding light and the sheer insecurity of the place: the effect of these elementary facts of life on settlers attempting to adapt to a strange new world have 'perhaps not been emphasized enough by historians'. 'It requires an effort of the historical imagination to understand the mental world of these poor peasants, who knew hardly anything about conditions outside their native area.'[70] We are in the realm of speculation here. What knowledge of Spanish conditions was available to the Northumbrian witness who reported in the 1150s that volunteers were being sought in England for service in those parts?[71] And in 1263, was

---

[68]   Menjot, 128–31.
[69]   Above, 68; Cantiga 345, cit González Jiménez, *Repartimiento de El Puerto de S. María*, xxi.
[70]   Linehan, *History*, 264–5; Cabrera, 475–6.
[71]   By the bishop of Lisbon, Gilbert of Hastings: John of Hexham, *Chronicle*, 324.

it not significant that after Écija had been 'emptied of Moors' all but one of the Christians who replaced them were Castilians, and that despite the inducements offered precious few even of them were interested in venturing into 'Spain's frying pan', the hottest corner of the peninsula?[72] With Seville unable to retain its earliest contingent of settlers after 1248, what hope was there for places such as Écija?[73]

We do know something about the methods used by Castile's rulers in order to increase the supply of population ('facer linage'). Their subjects were encouraged to marry young so that, in the event of death, there would be time to try again for children. Penalties for negligence regarding infants were severe; those for contraception and abortion correspondingly capital.[74] Enhanced social cachet attached to widows of child-bearing age. Concurrently, women were at an advantage in respect of inheritance, as they were in other respects, some of them apparently exorbitant.[75] Custom encouraged betrothed couples to remain betrothed and if they had slept together before the wedding allowed a spurned woman to retain the matrimonial dowry, regardless of papal rules to the contrary. Likewise, both Alfonso X and Fernando III licensed clergy to bequeath property to their offspring, while members of the laity were encouraged by a law of the First *Partida* to ignore the bell summoning them from bed to mass of a Sunday and settle down again for a spot of procreation, while if their union was blessed, in order to prevent the proliferation of canonical impediments to marriage they were limited in the number of godparents they were permitted to recruit.[76]

---

[72]   Sanz Fuentes, 546; González Jiménez, 'Población', 706–7. Of the 240 identifiable individuals involved in the *repartimiento* of El Puerto de Santa María in 1268, twenty-seven came from regions of the peninsula beyond Alfonso's control, though more than half hailed from Castile's regions attracted doubtless by the maritime opportunities the region appeared to offer: idem, *Repartimiento de El Puerto de Santa María*, cxxxii–cxxxv.

[73]   Above, 73–4.

[74]   Dillard, 210; *Fuero de Teruel*, c. 378; Powers, *Code*, 84. Cf. the remarkable contention that 'the purpose of abortion and infanticide was to regulate children, not eliminate them': Coleman, 63.

[75]   For example, the reception of Elvira Rodríguez as canon of the male community of S. Isidro de León in 1291 and the listing of Inés Rodríguez (no relation) as canon of León cathedral in 1293, in expectation of the ladies' landed property and, in the second case, burial within the church: Martín López, no. 321; Ruiz Asencio & Martín Fuertes, no. 2574.

[76]   Dillard, 56–8, 99–126; Linehan, *History*, 416–17, 510; above, 61; *Part.* 1. 5. 36; 4. 2. 12. In more cerebral Barcelona, by contrast, 'often a younger son was encouraged to pursue his studies as a means of limiting the number of heirs and delaying marriage; the classroom could provide as effective a means of birth control (at least of legitimate children) as the monastic cell': Bensch, 380–1.

Social engineering did not end at the baptismal font. Other Alfonsine expedients sought to lure human resources to where they were needed. One, which may instead have had the effect of causing Muḥammad I to bring his co-religionists across the straits in 1264 (according to the Chronicle, the first mounted warriors to have done so since 1212), was his recently stated intention of having himself buried, when his time came, in the newly established cathedral of Cádiz opposite Africa. What 'surer sign of the monarch's consummate religion and piety' could there have been than his thoughts of death at the age of forty-two, the seventeenth-century Marqués de Mondéjar wondered. Contemporaries may have wondered otherwise. In the funerary schemes of a king of Castile with eyes set on Ceuta and points south and no existing ceremonial capital, his opposite number in Granada might reasonably have suspected a worldlier purpose.[77] Various of the king's *Cantigas de Santa Maria* would recount miracles performed by the Virgin in favour of pilgrims who had made the initial mistake of visiting such *passé* shrines as Santiago de Compostela. On his way to the Galician shrine, a paralytic German is struck blind. As he limps back along the pilgrim road, hardly the better for his outing, he comes to spend the night at the Templar church of S. María de Villalcázar de Sirga. Here the Virgin appears to him and all is made well. Villalcázar de Sirga in the diocese of Palencia was on the pilgrim road. Altogether more to the point were various miracles performed at El Puerto de Santa María in the Bay of Cádiz. The manipulation of popular religion for the purpose of attracting settlers to where they were required was one of the many initiatives of Alfonso X which came to not very much in his own lifetime but which his successors would emulate to greater effect.[78]

Less subtle methods involved the use of the (presumably royal) recruiting agents reported to the pope by Bishop Pedro of Cuenca in the early 1260s to be at large in his diocese, 'daily robbing it of settlers in favour of Seville and other frontiers' while 'we are fully occupied in continuous warfare in God's service and the king's against the Saracens of Spain and Africa and in repopulating the land brought back to Christian observance'. At about the same time the same pontiff received a complaint from the Castilian clergy that with the departure of their parishioners for 'newly acquired places where they have possessions for nothing and pay no taxes' their tithe income had disappeared.[79] It was a seller's market. In Old Catalonia landowners found themselves obliged to grant relief from evil customs and

---

[77]   *CAX*, c. 13. Mondéjar, *Memorias*, 436; *Reg. Urb. IV*, 348 (RdLU, no. 90).
[78]   Procter, *Alfonso X*, 32; Linehan, 'Beginnings of Guadalupe'.
[79]   Idem, '*Gravamina*', 749; Benito Ruano, 14–15.

usages in order to deter their workforce from emigrating southward. Not that the frontier was the only area towards which they were being lured. Alfonso X was also engaged in a process of in-filling the hinterland of his kingdom, establishing settlements in the north and north-west about which the rebellious nobles would protest in 1272–3 'because they said it was costing them what they had'.[80]

The Murcian uprising of 1264 was the latest indication of demographic bankruptcy, Castile's in particular. Thanks to the king of Aragón, but not to the Aragonese whose response to the call was negligible, the situation was saved, though at a price. For

> first, [the Saracens] asked that they would be able to remain there with all their inheritances. Second, that they would be able to practise their religion, as to shouting from their mosque. And the third, that they could be judged according to the custom of the Saracens, and were not to be compelled by any Christian, but that Saracens should judge them.[81]

All this Jaime readily granted, and assurances were given 'that we would make the king of Castile observe all the agreements that they had with us', though without consulting the king of Castile himself. In the same spirit the Castilian Chronicle of the reign failed even to mention the Aragonese relief of Murcia. The dietary practices of the defeated Moors were punctiliously observed. There was just one sticking point: the question of possession of the major mosque. That was non-negotiable. The terms in which the surrender of the place was recorded speak volumes of the different criteria adopted in Murcia by the king of Castile before 1264 and the king of Aragón after his experiences with the rebel al-Azraq:

> On gaining the church, we ordered an altar to be set up to Our Lady Saint Mary, because in all the great towns that God has given unto us to win from the Saracens we have built a church to Our Lady Saint Mary. And as this was the greatest town of Andalusia, except for Seville, we wished to honour the name of the mother of God, so that she should be honoured there for all time . . .[82]

With the bishops of Barcelona and Cartagena and richly arrayed clergy in attendance, Jaime then approached the altar with the reflection that

---

[80]   Font Rius, xx; *CAX*, c. 23; Ruiz de la Peña, 'Procesos tardíos', esp. 765–6.
[81]   *Book of Deeds*, cc. 406, 418.
[82]   Ibid., cc. 438–9, 450.

We had never gone past Murcia without praying that we might be able to place the name of the glorious virgin Saint Mary there, and she, praying to her beloved Son, caused our wish to be fulfilled. Embracing the altar, we wept so strongly and so heartfeltly that for the time it takes to go a mile, we could not stop crying nor leave the altar.[83]

'We had never gone past Murcia . . .' Here was reconquest as an act of love or religion in contrast to reconquest as investment opportunity, the aspect of it with which the account of the siege of Lisbon in 1147 is suffused as well as other sections of Jaime's memoirs, with their tales of the king courting injury in order to justify withdrawal from a siege, and, in the absence of territory recovered, the paramount need to ensure a return from the front either loaded with plunder or supplied with currency in the form of negotiable slaves.[84] Here was the cordial rather than cerebral response, the emotional rather than the calculating reconquest, the expression of sentiments which, unless they were wholly artificial, demand qualification of the view that in the recovery of the kingdom of Valencia religion was invariably subordinated to politics.[85] The celebratory mass in the reconquered mosque of Córdoba in 1236 had been in the same register.

For the bishop of Huesca the losses suffered in 1264 were the whole of Christian Spain's losses, not just Castile's. So too for the king of Aragón, for whom the consideration provided justification for hastening to Castile's aid – though with the qualification that he had to because the king of Castile was 'one of the most powerful men in the world' and the practical consideration that there was advantage in defending his own kingdom on another man's territory. These sentiments were not shared by the Aragonese nobility. They were not impressed when at the Cortes of Zaragoza, to which they had been summoned in order to secure their collaboration, a Franciscan friar revealed a dream he had had in which an angel had predicted that the king of Aragón would reconquer the whole peninsula. 'Men of that time were not so simple as to be incapable of understanding the purpose of such a vision', Jerónimo Zurita observed in the sixteenth century.[86] Whereas the Catalans, albeit grudgingly, had contributed to the task of 'saving Spain' in their persons and from their purses by means of the *bovatge*,[87] the Aragonese refused to do so, partly, perhaps, because they

[83]   Ibid., c. 451; Torres Fontes, *Reconquista de Murcia*, 152–4.
[84]   *Book of Deeds*, cc. 169, 174, 196, 200–5.
[85]   Thus Guichard, 397.
[86]   *Book of Deeds*, c. 382; Zurita, III, 66.
[87]   Hitherto levied exclusively as an accession tax: Bisson, *Medieval Crown of Aragon*, 54, 79.

were antagonized by Jaime's hardly diplomatic description of Catalonia as 'the best kingdom in Spain, the most honourable and the most noble', but also on account of anti-Castilian resentment, a sense of marginalization in the kingdom of Valencia, and the widespread adoption there of a law code of strongly Catalan character.[88] As the handiwork of Roman lawyers in the king's entourage, the *fur* of Valencia was deeply suspect to adherents to an indigenous feudal tradition, just as Alfonso X's legal innovations were to the Castilian territorial aristocracy. The Aragonese complaint that Jaime 'had ignored the *fueros* of Aragón and [was] always attended by pleaders in law and the decretals' might equally have been made by the Infante Felipe of Castile and his associates.[89] Throughout the later years of Jaime I's reign the Aragonese nobility was in a state of permanent mutiny.

As soon as he had had control of the kingdom of Murcia restored to him Alfonso repudiated Jaime's policies and disowned his promises. As in the aftermath of al-Azraq's rebellion a process of expulsion to the suburbs and beyond occurred, but because it could not be afforded no decree of compulsory exile was issued. The record of the successive *repartimientos* of territory between 1266 and 1273, Murcia's third to fifth such processes, reveal an 'extremely feeble rhythm' of settlement and, as at Seville after 1248, a persistent tendency amongst settlers to abandon holdings before satisfying the five-year residence requirement. The result, according to the most recent and exhaustive analysis of the process, was an unstable and heterogeneous colonial society that was anything but Castilian.[90] 'Politically Murcia belonged to Castile, but in human terms it was an Arago-Catalan colony',[91] with the emphasis on Catalan. Similar patterns and problems are observable elsewhere in the kingdom, at Alicante (whose coastal location made it the more attractive to Catalans) and Orihuela. 'Because the territory [of the kingdom of Murcia] was large and the king could not then get sufficient numbers to people it, he allowed many of those Moors who lived there before to remain.'[92]

Meanwhile, in time-honoured fashion rifts developed between Muḥammad I and the Banū 'Ashqilūlah; the latter, fearing their ascendancy in Guadix and Málaga to be threatened by the Marīnids, made common

---

[88] *Book of Deeds*, c. 392. First promulgated in 1240, the *fuero* (*fur*) of Valencia was revised in 1261: Zurita, III, 66; Soldevila, *Hist. de Catalunya*, 289–90.
[89] *Book of Deeds*, c. 395; below, 165–6.
[90] Ayala Martínez, 'Jaime I', 106–7; Menjot, 141–219 (esp. 137–8, 152).
[91] Ibid., 160, 170; also Moxó, *Repoblación*, 375–82.
[92] CAX, cc. 15, 16. At Orihuela more than twice as many settlers came from the Crown of Aragón as from Castile: Torres Fontes & Veas Arteseros, 'Procedencia'.

cause with Alfonso; and the Nasrid Muḥammad felt constrained also to resume his vassalage in the form of an annual payment of a quarter of a million *maravedís*.[93] What of Alfonso's Christian vassals though, who had failed to come to the host? As he complained in his *cantiga*, when most he needed them,

> Nen Pero Garcia nen Pero d'Espanha
> nen Pero Galego non irá comego.[94]

Nor was it not only Pero Garcia etc. who had failed to provide the three months of service due from them. Neither had the urban militias, since, according to the Chronicle, 'many horses were lost' in that war.[95] And possession of a horse was both the means of making war and the symbol of social rank of those upon whom Alfonso's alternative political strategy depended. Particularly significant was the fact that the warriors of Extremadura were proving reluctant, because (again in the words of the Chronicle) 'he depended more heavily on the towns of Extremadura than on any other towns of his kingdom', and set out to woo them and the *caballeros villanos* from further afield by constituting them an elite class of royal vassal and setting them to challenge the political hold of the *ricos homes* within the cities.[96] Yet if the peril to the *patria* was not felt in that region, just behind the front line, where was it felt? In Cuenca, reconquered eighty years before, whose bishop had recently been complaining about royal agents systematically depopulating his diocese? In Toledo, which the incoming archbishop was about to declare a safe haven because 'the Saracens are now, thank God, operating far away'?[97] Or in Burgos? What did they know in Burgos who only Burgos knew? What sense was there in Burgos that the affairs of Jerez were their affairs too? Had not the reconquest of the peninsula run ahead of itself, not only in terms of resources but also in terms of imagination? How far had Alfonso X succeeded in breaking down the commitment to local loyalties and local *fueros*, in favour of something akin to a national plan? If even the *concejos* of Extremadura chose to stay at home whilst Andalusia suffered, not *very* far.

[93]   *CAX*, c. 15; Harvey, *Islamic Spain*, 31ff., who (p. 38) states that the payment was ten times as much.
[94]   Lapa, no. 2; also nos. 16, 24.
[95]   *CAX*, c. 12.
[96]   Ibid., specifying the inducements offered; Iglesia Ferreirós, 'Privilegio general', González Jiménez, 'Alfonso X y las oligarquías urbanas', 205–14.
[97]   Above, 154; Linehan, *Spanish Church*, 179n.

In adhering to the Banū 'Ashqilūlah and refusing to hand them over to the tender mercies of the king of Granada,[98] Alfonso had acted astutely – in the short term. But he had enraged King Muḥammad and rendered him more inclined to lend a sympathetic ear to the disaffected Castilian nobility, 'thus making a symmetrical pattern with on each side a band of rebels in opposition to the monarch'.[99] All that remained was for Alfonso to provide the opposition with a focus for their generalized discontent. This he did at Badajoz in 1267 by surrendering Castile's rights in the Algarve to his son-in-law, Afonso III of Portugal. The chronically unchronological Chronicle of the reign, hopelessly at fault though it is regarding the circumstances of the concession, is nevertheless credible in its account of Nuño González de Lara's protest. There could be no objection to the king indulging his grandson from his own resources ('de vuestro aver'). But it was another thing entirely for him to diminish 'the crown'. 'Sire, that you should deprive la corona of your kingdoms of the tribute due from the king and kingdom of Portugal, that, Sire, I shall never advise you to do.'[100] Although the principle of inalienability of the fisc, here enunciated perhaps for the first time in Castile's chronicle tradition, may conceivably belong to the 1340s when the Chronicle of the reign was written, rather than to the 1260s to which Lara's protest is ascribed, it was also at about this time, when at the 1269 Burgos Cortes the nobles permitted taxation of their hitherto exempt vassals for the defence of the frontier until (in the words of the Chronicle) 'the imperial business was completed', that a shift is discernible 'from fiscal arrangements of the seigneurial type to a different system in which elements typical of state sovereignty preponderate'.[101]

The king was not best pleased by Nuño González's intervention, the author of the Chronicle reports. Yet the two parted on apparently the best of terms, with the one assuring the other that 'never had he had such great desire to serve the king as he had then' and asking as a favour that 'he should not believe anything they said about him.' The next chapter opens with the Infante Felipe, D. Nuño 'and many noblemen and knights and others of the towns' assembling at Lerma and vowing to combine against the

---

[98]   CAX, c. 16.

[99]   Harvey, Islamic Spain, 37.

[100]   CAX, c. 19, placing the encounter in 1269 and associating it with Alfonso's knighting of his grandson D. Dinis, born Oct. 1261 but reported by the Chronicle to have been twelve or thirteen at the time: a request which 'because this infante was his grandson and because other heirs to thrones had come to receive knighthood from him, gave him much pleasure.' Cf. O'Callaghan, Learned King, 160–1; González Jiménez, Alfonso X, 187–90.

[101]   Linehan, History, 651; Ladero Quesada, 'Transformaciones', 331–2, 405; CAX, c. 18.

king and 'bring him down so far as they could if he failed to grant them the things they would demand'.[102] From 1267 the skies darken as the story moves inexorably on.

Yet even while war was being waged the Latin translation of Muḥammad's Ladder, arguably Dante's source, was completed by the royal notary, Bonaventura of Siena (May 1264), the process of centralization serenely continued with the completion of the first redaction of *Las Siete Partidas* (August 1265), and work began on the earliest version of the *Cantigas de Santa María* and on the *Estoria de Espana*.[103] It was almost as if political reverses inspired Alfonso to renewed efforts on other fronts.

The assembly at Lerma, to the south of Burgos, in the spring of 1271 provided the malcontents with a talking-shop. They had previously met at Burgos itself in November 1269 for the solemnization of the marriage of the heir to the throne, Fernando de la Cerda, and Blanche, daughter of Louis IX of France:[104] an event which revived French claims to the Castilian throne as well as coinciding with an undertaking given by Alfonso calculated to enrage his hard-pressed subjects. The king's promise of six hundred warriors to join Charles of Anjou's projected attack on Constantinople provided almost a third of the latter's promised force while the 80,000 marks of silver (£200,000 Tours) pledged with Louis IX for their payment was almost thirty times the sum *not* paid by the French king as his daughter's dowry on that occasion.[105] And all this just a matter of months after the capture and beheading of Conradin of Hohenstaufen after the battle of Tagliacozzo.

At the conclusion of the Burgos festivities, Nuño González de Lara fell in alongside the king of Aragon as the pair of them were riding by the river, and offered him his services. Though his advances were rejected (Jaime claimed,[106] perhaps rightly), here was a further attempt by a Castilian nobleman to 'denaturalize' himself, performing an act of political self-mutilation by severing relationships with his natural lord.

---

[102]   *CAX*, c. 20. According to the documentary section of the Chronicle covering the rebellion of 1272–3, Alfonso had earned Nuño González's further displeasure by obstructing his attempt to dispossess the youthful Lope Díaz de Haro of the lordship of Vizcaya – though scant gratitude the young man was to show him: ibid., c. 31.

[103]   Holloway, 'Road through Roncesvalles'; Craddock, 'Cronología'; Montoya Martínez, 'Cancioneiro marial de Alfonso X'.

[104]   Celebrated at Toledo five months earlier: Daumet, *Mémoire*, 153–6. Unlike Wifred the Hairy, Fernando de la Cerda was bristly only on his back.

[105]   del Giudice, 118–19. Cf. Geanakoplos, 197–8.

[106]   *Book of Deeds*, c. 496.

Jaime was Alfonso X's father-in-law, just as Alfonso VIII had been Jaime's, and according to Muntaner looked upon him as a son.[107] As Alfonso accompanied him out of his kingdom, Jaime offered him seven (in fact, six) pieces of paternal advice, four of which are of particular interest. These were, first,

> that if ever he had given his word to anybody that he must in all ways fulfil it,

and fifth,

> that the charters we had drawn up with the settlers of Murcia, and those that he had drawn up afterwards, were not being fulfilled but had been infringed;

inserted between which were,

> third, that he should retain all his people under his lordship, for it was necessary for all kings to know how to retain the people God had commended to them, willingly and gladly. The fourth was that if he was to retain any, he should at least retain two parts, if he could not retain all. They were the Church, the people and the towns of the land, because God loves these people more than the knights since the knights rise up more readily against their lord than the others. And if he could retain all parts, that would be better, but if not, then he should retain these two, for with them he could destroy the others.[108]

Jaime had been king almost forty years longer than Alfonso, and it may well be that as he spoke he was thinking of home, that when he said Castile he meant Aragón. But it was good advice. And it was not followed.

Owing to the advent of Charles of Anjou and Jaime's intervention in the kingdom of Murcia, since 1264 Castile's relations with Aragón had improved, if only superficially.[109] After D. Felipe's abandonment of the cloth and the death in October 1261 of the still youthful Archbishop Sancho of Toledo, the primatial church was transformed from a political to a diplomatic pawn by the imposition in 1266 of another under-age Infante Sancho, this time of the Aragonese variety.[110] In the previous year work had commenced on the king's latest venture.

[107] *Crònica*, c. 11 (Goodenough, 30).
[108] *Book of Deeds*, c. 498 (transl. adjusted).
[109] Valls Taberner, 35; Ayala Martínez, 'Alfonso X', 51–60.
[110] Hernández & Linehan, 113–15.

The Alfonsine Histories

Having determined the future direction of his kingdom by means of the most recent of his legal codes, Alfonso now embarked upon the direction of its past. Although in both cases his continuing dialogue with an insistent present was to necessitate subsequent revisions and recasting, he may be said to have been spurred into action on the historical front by knowledge of the existence of *two* translations of D. Rodrigo's *History*, one Aragonese (apparently by a Navarrese author), the other a Catalan version of the work in which the Romans, the Franks and Charlemagne loomed as large in the history of 'Spanya' as the Goths and D. Pelayo.[111] Insistence on the value of the written record and the importance of controlling what went into it were principles firmly established before 1252,[112] while the process of compilation of both of Alfonso's vast vernacular histories – the *Estoria de España* and the *General Estoria*, with its beginnings in the Garden of Eden – must have been under way by early 1270, when the king acknowledged receipt of various volumes 'in ancient script' borrowed from the church of Albelda and the monastery of Nájera, promising their return 'as soon as I have had them copied', and in the case of the former the completion by 1274 of its primitive version down to the beginning of Alfonso IX's reign, albeit only in draft form after that of Vermudo III (1037), was a monumental achievement.[113] Indeed, according to the hypothesis that the purpose of the *Estoria de España* was to enhance the king's imperial credentials,[114] by early 1270 it must have been *well* under way – though curiously, while assigning to the year 1260 preliminary work on the balance of Alfonso's entire cultural programme – biblical translation, the legal works, 'all the ecclesiastical', the natural philosophy and the astrology – in fact, the Chronicle makes no mention at all of the histories.[115]

To those scholars who have considered the Learned King's cultural activities as no more than light relief from a succession of political disappointments, 'as though such systematic exertion could have served as a mere "hobby", a pastime far removed from the business of transforming

[111]   By 1268: Catalán & Jerez, esp. 27–43, 394–410.
[112]   'G. Petri Rithmi', lines 169–72, 207, 295–6, 339–40.
[113]   *MHE*, I, nos. 117–18; Procter, *Alfonso X*, 89–96; Catalán, *De Alfonso X al Conde de Barcelos*, 102–5; Fernández-Ordóñez, Estorias *de Alfonso el Sabio*, 71–95; eadem, 'Taller de las "Estorias"', 74.
[114]   Fraker, 101. But in that case why the suspension of work on the project in 1274, just as the imperial campaign was peaking?: Brancaforte, 22–4. Cf. Catalán, *Estoria de España*, 51–2.
[115]   *CAX*, c. 9.

the structures of the kingdom', a reading of the Alfonsine histories must come as a salutary shock. By contrast with his legislative works, 'the extent to which in his historical works Alfonso recruited History to the service of his tasks of government has not been sufficiently understood'.[116] As to the national history, in its exploitation and manipulation of the histories of Lucas of Tuy and Rodrigo of Toledo, Alfonso's ideological purpose is never far from the surface, and in his treatment of those volumes 'in ancient script' – Statius, Virgil, Ovid etc., the Bible, and many others – it was rampant.[117] The two historical enterprises proceeded together, whether they were conducted across a common corridor between the royal chancery and the royal scriptorium, or, less probably, they progressed along a wide avenue within which each team ploughed its own furrow.[118] In the *General* Estoria, with whatever civilizing purpose they begin – whether with Jupiter, Alexander the Great or the Trojans – all furrows lead to Rome, and from Rome, and most recently from the Emperor Frederick II, to Alfonso X. In this reading of the past with its regular reference to the present, 'universal history becomes family history'. The tone is severely and relentlessly didactic, with the message addressed to such 'high princes' and 'other good men' as should have ears to hear it. Such hearers, and readers, of the *General Estoria* were expected not to miss the significance of the fact that Hercules, despite all his labours, was 'always very shrewd and very wise, always applied himself to *los saberes* and took great pleasure in them, and no matter where he was always had something to learn, as long as he could find a brain to pick',[119] and that whereas until Jupiter's time men had lacked for *fueros* and stable laws, depending instead on custom (*uso* and *alvedrío*), Jupiter 'organized the *fueros* and laws and turned them into writing and made a book of them'.

Because 'all men by nature desire to know' (Alfonso is quoting the opening phrase of Aristotle's *Metaphysics*) 'the things that happened before their time', he continues, equally they must be ready to learn from them that the good ended happily and the bad unhappily. With the history of Perseus and the Gorgons and Xerxes in mind, they must be aware that division of the

[116] Catalán, *Estoria de España*, 13–14; Fernández-Ordóñez, 'Taller historiográfico', 115.
[117] Linehan, *History*, 413–505; Catalán, *Estoria de España*, 11–44; Rico, *Alfonso el Sabio*; Fernández-Ordóñez, Estorias *de Alfonso el Sabio*, 19–68.
[118] Fernández-Ordóñez (conclusively demonstrating the degree of shared endeavour): Estorias *de Alfonso el Sabio*, 71–158. Cf. Funes, *Modelo historiográfico*, 19 (a judgement compromised by the author's neglect of the *General estoria*); Linehan, *History*, 478.
[119] Cárdenas, 'Myth', 11–12, registering the resemblance to the descriptions of Alfonso himself in the prologue to the *Libro de las cruzes* ('whom God endowed with practical intelligence, understanding and wisdom, above all other princes of his time, instructed by the various books of wise men') and elsewhere.

kingdom and its *señorío* was not to be countenanced and that primogeniture was the only possible course. With biblical exemplars before them, they would acknowledge that it was 'as a good judge who judges rightly' and 'as king and emperor and lord' that God had given the inhabitants of Sodom and Gomorrah their just deserts.[120] In the *Estoria de España* this 'monarchical' reading of the past applied *a fortiori* to the Spanish past. Whereas by failing to observe the laws of succession the Goths had incurred divine wrath, and that had cost them the *señorío* of Spain, in its uninterrupted passage from the last Visigothic king via Pelayo and his band of brothers to Alfonso himself Alfonso's ancestors had never either shared or compromised that *señorío*. It followed that for Alfonso, as heir to the pan-peninsular Visigothic kingdom, none of the rulers of the kingdoms that had sprung up since 711, of Aragón, Navarre or Portugal, even less those of al-Andalus, had enjoyed legitimacy. So in the narration of events they are invariably presented in a subsidiary role, programmatically degraded. To achieve this effect, compilatory feats of legerdemain were called for to demonstrate the consensual character of *coups d'état* by the nobility, such as that which had led to Castilian independence from León in the tenth century – not least since by 1274, when the text of the *Estoria* was already far enough advanced for its Visigothic part to undergo emendation, attempted *coups d'état* by the nobility were a thing of the very recent past.[121] According to Alfonso's nephew, don Juan Manuel, this improving tale was meant for the instruction of 'high princes' and 'other good men'.[122] What they made of it is another matter.

In April 1272 the death of Richard of Cornwall contributed to the process that was to cost the king the sympathy of those sectors of Castilian society his father-in-law had urged him to retain by reviving the imperial question and prompting Alfonso to hasten to Lombardy to rally his supporters. The following autumn saw a hard core of nobles at the Burgos Cortes led by the Infante Felipe raising the stakes and demanding all manner of concessions both fiscal and judicial. To the general discontent the climate contributed, with 'great snows' at the end of October and earthquakes in 1273.[123] Although

[120]   Rico, *Alfonso el Sabio*, 114; Martin, 'Modelo historiográfico', 39, 46, 47; Fernández-Ordóñez, Estorias *de Alfonso el Sabio*, 42.
[121]   Eadem, 'Variación', 43–8; Martin, *Juges de Castille*, 360–1; Catalán, *De la silva textual*, 134–41.
[122]   Recalling that among 'many noble things' his uncle had done had been 'to organize the Chronicle of Spain most thoroughly so that every man who read it could understand the work': *Crón. abreviada*, 576. For the shift from reader to listener as the envisaged audience of the pre-Alfonsine and Alfonsine chronicles: Fernández-Ordóñez, 'De la historiografía fernandina a la alfonsí', 96–9.
[123]   Lomax, 'Crónica inédita', 332.

in order to secure a grant of subsidies (*servicios*) sufficient to enable him to persevere with his quest the king yielded on every particular, even so the malcontents broke their bond of vassalage and pledged themselves to the service of the ruler of Granada.[124] Little good royal exegesis of the history of tenth-century rebellion had done them. What they remembered were the intrusive measures of an obsessively interventionist ruler who forbad them to marry, create knights, acquire more than four new outfits a year of a particular design and colour, or have silver buttons on their capes.[125] By 1272 Alfonso X and his principal subjects were speaking a different language.

The king appeared to be in full flight. Amongst the measures withdrawn by him were the further restrictions imposed by the Jerez gathering of 1268 (the 'ayuntamiento' to which connoisseurs of the matter deny the name 'cortes') – the export controls, the minute price-fixing (two *dineros* for a skinned rabbit), the normalization of weights and measures, the prohibition on dicing on pain of exile, regulations on the size of arms and that old nightmare, subversive wedding breakfasts[126] – together with the centralizing procedures envisaged by the *Espéculo*, the *Fuero Real*, and by that date summarized in the *Partidas*, at the expense of the municipal *fueros*. Liberties granted to the localities by his predecessors from Alfonso VIII onwards were confirmed.[127] There appeared to be no level of political abasement to which the king of Castile was not prepared to descend in order to secure the empire: a process which may be said to have been completed in June–July 1274 at the Cortes of Zamora, a region of his realm hitherto largely neglected by him.

But the reality was rather more nuanced, for even now Alfonso was not prepared to preside over the dismantling of his entire system. Indeed, it was at the Zamora Cortes that what amounted to a list of offences against the king's peace was established, with judgment reserved to the king's tribunal of 'cases of court', crimes such as murder, rape, arson, treason etc. In the municipalities, moreover, the king's judges remained a powerful force against the likes of Zamora's own bishop and other entrenched representatives of regional interests.[128]

For what was the essence of these local *fueros*, which at this critical juncture the king was prepared to see restored regardless of his earlier commitment to principles that had been represented as central to his entire political

[124]   *CAX*, c. 27; O'Callaghan, *Learned King*, 214–25; González Jiménez, *Alfonso X*, 239–70.
[125]   *CLC*, I. 57, 59 (Cortes of Valladolid 1258, cc. 14, 23, 25). The Seville cortes of 1261 had decreed measures even more draconian: Rodríguez Díez, 715–20; González Jiménez, 'Cortes de Sevilla'.
[126]   Ibid., 64–85 (cc. 14, 19, 26, 35, 38, 40–1); Fita, 'Igualación de pesos', 139–41.
[127]   González Jiménez, *Alfonso X*, 210–13.
[128]   Iglesia Ferreirós, 'Cortes de Zamora'; González Jiménez, *Alfonso X*, 275–8; above, 128.

system? The essence of them was selfishness. The rebels were selfish and faithless. At the beginning of his reign, according to the Chronicle, Alfonso greatly increased the rewards made to the *ricos homes* above the levels set by his father. This he did in order to be more certain of their services when he needed them and out of his 'greatness of heart' (a detail which, incidentally, casts doubt on the doctrine that the *Crónica de Alfonso X* was designed to do damage to its subject).[129] In the spring of 1273 the king reminded one of them, Nuño González de Lara, of all that that grandee owed him. As infante he had provided him with the protection of his household and advanced his interests in the face of the (well-merited) suspicions of his family entertained by Fernando III. As king, Alfonso had lavished inheritances, gifts and holdings upon him and in order to secure his loyalty the more firmly had taken his part even when he knew him to be in the wrong. He had made him the most powerful, the best provided man in the kingdom. As for the rebels' concern for the *fueros*, when the king had asked him whether the taxes imposed by him were legal ('si era fuero') Nuño had replied that they were not but that they were customary, to which the king had replied that in that case they were tantamount to robbery and must never be repeated.[130]

In what has been called the 'first political essay in the Castilian language', Alfonso wrote to Fernando de la Cerda in the same year that it was not in defence of their 'fuero' that the *ricos homes* had moved against him. What it was in defence of was aristocratic self-interest, the desire to limit the monarch's power and the determination to enrich themselves at the expense of the crown, just as their forefathers had done:

> They did not move against me on account of any *fuero* or for any wrong I had done them. (. . .) They cannot claim to be acting for the good of the land since their concern for the land cannot possibly be greater than mine whose inheritance it is, and only with my good will can they profit from it. No, the reason they rose against me was that they want to keep kings permanently in leading-strings so as to rob them of what is theirs, looking for ways of disinheriting and dishonouring them, just as those from whom they are descended did. (. . .) The kings who had enriched them they have striven to disinherit by making common cause with their enemies, seizing the wealth of the land, little by little depriving them of what is theirs, and denying them it. Just as kings empowered and honoured them, so do they seek to weaken and dishonour kings in so many ways that it would be too long and shameful to describe. *This* is the law (*fuero*) and the good of the land that they have always wanted. Now you may understand this, for everything

---

[129]   *CAX*, c. 1. In the same sense, Iglesia Ferreirós, 'Alfonso X', 45–7.
[130]   *CAX*, c. 30.

by which I was moved to do what they wanted they opposed, especially the pursuit of the empire, which is what matters most ('que es lo mas').[131]

All of which reads almost as an exegesis of Blasco de Alagón's outburst at Burriana in 1233: 'If you kings were to achieve everything you wanted all the land would be yours'.[132]

Though framed in cosmic terms, Alfonso's reproachful analysis on that occasion – with its echoes of the *improperia* uttered by the crucified Christ in the Good Friday liturgy: 'O my people, what have I done to thee? Or wherein have I afflicted thee?', with the haunting plea 'Answer me' – centred on his kingdom (*tierra*), and, for all that its characterization of the *ricos homes* was as much caricature as generalization, nevertheless it is in terms of the complicated, largely human, chemistry involving king, *tierra* and *fueros* that its account of the domestic history of his reign is presented. With Church, people and towns, as well as the military orders,[133] excluded from the equation altogether, this was not much of a look-out for empire.

Only four years earlier the nobility had consented to the taxation of their vassals until 'the imperial business was completed'. In the event, however, the empire hardly came into it. Men had been asking why Alfonso had failed to confront Charles of Anjou in Southern France. Cerverí de Girona lamented the decay of Castilian qualities. The question being asked was whether this was due to its king or its people ('del reys o de las regios'). But whichever way you looked at it, France was on top and the others underneath.[134] Amongst others, Cerverí's co-*jongleur* Paulet de Marseilles (*fl.* 1262/8) was troubled that the king's brother D. Enrique was still in Charles of Anjou's prison where he had been languishing, none too uncomfortably, since his capture at the battle of Tagliacozzo. If Alfonso, a valiant and noble-hearted king, suffered him to remain there he would have deceived his admirers, and Spaniards failing to hasten to his assistance would be guilty of villainy and cowardice.[135] Another account of the aftermath of that battle, related in the 1450s by Aeneas Silvius Piccolomini, reported how before his beheading,

---

[131]   Ibid., c. 52; Rodgers, 62 (with edition of the letter, here lines 50–1, 57–65, 68–79; translation my own). Copies of this and other letters concerning the rebels were made, perhaps by the notary for Castile, Gonzalo Pérez, with the evident purpose of creating a dossier from which to demonstrate, possibly at the papal chancery, Alfonso's good lordship and his opponents' faithlessness: Hernández & Linehan, 128–9. They were incorporated in the Chronicle of the reign when it was composed in the 1340s.

[132]   Above, 63.

[133]   For whose role in 1272–3: Josserand, 503–4.

[134]   Riquer, *Cerverí de Girona*, 94–5.

[135]   Levy, 279–80.

the marvellous boy Conradin took his gauntlet and 'falling flung to the host behind' this symbol of his 'betrayed kingdom'.[136] Thus the charismatic grandson of Frederick II passed on whatever rights he enjoyed there to the Infant Pedro of Aragon, at whose court he would be remembered as 'King Conradin II'.[137] It was the killing of him that brought to the surface the hatred of Charles and Frenchmen that Pedro had harboured since boyhood.[138]

Meanwhile, in early April 1274, while the Cortes of Burgos was discussing the matter of 'sending knights to the Roman empire', on his way to Palencia the king stopped off at Pampliega where King Wamba (†680/681) was buried. Fernando III, whose knowledge of Wamba's whereabouts came from D. Rodrigo's History, had intended to have him moved to a 'more honourable' place but had died before doing anything about it. (Since he survived the publication of De rebus Hispanie by all of nine years he can hardly have been in any hurry to do so.) However, he did do Wamba the honour of having a new door cut in the church so that when he visited his remains he did not have to exit by the door next to which his predecessor was buried.[139] Alfonso did better. He arranged for Wamba's re-interment within the church of Santa Leocadia at Toledo 'which in the time of the Goths was the capital of Spain and the place where of old emperors were crowned'. Never was his sense of history's possibilities demonstrated to better effect.[140] In 1274 the possible parallels with Wamba – the last reputable king of Visigothic Spain, and according to the near contemporary 'Poema de Fernán González' a popular king, the peninsular Cincinnatus crowned in Toledo, the victor of trans-Pyrenean encounters and the flail of domestic insurrection – would not have been lost on him. Might Spain's new emperor be crowned in Toledo too, therefore? Be that as it may, the detail of Wamba's reburial was entered into the amended text of the Estoria, which is how we know the date of it, more or less, as Alfonso prepared to travel to Provence to receive the new pope's blessing of his new empire.[141]

---

[136]   Hist. rerum Frederici III, 72–3.
[137]   Added point being given to the incident by the romantic legend that the man who conveyed the emblematic gauntlet to the heir to the Aragonese throne was Giovanni da Procida, the reputed impresario of the Sicilian Vespers: Soldevila, Pere el Gran, 226, misidentifying Piccolomini's source as his Commentaries. Cf. Wieruszowski, 20.
[138]   Gesta comitum Barcinonensium, 69; above, 85.
[139]   Presumably the west door: a detail deserving consideration by students of the location of seventh-century royal remains.
[140]   Although not well enough for those who imagine him to have been reburied in the cathedral: Gonzálvez, ' "Bible of St Louis" ', 114, n. 65.
[141]   Linehan, History, 386–7, 455–60; Catalán, De la silva textual, 137–9 (observing that the emendation to the Estoria is likely to have been made soon after the event).

7

1275–84

A Reign in Ruins

'La ida al imperio, que es lo mas': for eighteen years the drive towards empire had been everything. Then, at Beaucaire in May 1275, Gregory X administered the king of Castile a humiliating rebuff. Declaring Alfonso X's imperial quest over, the pope ordered him to cease using imperial titles and regalia and sent him on his way with no more than a licence to mulct the long-suffering Castilian Church further as compensation. In a face-saving letter to the *podestà* of Pavia, Lanfranco Pignatorio, Alfonso claimed that it was all much as he had expected. He had only subjected himself to the sham of submitting his case to the pontiff in order to reveal the hypocrisy of 'him who ought to be the fount of justice on earth' and to demonstrate how little consideration Gregory had given to the merits of the case and the deserts of him and his ancestors.[1] In one of his *Cantigas d'escarnho e de maldezir* ('Songs of Scorn and Derision') he excoriated Gregory and the cardinals who had stripped him naked.[2] He also continued to describe himself as king of the Romans.[3]

While the king was away his kingdom had suffered a series of disasters. Via Montpellier, where the Virgin delivered him from death's door, a despondent Alfonso arrived home at the end of 1275 to be greeted by a casket containing the mutilated remains of the archbishop of Toledo,

---

[1] *Annales Italiae* ('Annales Placentini Ghibellini'), 561. Details in Hernández & Linehan, 142–7.
[2] 'Se me graça fezesse este Papa de Roma!' (Lapa, no. 32). (Alternatively this outburst may have been occasioned by Gregory's promotion of Gonzalo Gómez García as archbishop of Compostela, an action resulting in a decade of royal persecution for that church: López Ferreiro, *Historia*, V, 239–54; Linehan, 'Spanish Church revisited', 141–2.)
[3] González Jiménez, *Alfonso X*, 285–6; Ayala Martínez, 'Relaciones', 147–50.

slaughtered at Martos by the latest army of warriors from across the straits. Another casualty, at Écija, had been Nuño González de Lara, *adelantado mayor de la frontera* (so rapidly might fortunes change in the Castile of the 1270s). Worst of all, the heir to whom the kingdom had been entrusted in his father's absence, Fernando de la Cerda, had dropped down dead. And yet, even in such desperate circumstances even the Dominicans were fighting shy of preaching the Crusade. 'For if the trumpet give an uncertain sound, who shall prepare himself to battle?', it occurred to the prior provincial of the Order to wonder.[4]

The armies of the Marīnid ruler of Morocco Abū Yūsuf, which had crossed from Ceuta and Tangier in the previous summer, 'as if', in the words of the Marīnid chronicle, 'the ocean were a pavement for their steeds' – shocked the peninsula's Christian rulers back into the age of Alarcos and Las Navas. Yet it was with precisely those precedents in mind that, despite the emir's intervention in peninsular affairs in 1263 and his dealings with the rebel nobility in 1272–3, Alfonso had discounted the possibility of any such eventuality. Where would Abū Yūsuf find sufficient ships for the passage, he had asked in his letter to Fernando de la Cerda, or even the means of feeding his troops?[5] In the event the emir had no difficulty in doing both.

Emerging from the withered chrysalis of the Almohads, the Marīnids had been fostered in their development by Jaime I. In helping Abū Yūsuf to capture Ceuta in the interests of Catalan commerce, the Aragonese monarch had shown as little strategic nous as his Castilian counterpart. Further assistance to the invaders was provided by the new king of Granada Muḥammad II (1273–1302) in revenge for Alfonso's continuing support of the Banū 'Ashqilūlah.[6] In the spring of 1276 a two-year truce was reached, in the course of which, after dealings of considerable complexity between the Banū 'Ashqilūlah and the Marīnids, the Nasrid ruler of Granada regained control of Málaga, the port without access to which Granada would have been reduced to 'no more than an isolated, mountain-girt city'.[7]

According to at least one Muslim source, when Nuño González de Lara perished at the battle of Éjica another eighteen thousand or more Christians perished with him, and the muezzins clambered up the heap of decapitated heads to recite their evening prayer. By the same account, just twenty-four

---

[4]   Linehan, ' "Quedam de quibus dubitans" ', 143. For particulars of Fernando's brief administration: González Jiménez, 'El Infante don Fernando', 547–54.

[5]   *Al-Dhakhira al-saniyya*, cit. Harvey, *Islamic Spain*, 155; *CAX*, cc. 13, 22; *Book of Deeds*, c. 378; Rodgers, lines 118–33.

[6]   Dufourcq, *Espagne catalane*, 161–6; *CAX*. c. 58.

[7]   Arié, 68–75; Harvey, *Islamic Spain*, 158.

Muslim lives had been lost in the engagement: a nice reverse of Las Navas therefore.[8] 'Because he was not prepared to make war and because he knew nothing about the affairs of his kingdoms', the Chronicle states, Alfonso X refused to enter Toledo.[9] To the political classes, it did not need to be emphasized either that when he was most needed at home the king had been following his imperial will o' the wisp or that the one man who had come well out of the recent rout was the Infante D. Sancho. If only Alfonso were as martial as he was munificent, men would honour him, the troubadour Guiraut Riquier reflected. Instead they were reviling him. That it should have come to this: that the king's stock should have fallen so low that it pained the poet to praise him. Could anyone imagine such things being said as recently as two years before?[10]

By successfully blockading Algeciras and Tarifa, the seventeen-year-old prince had saved the day. But his first thought, if the Chronicle of the reign is to be believed, was the succession. The death of the Infante Fernando, leaving as his heir the five-year-old Alfonso, created divisions within the political establishment that would last until the end of the reign and well beyond. As the oldest of the surviving brothers, Sancho was determined to 'inherit the kingdom after the days of his father', and told Lope Díaz de Haro so even before his father's return from Beaucaire. Haro promised his support, and from that day on, the Chronicle continues, letters issued by Sancho's chancery styled him 'eldest son and heir of the king D. Alfonso'.[11]

But on his deathbed the Infante Fernando had extracted a promise from his vassal Juan Núñez de Lara, successor of Nuño González and lord of Albarracín, to defend young Alfonso's rights to the throne.[12] The promise given by King Alfonso at the wedding of Fernando and Blanche of France that these rights would be respected ensured that the approaching conflict would have an international dimension. It was also part of the reason why, on the advice of Jaime of Aragon, the Infante Sancho refused to be knighted by D. Fernando on that occasion.[13]

---

[8]   Ibid., 157, quoting *Al-Dhakh»ra al-saniyya*. O'Callaghan, *Learned King*, 235, cites Ibn Abū Zar' to the same effect, 'with grotesque exaggeration', he says.

[9]   *CAX*, c. 67: an astonishing proposition, and the point perhaps at which the Chronicle's fourteenth-century author finally loses patience with his thirteenth-century subject. It is noticeable that Gil de Zamora's history of Alfonso ignores the king after 1266 while continuing with Louis IX and other crusading monarchs and providing some account of foreign affairs down to 1270: Fita, 'Biografías', 325.

[10]   Riquer, *Trovadores*, 1621–3.

[11]   *CAX*, c. 65.

[12]   Ibid., c. 64.

[13]   Craddock, 'Cronología', 401; *Book of Deeds*, c. 495; *CAX*, c. 18.

The law was not on D. Sancho's side. What the *Espéculo* had stated, that

> if there be not son or daughter or grandson or granddaughter or heir in the direct line of descent to inherit the kingdom then let them take as their lord the eldest brother of the king, *and if there is no eldest brother then the closest relative available*[14]

had recently been replaced by the law of the Second *Partida* which ruled that

> should the eldest son die before he inherits, if he leave a son or daughter begat of his lawful wife, *then that child shall succeed and no other.*'[15]

This provision, enshrining a fundamental change to the law of succession and enshrining the so-called right of representation, had been enacted sometime before August 1265, at a time when no one had envisaged the circumstances that would obtain ten years later, with the Marīnids at the gate, a five-year-old heir in the offing, and the five-year-old heir's grandfather ill – indeed very ill.

Although, according to *Cantiga* 235 (the *cantiga* that records the king's regular deliverance from death courtesy of the Virgin), when Alfonso returned to Castile men wished him a civil good-day ('Sennor, tan bon dia vosco'), he was, the Catalan chronicler Desclot reports, 'very angry and sick' – and not only that, also ready for retirement.

> But later, believe me,
> Never was Sancho in Portugal thus betrayed,

Cantiga 235 continues, referring darkly (whenever the *cantiga* was written; Kinkade suggests mid-1278) to Sancho II, deprived of the administration of his kingdom by Innocent IV in 1245. Might not Alfonso also be sidelined as a 'useless king' (*rex inutilis*), like the Portuguese monarch to whom in his youth he had played host at Toledo? On account of the imperial fiasco, men were mocking him, the Chronicle reports, and the king knew it. The majority view, reported by Riquier, was that he would soon be 'dispossessed' by his son.[16] That was the ever-present possibility during the last seven years of his effective reign against which the extraordinary intellectual achievements of that period have to be measured.

At the beginning of his imperial adventure another troubadour, Guilhem de Montanhagol, had said that the empire was awaiting him, but had added,

---

[14]   *Espéculo*, 2.16.3: ed. Craddock, 'Cronología', 406.
[15]   *Part*. 2. 15. 2: ed. Craddock., 407.
[16]   Kinkade, 'Alfonso X', 312, 321; Hernández & Linehan, 48, 234; *CAX*, c. 66; Riquier, *Trovadores*, 1622.

ominously, that 'when a great king undertakes a great action, he must either achieve it or accept the consequences'.[17] Now the consequences were upon him. Moreover, he was ill at both extremities, in the face and the leg. As to the former, what has been diagnosed as a cancerous ulcer, we have the regular *communiqués* of *Cantiga* 235. But, whatever the pathological origin of his illness, the state of his face will have caused him chronic pain as well as enabling his enemies to describe him as leprous, with all that that implied.[18] Some camp followers of the political theology preached by the late E. A. Kantorowicz have been quick to descry 'sacral' characteristics in Castile's thirteenth-century rulers.[19] But reflection on the king's two bodies can be of only limited use in the case of a king whose gammy leg and decaying nose left him without full control of one. The leglessness was particularly damaging. As the case of another Portuguese ruler, Afonso II, had demonstrated fifty years before, a thirteenth-century king unable to ride hardly deserved the name of king,[20] even one as firmly convinced as Alfonso X

---

[17]   Ricketts, 135–7 (above, 114).

[18]   Presilla, 435–7 (a diagnosis based on an autopsy on the king's exhumed remains in 1948: Delgado Roig, 'Examen medico-legal'), while more recent medical opinion has suggested either recidivant infectious sinusitis or an infectious granulomatosis of tubercular, syphilitic or leprous origin, both of which conditions were capable of sudden, apparently miraculous improvement: Salvador Martínez, 'Locura alfonsí', 46–7; González Jiménez, *Alfonso X*, 352 n.88. (It may be noted that in 1272 Alfonso had provided the monks of S. Pedro de Cardeña with a new tomb for the Cid. As he will have known from the *Estoria de España*, after sitting bolt upright for ten years the Castilian hero had first been entombed because the tip of his nose had fallen off: *PCG* c. 961; Linehan, *History*, 460).

[19]   Nieto Soria, *Fundamentos ideológicos*, 58–62, referring to Kantorowicz's *The King's Two Bodies. A study in mediaeval political theology* (Princeton, N.J., 1957).

[20]   Kinkade, 'Alfonso X', 289–90, is responsible for the universal belief that the origin of the king's medical troubles was a blow to the face that felled him in late 1269–early 1270. This is mistaken, the misunderstanding deriving from (i) the certain fact that the king had problems with his face later; and (ii) the assumption that the origins of the injury must have been the horse's hoof that sent him to his 'cama' (Castilian for 'bed'). However, the language of the *Book of Deeds*, in which (c. 499) the report occurs, is Catalan, in which language 'cama' means not bed but leg (thus discrediting Kinkade's description of Forster's correct translation of the word as 'gratuitous'). The king having been kicked not in bed but in the leg, significance attaches to the incident (?Dec. 1281), reported by Kinkade n. 154, citing *Cantiga* 367, of his legs swelling 'to such an extent that they no longer fit[ted] into his boots, and, what is more, the skin on them split and yellow fluid came out'. On the basis of this description and of the (inadequate) photographs of 1948, Dr Michael Petch proposes a diagnosis which would account for both sets of symptoms, the crural as well as the facial: a tuberculoma deforming the face and constrictive pericarditis (Pick's Disease: a cardiac condition caused by tuberculosis) leading to congestion of the body and calcification of its organs. However, confirmation of this must await the agreement of the authorities of Murcia Cathedral to allow an autopsy to be done on Alfonso X's heart. According to Guillaume de Nangis, when Alfonso ('that Pharaoh') began to co-rule with his son he was already afflicted by a 'contagion of paralytic illness': *Gesta Philippi III*, 498. For the medical condition of Afonso II of Portugal: Vilar, 120–5.

had been just two years earlier that law, right and truth ('ley, derecho & verdat') were all riding with him.[21] The varicose ulcers also prevented him from confronting the Marīnids when they invaded the kingdom again in August 1277.[22]

At the Burgos Cortes of 1276, with the Infante D. Manuel, as the 'highest branch' of 'the royal tree', acting as Sancho's principal advocate,[23] Alfonso had sought to resolve the succession issue by the simple expedient of changing the law of the *Partidas* yet again so as to read:

> Should the eldest son die before he inherits and leave a legitimate son then that son shall succeed. However if another son of the king should survive then let him and not the grandson inherit,

and by reducing from twenty to sixteen the age at which that survivor might succeed without the inconvenience of a regency council.[24] He had sought to resolve it, but when the succession of Sancho was eventually confirmed in 1278 and, as Gil de Zamora reports, he began to share government with his father,[25] neither amongst the la Cerda partisans within Castile nor further afield was his decision regarded as settling the matter.

Further afield Philippe III of France was outraged by the disinheritance of his nephew, and threatened war. Here was another *casus belli* to add to the already simmering issue of the kingdom of Navarre, which under Teobaldo II had been subject to a process of creeping French colonization. Teobaldo had entrusted the government of Navarre to French seneschals, spending two-thirds of his reign either in Champagne or in the company of his father-in-law, Louis IX. It was on Louis' ill-fated crusade that he died at Trapani in 1270. His brother and successor, Enrique I, whose monumental fatness (a condition perhaps inherited from his grandmother, sister of the equally unwieldy Sanç VII) prevented from riding, followed him to an early grave in 1274, at the age of twenty-four. There ensued a race for the infant heir to the throne, another Teobaldo, one in which the king of Castile triumphed, securing the child's betrothal to his daughter, the Infanta

---

[21]   Rodgers, lines 155–60.
[22]   As to whether or not he was reduced to suing for peace at this point: González Jiménez, *Alfonso X*, 324; cf. O'Callaghan, *Learned King*, 244.
[23]   *CAX*, c. 67; Craddock, 'Dynasty in dispute', 208, showing the passage to have been expanded in later manuscripts of *CAX* by the addition of words spoken by the king as though in Sancho's favour which in fact derived from the will which disinherited him.
[24]   Maldonado, 'En torno a un texto modificado'; Craddock, 'Cronología', 409–11; MacDonald, 'Alfonso the Learned', 650–2.
[25]   González Jiménez, *Alfonso X*, 310–11, 327–8.

Violante. However, little Teobaldo perished on being dropped by his nurse from the ramparts of Estella when reaching out to stroke a squirrel, whereupon the succession passed to young Jeanne who, while Alfonso X was with the pope at Beaucaire, became betrothed to Philippe III's son, the future Philippe IV (the Fair).[26]

Gregory X's consent to this grossly incestuous proposal, which was as prompt in the granting as it was anguished in the asking, proved that the Roman Church's commitment to the ecclesiastical model of marriage remained contingent on dynastic, and especially French dynastic, considerations.[27] It coincided with Jaime of Aragón's claim to the orphaned kingdom, based on his forty-three-year-old agreement with Sanç VII,[28] and the conspiracy of disaffected elements in Castile with Philippe III. As the latter moved his army towards the Pyrenees, Pope John XXI urged restraint. The Portuguese pontiff will have been mindful not only of the parlous state of Castile's southern frontier but also of the new regime in Aragón where in July 1276 the apparently indestructible Jaime I had abdicated his royal authority and, garbed in the Cistercian habit to help him to a better world, had shortly after expired and been buried at Poblet.[29]

France and Aragón

The new king of Aragón promptly gave notice of a new style of management. Pedro III's (Count Pere II's) long, and frequently strained, apprenticeship had provided him with a firm power base in Catalonia, where he had represented his father as procurator since 1257. He was to that extent well placed to deal with the rebellion of the Catalan baronage which had its origins in Jaime I's attempt to impose control over the county of Urgell by marrying his niece, Constança of Moncada, to Count Àlvar II, with the damaging consequences of the ensuing bigamy suit aggravated by the protest produced

[26]   Lacarra, *Hist. política*, 163–205.
[27]   'Exceedingly troublesome' the pontiff found the king of France's petition since Jeanne was Louis IX's great-niece, 'but in view of the dangers encompassing your most Christian kingdom . . .': *Reg. Greg. X*, 907.
[28]   Above, 67. He had previously reminded Fernando de la Cerda 'that the kingdom of Navarre used to belong to the kingdom of Aragon, but when King Alfonso [the Battler] perished at the battle of Fraga the Navarrese elected their own king', and then there had been the agreement with Sanç VII: *MHE*, I, no. 136 (25 Aug. 1274). 1275 therefore provided an opportunity for righting an ancient wrong. However, the interest of Jaime's successor would be focused elsewhere.
[29]   Soldevila, *Pere el Gran*, 421.

by the demand for *bovatge* at the start of the new reign. The magnanimity displayed by Pedro in neutralizing the Catalan mutineers was matched by his effectiveness in suppressing another uprising he had inherited, that of the Valencian Mudéjars. This he did with such thoroughness that not even in 1285, when his situation was at its most perilous, was there further trouble from that quarter. By having himself crowned in November 1276 at Zaragoza ('the first coronation celebrated by a king in Aragón itself') before even visiting Barcelona, and by abstaining from use of the royal title in advance of that ceremony, he repudiated the kingdom's subjection to Rome which his grandfather had contracted in 1204, and declared Zaragoza its ceremonial capital. The kingdom of Mallorca he regarded as part of the kingdom of Aragón for which his brother owed him homage and fealty, with his own inclusive title replacing the litany of its territorial components employed by his father. In 1281 he married his daughter Isabel to Dinis of Portugal and in 1282 his heir Alfonso to Eleanor, daughter of Edward I of England.[30] He had already wrong-footed both Castile and France by providing refuge for his sister, Alfonso X's queen Violant, when in January 1278 she fled her husband, bringing her la Cerda grandsons with her.[31]

In November 1276 Alfonso X had entered into a truce with Philippe III at Vitoria, undertaking to submit the succession question to a meeting of the cortes at which the French king would be represented and to abide by its decision. Because the French king was to abide by it too, the French historian Georges Daumet considered the outcome a diplomatic disaster. Castilian opinion will have judged differently. Within six months of ruling in Sancho's favour, and two of surrendering the Navarrese of Pamplona to the tender mercies of the French invaders, Alfonso was seen to be willing to treat the succession as negotiable and rehabilitate the denaturalized Lara without penalty.[32] The twofold consequence of such indecision was to alienate the Infante Sancho and to encourage D. Fadrique to wonder whether, if after all the law was as the *Espéculo* had defined it, as the king's eldest brother *he* may not have possessed the strongest claim to succeed.

For twelve years after the Norwegian lady had decided against him D. Fadrique had sought solace in the service of the sultan of Tunis and elsewhere. In 1272 he returned to Castile, now in his fifty-third year.[33] He did not figure amongst the rebel nobles in 1272–3; indeed in discussion of the

[30] Swift, 269–72; Brundage, 'Matrimonial politics'; Soldevila, *Hist. de Catalunya*, 342–8 (cf. Palacios Martín, *Coronación*, 91–112). The English match had been negotiated in 1273.
[31] Kinkade, 'Violante of Aragon', 9–10.
[32] Daumet, *Mémoire*, 40–7; Goñi Gaztambide, *Hist. de los obispos de Pamplona*, 663.
[33] *CAX*, c. 24. The references in cc. 18 and 19 are to be discounted.

king's differences with them he had been counted 'on the king's side', and according to Jofré de Loaisa in 1276 he was amongst those who did homage to D. Sancho as 'future king'.[34] It would be interesting to know what he had been doing in the previous four years because in 1277 the king had him strangled (or, as the Silos Annals preferred, entombed 'in a box of sharp irons') and his son-in-law, Simón Ruíz de los Cameros, consigned to the flames by D. Sancho, on account, in Loaisa's words 'of certain things that the king knew about them,' by most accounts without any semblance of legal process.[35]

Since in the previous year Alfonso had been prepared to contemplate the subsidized restoration to favour of men who had denaturalized themselves by becoming the vassals of a foreign king committed to thwarting his plans for the succession, the severity of his action now, as well as its apparent arbitrariness, sent shock-waves through the political establishment. Most contemporaries seem to have been in the dark regarding the nature of those 'certain things'. Posterity certainly has, and has preferred various lurid possibilities to the simple explanation of political ambition.[36] Although he and the king had co-existed for five years, the fact remarked by Mondéjar that as heir to the Swabian inheritance Fadrique may have felt aggrieved by Alfonso's imperial antics deserves consideration; as does the 'notable thing' reported by Zurita in his account of the execution of Conradin of Hohenstaufen. This was that Conradin's gauntlet had been taken up by Fadrique and handed by him to an Aragonese knight for

[34]   Ibid., c. 26, 40, 41, 47; *Crónica*, c. 21.
[35]   Lomax, 'Crónica inédita', 332. Loaisa, *Crónica*, c. 23; *CAX*, c. 68. *Anales Toledanos III*, 173, states that the pair were dispatched 'mediante iusticia': in view of the prominence given to this act in 1282 a notable assertion.
[36]   See González Jiménez, *Alfonso X*, 316–22; Salvador Martínez, *Alfonso X*, 408–18, and, for a plausible selection of possible explanations, O'Callaghan, *Alfonso X and the* Cantigas, 147. In view of his choice of executioner it can hardly have been a conspiracy 'in favour of D. Sancho, without D. Sancho', as suggested by Ballesteros, *Alfonso X*, 824. Nor, despite Zurita, IV. 3, can Alfonso's ire have been caused by the queen's flight to Aragón since the killings preceded that event by ten months. Moreover, the punishments inflicted seem disproportionate to the pair's responsibility for failure to relieve the *Navarrería*, as proposed by the Prince of Viana (d. 1461): *Crónica de los Reyes de Navarra*, 151. As to the suspicion of a homosexual relationship, favoured by Kinkade, 'Alfonso X', 315–18, although such considerations might have offered a pretext they did not necessarily involve public castration and hanging upside-down, the penalties prescribed by *F.Real* 4.9.2: below, 196. Montoya Martínez, '"Gran vingança"', suggests Catharism (an impression thought to be conveyed by the illustration of the scene of Simón's burning in the Florentine codex of the *Cantigas*: Kinkade & Keller, 'Orphaned miniature', 43). González Jiménez notes that the pair were the only significant figures absent from the Burgos Cortes of 1274: *Alfonso X*, 274.

transmission to the Infant D. Pedro.[37] So was Fadrique guilty, or (wrongly perhaps) thought to have been guilty, of collusion with the new king of Aragón in surrendering his family's claims to the Hohenstaufen bequest? Or was the king simply mad? Was he safe to be with? Just to be sure, Fernán Pérez Ponce, no supporter of the la Cerda cause and a man who would be with Alfonso at the end, took himself off to France.[38]

Queen Violant's return to Castile in July 1279, without her grandsons, coincided with the arrival of Nicholas III's nuncio, Bishop Pietro of Rieti, demanding action on a whole dossier of episcopal grievances. To many of these Alfonso and Sancho were ready enough to reply as suggested in the pope's own instructions to the nuncio, namely that if such abuses had occurred in the past they ought not to be repeated in the future.[39] Most of the institutional practices complained of were not new, though the personal vendettas were. They dated from well before Alfonso's accession and were to continue long after his death, extortion of the *tercias* and pro-hibition of episcopal assemblies in particular. Writing in these very years, the infante's tutor Gil de Zamora commended the principle of divide and rule as a 'most useful practice'.[40] But for Alfonso X at the end of the 1270s it was not sufficient. With Alfonso seeking to suborn the king of France's discontented vassal, the *vicomte* of Narbonne with the offer of the vacant archbishopric of Toledo for his younger brother, and Lope Díaz de Haro, formerly the infante's principal supporter, defecting to the king of France and the la Cerda cause, treachery was at a premium. Its ramifications extended to Rome and the household of Cardinal Ordoño Álvarez, whose father Alvar Díaz de Asturias had been a ring-leader of the rebellion of 1272–3.[41]

Amongst the complaints raised by the nuncio was one concerning the king's unlicensed establishment of the hierarchically hybrid maritime military order of Santa Maria de España (or of the Star), with the Infante Sancho as 'ensign of St Mary and admiral' and its exclusively coastal convents facing the North Atlantic as well as North Africa. His purpose in doing so may, again, have been to counter-balance the long-established and now increasingly hostile

---

[37] *Memorias*, 344–5; above, 168; Zurita, III. 78, describing Fadrique as the son of Conradin's aunt and Pedro of Aragón as 'the great avenger of the injuries' done to the prince and his line. Although Zurita attributes the story of Fadrique's intervention to Piccolomini, Piccolomini does not mention it.

[38] Daumet, *Mémoire*, 163–4; *CAX*, c. 68.

[39] Kinkade, 'Violante of Aragon', 9–10; Domínguez Sánchez, *Nicolás III*, 344; Linehan, 'Spanish Church revisited', 134–5.

[40] 'And it is excellent practice ('doctrina perutilis') for the king never to consult clergy and laity together, or let one group know what the other is doing, until both have agreed to whatever is proposed': *De preconiis Hispanie*, 210–11; Linehan, *Spanish Church*, 101–87.

[41] Hernández & Linehan, 160–5; Kinkade & Keller, 'Orphaned miniature', 38; Daumet, *Mémoire*, 178–81 (Oct. 1281); Linehan & Torre Sevilla, 'Misattributed tomb', 58–9.

military orders. But it was the churches that claimed to be oppressed thereby, a charge which remained unanswered at the time and has given rise to all manner of interpretations since.[42] Also unanswered was another grievance which must have arisen in the course of the nuncio's conversations with senior churchmen since it was not mentioned in his instructions from the pope. This was specific to the king and was to the effect that his court was a hive of Jewish and other free-thinkers who referred slightingly to the Almighty and where 'almost all things are attributed not to God, who is *natura naturans*, but to *natura naturata* by certain persons' who, 'asserting that there is no God, proceed in almost all their actions according to the fallacious judgement of astronomers, augurs and soothsayers'.[43] Now this charge may either have had a general context (for example, a tendency amongst rulers to put their trust in soothsayers, sneezers and the like, and not to go out on Tuesdays or Wednesdays) or it may have been occasioned by specific activities regarded as especially iniquitous.[44]

Either way, at a time when the swarms of agnostics preaching similar heresies had caused the closure of the arts faculty at the University of Paris, the characterization of the intellectual activities of the royal court was calculated to ring warning bells at Rome, regardless of the king's acknowledgement that the stars were God's servants.[45] For while the gigantic task

---

[42]   Domínguez Sánchez, *Nicolás III*, 342; Linehan, 'Spanish Church revisited', 145; Ayala Martínez, *Órdenes militares*, 108–12. Gregory X had declined to approve the Order, having learnt 'some sinister things' not to the credit of such confraternities: Domínguez Sánchez, *Gregorio X*, 150. The pope's objection to 'a new order or religion' ('novum ordinem seu religionem') was related neither to the clergy's exclusion from knight-making ceremonies, as suggested by Lizabe de Savastano, 397, nor to a heterodox 'new religion' espoused by Alfonso and associated with the Spiritual Franciscans, evidences of which Domínguez Rodríguez observes in *Cantigas* illustrations of the Virgin by the Cross and at the Last Judgement: ' "Compassio" y "co-redemptio" ', 34. Alfonso's offence was his breach of 'Ne nimia', the decree of IV Lateran prohibiting the founding of new orders ('ne quis de cetero *novam religionem* inveniat': X 3. 36. 9: Friedberg, II, 607): a transgression in which he persisted regardless of the nuncio's remonstrations, with his patronage of the Order continuing until it was combined with the Order of Santiago in 1280: Torres Fontes, 'Orden de S. María', 109–15.

[43]   Linehan, 'Spanish Church revisited', 147.

[44]   Cf. Walsh, *Libro de los XII Sabios*, 112: 'Do not trust to sorcerers or augurs and have no regard for soothsayers or *estornudos* (sneezers).' According to the Count of Barcelos in the fourteenth century, wishing to know his end Alfonso consulted many astronomers who informed him that he would die disinherited 'by a man of his blood', which was why he had D. Fadrique and his son-in-law killed, 'reasoning that it was through them that he would meet his end': Lindley Cintra, 511; Craddock, 'Dynasty in dispute', 206.

[45]   Millás Vallicrosa, *Traducciones orientales*; Gil, *Escuela de traductores*, 57–87; Samsó, 'Sevilla y la obra científica de Alfonso X'. For the possibility that it was a Toledan at the centre of royal government, Bishop Gonzalo Pérez of Burgos, who was responsible for bringing the accusation: Hernández & Linehan, 180–1; *Libro de la espera*, cit. Cárdenas, 'Alfonso's scriptorium', 105.

of translating the historical materials from Latin was proceeding, and while the Marīnids were at the gates and the *ricos homes* within the walls, there had been no interruption in the transmission of the 'wisdom of the Arabs'.[46] Between 1262 and 1272 Alfonso's great work, the Astronomical Tables, based on the Toledo meridian, were constructed there and at Burgos, with Jewish scholars providing the essential link between the semitic languages and Romance. Between 1276 and 1279 the sixteen books that comprise the *Libros del saber de astronomia/astrologia* and its counterpart the *Libro de las formas et de los ymagenes* (an expansion of both the *Lapidario* and a 'more excellent' *Liber Razielis*), of which only a summary of contents survives, were perfected, and before 1279 the *Libro de astromagia* was completed.[47] Plainly, Alfonso's court possessed an astromagical library of consequence from which texts and parts of texts could be extracted for the king's purposes. Plainly also, most of this activity was at best only marginally orthodox in terms of the 'science of the stars' as classified by Albertus Magnus in his *Speculum astronomiae* at the end of the previous decade, which firmly stated, contrary to the assurances of the *Liber Razielis*, that 'the angels do not move the celestial bodies' and proscribed all attempts to achieve that effect by means of talismans, auspicious times and other Salamonic and cabbalistic devices.[48] But with the would-be emperor needing to express himself in a language intelligible to all, now the works of astronomy, as well as those of astrology and magic, were perfected and for the benefit of his eventual imperial subjects translated back into Latin, largely by Italians, thereby providing a corpus of scientific knowledge which would still be admired long after his claims to empire had been forgotten.[49]

Always supposing that they were able to distinguish one thing from another, it was Alfonso's astrological interests that would have provided his local critics with their chief cause for complaint as the enemy was gathering. These were an obsession. The magical treatise *Picatrix*, for example, said to be one of the 'spiritual works' of Aristotle, which had been translated from the Arabic in 1256–8, purported to enable a man 'to do all, know all, remember all, say all and hear all' (provided he knew the trick).[50] While acknowledging that to engage in divination was to disparage the Almighty,

[46]   Procter, 'Scientific works', 27, Menéndez Pidal, 'Cómo trabajaron', 368, to the contrary.
[47]   García Avilés, 'Alfonso X y el *Liber Razielis*', 33–5; idem, 'Alfonso X y la tradición de la magia astral', 95; above, 143. A. d'Agostino's edition of the *Libro de astromagia* (Naples, 1992) has not been available to me.
[48]   García Avilés, 'Alfonso X y el *Liber Razielis*', 25; idem, 'Alfonso X y la tradición de la magia astral', 84–5.
[49]   Procter, 'Scientific works', 13–14; Gingerich, 'Alfonso the Tenth'; Burnett, 122–39.
[50]   Idem, 136, 138.

the law of the *Partidas* on the subject stated as much; the lessons of history proved the rest. 'The historian and the divinator were two of a kind: the function of the one defined the practice of the other.'[51]

This was all very well, yet in the south the Marīnids had returned in 1277 and were pressing hard, revealing the desperateness of the situation. And what benefits did astrology, the lessons of history and knowledge of the *Picatrix* provide, those critics may have asked, when in a series of dizzyingly complex manoeuvres, at one time or the other over the next four years Alfonso was allied to all three players in the great game, the Marīnids, Muḥammad II of Granada and the Banū 'Ashqilūlah, yet still managed to finish up on the wrong side? Too ill to confront the foe, first he sued for peace, then, while the papal nuncio was fussing around behind the front line, had his army routed by Abū Yūsuf's forces and was forced to raise the siege of Algeciras. Defeat at the hands of Muḥammad II followed at Moclín to the south-west of Granada (June 1280), involving the loss of the Master of Santiago and many of his knights and resulting in its unification with the Order of Santa María de España under the leadership of its Master, Pedro Núñez.[52] The king's dismay at the speed and extent of these reverses seems to have been largely responsible for his concentration at this time on the encouragement of repopulation of the extreme south-west by means of miracle stories associated with El Puerto de Santa María contained in his *Cantigas*.[53] By now though his eye was hanging out.

The failure of the siege of Algeciras had been partly due to the lack of funds created by D. Sancho's diversion of revenues from Alfonso's farmer of taxes and *almoxarife mayor*, Çag de la Maleha, in order to assist Violant return from Aragon. In revenge Alfonso arrested the Jewish tax collectors and had Çag dragged past the convent of San Francisco at Seville where Sancho and his brothers were staying, and burnt alive. The act was meant to serve as a warning to his heir. 'And when D. Sancho learnt of it', the Chronicle reports,

> he was minded to arrest his father and was only dissuaded from doing so by his followers. But he remained greatly incensed against him on account of the Jew's death, which he reckoned had been ordered because of the service the Jew had done him.[54]

[51]   Solalinde, 'Alfonso X astrólogo', 354; *Part.* 7. 23. 1; Linehan, *History*, 489.

[52]   *CAX*, c. 74; Harvey, *Islamic Spain*, 158–9; Torres Fontes, 'Orden de S. María', 95. For Castilian confusion at the papal curia as to the state of Alfonso's alliances: Hernández & Linehan, 445.

[53]   Snow, 'A chapter'; O'Callaghan, *Alfonso X and the* Cantigas, chap. 9.

[54]   *CAX*, c. 74.

Tension was further increased when, at Bayonne at the end of the year, Alfonso suggested making the la Cerda prince his vassal for the kingdom of Jaén: a solution to the succession problem inadequate so far as the French king was concerned and to the Castilian infante, like the king's eye, exorbitant.[55]

Starved of satisfaction on the French front, Alfonso now embarked on a final round of hectic activity, resuming the imperial title which in 1275 he had promised to disclaim, marrying his son D. Juan to Margarita, the daughter of William VII, marquess of Montferrat the long-time upholder of Ghibelline interests in Lombardy, and granddaughter of Richard of Cornwall(!), and in a letter to the Genoese authorities announcing the dispatch of a contingent of three hundred knights and a hundred archers. In conformity with his anti-French stance his son D. Pedro was married to a sister of the *vicomte* of Narbonne and, at Campillo on 27 March 1281, agreements were reached with Pedro of Aragón for the partition of Navarre and the ejection of the French king's Lara and Haro allies from the Lara stronghold of Albarracín.

But the proceedings at Campillo were a sham, in Ayala Martínez's words 'a diplomatic farce'.[56] For at Agreda on the following day, with neither party taking the king of Castile into account, D. Sancho agreed to make substantial territorial concessions to Pedro III and promised him Navarre entire.[57] While the king of Aragón contemplated his interests elsewhere, as the *Chronicle of Alfonso X* makes clear the infante remained deeply sceptical of the strength of his father's commitment to the integrity of the kingdom. Was it because word had reached the king of the infante's double-dealing at Agreda that the possibility of making the kingdom of Jaén a state within a state for Alfonso de la Cerda had been revived? Whether or not, when the bishop-elect of Ávila, D. Aimar, raised the question with Sancho, Sancho rounded on him, branding him as both insolent and mad. But for his Franciscan habit, the infante would have made such an example of him that no one would ever have dared to broach the matter again. He would not even have it raised by Alfonso, and, when it was, the exchange ended with the father reminding his son that he was not yet king and that he never would be unless he agreed to the proposed settlement. At the mention of disinheritance, the Chronicle records Sancho berating Alfonso and addressing him as follows:

---

[55]   Ibid. The Dominican hotline ensured that Ptolemy of Lucca learnt of the proposed grant of 'certam terram' to the king's grandsons: *Annalen*, ed. Schmeidler, 183–4.
[56]   Doubleday, 84–7; Ayala Martínez, 'Paces', 163.
[57]   Zurita, IV. 6, 8, 11; Ayala Martínez, 'Paces', 160–3.

Sire, you did not make me your heir; God did. And in order to achieve this
he did much. For he killed my brother who was older than I and who
would have inherited these kingdoms if he had lived longer than you. And
he killed him for no other reason than that I should inherit when your days
are over. And the word that you have allowed yourself you might better have
swallowed, for the time will come when you will wish that you had never
spoken it.[58]

Whether or not any such words were ever really uttered (as reported they
do have an exculpatory fourteenth-century ring to them)[59] the point of
no return had now been passed. In November 1281 the cortes had already
assembled at Seville and the political heavyweights were signing up to the
infante's cause. To that extent, the summoning of the assembly was a serious
miscalculation, urgent though the need was to reform the currency, since as
a plenary session of the institution, 'perhaps one of the largest of the Middle
Ages',[60] it provided an ideal opportunity for the disaffected from all over
the kingdom to conspire and take courage from one another's adversity.
According to *Cantiga* 386, it ended in a great display of harmony and concord and with a lavish banquet courtesy of the Virgin Mary who supplied the
fish.[61] In reality, 'more out of fear than love', the meeting had agreed to Alfonso's
proposal to provide the silver he needed to finance the struggle against the
ruler of Morocco by withdrawing the already devalued billon coinage and
issuing coins of copper only for the people's everyday needs, in effect a type
of intrinsically valueless paper money the equivalent of tokens.[62]

As the infante traversed the country, strewing charters of exemption,
confirming municipal *fueros* and – as Alfonso would later claim, not without reason – fomenting disaffection, everywhere he went he encountered
abandoned settlements and complaints about levels of taxation beyond
endurance and the new 'copper money'.[63] His course was now clear, and when,
by way of Córdoba (where according to Alfonso, when he came to present
his account, the plot was hatched)[64] he reached Valladolid in the second

[58] *CAX*, c. 75. The manuscript of the *Chronicle* used by González Jiménez (p. 219) gives the
concluding words of Alfonso's reported outburst as 'e quél le fiziera e que lo desfaría' rather
than 'é que él lo ficiera, ó que él le desheredaria', rendering the Infante's response unintelligible.
[59] Cf. the remarks in similar vein found in [Sancho's] *Lucidario* and *Castigos*: below, 224–5.
[60] O'Callaghan, *Learned King*, 256.
[61] Idem, *Alfonso X and the* Cantigas, 166–71.
[62] *CAX*, c. 75; *Crónica*, ed. González Jiménez, 217; Hernández, *Rentas*, I, clxxxiv.
[63] Lomax, 'Crónica inédita', 332–3; González Jiménez, 'Sancho IV, infante', 167–9.
[64] Reportedly it was there that he entered into alliance with the king of Granada: Zurita,
Indices, 171. The Chronicle (c. 75) reveals the double game Sancho was playing at this stage.

week of April, awaiting him was the queen who, the Chronicle reports, was delighted to know of his decision to break with his father. Also there were the Infante D. Manuel, the king's dearest, indeed only surviving brother (other than the indestructible but unmentionable D. Enrique, who had he not remained imprisoned in Apulia, would certainly have relished the opportunity of making mischief in Castile), and – and it was this that mattered – the spokesmen of the kingdom.[65] The *soi-disant* Cortes of Valladolid – the assembly called by D. Sancho that he lacked the authority to summon – was to have met at Easter, which in 1282 fell on 29 March. In the event, the Valladolid gathering had to be delayed until mid-April.

One of the animal fables included in the Hebrew *Meshal Haqadmini*, the volume on which Isaac ibn Sahula began work in Egypt in 1281, tells of the meeting of the animals summoned to consider how to respond to the ceaseless depredations of their king, the Lion. The author's tantalizing allegory describes the Ox opening the debate and urging all the horned beasts to surround their tormentor and do him to death. But the Onager urges caution. For

> Was not the Lion's sire liege-lord long since
> Of our sires who now have his son for prince?
> Repression on himself he needs must bring
> Who insurrection moves against his king.
> Was ever there a subject raised his arm
> Against the Lord's anointed, without harm? . . .
> This kingdom is the Lion's, down a chain
> Of sires, passed to their sons: long may he reign!

Instead the Onager recommends repairing 'to some far distant territory' and, led by the Wild Ass, this they duly do, discovering there 'an ample land, of plenty and of peace'.[66] Ibn Sahula, who hailed from Guadalajara, clearly had the Castilian situation and the exiles in France and Rome in mind with Alfonso in the role of the Lion (and, in another tale, of the Eagle), and though his account of it remains provokingly allusive, his tales are replete with contemporary references.[67] The significance of the Wolf's opposition

---

[65] *CAX*, c. 76; del Giudice, 72–83.

[66] Loewe, 60–6. Cf. Oldradus de Ponte (*c*.1330): 'Saracens are called beasts literally, because their father Ishmael was called Onager by the Lord' (transl. Zacour, 51).

[67] With the Hart (a Jewish symbol) ennobled, the Fox complaining about the Lion 'ennobling those who Are quite unsuitable, whilst none of true Nobility are near him' (an allusion to the advancement of the *caballeros villanos*?) and seeking to induce the Wolf to rebel against his master, only to be betrayed by him: ibid., xv–xvii, lxxxvi–ci, 112, 132–6.

to the Lion's attempt to make the Fox pay with his head, whether or not he pleaded guilty as charged –

> "Nay", said the Wolf, "the judge of all the land
> Ought not give final sentence out of hand.
> The law gives warning, none may be despatched
> On single evidence – it must be matched –

would not have escaped his readers in 1281, nor would the plot he then hatches to incriminate the other.[68] But in 1282 when the call went out and the exiles returned, it was the course of action proposed by the Ox that prevailed.

1282

The year 1282 was a significant one in Spanish history and Easter Sunday, which fell on 29 March, was a particularly significant day. While infantes and *procuradores* were gathering in Valladolid, in Palermo a tipsy French soldier made a pass at the wife of a Sicilian and within no time the Angevin garrison was being slaughtered, the unborn children of Frenchmen reportedly being spiked out of Sicilian wombs, the process of putting the French out of southern Italy was under way, and Muret and Corbeil were avenged. The events of that March weekend put paid to Castile's European pretensions for the next two hundred years. No matter that the kings of Castile were, or can be calculated to have been, materially so much wealthier than their Aragonese neighbours. After 1282 the kingdom increasingly turned in upon itself while Aragón turned outwards, not that it is altogether easy to synchronize the development of one with the other. Annalizing just the history of Aragón, that seasoned story-teller, the *cronista real* Jerónimo Zurita, found it necessary to bob and weave around the year 1282: in his narrative we reach 1281, we are then back in 1277.[69]

That said, in 1282 the prospect revealed to Alfonso X in 1256 of a Spanish empire based on Africa and with a foothold in Italy had been realized by the Aragonese established in Sicily opposite Tunisia. So had Urban IV's forebodings of twenty years before. Ironically (because it was one of Urban's most anti-Ghibelline predecessors who had first encouraged the Aragonese to fish in Sicilian waters) the Aragonese had emerged as the Ghibellines of

---

[68] Ibid., 136–8.
[69] Hillgarth, 'Problem', 8–9; Zurita, IV. 12–13.

their generation.[70] Alfonso X had been right to be alarmed by the Aragonese marriage to the Hohenstaufen heiress.[71] But after 1260 he had allowed his attention to be diverted. Grateful for his father-in-law's assistance in recovering Murcia, he had lowered his guard, and received Jaime's son as archbishop of Toledo. (It was oddly symbolic that the man he had actually wanted for the job, Bishop Pascual of Jaén, had ended up as a debtor of the king of Aragón.)[72] The arrangements reached at Agreda had set the seal. Reversing the diplomatic alignment that had obtained in 1252, the rulers of Aragón and Portugal were now in league with the Castilian rebel, despite the fact that as late as January 1282 Pedro III had been duping Alfonso into believing that he was fully paid-up member of the Great Conspiracy for 'the recovery of the kingdom of Sicily, for which you [have] freely offered your aid'.[73] So much for the fiction of the king of Aragón as a disinterested innocent who happened to be cruising along the African coast at the time sunk in crusading speculations who, when invited to intervene in the affairs of the island, calmly submitted the matter to the barons of Catalonia *and Aragón* for their advice on the merits of the case.[74]

Pedro III had also known in advance about the gathering at Valladolid. As he had the goodness to inform Alfonso two days after the event, the Infante Sancho had invited him to be represented there. But now, as he had learnt, there was some unpleasantness in Alfonso's kingdom, which he was very sorry to hear of. He was unable to be present at Villareal fifteen days later for the cortes to which Alfonso had invited him, but which Alfonso had now had to postpone since, as his correspondent understood, he was otherwise occupied.[75]

This was a carefully crafted letter, and as soon as the Valladolid meeting got under way the reasons for the need to finesse became apparent. Indeed it may well have given Alfonso the clearest if not the earliest intimation of

[70]   Dufourcq, *Espagne catalane*, 238–59 ('the Tunisian issue and the Sicilian issue were always linked', p. 250); Soldevila, *Pere el Gran*, 99–100; above, 44.

[71]   Above, 146; Boscolo, 83.

[72]   Fleuchaus, no. 670.

[73]   Hillgarth, 'Problem', 25. Confirmation of Pedro's Sicilian intentions and of his alliance with the Eastern emperor is provided by his letter of the same month to the commune of Pisa: Geanakoplos, 348–9. Alfonso was regarded as a third 'abettor' and the Infante Sancho was also in contact with Constantinople: Salimbene, *Cronica*, 772; Hernández & Linehan, 233.

[74]   Thus Desclot, c. 88, denying prior knowledge of Sicilian affairs (Critchlow, II, 54). Cf. Wieruszowski, 173–314; Runciman, *Sicilian Vespers*, chaps. 12–13; on the N. African front, Dufourcq, *Espagne catalane*, esp. 238–59.

[75]   MHE, II, no. 197 (1 Apr. 1282).

the extent of the problem facing him. Still, the outcome was far from certain, particularly for the rebels for whom the achievement of a favourable outcome necessitated the use of strong-arm tactics. Despite the adherence to the cause of the queen and the infantes, bringing kings to book was not something to which Spaniards were much accustomed. The English were better at that. As for deposing them, they had not done that for almost four hundred years. So those present were unsure how to proceed. But perhaps the bishops would know. They were sure to, particularly since it was through their pulpits that any changes would be made known in the country. Time and again churchmen had protested at the king's mistreatment of them. It was even rumoured that it was because of reports received from the exiled bishops that the pope had refused the king the imperial title.

Even so, there were some at Valladolid who were reluctant to make the final break, most notably the bishops of Burgos and Palencia, Fernando de Covarrubias and Juan Alfonso de Molina. In view of the staunch Alfonsine sympathies of the archbishop of Seville and the absence abroad of those of Toledo and Compostela, these were the kingdom's senior prelates *in situ* and, more than that, the first was a member of the influential Franciscan order, and the other the uncle of D. María de Molina, Sancho's future wife. When therefore the king's brothers the Infantes Pedro and Juan 'suddenly and unexpectedly' broke into their quarters on 22 April and required them to wait upon the infante in order to subscribe a sentence depriving the king of authority to rule, they refused to do so. The matter was 'one most arduous and requiring careful consideration', they protested. When threatened with death if they did not comply, however, comply they did, though having been informed of the three articles on which the king was held to be culpable, they absented themselves from publication of the sentence ('if sentence it can be called') and in a confusing narrative protested *inter alia* that if their seals were found to be appended to the instrument that would be because they had been affixed either unbeknownst to them or under duress. Furthermore, since 'a curia for the purpose had not been summoned' (that being something only the king could do), they dissociated themselves from any involvement in Alfonso's *de facto* deprivation or Sancho's election, nomination to or assumption of the kingdom.[76]

From the heavy-handedness evident on 22 April it is evident that the infante was not winning all the arguments. Over the weekend of 2–4 May, though, the assembly experienced a change of temper. On Saturday the 2nd, some forty Cluniac, Cistercian and Premonstratensian abbots of the monasteries

[76]   Linehan, *History*, 509; Pereda Llarena, 237–41.

of León and Castile, having been summoned by the infante 'by general edict', while continuing to record all the kingdoms of which Alfonso X was king, entered into a 'unity and brotherhood' for the purpose of . . . praying for one another.[77] By the Monday a firmer note was being struck.

In order to observe the process of mutiny developing it is necessary here to slow the narrative down to walking pace. For by the Monday the Leonese contingent had formed a group of its own, seven of the Saturday monasteries having defected to combine with another fourteen of their national colleagues. With no Castilians in view,[78] it was headed by five Leonese bishops, one of them that model civil servant D. Suero Pérez for whom the king was now merely the 'most illustrious lord Alfonso'. The bishop of Zamora's defection represented a resounding vote of no confidence in the man whom just two days before he had described as 'king of Castile, León, Toledo, Galicia, Seville, Córdoba, Murcia etc.'[79] By now he and his colleagues were agreeing to meet biennially in the defence of their liberties and immunities. As the day wore on, newcomers attached themselves to the cause, literally attached themselves by their signatures and seals to what quite suddenly they had persuaded themselves was the final life-raft destined for the harbour of political salvation.

The process can be followed almost by the hour.[80] In an attempt, as prudent as it was futile, to secure the support of the other mendicant order after its leaders had associated themselves with the two reluctant bishops, on the same day Queen Violant prevailed upon her rebel son to take the Dominicans under his protection.[81] On the next Sancho made a gift, to be made effective after the queen's death, of the churches of Moura, Serpa and Mourão 'and of all other places belonging to these castles' to Fernán Pérez, prior of the Hospitallers. Within the year Alfonso would assign the same properties to the Infanta Beatriz, the offspring of his early affair, now

---

[77] *MHE*, II, 67–8; Fernández Martín, 9, preferring the date the 3rd; Linehan, 'El cuatro de mayo', 155.

[78] Significantly perhaps, it was the bishops of Palencia and Burgos, together with their colleague of Zamora, whom the Silos annalist particularly mentioned in his account of these events: Lomax, 'Crónica inédita', 333. Certainly the absence of any corresponding declaration by the Castilian episcopate cannot be attributed to vacancies in the Castilian sees at this date: González Jiménez, *Diplomatario andaluz*, no. 501.

[79] *MHE*, II, 67. Ballesteros could not believe that the bishop was amongst the conspirators (*Alfonso X*, 584), despite the fact that (*pace* O'Callaghan, *Learned King*, 262) it was almost thirty years since he had acted as royal notary for León.

[80] Linehan, 'El cuatro de mayo', 159–61, for an analysis of the process on the basis of three surviving engrossments of the agreement.

[81] Madrid, AHN, Clero, carp. 3501/1; Pereda Llarena, 238. The Dominican bishops remained faithful to the king to the end: Hernández & Linehan, 240 n. 103.

Figure 2 May 1282. The Zamora copy of the instrument of allegiance of the bishops and abbots of the Leonese Church to the rebel Infante Sancho. The plethora of seals and the signatures squeezed onto the document (invisible here) graphically illustrate the urgency of the prelates' anxiety to dissociate themselves from their rightful king.

Archivo Diocesano de Zamora, 13/23. Reproduced by permission.

queen-mother of Portugal and estranged from *her* son, and with them the kingdom of Niebla in the extreme south-west.[82] Castile-León was now divided from top to bottom.

The two bishops who had been taken so much by surprise remembered three accusations being levied against Alfonso, which Alfonso's great-grandson, the Count of Barcelos, described as follows: the unlawful killing of the Infante Fadrique, Simon Ruiz de los Cameros 'and others', depriving the *fijos dalgo* and *concejos* of their *fueros*, and ruination of the land by taxation and the issue of bad money. For these failings the king was deprived

[82]   Ayala Martínez, *Libro de privilegios*, 584; *As Gavetas*, IX, 489–95; Linehan, 'Conquista de Sevilla', 240–2.

of his judicial, executive and fiscal functions.[83] The indictment was read out by D. Manuel and concluded with a call for Sancho to replace him on the throne. To this the *alcalde mayor* of Toledo, Diego Alfonso, responded that although on behalf of all he approved everything that had been said, 'if the infante agreed, it seemed to him an honest thing that during his father's lifetime he should not be called king.'[84] The infante did so agree and, while his father lived, scrupulously refrained from describing himself as anything other than his 'eldest son and heir'. But meanwhile, says the Chronicle, he granted petitioners 'whatever they demanded'.[85]

In theory at least there was a substantial difference between deposition and deprivation of the exercise of government, a difference that had been demonstrated in 1245 when Sancho II of Portugal had fallen foul of Rome, but although at the time men took refuge in the pretence, and albeit well-informed modern historians of the reign have wavered, deposition was what it amounted to. That is what the author of the Silos annals actually called it[86] and how less punctilious contemporaries doubtless viewed it.[87] The case of the king of Portugal had been in Castilian minds for almost a decade,[88] providing, it seems, something of a bench-mark. However, Castile was not beholden to the Roman Church, as Portugal was – and arguably Aragón.[89] Anyway, as soon as the French king gave him leave, the French pope would declare for Alfonso and against Pedro. And then what would happen? Although the king was already in his sixty-first year in April 1282 (the same

[83]   Lindley Cintra, 512. Thus, very summarily and without reference to the judicial murders, *CAX*, c. 76. In another version of the *Crónica de 1344*, cit. Catalán, *La Estoria de España*, 12 (and corresponding to Jofré de Loaisa's account, *Crónica*, c. 28), Alfonso was further charged with having disinherited the *fijosdalgo* of both kingdoms, their citizens and municipalities, in return for which he was himself deprived of his cities and strongholds and denied entry to them, and was alleged to have killed 'many others'.

[84]   Lindley Cintra, 512–13.

[85]   *CAX*, c. 76. The two alleged exceptions are both late copies: Estal, 'Documentos', 119; Ayala Martínez, 'Monarquía', 460 n. 160.

[86]   Lomax, 'Crónica inédita', 333. (The alleged entry in 'Anales Toledanos III', 175, is an editorial error: Catalán & Jerez, 553–4; cf. *Crónica*, ed. González Jiménez, 237 n. 375).

[87]   Thus González Jiménez: 'El motivo de la convocatoria – la deposición del rey legítimo (. . .); la deposición o, mejor, la inhabilitación del rey legítimo (. . .). A la hora de la deposición . . .': ibid., 223–4 n. 337.

[88]   Above, 172.

[89]   For the curious notion that Castile was a papal fief and that the 'ecclesiastical organization of the districts liberated after [the battle of Las Navas in] 1212' was thereby 'greatly facilitated': Ullmann, *Short History*, 214–15. Cf. the declaration of the jurists of the Castilian court when Diego López de Haro attempted to appeal from the king's court to the pope's *c*.1306, that 'the king and his kingdoms were exempt from the Roman Church . . . and (. . .) always had been': *CFIV*, cap. 13 (p. 139b).

age as Alfonso IX and two years older than Alfonso VIII when they died) there could be no knowing how long he might last. The whole issue was, as the bishops of Burgos and Palencia had stated, 'one most arduous and requiring careful consideration'. The Infante Sancho needed to keep all options open.

We may be reasonably sure that his advisors had those options in mind. With both France and England having a particular interest in Castile, European public opinion could not be easily flouted. True, Alfonso X was not an anointed ruler, which perhaps made it marginally easier for those of his bishops who did so to square their consciences to parting company with their king, even though he was king 'by the grace of God'.[90] Yet the issue of hierarchy still mattered, and to no one more than to the infante who, in order to avoid incurring obligations akin to those of a godson, as well as to distance himself from a matrimonial alliance designed to prejudice his place in the succession, had refused in 1269 to be knighted by Fernando de la Cerda.[91] Despite the exhaustive treatment accorded to the topic in the second of the *Siete Partidas*, to Alfonso, curiously, such obligations were nugatory. Although in his will he denounced the kings of England and Portugal for abandoning him, nowhere did he refer to the duties they owed him because he had knighted them.[92]

As the infante's supporters departed from Valladolid the euphoria of the occasion was already evaporating. For all of six years Sancho had shared the government of the country with his father. But throughout that time his father had always had the last word. Now Sancho had declared himself in charge. The currency was in chaos. At Valladolid he had promised a return to the golden age of Alfonso VIII and Fernando III. So the 'wise men who understood about money' were called in, and their advice was to allow the national currency to separate into its local elements, *burgaleses* for Castile and *leoneses* for León.[93] Antonio Ballesteros, writing in the age of Franco when questions of the currency and the succession were so much more efficiently handled, dismissed D. Sancho's attempted reforms as a piece of democratic posturing, and in Burgos itself, the united kingdom's

[90]   Linehan, 'Accession of Alfonso X'; idem, *History*, 449–53.
[91]   Above, 171. In 1332 the involvement of any human agent was avoided by having Alfonso XI knighted by a mechanical statue of Santiago. Might such possibilities explain Alfonso X's interest in the Arabic treatise on automata translated by Isḥāq ibn Sīd in May 1266?: Linehan, 'Alfonso XI'; Vernet, 'Un texto árabe'.
[92]   Part. 2. 21. 16; Linehan, 'Alfonso XI', 130–3. *Pace* Salvador Martínez (*Alfonso X*, 503), even less did Alfonso claim such a hold over the king of Aragón, which was in any circumstances unthinkable.
[93]   '. . . and *pepiones* and *sallamanqueses* as they used to have in the time of King Alfonso, my great-great-grandfather, and King Fernando, my grandfather': E. González Díez, no. 118.

mercantile capital, the *concejo* prohibited the minting of the new money – to the infante's feigned astonishment at such defiance of the popular will.[94] The fact was that by feigning concern for popular sentiment, and in particular by fostering the *hermandades*, the infante had unleashed the furies, while meanwhile having either to govern, and do so by himself, or risk being judged unfit to govern at all.

The king's response to the Valladolid *pronunciamiento* was tremendous but deceptive. On the face of it, the privileges he continued to issue were witnessed by almost the entire political community. But the roll-call of witnesses is misleading. In mid-July, for example, the transfer issued at Seville of the *villa* of Montemolín from Pedro Núñez, Master of Santiago, to the *concejo* of Seville was confirmed by all the grandees, other than his rebel son, the queen, and the said Master. Ostensibly, not only D. Manuel, the proposer of Alfonso's deposition, but also the masters of the other military orders as well as all prelates not in exile, including Suero Pérez of Zamora, were in attendance. In reality, pitifully few of them were. In particular, the king's entire family had defected, though before the end one or other of his sons would shamefacedly come creeping back. The list of *confirmantes* attached to the privilege was therefore as much a fiction as was Sancho's claim to be acting on his father's behalf, and scarcely less of one than Alfonso's delusion that Pedro Núñez and the brothers of his Order alone were responsible for persuading 'his lineage' to abandon him.[95]

Historians have been misled because that is what Alfonso wanted. When issuing instructions to restrict abuses of the practice of ecclesiastical asylum, he claimed to be doing so only after consulting 'our brothers and our sons, (...) the bishops and the Masters and other good men of the Orders', though with few if any of them can he have had any dealings during the previous four months.[96] He was deprived of the support of his wife, 'his lineage', and,

---

[94]   Ballesteros, *Alfonso X*, 975; Infante to *concejo*, 4 June 1282: 'and I cannot believe that you could have ordained the like, particularly after everyone had demanded the change at the cortes I held.' Two days later he wrote again in similar vein but omitting the reference to the cortes: E. González Díez, nos. 120, 122.

[95]   González Jiménez, *Diplomatario andaluz*, no. 501. In that author's judgement, by this means the king may have been providing a causeway along which the rebels might climb back on board: *Alfonso X* (1993), 138, whence Salvador Martínez, *Alfonso X*, 481–2. Yet the name of the bishop of Zamora should suffice to raise doubts. Not for decades had lists of *confirmantes* attached to privileges provided reliable accounts of those present at their granting. Only in September 1283 did Alfonso's chancery provide a credible (and meagre) list of the loyalists: *Diplomatio andaluz*, nos. 515, 520. Cf. Hernández & Linehan, 240 n. 103 and, for the alignment of the military orders, Josserand, 504–6.

[96]   Rodríguez Molina, no. 42 (21 July 1282).

as he was to complain in his will, of the kings of England, Portugal and Aragón – and of the last of these in particular since with his fleet poised to make landfall in Sicily nothing could have been more untimely for Pedro than a Marīnid assault on the kingdom of Valencia. Accordingly, a fortnight after the Valladolid *coup* and little more than a year since the treaty of Agreda, he had written offering Alfonso, and Sancho too for that matter, safe haven in Aragón should it become necessary and, with the la Cerda children in his custody, disingenuously declaring a position of strict neutrality.[97] Whereupon Alfonso turned to the emir of Morocco, Abū Yūsuf, for help. This the emir was glad to supply for the tactical reason that by backing the weaker side he was extending the struggle and undermining the kingdom, as symbolized by his receipt of the crown of the kingdom pledged to him as surety for a loan of a hundred thousand dinars.

This extreme, which led to his being represented as the modern counterpart of Count Julian, the man held responsible for ushering in the invaders in 711, was one to which none of Alfonso's predecessors had been reduced.[98] Did his father's deathbed admonitions now return to haunt him?[99] During the melancholy summer of 1282 he had ample opportunity to consider his position. It was a summer that continued until the first Saturday of November, by which time the emir had returned to Morocco for the time being and the king had recovered the use of his legs. As recorded in his will, he was now able to walk and ride again, which was as much *lo mas* (what mattered most) in 1282 as the prospect of empire had been ten years earlier.[100] Then on 8 November, six months after the infante had shown his hand, the old man retaliated by publishing that will and calling down divine vengeance upon his son.[101]

After protesting his absolute orthodoxy, the king proceeded to provide a narrative account of the perfidy of his thankless child and his treachery 'against God, us, all our lineage, Spain, and the whole world', contrasting

---

[97]   *MHE*, II, no. 208.5.
[98]   Hijano Villegas, 139.
[99]   Ibn Abū Zar', II, 636; Ibn Khaldūn, *Hist. des Berbères*, IV. 107.
[100]   Solalinde, *Antología*, 230.
[101]   The dates traditionally assigned to the will and the codicil are both incorrect, with serious consequences for the narrative of the end of the reign. Ballesteros (*Alfonso X*, 1000), followed by Salvador Martínez, in so many respects the Ballesteros of his generation (*Alfonso X*, p. 529), give the date of the former as November 1283 rather than November 1282. Moreover, the Latin version of the codicil reveals a number of differences in respect of its Spanish form, suggesting that some changes had been made to its text between 10 January and the date of its Latin translation, 20 April 1284: Hernández, 'Alfonso X in Andalucía', 295–6; Daumet, 'Les testaments'; below 201.

his own paternal indulgence towards Sancho with Sancho's dereliction of all filial duty. Accordingly, the infante was declared 'accursed of God, the Virgin and all the celestial court' and pronounced defamed, and he and his succession disinherited for ever ('por siempre jamás'). From the kings of Europe Alfonso has had nothing but fine words, and from the pope, despite all his and his lineage's sacrifices for the Faith, nothing at all. His *señorío mayor* (his 'major lordship', the kingdoms of Castile and León) he bequeathed to Alfonso de la Cerda with reversion to the king of France, 'because he is directly descended from the Emperor of Spain (that is, Alfonso VII)' and, like the testator was the great-grandson of Alfonso VIII, resulting in the permanent union of the kingdoms of Castile and France in a marriage of valour and riches under a single ruler with the Roman Church acting as guarantor of the settlement.[102] On the same day, in a carefully choreographed imperial act, 'presiding as judge' and speaking from a decorated throne (in Latin of course for dissemination abroad), the king particularized further concerning his son's enormities and the proceedings of the Valladolid Cortes ('if it merit the name of cortes') which had purported, without any semblance of legality, to deprive him of his kingdom. In conclusion he announced his dreadful sentence to the world.[103]

As he toured the country 'preaching against him', Sancho had called him mad and leprous, Alfonso recalled.[104] If so, it must have been in order to demonstrate that Alfonso was not competent to govern; that he was 'useless'. Meanwhile, the combination of facial disfigurement and suppurating legs rendered the king's condition increasingly wretched. Portraits of him in products of his *scriptorium* had regularly shown him as a young, vigorous man. Now, on the first folio of his translation of the book on chess, which was in progress in 1283, we see him with his left eye blanked out, as though by glaucoma,[105] and in the introduction to the text the game is recommended for women, for men who are old and feeble, or in prison,

[102]   Solalinde, *Antología*, 224–33; Martin, 'Alphonse X maudit son fils', 155–65. The eternal ('para siempre') consequences for a traitor's male descendants had been summarized in *Part.* 7. 2. 2.

[103]   Zurita, *Indices*, 173. The combination of the formula 'nobis non citato, non monito, non confesso, non convicto (. . .), non a iudice, immo per hostes & conspiratores', the six-month period between the Valladolid 'cortes' and the Seville commination (in accordance with the time allowed for appeal to the imperial court) and the language of canonical procedure ('sedente pro tribunali') suggests a rich mixture in the king's mind. Cf. *Part.* 3. 8. 7.

[104]   Zurita, *Indices*, 172. 'Preaching' is the term used by the Chronicle of the Infante D. Juan as he recruited support for Sancho: *CAX*, c. 76; Peters, 116–34.

[105]   For treatment of which condition Ibn Sahula's Eagle had recommended a salve made of equal parts of grouse gall, olive oil and honey: Loewe, 320.

or . . . 'who cannot ride'. The instructions for checking the king ('which is the best piece on the board'; Alfonso, be it remembered, had already lost his queen) are surely also autobiographical. For this 'is how you affront him *con derecho* (properly)', while mating him 'is a move of great dishonour, equivalent to defeat or death'.[106]

More or less immured in Seville, and dependent on a shrivelled establishment of men not his *naturales*, in his post-imperial *tristesse* Alfonso was the 'miserable old man', the 'mezquino viejo' as the Chronicle reports he described himself when found weeping at the (false) report that D. Sancho was dead.[107] So striking was the resemblance to King Lear that it comes as no surprise to find that his *General estoria* workforce were familiar with the British king's misfortunes, as related in Geoffrey of Monmouth's *History of the Kings of Britain*.[108] The attention he received from his Cordelia figure, his bastard daughter Beatriz exiled by her son the king of Portugal, adds poignancy to the possibility, though amongst Shakespeare's exemplars from antiquity with any degree of self-knowledge perhaps Cleopatra would have been no less appropriate a precursor.

> 'Against the blown rose may they stop their nose,
> That kneel'd unto the buds.'[109]

By some the hauntingly melancholic *cantiga* whose author imagines himself escaping from the scorpions' nest and, sailing in his 'fine galleon' 'along the shore, peddling oil and flour', has been read as an autobiographical account of the king's state of mind at this stage of his career.[110] Yet the intellect remained as sharp as ever and forever voracious for ancient instances of modern treachery. It is to this final period of his life that the so-called 'Versión crítica' of the early part of the *Estoria de España*, with

---

[106] Cómez Ramos, 'Retrato', 38–9; Steiger, 4, 10, 386. The 'Historia hasta 1288 dialogada' (p. 17) tells the story of a game of chess staged by Alfonso's *ricos homes* in 1275 the outcome of which persuaded him to return home from Provence.

[107] For the increasing proportion of Portuguese nobles in attendance during his final months: González, *Alfonso X*, 354; *CAX*, c. 77.

[108] Kasten, 98n. The letter printed by Ortiz de Zúñiga in 1677 lamenting his misfortunes, pathetic though it is, looks suspect if only on account of its date ('fecha en la mi sola leal Cibdad de Sevilla, á los treinta años de el mio regnado, y el primero de mis cuitas'): *Annales*, I, 274–5.

[109] Or, as Ptolemy of Lucca, expressed it, more prosaically: 'so constrained was he by his son that, having in his youth outshone all other Westerners, he died in utmost poverty and misery': *Hist. ecclesiastica*, col. 1178.

[110] Lapa, no. 10; Snow, 'Satirical poetry', 123. Cf. Paredes, 210–11.

its insistently moralizing interventions, what Fernández-Ordóñez has called 'the radicalization of the Alfonsine model', is to be dated. In this version of the History the pretensions of the territorial nobility are systematically cut down to size and allusion to contemporary events allowed to intrude upon the previously serene account of the national past.[111] Though evident in all his works, the king's perfectionism, his obsession with revising and recasting are here observable at their most developed. Here, and nowhere else other than in the *Cantigas*, the authorial 'I' rather than the majestic 'We' is employed.[112] Of particular interest to the old king was the theme of treason in the blood. The tendency to treason was inherited. It was a genetic defect like . . . leprosy. The notion, derived from the 'wise ancients who understood things aright' had been promoted in the *Partidas*. It had been apparent in the letter of 1273 to Fernando de la Cerda in which Alfonso had derived rueful satisfaction from the fact that Diego López de Haro, the great-grandfather of one of the rebels of the day and the man on account of whose cowardice the battle of Alarcos had been lost, was remembered as Diego 'the Good'.[113] Now it took wings. The king discovered, or thought he had, that the dean of Seville, Fernán Pérez, who after a lifetime in the royal chancery had defected to D. Sancho was, as well as a sodomite, a descendant of Vellid Adolfo, the regicide who had done Sancho II to death more than two centuries before.[114]

Once he started rootling around for evidences of that sort in the belief that the story of the ancients was the key to the present, there was no end to it. The Old Testament for example, and therefore the earlier books of the *General Estoria*, abounded with examples. The treatise on royal taboos which interrupts the *Estoria*'s text after the anointing of Saul, described as 'a rule which the children of Israel observed as a law or decree to maintain the rights and honours of their kings', was particularly suggestive, with its description of the custom whereby, whether or not he has inherited a law-code from his father, a new king has his own law-book ('libro de ley') compiled, and its insistence on the ruler's entitlement while on campaign to appropriate the property and rights of individuals 'for the king is the law and the *fuero* and all the kingdom': the corollary of the apophthegm pronounced in *Estoria de España* apropos the death of Visigothic Spain

---

[111]   *Versión crítica*, ed. Fernández-Ordóñez; eadem, 'Variación', 49–61.

[112]   Eadem, 'Taller de las "Estorias"', 62–5.

[113]   *Partida*, 7. 2, *De las trayciones*, proem.: 'So ill did the wise ancient regard it [treason] that they likened it to leprosy (*la gafedat*)'; Rodgers, lines 109–14. This madness ('locura') was in such people's blood: 'viene de linage que siempre perdieron quanto avian & por esta rrazon murieron mal andantes' (lines 183–6).

[114]   Linehan, *Spanish Church*, 231.

that 'all men are formed in the likeness of their king and resemble him'.[115]
Likewise, the rebelliousness of the sons of King David in the First Book
of Kings became indistinguishable from that of his own sons, albeit this
parallel did perhaps provide some reason for optimism.[116] And in the same
spirit, at this late stage, the king embarked on the composition of the
Setenario, reading history backwards and celebrating both Seville, the city
that almost alone had remained loyal to him, and the father whose hopes
he had disappointed.[117]

To take just one example, as recently as 1274 Toledo had been accorded
the accolade of being 'the place where of old emperors were crowned'.
Since then though there had been the so-called Cortes of Valladolid at which
one of Toledo's *alcaldes* had acted as the spokesman of those in favour of
sending Alfonso X into early retirement. Now therefore it was Seville that
was remembered as 'of old the residence and dwelling place of emperors
and where they were crowned'.[118]

Whether or not as a result of the sentence on Sancho, by the spring of
1283 Murcia had declared its allegiance to Alfonso, as had the Masters of
two of the military orders, and the ecclesiastics of León and Galicia, meeting at Benavente, were having to ask the infante to do 'as he promised' in
respect of protecting churches and monasteries and restrain his forces from
harassing both the secular and regular clergy.[119] A return to a golden age
had been promised, but, as sometimes happens on such occasions, reality
proved more leaden. Things were going badly for the infante in the south,
with the Marīnids trouncing his ally the king of Granada, and there was
talk of truce with the old king. Having nailed his colours to a popular mast,
however, the infante felt himself constrained from acting 'other than with
your counsel and that of other good men of all the land', as he wrote to

[115]   Above, 138.
[116]   Linehan, *History*, 493–5. Like Alfonso, David had been thirty years old when he began
to reign, 'and he reigned for forty years': *GE*, II.ii.358b$_{26-28}$.
[117]   The dating of *Setenario* is controversial, Gómez Redondo for example thinking it to belong
to the beginning of the reign. In view of the laborious rehearsal of the arguments provided
by that author they need not be rehearsed here (cf. Martin, 'De nuevo sobre la fecha del
Setenario'). Suffice it to say that, contrary to Martin ('Alphonse X ou la science politique',
79) and Salvador Martínez (*Alfonso X*, 299–300), the case for a late date occurred to
Linehan ('Politics of Piety', 388 n. 15) and Craddock ('*Setenario*', 451 n. 22) independently.
Programmed as they are always to look for *influences*, the notion of the same idea striking
simultaneously in different places is something that some medievalists have still to come to
terms with.
[118]   *Setenario*, 19; above, 122.
[119]   González Jiménez, *Alfonso X*, 354–5; Linehan, 'Conquista de Sevilla', 242; *MHE*, II,
no. 220.

the *concejo* of Burgos at the beginning of April.[120] And then the moment passed, and that autumn the other side secured the initiative when Pope Martin IV, no doubt influenced by knowledge of Alfonso's changed (i.e. pro-French) stance regarding the succession, came out strongly for him, directing all his subjects to reaffirm their obedience to him, excommunicating Sancho and his supporters, and interdicting their territories.[121]

In the previous March, with Apulia and Calabria joining Sicily in welcoming the Aragonese liberator and his admiral Ruggiero di Loria, the pope had declared Pedro deposed, ordered Philippe of France to invade Aragón, and awarded the kingdom and county of Barcelona to Philippe's son, Charles of Valois, though with the stipulation, in contrast to Alfonso X's recent dispositions, that Aragón-Catalonia should never be held by the ruler of France, Castile or England.[122] So the disinherited Infante Sancho, whose resistance to his father's bequest of Castile and León to the king of France had already qualified for mention in dispatches, was now driven into even closer embrace with his deposed Aragonese uncle, the intended quarry of the pope's French-led crusade.[123]

Though the pope's injunctions made not the slightest impression on the Castilian bishops[124] (so much for papal jurisdiction), they enraged the infante. By slaughtering more than four hundred people at Talavera[125] (so much for the infante's moral indignation at the elimination of poor Uncle Fadrique) Sancho had already shown what he was capable of. Now he threatened anyone found in possession of the papal letters with a bloody end (as did his uncle in Aragón) and vowed to appeal to the next pontiff or to a general council against the 'aggravation that the pope [was causing] his land'.[126] On being required to declare for Alfonso, the archbishop of Toledo, who had been equivocating his way around Provence for some time, appealed to Rome on the grounds that to do so would be

---

[120]   E. González Díez, no. 128.
[121]   Bull 'Insurgentis fremitus' (9 Aug. 1283): Hernández & Linehan, 234–5.
[122]   Zurita, IV. 41.
[123]   Ibid., IV. 36; Soldevila, *Hist. de Catalunya*, 358–9. For his determination that 'the French should not enter the land', Sancho is twice acclaimed in the 'Historia hasta 1288 dialogada', 17, 24–5.
[124]   In March 1283 the archbishop of Seville had been in attendance together with two Dominican bishops, the hated foreigner Fredolo of Oviedo, and six sees were recorded as vacant. By January 1284 the only change was an increase in the number of vacancies: Linehan, 'Conquista de Sevilla', 241–2; González Jiménez, *Diplomatario andaluz*, no. 520.
[125]   *CAX*, c. 77. Not even the author of the *Crónica* attempted to extenuate the brutality of the act.
[126]   Ibid.; Vincke, no. 24 (May 1283).

to expose his friends and relations to revenge at the infante's hands, and resumed his equivocation.[127]

As the infante entered his second winter as the 'eldest son and heir of the most noble don Alfonso', pressure was mounting. Already in July 1282, when the *concejo* of Segovia, speaking on its own behalf and that of 'the towns of the bishopric of Segovia', attached itself to the cause in the person of the Master of the Order of Santiago, it was made clear that it was not only the king that they had in their sights but also 'the Infante D. Sancho and other kings who come after them'. If any of these should infringe the 'privilege that D. Sancho granted at Valladolid' because they had been 'deprived of their fueros and mistreated' (their grievances had already become something of a mantra), then let them be aware that they would 'defend themselves and their *fueros*, customs, uses, liberties, freedoms, privileges and charters' against not only the infante etc. but also 'every man in the world'.[128] By the spring of 1283, royal authority had effectively devolved upon the *hermandades*.

Aragón Alone

In Aragón meanwhile papal fulminations contributed significantly to the disquiet caused by the domestic consequences of Pedro III's foreign adventures. In June 1283 word reached Pedro of 'conjurations' in the town of Sos. By the following February the word 'ermandat' had become part of the language of discourse.[129] As at Valladolid in the previous year, the gathering at Tarazona in September 1283 protested about *fueros* being trodden underfoot. But at Tarazona there was no heir apparent to make the complaint his own. The fact that the land was beset by French invaders and papal sanctions the Aragonese nobility regarded not as a matter of national concern but attributable to personal and family ambition. As in 1264, they therefore refused to provide the king with military assistance, instead demanding confirmation of their privileges and liberties. And as in 1264 their demands fell on deaf ears. Having recently returned from what was to have been an armed contest between him and his Angevin adversary and equal numbers of knights which, although cancelled (Bordeaux, 1 June

---

[127]   Hernández & Linehan, 232–43, 454–5. Gonzálvez's report to the contrary derives from his misdating of the record: *Hombres y libros*, 359–60.
[128]   Asenjo González, 83–4. The bishop of Segovia, D. Rodrigo, an Alfonsine loyalist, was abroad: Hernández & Linehan, 238.
[129]   González Antón, II, 105–6, 154.

1283), was to earn him a universal reputation in chivalric circles, the king
was perhaps euphoric.[130] He was also at pains to bring peace to Castile.[131]
But the malcontents were not impressed by his hawkish determination
to brazen things out. Like the Valladolid malcontents they hankered after
a Golden Age and restitution of their 'manifest and notorious' losses at the
hands of the last two kings and discussed openly the possibility of expelling
Pedro from the kingdom and replacing him with his son, the Infant Alfonso.
So far, so much alike.[132]

By confirming privileges granted to the chapter of Salamanca by Alfonso
VIII and Fernando III the *hermandad* of the kingdoms of León and Galicia
celebrated at Benavente four months previously had assumed quasi-royal
powers. Developments in Aragón provided further evidence of a world
turned upside-down. For a cortes summoned by *ricos hombres* was no more
of a cortes than one summoned by a disaffected infante, and initially there
were some signs of tentativeness akin to that which had marked the early
stages of Castilian insurgency, with the *concejos* of Borja and Magallón,
for example, asking the king how they ought to respond to the nobility's
instruction to send representatives to Zaragoza.[133] But in the event the curdled
resentment of decades secured the king's submission to the Aragonese
'Union' whose programme of demands consisted not of constitutional or
national issues but rather of local and particularly fiscal grievances and the
aggregated complaints of municipal memory: a miscellany of customs and
prerogatives confirmed by the 'General Privilege' and the establishment of
the *Justicia* as mediator. In the circumstances in which he found himself
Pedro had little option but to comply, though little immediate good it did
him other than in enabling him to resist the recurrent demand for the *fueros*
of Aragón to be imposed on the kingdom of Valencia.[134]

The very different tenor of the king's relationship with the Catalans was
reflected in the conduct of the Corts of Barcelona (1283–4). So too was
the degree of Catalan commitment to his Mediterranean undertakings,

[130] Desclot, cc. 99–104 (Critchlow, II, 109–22); Zurita, IV. 32; Soldevila, *Hist. de Catalunya*, 359–61.
[131] He is reported to have visited Logroño and other places in Castile for this purpose: *Gesta comitum Barcinonensium*, 74. Cf. *CAX*, c. 77 (p. 64ab) where Pedro's main purpose in being in Castile was survival. Sancho was at Logroño in mid-June: Serrano, no. lxxxiii.
[132] Zurita, IV. 38, 45; González Antón, I, 52–66 (nowhere in whose lengthy monograph is the possibility considered that developments in Castile might have influenced, as distinct from paralleling [p. 348], events in Aragón).
[133] Martín Martín, *Documentos de Salamanca*, no. 391; González Antón, I, 83 ('poco regulares Cortes'), II, 122.
[134] Ibid., I, 70–101.

prompting Soldevila to point yet again to the contrast between the nimble, clever, urban Catalans and their country cousins, the lumbering Aragonese feudatories, as well as to remark on the paradox that it was 'the king so wedded to personal government and to the strengthening of his own author-ity free of all parliamentary trammels who was responsible for establishing the bases of [Catalan] representative constitutionalism and the role of the Corts in the life of the state.' As well as promulgating the constitutions *Una vegada l'any*, binding Pedro and his successors to convene annual meetings of the General Corts comprising members of the three estates, and *Volem, statuïm*, entrusting that consultative body with legislative powers to be exercised in concert with the king, by the decree *Recognoverunt proceres* the 1283 assembly confirmed such customs and privileges of the city as the city desired to have confirmed, 116 in number.[135]

Having already disposed of the *señorío mayor*, in a codicil of January 1284 Alfonso X distributed the territories still under his control, the kingdoms of Murcia, Seville and Badajoz, amongst the few members of his family who had either remained loyal or had returned to his allegiance (subject always to the consent of the king of France, of course).[136] In distinguish-ing between the *señorío mayor* and other places of more recent acquisition Alfonso was treating the entirety of the royal fisc as a partible inheritance available for distribution within the family in a manner reminiscent of the actions of Sancho III of Navarre in 1035, Alfonso VII, Emperor of León, in 1157, and Jaime I of Aragón in 1276. In reverting to ancient Navarrese, Leonese and indeed Aragonese practice not only was he violating the com-mitment to the principle of territorial integrity that once he had shared with his son and which inspired the contemporaneous revision of his national history, he was also ignoring Nuño González de Lara's defence of the integrity of the *corona*. Hence perhaps his ultimate reluctance to confirm the bequest of Seville and Badajoz to the Infante D. Juan when he learnt that, despite rumours to the contrary, D. Sancho had not preceded him to the grave.[137] With Alfonso himself stubbornly refusing to die, the rumour that Sancho had instead succumbed strengthened the case for some sort

---

[135] Zurita, IV. 40; Soldevila, *Hist. de Catalunya*, 361–6.

[136] Solalinde, *Antología*, 233–42 (esp. pp. 238–9). The Spanish and the Latin texts of this so-called second will reveal some curious differences: while the former states (p. 239) that 'all France and all Spain were once ('antiguamente') in Christian hands and in the lordship of our lineage and by our sins were then lost', the Latin text refers not to 'all France' but 'all Africa': Daumet, 'Les testaments', p. 93.

[137] Lacarra, 'Lento predominio', 69; 362–3, 367–8; Fernández-Ordóñez, *Versión crítica*, 174; *CAX*, cc. 19 (above, 159), 77.

of settlement. The father whose son had denounced him as mad, leprous, false and perjured might not have been expected to shed tears at news of his decease. But the report is that he did, and the report is that of the Chronicle said to have been written in the other party's interests. Here Alfonso laments the loss of the 'best man of his lineage'.

Now the king knew his Bible and its cadences. There had been echoes of it in the letter he had earlier sent his elder son.[138] And the signs are that the rebellion of David's sons, Adonijah. Absalom, and his brothers, 'doing those things they do to kings', was not far from his mind.[139] Assuming that the king's tears are faithfully reported, we may therefore picture him reading David's lament for his dead son – 'O my son Absalom, my son, my son, Absalom! Would God I had died for thee, O Absalom, my son, my son!' (2 Sam. 18:33) – and seeing the dead infante staring him in the face: sentiments that combined with the further consideration voiced by him that it would have been easier for him to have dealt with one man than with the assembly of *ricos homes* and masters of military orders that D. Sancho had unleashed.[140] At any event, on learning that *his* Absalom had recovered (the Chronicle continues), as well as suspending his dismemberment of the kingdom, Alfonso 'stated before witnesses that he was pardoning D. Sancho his son and heir because what he had done he had done out of youthful high spirits (*con mançebia*) (. . .) and, before expiring himself fortified by the rites of Holy Church, ordered charters to this effect sealed with his gold seals to be issued'.[141]

The deathbed reconciliation as recounted by the Chronicle might seem too convenient for the Chronicle's compilers in the 1340s to be credible. However, there is evidence of overtures from the other side to be considered. In November 1283 the infante had summoned his supporters to Palencia to discuss the possibility of 'restoring relations of love and accord between the king my father and me and all others of the land': an initiative brought to nothing by the implacable opposition of his supporters and the death of D. Manuel, the one man of sufficient stature to have engineered a reconciliation.[142]

Ibid., above, 166–7.
[139]   Linehan, *History*, 493. A similar refrain occurs in the admission in the king's will of Nov. 1282 that he had sometimes caused the Infante grief, 'as fathers do to sons': Solalinde, *Antología*, 226.
[140]   ' . . . que no de tantos' (or: 'que de todos'): *CAX*, c. 77; González Jiménez, *Crónica*, 241.
[141]   *CAX*, c. 77; *Gesta comitum Barcinonensium*, 74.
[142]   Ruiz Asencio & Martín Fuertes, no. 2429; Ballesteros, 'Burgos y la rebelión', 187–91.

However, the Chronicle also reports that for some time Beatriz of Portugal and María de Molina had been attempting to mend the rift while, according to a Catalan source, the parties were brought to a 'treaty of love' by the king of Aragón *en route* from Bordeaux.[143] Moreover, just twelve days before the end Alfonso sent the pope a letter, a copy of which, made in the following October, found its way into the English public records. 'Sealed with our small gold seal', this informed Martin IV that 'our very dear son' the infante had been induced into rebellion 'by his juvenile condition rather than willingly' but had now seen the error of his ways and tearfully begged to be restored to his father's favour. This Alfonso, ever the indulgent parent, had granted, 'recognizing the need for sons to be educated by human and divine laws and by their parents' and acknowledging the curious doctrine 'that father and son are the same person'.[144]

In view of D. Sancho's later involvement in the forging of papal letters, a degree of scepticism is also inevitable regarding the authenticity of this communication.[145] But the survival in a contemporary formulary of papal letters of two undated communications to an unnamed king of Castile and his son in which both parties are congratulated on the resolution of their differences, tips the balance.[146] Nor does the fact that Alfonso was dead by the time his letter reached Orvieto detract from their significance. Nor would it have been in Alfonso's interest to encourage the pope to moderate his measures against the infante before a settlement had been reached or to have omitted to inform his son that he was willing to pardon him.[147] But, as Jofré de Loiasa reported, despite all this the king's death on 4 April prevented the completion of the process and in particular the annulment of the curse in a physical embrace of reconciliation.[148] So there followed all the ominous consequences that D. Juan Manuel was later to report. And with powerful forces at work at the papal curia promoting French and la Cerda interests, as the reign of Sancho IV began uncertainties of this sort were bound to be encouraged.

---

[143] *CAX*, c. 77; above, n. 131.

[144] London, National Archives, E36/275 (*Liber munimentorum B*), fo. 157rv (printed Rymer, 640: 23 March 1284). The letter concluded with a tribute to the Roman Church that had sustained him when 'others on whom we had pinned our hopes, instead of assisting, derided us': a very different account from that of his will seventeen months earlier.

[145] Thus Zurita, IV. 47.

[146] Hernández, 'Alfonso X in Andalucía', 298–301; Linehan, 'Conquista de Sevilla', 237, 243–4.

[147] As suggested by O'Callaghan, *Learned King*, 269.

[148] *Crónica*, c. 32.

The Learned King

It remains to attempt some estimate of the man who had just died and the reign that had just ended.

One of nature's optimists once described the period between 1260 and 1290 as 'the most hopeful period of the Middle Ages'.[149] But with Christendom's most learned king espousing the singular doctrine that the interests of the Church of Rome and the king of France would always be identical, with the crown of Castile pawned to the emir of Morocco and its moribund monarch reduced to a single city bearing all too little resemblance to Spain's Rome, it was not so for the kingdom of Castile.[150] On the basis of a rather strained interpretation of the text in Isaiah 18:1, apropos 'the land shadowing with wings, which is beyond the rivers of Ethiopia', in the second year of his reign Alfonso had been identified as Antichrist.[151] It was a parallel which two years before its end many of his bishops would have approved, since by then the description in Isaiah 18:2, of 'a nation scattered and peeled', clearly applied. As it did on Mr Casaubon, time ran out on Alfonso X. There are some now who would say it is less the attention of the historian he requires than that of a forensic psychiatrist.

This he has already received though. Since Mariana described him as a 'king who would have been a great and most prudent king if only he had aspired to self-knowledge', more perhaps has been written about this ruler's personality than the evidence strictly justifies. Was he also schizophrenic (a condition whose very meaning the experts are at odds about)? Or cyclothymic, a disorder manifested in alternations of mood from exhilaration to depression with a tendency to manic depression, and attributed by some historians to another thirteenth-century king whose reign ended in a similar sorry state, namely John of England?[152] To some, the size of what was left of his nose (so far as its size could be established by the investigations on his skull done in 1948) has been thought suggestive of both cyclothymic and cerebrotonic tendencies, indicating an intellectual but inverted and immature personality as well as paternal neglect in the subject's early years.[153]

---

[149]   Southern, *Western Views of Islam*, 65.
[150]   Cf. Engels, 'Idea imperial'.
[151]   Thus the Joachimite Gerard of Borgo San Donnino, reported by Salimbene, *Cronica*, 689 (admittedly even Salibene was sceptical).
[152]   Mariana, XIII. 9, XIV. 7; Socarras, 111–12; Petit-Dutaillis & Guinard, IV.ii, 137.
[153]   Torres González, 110–11, 119–20.

His reputation had preceded him. Two years before he ascended the throne a contemporary noted his erudition 'in all things'. One wonders where he got his genes from; surely not from his prudish father. In the 1580s, three hundred years after the event, the Aragonese chronicler, Jerónimo Zurita, passed sentence on 'a great and most remarkable example of princes whose ambition and lack of judgement divert from the true path of equity and justice.'[154] But this was a view observed across austere territory, and uttered in the reign of Philip II.

Over the course of time Alfonso X's reputation for universal learning has caused some admirers to claim for him literary prowess beyond the capacity of any individual: not only the authorship of both the National and the General History, but also credit for giving Castilian poetry its 'metric rhymed method' well ahead of the Provencaux and the Italians.[155] Yet he was capable of penning some at least of the most exquisite hymns of praise to the Virgin that survive as well as some of the most obscene and imaginative verse conceivable:

> All which apart, the learned dean can do
> Things with his books to which you'd not aspire.
> If, let us say, he finds a lady who
> Is writhing ravaged by St Marcoul's fire,
> What with his manual, tool-kit and his know-how,
> He'll quickly turn her smould'ring ash to snow. How?
> By dousing with his bookish balm, of course, and easing with his
> literary screw.[156]

This was a talent perhaps best reserved for *soldadeiras* who managed to evade the expulsion from court in accordance with the king's decrees and who remained to service (or to fail to service) the dean and his likes.[157] When applied to sacred subjects, as in the burlesque *cantiga* interweaving the Passion of Christ with sexual passion in its relation of the agonies of abstinence suffered by the *soldadeira* as she restrains her partner from bringing her to climax on Good Friday, it achieved a level of profanity and a degree of sacrilege without parallel. 'No liberty grosser than this is imaginable in the use of religious material for other ends', one critic has

---

[154]   Zurita, IV. 15.
[155]   Mondéjar, 457–60, 467, 472; above, 136.
[156]   Lapa, no. 23 (trans. Linehan, 'The King's Touch', 202–3); Márquez Villanueva, 'Lecturas del dean de Cádiz'.
[157]   The most renowned of whom was María Pérez Balteira, perennial butt of the poets' scorn: Menéndez Pidal, *Poesía juglaresca*, 167–9.

ruled.[158] The most repulsive parody in the whole of universal literature, no less, which is how another expert in the genre describes the same exhibit can hardly have contributed much to the poet-king's reputation as a prince imbued with a 'sacred intent to benefit and enrich the churches' and as a 'model of religiosity'.[159] For that matter, it was not as a builder of churches that the Castilian bishops in 1279 regarded him. It was as the man who, by appropriating the third of the tithe reserved for the purpose, prevented churches even from being kept standing, let alone built in the first place.[160]

All this was of a piece with other facets of Alfonso's personality. His so-called blasphemy, the claim that had he been present at the Creation things would have been better arranged, only began to be reflected on later, so will not be considered here.[161] He was not interested in the business of sacral monarchy or in touching for illnesses. For the claims to curative powers made by the anointed monarchs of England and France he gave 'not a rotten fig', an attitude likely to have further alienated the bishops by excluding them from profitable business. As their response to the divisions of 1282 revealed, the military orders also felt excluded. And throughout he indulged that mania for controlling, and for controlling everything, which has been said to have necessitated the adoption of an intelligible vernacular as the means of expressing the directives of government. Although the sumptuary provisions of meetings of the cortes over which he presided were not unprecedented, they were extended by him into areas of activity into which his predecessors had not ventured. What other king, with his territorial nobility in turmoil and while himself preparing for a crucial interview with the Supreme Pontiff, would have responded in kind to a poetical enquiry regarding the definition of licensed entertainers?[162] Even at

[158] Lapa, no. 14; Paredes, 237–9; Scholberg, 86.
[159] Filgueira Valverde, 147. Cf. Mondéjar, 436; Ballesteros, *Alfonso X*, 584.
[160] Linehan, *Spanish Church*, 177–81; idem, 'Spanish Church revisited', 145–6.
[161] I am grateful to Professor Raphael Loewe for notice of the parallel with a quatrain of the *Rubáiyát* of Omar Khayyám (no. 228 in A. J. Arberry's translation, London 1952):

> If yonder Heaven had been mine,
> Not God's, to hold at my desire,
> I would have rooted up entire
> And utterly its old deign,

and the suggestion that the germ of the idea might have been picked up by Alfonso's embassy to the Ismailis (unlikely though it is that any of its members would have known Pahlavi).
[162] Linehan, *History*, 504; Ayala Martínez, *Órdenes militares*, 710–14, noting a 'qualitative change' in the king's relationship with the military orders during this reign; Rojinsky, 299–303; Menéndez Pidal, *Poesía juglaresca*, 132; Bertolucci Pizzorusso, 'Supplica di Guiraut Riquier'.

this point Alfonso found time to write verse. With forces gathering capable of removing him from power, what other king would have concerned himself with the question of protecting Écija from imports of foreign wine between the months of January and June?[163]

With Jofré de Loaisa, posterity would attribute his downfall to his prodigality rather than his bookishness, and to the cost of maintaining the exotic denizens of his cosmopolitan court – the king of Granada, the rector of Harrow, and all those Italians – in the style to which they so readily became accustomed.[164] That was not the problem though. For a king with Alfonso's horizons lavishness was all. The Genoese troubadour, Bonifaci Calvo, thought it necessary to beg him to not to create *privados* since every *privado* was principally concerned to destroy his reputation. But as the fictional king in Ibn Sahula's tale professed, it was always necessary to make a good show:

> Honour and wealth I'll give thee, yea, a store
> Of silver and of gold, enough and more.
> For to my realm no man of intellect
> Yet came, whom to promote did I neglect,
> No sage I failed to honour, or invite
> His views on questions as to wrong and right

It was his impenitent cosmopolitanism that compelled him to send one embassy to the Persian Ismailis in 1265 and another to the Mongols of Tartary in 1279. It was typical of him that in 1277, while the cortes were petitioning the pope for permission to correct the over-valued currency, he should have been offering to provision Navarre from his stricken land, claiming that it was 'all planted up'.[165] The trouble was that, like many more otherwise quite clever men, he failed to master the laws of economics, and that, in common with some not unusually intelligent kings, he neglected to notice how seriously mismanagement of the currency affects ordinary people.

Take for example the case of Fernán Potas of Zamora who in 1269 borrowed seventy *maravedís* of León for a year from the Jew Hebrasan

---

[163] González Jiménez, *Diplomatario andaluz*, no. 498 (1 May 1282).

[164] For the rector of Harrow (Geoffrey of Everley, notary and nuncio both of Alfonso and of Edward I of England and author of an 'Ars dictandi' dedicated to the former): Bertolucci Pizzorusso, 'Un trattato'; Hernández & Linehan, 97, 178.

[165] Branciforti, 119; Loewe, 474; Vernet, 'Alfonso X el Sabio: mecánica y astronomía', 26; Rymer, 564; Escudero de la Peña, 'Variedades'; Guillaume Anelier de Toulouse, *Hist. de la guerre de Navarre en 1276 et 1277*, 126. Cf. above, 100.

Catalan with a penalty clause of two soldos a day for late repayment. In 1284 his executors found his estate encumbered to the tune of

> seventy *maravedís leoneses*, at eight *soldos* to the *maravedí* equivalent to 420 *maravedís* in the (newly minted) *dineros menudos dela guerra* (also at eight *soldos* to the *maravedí*), counting six of these to one of the *leoneses*. (. . .) And so these seventy *leoneses*, lent *al tanto e medio* (150) are worth 1050 *leoneses* of the aforesaid *dineros menudos* at eight *soldos* to the *maravedí*.[166]

Fernán Potas had only himself to blame for not repaying on time. His executors, however, in common with every other executor of the period, had only Alfonso X to thank for the effects of the successive complications of the currency over the previous fifteen years.

The monetary history of the reign constitutes a sort of allegory of its progress in other departments. Intent on blackening his memory, the Chronicle gave prominence to his handling of the matter, by beginning with the subject and then raising it again in its account of the Seville Cortes of 1281.[167] But it failed to make allowance for two developments for neither of which Alfonso could be held responsible: the inflation resulting from the booty released from reconquered Seville into the Castilian economy while human resources were drained from further north, and the striking of fine gold coins in Genoa and Florence in the very year of his accession to the throne, a development pregnant with consequences for any ruler intent on playing a part in European affairs. Even so, the seventeenth-century author had a point when he remarked on the shortcomings of the king who, for all his supposed acquaintance with the philosopher's stone, failed to secure sufficient quantities of the yellow metal to keep the crown of his ancestors out of Moorish hands.[168]

Despite those tendencies towards heterodoxy which so bothered his bishops, at times his disdain for the gods of Antiquity appeared to be as absolute as it was for the Prophet, his account of whose career in the *Estoria de España*, though chronologically integrated with the national story, comprises a farrago of fantasy and a mishmash of myth. Muḥammad begins his career as a learned cleric, possessing a level of expertise in the Old and New Testaments as well as in natural philosophy ('la sciencia de las naturas') which would have qualified him for membership of the king's inner circle. Thereafter, though, he turns vicious, taking eighteen wives and

---

[166]   AC Zamora, 16.II/39.
[167]   *CAX*, cc. 1, 75.
[168]   Lopez, 'Back to gold, 1252'; Ortiz de Zúñiga, I, 289.

promising those of his followers who embrace martyrdom a species of celestial Seville: paradise and virgins unlimited.[169]

Alfonso X might have been happier organizing a research institute and keeping an eye on theses in progress than in running a kingdom. Certainly his cerebral achievements earned him the most fulsome tributes, of 'intellect, understanding and knowledge greater than all the princes of his time', being judged 'seemingly of divine rather than human origin', with Egidius de Tebaldis, author of the prologue to the *Libro de las Cruzes*, praising him in particular for 'practical intelligence (*seso*), understanding and wisdom'. The Italian continued: 'I do not believe that nature could have created a more perfect man.'[170] This is going too far. Though we know about the *de luxe* items he disposed of in his will we know nothing about his bed-side reading.[171] Reputation was all. It was the reputation he enjoyed for wisdom (as well as gentleness), not his proven possession of these qualities, that at the beginning of the reign the king of England described as breaking upon the world 'like an exploding star',[172] and in the department of practical intelligence that the problem lay, in the department of wisdom rather than learning. The Learned King was, quite simply, not terribly sensible. 'Let your yes mean yes and your no mean no', the royal reader of the *Libro de los doze sabios* had been enjoined, and in 1269 Alfonso's father-in-law had proffered similar sound advice.[173] But it was not taken. There will have been other things on Alfonso's mind at the time. There always were.

---

[169] Lida de Malkiel, 'La *General estoria*', 127; *PCG*, cc. 466–94. Cf. above, 73.
[170] Cit. Procter, 'Scientific works', 22.
[171] Solalinde, *Antología*, 236. Rubio García's article entitled 'En torno a la biblioteca de Alfonso X' is about nothing of the sort. Cf. *Libro de las Cruzes*, ed. Kasten & Kiddle, 1.
[172] Rymer, 290.
[173] ed. Walsh, 113; above, 161.

8

The Changed Balance

We do not know how much the messenger was paid in April 1284 for bringing his successor news of the death of Alfonso X, how much, that is, the
son thought the information worth to him. But when Dr F. J. Hernández's
account of the fiscal records of Sancho's reign is published we will. Then
we will be better informed about the political structure, the operations of
the chancery, and particulars of royal income and expenditure than we are
about any comparable period in the history of medieval Castile. Then the
identities of the men in whose hands the government of the kingdom rested
in the last years of the thirteenth century will be revealed and the sinews
of state made available for anatomizing.[1] It is a happy prospect. But it is
also one that serves as a reminder of how much has been lost. For the comparative richness of these revelations is entirely due to the chance survival
of records indistinguishable from others which, if spared, would have provided no less detailed an account of previous reigns and placed study of
the history of the Castilian monarchy on a footing similar to that of its
Aragonese neighbour.

Castile after 1284

The old king's end cast a deep shadow over everything that followed. No
doubt affected by being paternally cursed and disinherited, Sancho IV chose
to lean on a succession of favourites, discarding in turn all but the latest
of them. With the La Cerda claim making him vulnerable to French and
Aragonese manipulation, his invalid marriage to his grandfather's niece

---

[1] Hernández, *Hombres del rey*.

kept the succession issue in suspense until his death and beyond.[2] Despite attempts to purchase biddable cardinals – Cardinal Ordoño Álvarez and the cardinal's cleric Master Rodrigo both figure in the list of 'those who have money from the king', for example – and fabricate a papal dispensation, brokered perhaps by the archbishop of Toledo, Sancho's heir remained a bastard. Moreover, the remoter origins of the problem also haunted Sancho alive and dead. When in August 1301 the question of legitimizing Fernando IV was under consideration at the papal court the French canonist, Cardinal Jean Lemoine, opposed the proposal on the grounds that because of undertakings entered into in 1269 Sancho had no 'right in the kingdom' anyway.[3]

Another cardinal involved in the same debate, Matteo Rosso Orsini, opposed Fernando's legitimization on the more pragmatic grounds that for as long as the issue remained unresolved Spain would have a multiplicity of kings and that the more kings Spain had the better it was for the Church. The remark expresses a generally neglected truth about the state of the Spanish peninsula at the end of the thirteenth century. There was no reason at the time to suppose that the union of the kingdoms of León and Castile in the person of Fernando III would oblige the teleological assumptions of Whiggish historians of the period by surviving the political stress of the decades ahead. Lucas of Tuy had written of the reign of the eleventh-century Fernando I as one in which the Saracens had been terrified by the spectacle of León and Castile in concord and under single effective rule. But that was Leonese idealism. As Rodrigo of Toledo, the empirical Castilian, acknowledged, for all the queen-mother's skill in achieving it, the union of 1230 had 'displeased almost everyone'.[4]

Alfonso X's kingdom was a dynastic contingency rather than a basis for territorial expansion. Between 1157 and 1282 the two kingdoms had spent more time apart than together, and when the Infante Sancho began his rebellion prospects for the survival of his father's *señorío mayor* were hardly promising, with the independent actions of the Leonese churchmen indicating where the fault lines and fissures ran, and the advice proffered favouring the issue of two separate national currencies.[5] Sancho had been

[2]   At the Cortes of Segovia in August 1386, Juan I felt obliged to base his title on his descent not from Sancho IV but from Fernando de la Cerda: *CLC*, II, 354; Craddock, 'Dynasty in dispute'.
[3]   'Nomina de León de 1285', 22.1; 22.26 (Hernández, *Hombres del rey*); Linehan, *Ladies of Zamora*, 117–20; Finke, *Acta Aragonensia*, I, 104–5.
[4]   Finke, *Bonifaz VIII*, xxix; *CM*, IV.49$_{15}$; *DrH*, IX.15$_{25}$.
[5]   Above, 191.

outraged by his father's proposal to grant the kingdom of Jaén to the La Cerda claimant, but the process of national disintegration into independent lordships ('señoralización') was hastened by Alfonso's bequests to his children, including the Infante Juan, and in 1295–6 by that infante's agreement, in his capacity as Fernando IV's tutor, to a process of territorial division which assigned León, Galicia and Seville to himself and Castile, Toledo, Córdoba, Murcia, Jaén and Murcia to Alfonso de la Cerda. In order to preserve the integrity of the kingdom, the Infante Sancho had gone to war with his father, in his *Castigos* was emphatic in counselling his son to maintain its unity, and in 1294 refused to contemplate alienating any part of it to France. But six years earlier he had been prepared to surrender Murcia and more in order to secure that alliance with as little commitment to unity as had been displayed in 1157.[6] As John de Balliol, claimant to the Scottish throne, argued in 1292, a kingdom partible was not rendered partible by its king's uncrowned or unanointed state; or such would be the fate of the Spanish kingdoms.[7] It was not relevant to his argument to state what it was that did do so, namely intrinsic incoherence and centrifugality without agreed centres, aggravated by strategies of jockeying for position, the perennial consequences of which were demonstrated by the insistence of Lucas of Tuy's fifteenth-century translator that Fernando III had made reconquered Seville subject to León and the *Fuero juzgo*.[8] Leonese-Castilian rivalry over Seville was matched by Aragonese-Catalan rivalry over Valencia, with kingdoms disposed of as though they were private property.[9]

As has been seen, in Aragón the practice of partibility had continued into the 1270s; in Aragonese Sicily it would last longer. In the case of Castile-León its survival was assisted by the scheming of generations of ambitious infantes of the stamp of D. Felipe[10] and by the refusal of the *hermandades* to die a decent death. For the first of these Sancho could hardly be held responsible (though he had done nothing to discourage the custom), for the second he would not soon be forgiven. By evoking the euphoria of 1248 but not allowing for the misery of the decades before then and since, he raised expectations both amongst the nobility and in the municipalities

---

[6]   *CFIV*, cap. 1 (p. 97a); *Castigos*, 150; Daumet, *Mémoire*, 117; below, 220.
[7]   Stones & Simpson, II, 320–1, 332.
[8]   Puyol, 445; Linehan, 'Invention of Toledo'. Cf. above, 73.
[9]   Thus González Mínguez, 46, who speaks of a reversion to practices prior to Fernando III but not of the will of Alfonso VIII and the sharply contrasting practices and attitudes elsewhere in contemporary Europe.
[10]   Appropriately it is from Sancho's reign that the magnificent tomb of that cultivator of sedition dates: F. Menéndez Pidal, 95–8; Sánchez Ameijeiras, *'Mui de coraçon'*, 247.

which neither he nor his successors would be able to satisfy. Operating over broken terrain, the combination of the two was fatal. One of Alfonso X's first tasks at the beginning of his reign had been to crack down on wedding parties and dismantle *cofradías* 'which were to the harm of the land'. (Similar bans on gatherings were also in force in Aragón, but significantly not in Catalonia.)[11] Now it was his son's to suppress the local associations for the defence of their *fueros* into which as rebel infante he had breathed new life as a means of dislodging his father. The spirit of local autonomy was nothing new, of course, and there is no need to search for its origins in the history of artificial fraternity or same-sex unions.[12] It was a matter of affliction, not affection. Only recently it had halted Alfonso X in his centralizing tracks. But the *hermandades* licensed by Sancho between 1282 and 1284 had been promised the novelty of meeting annually.

According to the Chronicle of his reign, on Sancho's accession the *hermandades* and councils themselves together with 'other men' petitioned the king 'in the *cortes*' to revoke the privileges he had been 'pressed' to grant them as infante, and this he graciously consented to do. 'And he ordered that they be surrendered and had them all destroyed.' But this was laundered history, the wishful thinking of a royal chronicler in the 1340s, by which time the principle was well established that history was what the royal chronicler said it was. Like modern political diaries, the fourteenth-century chronicles of Castile's thirteenth-century kings were highly political documents. In the autumn of 1284 it was Sancho, not the *hermandades*, who enjoyed the initiative; he who protested that two years before the *hermandades* had coerced him. At a meeting of the *corte* at Salamanca firmly under his control, rather than in an unpredictable gathering of the *cortes* (as the published version of the *Crónica* wrongly states), Sancho had the *hermandades* 'wholly abolished', as Jofré de Loaisa reported.[13] In 1282 the infante had disparaged his father for expenditure on Italians at court and intimidated his own bishops into submission. Ironically, it was Italian jurists who now advised the king on the law of intimidation and were richly rewarded for doing so.[14]

In his will of May 1285 that faulty episcopal weather-vane, Suero Pérez of Zamora, whom Sancho had groomed only to discard once he had played

---

[11] Above, 115; González Antón, I, 350 (Aínsa, Barbastro and Calatayud). Cf. Jaime I's licence to the inhabitants of various parishes of Barcelona to keep weapons in their homes and combine in self-defence against malefactors (Jan. 1258): *Docs.JI*, no. 933.

[12] Boswell, *Marriage*, 255, citing Hinojosa, 5.

[13] *CSIV*, cap. 1 (p. 70a); Loaisa, *Crónica*, 126.

[14] Hernández & Linehan, 111, n. 7; above, 187; Hernández, *Hombres del rey*, for details of the cost of collecting and destroying the offending charters.

his part in the dialectic of sedition, allowed himself the satisfaction of denying Sancho the royal title.[15] But the ebullience of local communities was less easy to wish out of existence. Moreover, the *hermandad general* was not dead, it was but concussed. In fact, in respect of both the development (or the 'virus', according to taste) of municipal autonomy and the 'aristocratization' of Castilian society, the seeds planted during those two years would continue to germinate and the growth they put up continue to flourish well into the next century and beyond.[16] As will be seen, this was in contrast to the ultimate fate of Aragonese Unionism.

But to remain in Castile. Here the corollary of the new king's repudiation of the *hermandades* was reconciliation with the territorial nobility, the political establishment of *ricos omes* that his father had alienated by promoting the urban *caballería villana*. It was on them and their *mesnadas* that he would principally depend for military effectiveness. The process began in April 1284 when Sancho held his first cortes at Toledo and was crowned in the cathedral there. By contrast with contemporary Aragón, where coronations were followed by the creation of large numbers of new knights,[17] at Toledo nothing of the sort happened. Instead, the king made Lope Díaz de Haro a handsome gift. With the humiliation (albeit temporary) of his Lara rival, Lope Díaz de Haro was the kingdom's leading *rico ombre*, and his *mesnada* easily the largest.

It was an indication of the extent of Sancho's discomfiture as both son and husband that he had chosen to submit himself and his queen to the first such ceremony in Castile-León since Alfonso VII's imperial coronation of 1135.[18] So also was the selection of Toledo as the setting for him first to be seen wearing his father's crown and, albeit in the absence of its archbishop, for María de Molina to be presented as his queen.[19] For just as there had been no coronation ceremony for a century and a half, neither was there a ceremonial capital in which to perform one – or any national capital for that matter. Latterly Alfonso X had favoured Seville (and Seville had loyally returned the compliment). But that had not made Seville his capital, any more than it had any of those places of residence previously preferred by him, Murcia and Toledo itself for example.[20]

[15]   Linehan, 'Economics of episcopal politics', 26.
[16]   Gautier Dalché, 'L'histoire castillane', 246; Suárez Fernández, 'Hermandades castellanas.'
[17]   *Gesta comitum Barcinonensium*, 65, 94.
[18]   Linehan, *History*, 390, 443, 446–7.
[19]   *Pace* Bizzarri: '*Castigos*', 18.
[20]   Above, 102.

In so far as he had a choice in the matter it was in the north and centre, in Burgos and Valladolid, that Sancho preferred to reside temporarily while alive, and in Toledo permanently thereafter. In the first year of his reign, and at the age of just twenty-six, he invaded the sanctuary space of the cathedral there and elected to be buried next to its high altar. Despite providing oil for burning before the royal tombs in Seville cathedral, after 1284 he only ever came to the place for military purposes, never in pursuit of domestic solace. The visits he paid to Compostela, perhaps because his father had never done so, did not serve to revive the fortunes of that place or its pilgrimage. So Toledo's friends felt encouraged to seek to attach the king even more firmly to the old Visigothic capital. Under the leadership of its archbishop, Gonzalo Pérez, their spokesman was the chronicler Jofré de Loaisa. According to Jofré, Sancho decreed that all future kings of Castile were to be crowned in Toledo cathedral.[21] This was wishful thinking too.

A Question of Alliances

Pedro of Aragón's problems were of a different order. With militant Unionists within and crusaders without under the French king's command, early in 1285 the French pope reassigned his kingdom to the French king's brother, Charles of Valois. Pedro's first move though was to dislodge Juan Núñez de Lara, the ally of France and Navarre, from the mountainous lordship of Albarracín, which he ruled as the 'vassal of Our Lady'. In besieging Lara, whose predecessors had been thorns in the sides of rulers of Aragón and Castile for more than a century, Pedro had the help of Sancho IV, though the Catalan chronicler chose to ignore the fact.[22] This alliance was short-lived, however, since as well as needing to remain on terms with the custodian of his La Cerda nephews, for reasons to which we will come Sancho had cause to curry favour with the French. It was in these circumstances, which were to ensure institutionalized instability in the foreign policies of the peninsular kingdoms for the remainder of the century, that the same chronicler observed of his master the count-king

---

[21]   Linehan, *History*, 483–5, 503, 447–8; Gutiérrez Baños, 167–9; Hernández, *Rentas*, I, 392; Gaibrois, *Sancho IV*, I, 46; (for Alfonso X's animosity towards Compostela), above, 154, 169n; Fernández-Ordóñez, *Versión crítica*, 173–4.

[22]   Above, 12–13; Desclot, cc. 117–18 (Critchlow, II, 153–60); Almagro, IV, 37–56; Doubleday; 86–7.

that he held the balance between the rulers of France and Castile, no matter that those kings were 'more mighty than all others upon earth'.[23]

He might no less appropriately have described the lord of Albarracín as holding the balance between the kings of Aragón and Castile. At any event, Juan Núñez was soon restored with Castilian assistance, just as Pedro's brother, Jaime II of Mallorca, was momentarily spared the fate he deserved for conspiring with the French invaders and allowing them passage through Roussillon and Cerdagne in the spring of 1285. Forced to withdraw to the Pyrenees, Pedro nevertheless triumphed, assisted by the effects of a plague of poisonous flies at Girona (as fatal to the French as the great heats of 1212), and the destruction of French naval supply lines by Ruggiero di Loria, Pedro's Sicilian admiral. Philippe III perished in the rout, Charles of Anjou and Martin IV had both died earlier in the year, and in the following November Pedro followed them, struck down at the age of forty-six as he prepared to deal with his treacherous brother.[24]

What made this outcome the more remarkable was that it had been achieved despite Aragonese hostility to their king since, while Charles of Valois was being invested with the Aragonese throne, the leaders of the *Unión* had been communicating with the French in Navarre.[25] Moreover, although because it was repelled by Catalan forces unaided the invasion had served to widen divisions within the Unionist ranks, with the cessation, albeit temporary, of the national emergency, Unionism reasserted itself.

One of the most remarkable manifestations of Europe's monarchical Middle Ages, Unionism dominated the short reign of Alfonso III ('el Franc': the Honest, 1285–91), hampering his every step as he sought to cope with invasion from Castile, France and his Mallorcan uncle and to reach a diplomatic solution with Rome.[26] By entitling himself king before setting foot in his kingdom and, at his coronation at Zaragoza, Unionism's heartland, like his father insisting that that city enjoyed no ceremonial monopoly, from the very outset of his reign Alfonso was on a crash course with the hard core of aristocrats and their demand that the king comply with every clause of the General Privilege of 1283. Acting as a corporation aggregate with its own seal, the oligarchs threatened Alfonso with defiance and deposition as well as the surrender of castles on the border with French Navarre (a bolt-hole permanently available should their plotting with Charles of Valois fail) should he dare to embark on international negotiations without

[23]   Desclot, c. 76 (Critchlow, II, 21).
[24]   *Gesta comitum Barcinonesium*, 78–92; Zurita, IV. 7; Soldevila, *Hist. de Catalunya*, 371–5.
[25]   Above, 198.
[26]   González Antón, I, 149–262.

consulting them. By requiring annual meetings of the cortes and then paralysing them by boycotting the sessions unless all but their supporters were excluded, they sought to control both the royal council and the royal household. While the king was attacking Menorca in 1287 their army invaded the kingdom of Valencia in order to maintain Aragonese domination there (albeit Valencia's only Aragonese feature was its absent nobility). Particularly remarkable were their attempts in the summer of 1287 to persuade foreign powers to intervene in Aragonese affairs, on the grounds that the king was destroying localities by attacking their *fueros*: a *cri de coeur* which Sancho IV, whom they approached as well as other rulers Christian as well as Muslim, will have found familiar.[27]

In fact, it was not the *fueros* of localities, large or small, that were at issue, but rather individual grievances, with the movement's composition, at some times numbering as few as five *ricos hombres*, twice that number of *mesnaderos*, and a failed bishop of Zaragoza, calling to mind Alfonso X's celebrated letter on selfishness as the essence of noble protest.[28] It must be revealing of the character of Aragonese high politics that, although numerically limited even with three of Jaime I's bastard sons flitting in and out of its ranks,[29] by inserting so inflexible an instrument into the sensitive interstices of the Corona de Aragón Unionism was more or less able to control the tempo of the reign. González Antón, the Unionists' most exhaustive recent chronicler, insists on their unrepresentativeness. But even if they failed to loosen the couplings of the pluralist monarchy, that defect did not limit their potential for mischief, a circumstance that seems not to surprise that author. True, as María de Molina was to demonstrate in Castile, in the 1290s such forces could only be defeated by the cortes. However, the extent of opposition in Castile was more widespread and of a different order. Alfonso III's attempt to prevail by force of arms in August 1287 having failed, thereafter he chose to surrender to his tormentors *outside* the cortes, perhaps in order not to flatter faction by treating it as a movement of national consequence, perhaps apprehensive of the extent of their influence within the assembly, perhaps like Sancho IV preferring the less unpredictable proceedings of his own narrow *corte*.[30] Even so, by the settlement made, the so-called Privileges of the Union, it was stated that

[27] Ibid., I, 359; II, 235–6; Palacios Martín, *Coronación*, 93–126.
[28] Above, 166–7.
[29] Jaime de Xèrica and Pedro de Ayerbe, the sons of Teresa Gil de Vidaura, and Pedro de Híjar, son of Berenguela Fernández.
[30] González Antón, I, 191–7, 352–61. In 1348 Pedro IV would proceed differently, shattering the Unionists' seal with the royal mace and rending their privileges: Zurita, VIII. 32.

> If, God forbid, we or our successors should contravene these articles in all or in part, it is our wish and express command that (. . .) you may make another, whomever you wish, king and lord (. . .) and even give yourselves to him as vassals.[31]

Although eventually Unionist disruption proved too much even for Zaragoza, and the locals lost patience, that was not until March 1291,[32] just weeks before the end of the reign, whereafter the movement forfeited such popular support as it had enjoyed, which in so far as it had any was anti-Catalan rather than anti-monarchical. Meanwhile, despite his conquest of Mallorca and the advantage of having both the Infantes de la Cerda and the Angevin heir, Charles of Salerno, in his custody,[33] notwithstanding Desclot's sunny confidence Alfonso III remained at risk from both his neighbours. Although promising to do so, the Castilian had failed to assist Pedro III in resisting the French invader: 'fine words; no action', Muntaner remarked, unconsciously echoing earlier Spanish applications of the same precept.[34] Probably for this reason there was no love lost between Pedro's son and Sancho IV, whose sensitivity regarding his shaky marriage was Alfonso's best safeguard against a Castilian–French alliance prospering at the start of both their reigns. As to Sancho and his queen, Philippe IV periodically undertook to put in a good word at Rome, and for as long as the papacy was French-dominated the French king's active sympathy was worth having. But after Martin IV's death (March 1285) French hold on that office was interrupted. Moreover, the French king who treated everything as negotiable included the Castilian marriage in that category, whereas Sancho IV did not. When in 1286 he learnt of conversations said to have taken place between Philippe and his *privado*, the abbot of Valladolid, Gómez García, regarding the possibility of Sancho separating from Maria de Molina in favour of the French king's sister, the abbot's days were numbered. Sensibly he died, and 'when the king heard of it', the Chronicle reports, 'he was very pleased'.

'For was there any other king anywhere as happily married as he?', Sancho wanted to know. And for that matter, why (he continued) was the pontiff proving so obstructive? Had not numerous of his ancestors also

---

[31]   transl. Giesey, 89.

[32]   González Antón, I, 260–1; II, 406–9.

[33]   Heir to the kingdom of Naples since the death of Charles of Anjou in Jan. 1285, the latter was in prison in Barcelona, after Constanza of Aragón had saved him from a Sicilian lynch mob: Zurita, IV. 50, 73.

[34]   Adding that it was Pedro's intention to declare Alfonso de la Cerda king of Castile in revenge: *Crònica*, cc. 120, 142; above, 55.

married their cousins without papal dispensation, and had not they proved splendid kings and defenders of the Faith? While the Aragonese Unionists spoke of appealing against their king to the king of France 'as the arm and most intimate son of the Church' during a papal vacancy,[35] Sancho declared himself minded to appeal from the pope to the Almighty, though this may have been a ruse intended to divert attention from the marriage he was in danger of being held to, the match with Guillerma de Montcada contracted for him in 1270. Sancho IV was known as 'el rey bravo', the fierce king. But according to Zurita, Guillerma de Montcada was both fierce and ugly, *very* ugly.[36] Perhaps she had inherited some of the characteristics of her grandmother, the formidable countess Garsenda, concerning whose gross and repellent aspect Matthew Paris was more than usually outspoken.[37]

The prospect of Guillerma contributed to the downfall of the man who now replaced the abbot in Sancho's affections. So besotted ('tan emaginado') with Lope Díaz de Haro (and doubtless with his military resources) was the king that on the first day of 1287 he bestowed upon him the title of Count (a badge of distinction long out of use), appointed him his *mayordomo mayor*, made over to him his castles and the keys to his chancery and, for good measure, declared the entire settlement hereditary. The creation of this 'alter ego' (who was the queen's brother-in-law, whose brother was the king's brother-in-law and whose daughter was the king's sister-in-law) confirms the impression that Sancho IV was a man unambitious for his posterity, one who, as he was to say on his deathbed, having been cursed by his father had nothing to bequeath to his son.[38]

The Count favoured an Aragonese alliance not least because the Laras, the champions of the La Cerda cause, were committed to the French. The continuation of the divisions within the territorial nobility opened up in the 1270s determined the diplomacy of successive decades. But, as was to be expected, before long the Count overreached himself, going so far as to propose marriage between Alfonso III and the five-year-old Infante Isabel of Castile.[39] When knowledge of the fact that the Count was also promoting the cause of the bogy of Béarn, his cousin the aforesaid Guillerma de Montcada, in place of the queen, at Alfaro in June 1288 the king demanded the return of his castles, adding that he would detain the Count and his

[35] González Antón, II, 234–7.
[36] Daumet, *Mémoire*, 92–4; Gaibrois, *Sancho IV*, I, 88–114; *CSIV*, cap. 2 (pp. 72b–73a); Linehan, *History*, 472–3; Marcos Pous, 14–33; Zurita, IV. 47.
[37] Described by him severally as a woman of 'gargantuan appetite', 'singularly monstrous', and 'prodigiously fat': *Chronica Majora*, IV. 224, V. 293; *Flores Historiarum*, II. 256.
[38] *CSIV*, cap. 3 (p. 75a); Gaibrois, *Sancho IV*, I, 132–40; below, 228.
[39] Zurita, IV. 100.

satellites until they complied. The Chronicle records the exchange that followed, culminating in what the lady historian of the scene described in 1922 as 'an indecent interjection'. In the ensuing mêlée the Count drew his dagger, the king's bodyguard struck him down, the king finished him off, and the queen intervened to prevent her husband from adding to the gory spectacle by despatching his own brother, the Infante Juan.[40]

Nothing better illustrates the volatile state of Mediterranean diplomacy in the years after the Sicilian Vespers than the speed with which Castile now reverted to an offensive–defensive French alliance. By the treaty of Lyons, initialled just one month later, in return for the renunciation of the claim to the Castilian throne, *inter alia* the Infantes de la Cerda were to be invested with the kingdom of Murcia and Alfonso X's foundation of Ciudad Real, together with certain revenues to be enjoyed by them and their heirs independently and forever; and the elder of them was to be betrothed to the Infanta Isabel and to succeed Sancho if he died without legitimate issue (a provision that made regularization of the royal marriage imperative, whence the Frenchman's undertaking to use his best offices at Rome). Sancho, Philippe IV and 'King Charles of Aragón' (alias Charles of Valois) were to combine as 'good and faithful friends' against 'Alfonso of Aragón' (so-called); Juan Núñez de Lara was to be restored to Albarracín; civil war exiles allowed to return to Castile; and all inherited French claims to the throne of Castile revoked.[41] At this, the infantes' mother, Blanche of France, protested to Alfonso III, who, with a view to forcing the hand of Blanche's nephew, Philippe IV, had the elder of them proclaimed king of Castile in September 1288. Later that year Alfonso III married the daughter of Edward I of England, and at the beginning of 1289 formally defied Sancho and prepared to invade Castile after 'King Alfonso of Castile' had ceded Murcia and Cartagena to him.[42]

In the event the treaty of Lyons remained a dead letter. But under the auspices of Archbishop Gonzalo Pérez of Toledo and Bishop Martín of Astorga the Castilian–French alliance survived. It was they who had reported the abbot of Valladolid's treasonable conversations, and the first of them in particular came to exercise a dominant influence over the queen and, more particularly, the king. When towards the end of the old king's reign Gonzalo Pérez had been in particular need of friends he had not hesitated

---

[40]   Zurita, IV. 89; *CSIV*, cap. 5 (p. 79a): 'What? Us prisoners? Oh shit! Get my men'; cf. Gaibrois, *Sancho IV*, I, 176–204, at 191.

[41]   Daumet, *Mémoire*, 184–98, esp. 192–3 (from the French archives). The summary provided by Zurita, IV. 100, contains particulars which must have come from elsewhere. Cf. Gaibrois, *Sancho IV*, 215 n.3.

[42]   Zurita, IV. 103–4; Gaibrois, *Sancho IV*, 236.

to remind the Infante Sancho how much, ever since he was a little boy, the latter had always 'loved and honoured' him. And although during the Castilian civil war the archbishop had remained firmly on the fence, after 1284 the influence he exerted over him was akin to that of a surrogate father, the position that ought to have been filled by his godfather, Remondo de Losana, the archbishop of Seville and unflinching supporter of Alfonso X. By May 1290 Gonzalo Pérez was chancellor-in-chief (*chanceller mayor*) of all Sancho's realms and investing the *ex officio* title with a significance that it not enjoyed since before his predecessor's loss of that office in 1230.[43] His survival from then until the end of the reign was remarkable, all the more so in view of the fate of his predecessors in a court notorious for rumour-mongering and the king's volcanic temperament and susceptibility to tittle-tattle.[44] In the *Castigos*, Sancho warned his son and heir against placing 'such trust in one man as you will have later to disavow, stating the opposite of what you first stated'.[45] Elsewhere in the same treatise he sketches his theory of the origin of the two powers, the ecclesiastical and the secular, in Aaron and Moses, twin vicars of God, with each bearing his symbol of office, the crozier and the sceptre, each having its own independent sphere of action yet also the ability to hone the other and thereby enable it the better to perform its task – all of which reads very much like an analysis of the illustration on the privilege of January 1285 whereby the king recently crowned in Toledo cathedral had ceded his body for burial there, an illustration in which croziered archbishop and sceptred monarch sit eyeing one another on absolutely level lineal terms.[46]

The archbishop it was who master-minded the *vistas* of Logroño in July 1293, the diplomatic high-water mark of the reign, celebrated in sumptuous style.[47] Nor was that the only indication of the international range of the man who while still infante had been in contact with Constantinople and in 1290 had the emissary of the Old Man of the Mountains on his payroll.[48] But impressive though it may have appeared that Benedetto

[43] Hernández & Linehan, 446; Ortiz de Zúñiga, I, 194; Linehan, 'Invention of Toledo'.
[44] Hernández & Linehan, 245–339.
[45] Cf. the advice of the author of the *Libro de los doze sabios*: above, 209.
[46] ed. Bizzarri, 150, 172; Linehan, *History*, 483–5, and Plate I.
[47] Hernández & Linehan, 299–300, 341–2; below, 232.
[48] Hernández & Linehan, 233n; Hernández, *Rentas*, I, 392, recording a monthly payment of seventy *maravedís* to 'Suia, mandadero del Vieio de las Montañas'. Though an embassy of Assassins had been present in the peninsula in 1276 in connexion with Sancho's proposed marriage to a daughter of 'the Sultan' (Zurita, IV. 2), contact with their leader at this date must refer to the Syrian branch of the Order and have had to do with the moribund Latin Kingdom of Jerusalem. Cf. Nowell, 514 ('After the return of St Louis to France, there are few records of dealings between Europeans and the Old Man').

Zaccaria had entered his service fresh from acting as Michael Palaeologus' go-between on the eve of the Vespers, the real significance of Sancho's employment of the pricey Genoese admiral lay not in his market value but in the fact that when Castilian forces seized Tarifa from the Marīnids in 1292 they did so with the assistance of the Aragonese fleet; the consideration that, when they retained the place two years later, it was for the same reason, combined with an outbreak of plague amongst the besiegers, that they were able to do so; and the presence amongst Abū Ya'qūb's allies at the siege of that 'sinister spirit', the Infante Juan.[49]

The presence at Tarifa of the king's brother, in open opposition to the king, showed Sancho's claim of 1285 to act as Christ's vicar in his kingdoms to be as febrile as by 1292 his physical condition had become and lacking resonance amongst his subjects. In reality, if the royal host turned up when it was summoned it did so not out of reverence for the Vicar of Christ but because it was paid to do so by the king, and if the silver content of the coins with which his troops were paid was reduced the impression of the king's crowned head on them, for the first time since the reign of Alfonso VIII, afforded no compensation. The same went for other examples of Sancho's attachment to crowns and crown-symbolism and for reports of his aping the kings of France and England in claiming to be able to exorcise a woman possessed. None of these – the vicariate of Christ, the crown, the royal touch – had played any part in the conduct of Alfonsine rule. For the attribution to foreign rulers of curative powers the old king had had particular scorn. But what Sancho's subjects will have remembered was how much Alfonso's worthless coinage had contributed to his downfall. Moreover, as the reign advanced the king took to counter-signing his own mandates, something that his father had never done. The king's authority was only worth the paper of his charters. The need to corroborate the products of his chancery with the words 'Nos el rey don Sancho', written in his own hand, proclaimed that, like the currency, unless enhanced they were devalued.[50] On one occasion, in an instruction to Archbishop Gonzalo Pérez to provide a favoured clerk with a benefice, the king is found stating that this was his third time of asking.[51]

[49]   *CSIV*, caps. 1, 11 (pp. 70a, 88b–9a); Geanakoplos, 356–8; Gaibrois, 'Tarifa', 144; Harvey, *Islamic Spain*, 161–2.

[50]   Linehan, *History*, 484, 503–4; Hernández, *Rentas*, I, clxxxv–cxci; Gutiérrez Baños, 64–81; Hernández & Linehan, 352, 359.

[51]   New York Hispanic Society of America, MS. B189. The clerk in question was one master Pedro, whose questionable identification with the author of the *Libro del consejo e de los consejeros* has caused the work to be associated with Sancho's reign: Gómez Redondo, 944–5.

Amongst the fiscal records soon to be published by Dr Hernández is a 'Book of Slackers' ('Libro de lo que mando el rey minguar') listing the names of those who failed to present themselves for service in 1285 when Abū Ya'qūb was attacking Jerez. The number of those absent without leave, most of them the king's own vassals, together with their military entourages, amounted to 868: a sizeable contingent. Rather than the corollary of some mystical relationship, what bound the king's vassals and their entourages to the king was a system of salaries, a bastard type of stipendiary feudalism which depended on money because by the mid-1280s there was no more land available for distribution as largesse, and which provided a 'simple but effective mechanism for ensuring (. . .) the continuity of the dynasty (. . .) and a right of succession that was recognized neither in Rome nor in many other places both within the peninsula and beyond'.[52] Another of Hernández's lists reveals the extent to which by 1285 money had come to control the affairs of the kingdom.[53] The payroll for that year included 942 persons of military competence, some with very elaborate obligations, and occupies 179 A4 typescript pages. But such expenditure could only be afforded, the king could only raise the six-figure sums that were needed to purchase if not the loyalty at least the quiescence of the Laras, by mulcting the kingdom at large and disappointing the hopes that in his salad days he had fostered.[54]

For it was not only the *hermandades* that had been promised restoration of local *fueros* throughout the kingdom. So also had the *ricos ombres* and *fijosdalgos* for whom cessation of the territorial reconquest meant the end of territorial largesse, with further acquisition of property having now to come not from the 'inheritances, gifts and holdings' which in 1273 Alfonso X recalled having been lavished upon Nuño González de Lara but by means of purchase from the royal fisc (*realengo*) and gifts from taxation voted by the cortes. With entire categories of royal income from both secular and ecclesiastical sources diverted *en bloc* to the kingdom's political establishment, the *concejos*, whose urban militias Alfonso X had courted had constituted themselves a *de facto* nobility, retaliated by insisting that *ricos homes* thus favoured reside in the locality and contribute to the fiscal

---

[52]   *Rentas*, I, xxxi.
[53]   'Nomina del año de la era de xxiii [1285] de los infançones τ mesnaderos τ de criazon e escriuanos τ clerigos de la capilla τ otros'.
[54]   Moxó, 'De la nobleza vieja', 39–40. For the sums involved: Doubleday, 87–92 (though what they were actually worth only closer study of the successive devaluations of the recent past would reveal).

burden of the place, and the crown responded by seeking to infiltrate the *concejos* with its own fiscal factotums, the *jurados*.[55]

As the gap widened between political ambition and the means of satisfying it so the king's temper shortened. Early in the reign, one of his agents described his master as the king of *pan y palo*, with a loaf of bread in one hand and a cudgel in the other, the symbols of reward and retribution. And there were those who were battered to death by that cudgel, thereby confirming one of the etymologies of his name proposed by his old tutor: Sancho the man of sanctions. While not invariably grim – on at least one occasion a royal chaplain dared to josh with him and the king entered into the spirit of the thing – grimness does seem to have been his default position. Five thousand prostitutes were reported to have been expelled from his court and warned that if they returned they would have their breasts cut off, 'which was done to many'. The anecdote prompts consideration of the nature of that court in comparison with the court of Alfonso X, who had also adopted measures, albeit rather less drastic ones, to prevent the place from becoming overcrowded.[56]

As well as with firmness, Gil de Zamora associated the name Sancho with three cardinal virtues which he predicted would characterize his pupil's reign: fullness of grace and truth, holiness, and wisdom. However, to judge by two works both attributed to Sancho, in the matter of wisdom the contrast between the son's court and the father's could hardly have been starker. In the *Lucidario*, a didactic work based on the *Elucidarium* of Honorius Augustodunensis († *c.*1156), a master doggedly answers a series of his pupil's questions which, because, as the author's prologue states, theological knowledge far outranks philosophical speculation, is principally concerned with such questions as the characteristics of guardian angels, and only secondarily with such 'lighter' issues as why fleas and lice have many feet but horses and elephants only four, and why rabbits and hares sleep with their eyes open.[57] The author's stern rebuke to those intent on investigating 'heavenly things (. . .) which God did not wish men to understand', such as the precise dimensions of the Godhead or His whereabouts at the Creation, evidently has in its sights the Alfonsine intellectual programme as summarized by the disaffected bishops in 1279 and the rationalist climate

[55]   Hernández, *Rentas, passim*; above, 166; Cortes of Valladolid, 1293, cap.3 (*CLC*, I. 119–20); Ladero Quesada, 'Transformaciones', 392–7; Ruiz, *Crisis and Continuity*, 190.
[56]   'Historia hasta 1288 dialogada', 37; *CSIV*, cap. 2 (p. 71b); Hernández & Linehan, 260; Gil de Zamora, *De preconiis Hispanie*, 345–6; Linehan, *History*, 525; Alvarus Pelagius, *Speculum regum*, I. 368; above, 119.
[57]   Kinkade, 'Lucidarios', 79–80, 168–85, 230–33, 257.

also condemned by many Jewish and Islamic mystics.[58] Only one chapter (chap. 91) is concerned with the qualities of precious stones. The same spirit pervades the *Castigos y documentos*, a volume of moral precepts and advice on the art of government addressed to Sancho's heir, the Infante Fernando. Dated in the year in which Tarifa was conquered (1292), the *Castigos* can be read as an expression of the confidence that that victory inspired. Shedding for once the burden of guilt he had brought with him to the throne, Sancho is here heard speaking to his own carnal son on behalf of the celestial parent of that son's soul.[59] Here is the king operating as Vicar of God in an, as it were, private capacity. Not for the first time it is claimed that the divine scheme of things has been vindicated by his seed, and that, since the Almighty who might have wished him to be the son of a labourer had instead chosen him to be the son of a king, to interfere with the rules of succession would be to thwart that plan.[60]

For all that it required a remarkable degree of amnesia regarding the recent past, this insistence on strict adherence to the providential proprieties is common to both the *Lucidario* and the *Castigos*. It is a part of a sense they share that an age in which men were reaching beyond themselves by meddling in heavenly mysteries called for more strictly hierarchical and religiously orthodox government. The gamma-minus report of the *Castigos* on the episcopate of the day, so little different from Diego García's eighty years before, is of almost Manichaean clarity. The catalogue of qualities expected of the 'good prelate' that this allegedly royal work rehearses marks it off sharply from the sleazy environment to which its author's father's account of the energetic dean of Cádiz had belonged.[61]

But of course, in 1292 this was wishful thinking too. The proposition that Castilian society should be governed austerely, in accordance with hierarchical principles, signally fails to allow for the fact that in 1282 that social hierarchy had been undermined by the infante who was now king. Both the *Lucidario* and the *Castigos* are works of political fiction. In the latter's fifty chapters there is not so much as a word about the territorial aristocracy or the courtly nobility.

That absence from the scene has been remarked upon as in striking contrast to the attention the *Castigos* pays to the territorial episcopate

[58]   Ibid., 77; above, 178. *Sefer ha-Zohar* (The Book of Radiance), the 'canon of the Cabbala', dates from these same years: Baer, 261–70; *Zohar*, xlii–xlvi, lviii–lx.

[59]   Prol., ed. Bizzarri, 71–4.

[60]   Above, 182–3. Cf. Kinkade, *Lucidarios*, 81.

[61]   Above, 49, 205; *Castigos*, 171–81.

and the courtly clergy.[62] It is remarkable enough on its own account. And there are other unresolved problems, for example whether these works are Sancho IV's at all rather than those of a clerical elite associated with Toledo and so closely identified with María de Molina as to deserve the term 'Molinist', an epithet usually applied to certain theological controversialists of a later age.[63]

Be that as it may, it has long been customary to view the intellectual activity of Sancho's reign as an extension of his father's and as a link with or bridge to the age of D. Juan Manuel.[64] But bridges are only useful to the extent that those constructing them have the far bank of the river in sight. In this case, twentieth-century hindsight has nothing to tell us about the accuracy of thirteenth-century surveying equipment, even less about their builders' designs. It is not a question of whether cultural activity continued after 1284. With Pay Gómez Charino, Zaccaria's predecessor as admiral of the king's fleet also celebrated for his 'vibrant barcaroles', of that there is no doubt.[65] Rather it is one of the extent to which a controlling intelligence remained at work behind the scenes. We know (or soon shall) that the troubadour Arias Núñez was on Sancho's payroll as well as all about the poetical accomplishments of the disgraced abbot of Valladolid.[66] Even so, we must ask, would Alfonso have done as Sancho did in 1285 in agreeing to Abū Ya'qūb's demand for the return of all those Arabic texts, the thirteen loads of stuff collected from Christian and Jewish houses, works of law and theology, as they were described, *et cetera*?[67]

Would he have remained indifferent to the privatization of his national History in the interests of a particular institution? – a process completed (it has been suggested) at the end of 1289 to coincide with the translation of the remains of Alfonso VII and others into more spacious quarters within Toledo cathedral. Toledo also stood to gain in May 1293 by the foundation within its diocese of a *studium* at Alcalá de Henares. But, like

[62]   By Gómez Redondo, 927, to whose analysis of these two works (pp. 890–943) I am indebted.
[63]   Bizzarri, '*Castigos*', 40–6; Gómez Redondo, 857, 912. There are two problems about this: one, the assumption that the interests of the king and the church of Toledo were identical, and the long-established but mistaken belief (exemplified ibid., 861) that the archbishop of Toledo was out of the country after 1286. Cf. Hernández & Linehan, 271n, 423n; Linehan, 'Invention of Toledo'.
[64]   Kinkade, 'Sancho IV'; Gaibrois, *Sancho IV*, II, 382.
[65]   Eadem, I, 36, 61.
[66]   Catalán, *La Estoria de España*, 54–5, 144–5; Hernández, *Hombres del rey*; Lorenzo Gradín, 'Gomez Garcia, abade de Valadolide'.
[67]   Ibn Abū Zar', *Rawḍ al-qirṭās* (c.1326), trans. Melville & Ubaydli, 163–5. As Codera observed in 1890, it is the 'etc.' that is interesting: 'Catálogo', 380.

the University of Palencia before it, Alcalá failed for lack of funds.[68] So Toledo failed to profit from Alcalá's momentary flourish, despite the ingenuity of its contemporary champions and their creation of a Toledan golden age akin to the golden age of Castilian society in general evoked by the rebel infante. In all likelihood it was one of those partisans who was responsible for the *Philosophia* of Virgil of Córdoba, whose philosophy (a rather threadbare one, it has to be said) and whose description of the wonders of Toledo's twelfth-century *studium* were allegedly translated from Arabic into Latin there in the year 1290.

With his account of a *studium generale* of philosophy in its widest sense at Toledo (or Córdoba; that is never quite clear), to which scholars from Morocco as well as all over the peninsula flocked in order to absorb the wisdom of its twelve masters, including such luminaries as Beromandral, Dubiatalfac and Aliafil, not to mention Córdoba's representatives – Averroes, Avicenna, pseudo-Virgil himself, and (why not?) Seneca – and his questions whether the world had always existed or there had been a Big Bang, the pseudo-Virgil would have felt at home in the company of the Mozarabic scribes responsible for copying the liturgical manuscripts which until recently passed as Visigothic products, Jofré de Loaisa with his report of Toledo cathedral's monopoly of Castilian coronations, and the compilers of the 'amplified version' of the Alfonsine History with its affecting account of the archbishop of Toledo in attendance in 1157 at the deathbed of Alfonso VII.[69]

In accordance with that fictional tradition in April 1295 Archbishop Gonzalo Pérez was in attendance at Sancho IV's deathbed and presided over his burial at Toledo, crowned and garbed in the Franciscan habit, 'in the stone monument that he had had made while he lived, close by don Alfonso emperor of Spain'.[70] In the last week of February, on his final journey to Toledo, the tubercular king had been at Madrid, lodged in the convent of the Dominican nuns of S. Domingo el Real, and granting the ladies' tailor ('be he Moor or Christian'), their shoemaker and their *mayordomo* exemption from certain royal taxes. As with his father at the summit of his career, here at the depths of his we can observe the king attending to issues of a most trivial nature.[71] Here he took leave of his cousin Don Juan Manuel, in whose *Libro de las armas* an account of that final interview is preserved.

---

[68] Bautista, *La* Estoria de España, 51–4; Linehan, 'Toledo forgeries', 666–71; Hernández & Linehan, 331–8.

[69] Heine, 211, 217; Mundó, 'Datación', 2–8, 12–13; above, 215, 8.

[70] *CSIV*, cap. 13 (p. 90b). The emperor was of course Alfonso VII, not Alfonso X as reported by Bizzarri ('*Castigos*', 70); Linehan, *History*, 445.

[71] Gaibrois, *Sancho IV*, III, no. 591; above, 121.

Between spasms of his racking cough, the king was inconsolable. He was dying not of illness but of sinfulness, 'and in particular because of the curse I received from my parents'. Since 'no one can give what he does not have', he had no blessing to convey to his cousin. Nor for that matter had his own parents been blessed by theirs, neither Alfonso X (because Fernando III's blessing of him had been conditional and he had failed the conditions, presumably the requirement to extend the kingdom), nor Queen Violant (because Jaime of Aragón suspected her of having caused the death of her sister, Constança, by means of a punnet of poisoned cherries).[72] And so inevitably the story of the doomed and blasted line continued.[73] There would be no King Sancho V. Altogether it was a poor look-out for the six-year-old bastard waiting to take over Castile.

Also in his dying days Sancho did what he could to fire-proof this son and heir by calling in the latest of the Laras. According to the Chronicle of the reign, Juan Núñez II was another of the royal visitors at Madrid and there the king reminded him of how he had come to him as a beardless youth and of the rewards of wife and fortune lavished on him since – just as his father had once reminded Juan Núñez's grandfather.[74] Would Juan Núñez now undertake to assist the king's beardless son and his widow? The barometric baron accepted the task and did homage. And, according to the Chronicle, the king then died, as he did so perhaps recalling that a principal cause of the previous twenty-five years' dynastic problems had been the entrusting of the interests of Fernando de la Cerda's sons to Juan Núñez II's father.[75]

It has to be remembered that, when he wrote it in the 1340s, the chronicler of Sancho IV was well aware of what the Chronicle of Fernando IV recorded. Indeed it may well have been in order to demonstrate the faithlessness of vassals that he gave such prominence to this deathbed undertaking. For, as soon as Sancho was dead, Juan Núñez reneged on all his promises and, allying himself to the Haro clan, his family's ancient enemies, threatened María de Molina with defection to the La Cerda cause unless she consented to re-establish him at Albarracín. The breakdown of social order was further hastened by the intervention of the two infantes, D. Juan and D. Enrique. The former, fresh from his exploits in assisting the enemy

---

[72]   *Obras completas*, I. 128, 133, 136–8; Linehan, *History*, 487; Kinkade, 'Violante of Aragon', 3.

[73]   Though Sancho's apparently tubercular condition may provide some clue to his father's medical problems they do not to those of his son, who also died young, but of an immoderate lunch.

[74]   Above, 166.

[75]   *CSIV*, cap. 12 (p. 89b); above, 171.

at Tarifa, first staked a claim to the throne, then to the kingdom of León, and, on encountering the resistance of the queen-mother, finally contented himself with further delaying completion of the process of legitimizing the king by claiming as salary, in accordance with Sancho IV's control-system, the ten thousand marks of silver scrimped and saved by María de Molina for the purchase of the necessary papal dispensation. After twenty-six years in Italian prisons, D. Enrique, Alfonso X's younger brother and senior bane and sometime Senator of Rome, arrogated to himself tutorial responsibility for the child king and toured the country touting for support, 'preaching' and reminding his hearers of . . . the golden age of his sainted father. There seemed to be no possibility of reining in the 'great stirrer', as the Chronicle described him, until, nearing seventy, he married Juana 'la Palomilla' ('the little dove'), the teenage sister of Juan Núñez de Lara, who proved too much for his exhausted frame.[76]

'Neither Truth nor Faith'

With additional intervention by the rulers of both Aragón and Portugal, the reign of Fernando IV was a time of almost perpetual civil war. 'Oh, calamity,' Jofré de Loaisa lamented. The kingdom had lapsed into a state of nature. With no merchant daring to venture abroad and fields untilled, everywhere hares, banditry and arson were the order of the day. With no respect shown for churches, sex, age or order, everywhere *ricos homes* passed themselves off as kings.[77] Jofré knew what he was talking about. He finished writing his Chronicle in April 1308, when Fernando's seventeen-year reign still had four to run, and was traumatized by the times through which he had lived, particularly by the proceedings of the Valladolid Cortes of 1295.[78] In the course of that occasion, he reported, during a meeting stretching across the first long summer of the reign, the nobles, barons and prelates of the kingdom had suffered 'things unheard-of'.

They certainly had. The Cortes of 1295 witnessed full-blown social revolution, in the course of which all the accumulated fury and indignation of almost half a century was vented. As all across the country regional and general *hermandades* again rose up in defence of local interests, at Valladolid the representatives of the *concejos* combined against the aristocracy

---

[76]   *CFIV*, cap. I, 6–8, 11 (recording that amongst his effects were found various 'blank charters sealed with the king's seal'): pp. 94b–5a, 116a, 117b, 119a, 132a–b; Doubleday, 93–7.
[77]   *Crónica*, cap. 67–69.
[78]   Ibid., cap. 61; Hernández & Linehan, 327–9.

both secular and ecclesiastical. While churchmen were banished from court, the clerical proletariat made common cause with the disaffected laity.[79] The age of the mutually emollient collaboration of Moses and Aaron, as envisaged in the *Castigos e documentos*, had proved as brief as it had always been imaginary. Almost in confirmation of Boniface VIII's contention regarding the innate anti-clericalism of the laity published that year in *Clericis laicos*, María de Molina combined with the municipalities to preserve the union of the kingdom, just as in 1230 doña Berenguela had done in order to re-create it.[80]

In 1292, when Archbishop Rodrigo of Compostela informed his provincial council of measures designed to ensure that clergy serving in secular households returned to their benefices, 'all the deans, archdeacons, canons, capitular proctors and other clergy there assembled' howled him down and forced him to withdraw the legislation. With sedition in the air, anarchy in the undergrowth, and alliances dissolving as fast as they were formed, the verdict of a Portuguese Hospitaller on conditions in Castile was stark: they were 'hopeless, absolutely hopeless'. The king of Aragon's man concurred: 'There is neither truth nor faith to be found here on any side.'[81] Indeed, it was only with the assistance of a loan of three thousand gold florins provided by a couple of Portuguese churchmen resident at Rome at the time, the bishops of Lisbon and Porto, that Fernando IV's papal dispensation had been secured at any price: a matter of grave embarrassment for Castile, the particulars of which have fortunately remained well-buried in a Portuguese archive ever since.[82]

As the search continued for the means of neutralizing the effects of the Sicilian Vespers there was an authentically *fin de siècle* feel about the Spanish 1290s. By some it was believed that Pedro III on his deathbed had ordered that the island be returned to the Church, but with his elder son's accession to the Aragonese throne, Jaime the younger brother succeeded him there.[83] With the assistance of Edward I of England, profitless peace followed fruitless treaty, facilitated by the exchange of hostages in both

[79] Ibid., 349–63; Linehan, 'Ecclesiastics and the Cortes', 130–35.
[80] Above, 58–9. A comparative treatment of the role of the two queen-mothers, akin to that provided by Maddicott for the 'crises' of the years 1258 and 1297 in English history would prove instructive, not least regarding the parallel trajectories of the archbishops of Toledo on the two occasions.
[81] Costa, 'Concilio provincial', 452–3; Benavides, II, 170; Giménez Soler, 392.
[82] The debt was still outstanding in July 1305. The mediation of the papal referendary, the Castilian Pedro Rodríguez, is to be suspected. Cf. *CFIV*, 119; Linehan, *History*, 540.
[83] Soldevila, *Hist. de Catalunya*, 374–5, 379–80.

directions and on a massive scale, with the largest value attached to Charles of Salerno, the Lame (but otherwise in good working order to judge by his twelve children who constituted the small change of the system), Charles himself deposited with the Unionists at one stage, and at Oloron in 1287 three of his sons, sixty Provencal barons, the vassalage of Provence and fifty thousand marks of silver held as gages against failure to return into custody.[84] But more than that was not possible while the pontiff remained adamant. Either Alfonso must plead for pardon at Rome and prevail on his brother to retreat from Sicily and release the Angevin to rule it, or Aragón would remain under interdict and liable to invasion by 'King' Charles of Valois. Some observers then and since have regarded the release of Salerno, negotiated at Canfranc in 1288, as Alfonso's gravest error, because having promised not to take the title of king of Sicily Salerno then submitted to papal coronation and accepted papal dispensation from all the undertakings he had given. This, though, is to underestimate the strength of Alfonso's domestic problems and the international pressure on him to settle. By the treaty of Tarascon-Brignoles in February 1291 he agreed to do so, accepting all papal demands other than Jaime of Mallorca's reinstatement, payment of the papal *census*, and the undertaking to drive his brother out of Sicily.[85] However, on his death three months later the diplomatic agenda reverted to the starting point.

Or, when on his succession to the throne of Aragón Jaime II defied precedent and the policy of partition (in Soldevila's view his great virtue) by establishing his brother Fadrique not as king of Sicily but as his viceroy, to a stage even prior to that.[86] Then, at the end of 1291 Jaime made peace with Sancho IV, with whom his relationship was initially more harmonious than his predecessor's. With its agreement to divide 'Barbary' along the line of the river Moulouya, in all its essentials the treaty of Monteagudo-Soria might have belonged to the 1170s or earlier, with anxiety for the defence of Christianity after the recent loss of the Holy Land being claimed as justification for Jaime's flagrantly uncanonical and undispensed marriage to the already much-betrothed though still only eight-year-old Infanta Isabel.[87] As the celebrated jurist Oldradus de Ponte, currently studying at Bologna, was later to reflect, matrimony was a device 'of great utility to king, kingdom and the entire Christian faith, for many discords which had existed between the predecessors of the rulers of Castile and Aragón were

[84] Zurita, IV. 92, 104; Powicke, 260, 282–4; González Antón, I, 217–21.
[85] Ibid., I, 233; Soldevila, *Hist. de Catalunya*, 385–7; Zurita, IV. 112–13, 120.
[86] *Hist. de Catalunya*, 390.
[87] Zurita, IV. 124; Gaibrois, *Sancho IV*, II, 139–43; *MHE*, III, 456.

thus resolved'. Indeed, he added in an obiter of which Spanish kings of the preceding century would have approved, it was the duty of 'good princes' to procure peace by such means'.[88]

But as soon as peninsular victory was secured at Tarifa Castile allowed the amicable relationship with Aragón to cool in favour of France, so that when in 1293 Sancho seized the occasion of another papal vacancy to play the part of Sicily's arbiter and at the gathering of kings at Logroño high-handedly required his cousin to surrender the island, the sinuous Catalan refused to be browbeaten, citing the same legal objections to coercion as Sancho had regarding the *hermandades*.

The Castilian's diplomacy left him equally obliged to both parties and forced to choose between the French alliance and the Aragonese marriage. But Sancho was not so mad, he claimed, as to sacrifice both France and Rome for Aragón.[89] Even so, on his death Castile was left without either when Aragón reached a *rapprochement* with France, the still scarcely nubile Infanta Isabel dropped out of the marriageable first division (to be supplanted, subject to inspection, by Blanche of Anjou) and Jaime sent his armies to annex Murcia under cover of assisting Castile's La Cerda claimant.[90] Here again was a reversion to the pre-Cazola peninsula, but set in the infinitely more complex context of post-Vespers Mediterranean power politics.

Discarding Sicily was to prove more difficult than acquiring it. With Boniface VIII installed, however, Jaime reacted astutely to successive papal inducements to disengage from the island whose value to the pope was such that during a nine-year pontificate, it has been calculated, he committed a third of his total revenue to the project. At Anagni in June 1295 Jaime renounced the Sicilian throne and submitted the issue of the kingdom of Mallorca to papal judgement. This was swiftly delivered and uncle Jaime restored as king. On face of it, the count-king was facing total defeat.[91] But not in the longer term, for the king of Mallorca was now required to acknowledge his vassalage (a relationship destined to keep the feudal lawyers fully occupied until the kingdom's reincorporation to the Corona de Aragón in 1343) and the volatile Fadrique was staying put, as his successors would do for centuries longer. True to his Hohenstaufen ancestry, in May 1296 Fadrique had himself crowned king at Palermo and obstinately

[88] Oldradus de Ponte, *cons.* 95, concerning permissibility of alienating part of the fisc 'propter nuptias' (fol. 35ra); above, 18, 42, 110.

[89] Zurita, V. 7; Daumet, *Mémoire*, 115–23; Gaibrois, *Sancho IV*, II, 227–47.

[90] Zurita, V. 11–28; Finke, *Acta Aragonensia*, I, 37–41; Estal, *Corpus*, 47–85. Daumet, *Mémoire*, 196n (for the Infanta's declining exchange value); Salavert y Roca, 303.

[91] Ibid., 236–60; Solalinde, *Hist. de Catalunya*, 395.

refused to be dislodged, even in April 1297 when Boniface's offer to Jaime (now papal *gonfalonier* and admiral of the Holy See) was increased to the (for the time being nugatory) offer of the kingdoms of Sardinia and Corsica in exchange for Sicily, even after Jaime had defeated him in naval battle in the straits of Messina off Cape Orlando in July 1299. Called in by Boniface, Muntaner's realmless 'king of the hat', Charles of Valois, made no impression.[92] In the same year the Angevin king of Naples, Charles II, even mentioned the possibility of pensioning Fadrique off as king of Murcia. Instead, by the treaty of Caltabellotta (1302), he consented to be styled king of Trinacria and not to bequeath the island to his offspring.[93] But that was far from being the end of the story.

Since for Boniface VIII, the great moderator, marriage dispensations were 'small change' (the ecclesiastical equivalent of secular hostage-taking), for as long as Jaime II's policies were consistent with achievement of the papal objective any invalid marriage involving the Aragonese or with Aragonese ramifications was dispensable.[94] And when after 1299 Jaime's attention turned to Sardinia and Corsica as well as Murcia he was open to bids (but not low bids) from Castile for the legitimization of Castile's king. In 1301 the deal was done.[95] Even so, the Infantes de la Cerda remained in play, two of the many loose ends left at the end of the closing century.

Epilogue

The year 1300 is not a good place at which to interrupt the story. Spain's long thirteenth century ended as raggedly as it had begun, and the Spanish peninsula was as divided as at any time over the previous century and a half.

One thing that had perhaps changed since 1150 was the way some of them thought of themselves. Amongst historiographers of the period, and even amongst some of its historians, a shift in attitudes amongst contemporaries regarding their past (and therefore their present) has recently been discerned. After Lucas of Tuy's suppression of the description his sources had provided of Rodrigo as 'last king of the Goths', the Gothic myth continued in service.[96] Despite the denial of its political implications at

---

[92] Oldradus de Ponte, *cons.* 231 (fols. 95vb–96rb); Muntaner, cc. 119, 121; Zurita, V. 55.
[93] Ibid., IV. 71, 112, V. 29–50; Finke, *Acta Aragonensia*, III, 73.
[94] Le Bras, 385.
[95] Linehan, *History*, 540–1.
[96] CM, III. 63$_{15}$. Cf. Gil et al., *Crónicas asturianas*, 122–3. It was not Lucas, it was his editor Mariana, who ended Book III and began Books IV of CM at the year 711.

234 THE CHANGED BALANCE

Cazola in 1179 and its rejection as an historiographical contrivance by
Juan of Osma in the 1230s, the Alfonsine History depended on it and the
reassuring conviction it provided that its author's own legitimacy derived
ultimately from King Rodrigo. In Sancho IV's *Castigos*, though, Rodrigo was
finally buried, with his demise, like the division of the kingdom in 1157,
merited by sin.[97] The same effect, if not the same cause, is explicitly stated
in the Amplified Version of the Alfonsine Chronicle (aka the '1289' and
the 'Sancho IV' Version) where credit for the reconquest 'from the sea of
Santander to the sea of Cádiz' is accorded not to the etiolated descendants
of the sin-stained 'last king' but to the valiant natives of the place, 'los
naturales' of all levels of society who had advanced the cause – although
admittedly some students of its complex textual history have observed
stress-lines developing across the Alfonsine History before 1289 and the
break with the past already foreshadowed.[98]

In Castile in the century of Aquinas, nature attached you to where you
were born. It was somewhere not to do anything shameful. If he had to
renounce his clerical status, Alfonso X wrote to D. Felipe, let him do so
elsewhere than 'in the land of his birth'. According to the same king's pro-
nouncement in the Fourth *Partida*, *natura* bound men by lineage just as
naturaleza did by long-standing affection.[99] In that sense, the rebellion of
1282 had been an offence against both justice and *naturaleza*. Or so it had
seemed in 1283 to the *concejos* of Murcia and Seville, Alfonso X's final
faithful friends.[100] Whether it also seemed so to the inhabitants of the
peninsula twenty years later is another matter. With Castile in chaos, and
'deep divisions and worse dissensions' such as to cause the bishop and
chapter of Zamora (for example) to deliver themselves into the hands of
a lay protector, the significance of the transition from the ethnic to the
territorial and from the myth of Goths to the fiction of the *naturales* may
have seemed less momentous to contemporaries than it sometimes has to
innovative historiographers and fashionable historians.[101]

[97] Ed. Bizzarri, 138; above, 7.
[98] Catalán, *De Alfonso X*, 153; Fernández-Ordóñez, 'Variación', 49, 61–2; 'La técnica
historiográfica', 197.
[99] *CAX*, c. 29 ('en la tierra do erades natural'); *Part*. IV. 24. proem. (there is no corresponding treatment in *F.Real*). Thus Manrique de Lara at the beginning of our period: above, 28.
Cf. Maravall, *Concepto*, 488–9.
[100] Cit. González Jiménez, *Alfonso X*, 354.
[101] Hernández & Linehan, 376; Bautista, *La* Estoria de España, 60–7 (excellent summary).

Bibliography

Manuscript

Cambridge, St John's College, MS. G.9: *Liber provincialis.*
London, National Archives, E36/275: *Liber munimentorum B.*
New York Hispanic Society of America, MS. B189.
Documentation in ACA, AHN, AC Toledo, AC Zamora.

Primary

Abajo Martín, T., *Documentación de la catedral de Palencia* (Palencia, 1986).

Alberic of Trois Fontaines, *Chronica*, ed. P. Scheffer-Boichorst, MGH, SS 23 (1874).

Alexander of Roes, *Memoriale*, ed. H. Grundmann & H. Heimpel, MGH Staatschriften des späteren Mittelalters, I/l (Stuttgart, 1958).

Alfonso X, *El Cancionero profano de Alfonso X el Sabio*, ed. J. Paredes (L'Aquila, 2001).

——, *Cantigas de Santa María*, ed. W. Mettmann, 3 vols. (Madrid, 1986–9).

——, *Espéculo. Texto jurídico atribuido al Rey de Castilla Don Alfonso X, el Sabio*, ed. R. A. MacDonald (Madison, WI, 1990).

——, *Fuero real*, ed. G. Martínez Díez (Ávila, 1988).

——, *General Estoria*, I, II, ed. A. G. Solalinde *et al.* (Madrid, 1930, 1957–61).

——, *Lapidario; Libro de las formas & ymagenes*, ed. R. C. Diman and L. W. Winget (Madison, WI, 1980).

——, *Libro de las Cruzes*, ed. L. A. Kasten & L. B. Kiddle (Madison-Madrid, 1961).

——, *Libros de acedrex, dados e tables. Das Schachzabelbuch König Alfons des Weisen*, ed. A. Steiger (Geneva/Zurich, 1941).

——, *Setenario*, ed. K. H. Vanderford (Buenos Aires, 1945; repr. Barcelona, 1984).

——, *Las Siete Partidas*, ed. Real Academia de la Historia, 3 vols. (Madrid, 1807; repr. Madrid, 1972).

Alfonso de Palencia, *Gesta Hispaniensia ex annalibus duorum dierum collecta Libri I–X*, ed. B. Tate & J. Lawrence, 2 vols. (Madrid, 1998–9).

Altisent, A., *Diplomatari de Santa Maria de Poblet*, I *960–1177* (Poblet-Barcelona, 1993).

Alvarus Pelagius, *Speculum regum*, ed. M. Pinto de Meneses, 2 vols. (Lisbon, 1955–63).

Anales Toledanos II, III, ed. H. Flórez, *ES*, 23 (Madrid, 1767), 401–9, 410–23.

Annales Italiae, ed. G. H. Pertz, MGH, SS, XVIII (Hannover, 1863).

Appel, C. (ed.), *Provenzalische Chrestomathie* (Leipzig, 1895).

Ayala Martínez, C. de, *Libro de privilegios de la Orden de San Juan de Jerusalén en Castilla y León (siglos XII–XV)* (Madrid, 1995).

Bacon, Roger, 'Opus tertium', ed. J. S. Brewer, *Opera quaedam hactenus inedita* (Rolls Ser., London, 1859).

Barton, S. & R. Fletcher, *The World of El Cid. Chronicles of the Spanish Reconquest* (Manchester & New York, 2000).

Böhmer, J. F., ed. J. Ficker and E. Winkelmann, *Regesta imperii*, V. *Die Regesten des Kaiserreichs unter Philipp, Otto IV, Friedrich II, Heinrich (VII), Conrad IV, Heinrich Raspe, Wilhelm und Richard. 1198–1272*, 3 vols. (Innsbruck, 1881–1901).

Brut y Tywysogyon, transl. Thomas Jones (Cardiff, 1955).

Canellas López, A., *Los cartularios de San Salvador de Zaragoza*, 3 vols. (Zaragoza, n.d.).

Castell Maiques, V., *Proceso sobre la ordenación de la Iglesia valentina entre los arzobispos de Toledo, Rodrigo Jiménez de Rada, y de Tarragona, Pedro de Albalat (1238–1246)*, 2 vols. (Valencia, 1996).

Catalán, D. & M. S. de Andrés (eds.), *Crónica de 1344 que ordenó el Conde de Barcelos, don Pedro Alfonso* (Madrid, 1970).

Chaplais, P., *Diplomatic Documents Preserved in the Public Record Office*, I, *1101–1272* (London, 1964).

Chronica Adefonsi Imperatoris, ed. A. Maya Sánchez, CCCM 71/1 (1990), 109–248.

Cortes de los antiguos reinos de León y de Castilla publicadas por la Real Academia de la Historia, I–II (Madrid, 1861–3).

Crónica de Alfonso X, ed. C. Rosell (BAE, 66: Madrid, 1875), 3–66.

Crónica de Alfonso X según el MS. II/2777 de la Biblioteca del Palacio Real (Madrid), ed. M. González Jiménez (Murcia, 2000).

Crónica de Alfonso XI, ed. C. Rosell (BAE, 66: Madrid, 1875), 173–392.

Crónica de Fernando IV, ed. C. Rosell (BAE, 66: Madrid, 1875), 93–170.

Crónica latina de los reyes de Castilla, ed. L. Charlo Brea, CCCM 73 (1997), 7–118.

Crónica de Sancho IV, ed. C. Rosell (BAE, 66: Madrid, 1875), 69–90.

Crónica de la población de Ávila, ed. A. Hernández Segura (Valencia, 1966).

Crónica Geral de Espanha de 1344, ed. L. F. Lindley Cintra, IV (Lisbon, 1990).

Dasent, G. W. (transl.), *Icelandic Sagas. The Saga of Hacon and a fragment of the Saga of Magnus* [1894], II (Felin Fach, 1997).

Desclot, Bernat, *Llibre del rei en Pere* [*Chronicle of the Reign of King Pedro III of Aragon*, transl. F. L. Critchlow, 2 vols. (Princeton, 1928–34)].

Diego García, *Planeta*, ed. M. Alonso (Madrid, 1943).

Documentos de Jaime I de Aragón, ed. A. Huici Miranda & M. D. Cabanes Pecourt, 5 vols. (Valencia, 1976–Zaragoza, 1988).

Domingo Palacio, T., *Documentos del Archivo General de la villa de Madrid*, I (Madrid, 1888).

Domínguez Sánchez, S., *Documentos de Clemente IV (1265–1268) referentes a España* (León, 1996).

——, *Documentos de Gregorio X (1272–1276) referentes a España* (León, 1997).

——, *Documentos de Nicolás III (1277–1280) referentes a España* (León, 1999).

——, *Documentos de Gregorio IX (1227–1241) referentes a España* (León, 2004).

Duro Peña, E., *Documentos da catedral de Ourense* (Santiago de Compostela, 1996).

Estal, J. M. del., *Documentos inéditos de Alfonso X y del Infante su hijo Don Sancho* (Alicante, 1984).

——, *Corpus documental del reino de Murcia bajo la soberanía de Aragón (1296–1304/5)* (Alicante, 1985).

Fernández-Catón, J. M., *Colección documental del Archivo de la Catedral de León*, VI *(1188–1230)* (León, 1991).

Finke, H., *Aus den Tagen Bonifaz VIII.* (Münster-in-W., 1902).

——, *Papsttum und Untergang des Templerordens*, II, *Quellen* (Münster-in-W., 1907).

——, *Acta Aragonensia*, 3 vols. (Berlin, 1908–1922).

Fita, F., *Actas inéditas de siete concilios españoles desde el año 1282 hasta el de 1314* (Madrid, 1882).

——, 'Biografías de San Fernando y de Alfonso el Sabio por Gil de Zamora', *BRAH*, 5 (1884), 308–27.

Fleuchaus, E., *Die Briefsammlung des Berard von Neapel. Überlieferung. Regesten* (Munich, 1998).

Floriano, A. C., 'Anales Toledanos III', *CHE*, 43–4 (1967), 154–87.

Font Rius, J. M., *Cartas de población y franquicia de Cataluña*, I. *Textos* (Madrid-Barcelona, 1969).

Friedberg, E. (ed.), *Corpus iuris canonici*, 2 vols. (Leipzig, 1879–81).

El Fuero de Baeza, ed. J. Roudil (The Hague, 1962).

El Fuero de Teruel, ed. J. Castañé Llinás, 2nd edn (Teruel, 1991).

García y García, A. *et al.* (eds.), *Synodicon Hispanum*, 7 vols. to date (Salamanca, 1981–).

See also Martín Pérez.

As Gavetas da Torre de Tombo, 12 vols. (Lisbon, 1960–77).

Gervase of Tilbury, *Otia imperialia. Recreation of an emperor*, ed. S. E. Banks & J. W. Binns (Oxford, 2002).

Gesta comitum Barcinonensium, ed. L. Barrau Dihigo & J. Massó Torrents (Barcelona, 1925).

Gil, J.: see 'Guillermi Petri de Calciata'.

[Fray Juan] Gil de Zamora, OFM. De preconiis Hispanie, ed. M. de Castro y Castro (Madrid, 1955).

González Díez, E., *Colección diplomática del Concejo de Burgos (884–1369)* (Burgos, 1984).

González Jiménez, M., *Diplomatario andaluz de Alfonso X* (Seville, 1991).

—— (ed.), *Repartimiento de El Puerto de Santa María* (Seville, 2002).

Goodenough, Lady (transl.), *The Chronicle of Muntaner*, 2 vols. (Hakluyt Soc.; London, 1920–21).

Gross, G., 'Las Cortes de 1252. Ordenamiento otorgado al consejo de Burgos en las cortes celebradas en Sevilla el 12 de octubre de 1252 (según original)', *BRAH*, 182 (1985), 95–114.

Guillaume Anelier de Toulouse, *Histoire de la guerre de Navarre en 1276 et 1277*, ed. F. Michel (Paris, 1856).

Guillaume de Nangis, *Gesta Philippi tertii Francorum regis*, ed. C. F. Daunou & J. Naudet, *Recueil des Historiens des Gaules et de la France*, 20 (Paris, 1840), 466–539.

'Guillelmi Petri de Calciata Rithmi de Iulia Romula seu Ispalensi urbe', ed. R. Carande Herrero, CCCM, 73 (1997), 195–209.

Hahn, S. F., *Collectio monumentorum*, I (Brunswick, 1724).

Hernández, F. J., *Las rentas del rey. Sociedad y fisco en el reino castellano del siglo XIII*, 2 vols. (Madrid, 1993).

——, *Los hombres del rey* (forthcoming).

'Historia hasta 1288 dialogada', ed. Marqués de la Fuensanta del Valle, *Colección de documentos inéditos para la Historia de España*, 106 (1893), 3–46.

Humbert de Romanis, *Opusculum tripartitum*: E. Brown (ed.), *Appendix ad fasciculum rerum expetendarum & fugiendarum . . .* , II (London, 1690), 185–229.

Ibn Abū Zar', *Rawd al-Qirtas*, transl. A. Huici Miranda, 2 vols. (Valencia, 1964).

Ibn Khaldūn, *Histoire des Berbères et des dynasties musulmanes de l'Afrique septentrionale*, transl. Macguckin de Slane; new edn by P. Casanova, IV (Paris, 1956).

——, 'Histoire des Benou l'Ahmar, rois de Grenade', transl. M. Gaudefroy-Demombynes, *Journal Asiatique*, 9th ser., 12 (1898), 309–40, 407–62.

Isaac Ibn Sahula, Meshal Haqadmoni. Fables from the Distant Past, ed. & transl. R. Loewe, 2 vols. (Oxford/Portland, OR., 2004).

The Chronicle of James I, King of Aragon, surnamed the Conqueror (written by Himself), transl. J. Forster, 2 vols. (London, 1883).

Jaume I of Aragón, *The Book of Deeds of James I of Aragon. A translation of the Catalan Llibre dels Fets*, by Damian Smith & Helena Buffery (Aldershot, 2003).

Jofré de Loaisa, *Crónica de los reyes de Castilla*, ed. A. García Martínez (Murcia, 1982).

John of Hexham, *Chronicle*, in *Symeonis monachi Opera omnia*, ed. T. Arnold, II (London, Rolls Ser., 1885), 284–332.

Juan Manuel. *Obras completas*, ed. J. M. Blecua, 2 vols. (Madrid, 1981–3).

Kagay, D. J. (transl.), *The Usatges of Barcelona. The fundamental law of Catalonia* (Philadelphia, 1994).

Kehr, P., *Papsturkunden in Spanien*, II. *Navarra und Aragon* (Abhandlungen der Gesellschaft der Wissenschaften zu Göttingen; Phil-hist. Kl., n. F. 21.1; Berlin, 1928).

Kinkade, R. P. (ed.), *Los 'Lucidarios' españoles* (Madrid, 1968).

Lapa, M. R. (ed.), *Cantigas d'escarnho e de mal dizer*, 4th edn (Lisbon, 1998).

Liber Sancti Jacobi: Codex Calixtinus, transl. A. C. Moralejo, C. Torres & J. Feo (Santiago de Compostela, 1951).

El Libro de los doze sabios o Tractado de la nobleza y lealtad [ca.1237]. Estudio y edición, ed. J. K. Walsh (Madrid, 1975).

Limor, O. (transl.), *Die Disputationen zu Ceuta (1179) und Mallorca (1286). Zwei antijüdische Schriften aus dem mittelalterlichen Genua* (Munich, 1994).

Lomax, D. W., 'Una crónica inédita de Silos', *Homenaje a Fray Justo Pérez de Urbel* (Silos, 1976), I, 323–37.

Lucas of Tuy, *Chronicon mundi*, ed. E. Falque, CCCM, 74 (2003).

Mansilla, D., *La documentación pontificia hasta Inocencio III (965–1216)* (Rome, 1955).

——, *La documentación pontificia de Honorio III (1216–1227)* (Rome, 1965).

Martín Martín, J. L., *Documentación medieval de la iglesia catedral de Coria* (Salamanca, 1989).

—— *et al.* (eds.), *Documentos de los archivos catedralicio y diocesano de Salamanca (siglos XII–XIII)* (Salamanca, 1977).

Martín Pérez, Libro de las Confesiones. Una radiografía de la sociedad medieval española, ed. A. García y García *et al.* (Madrid, 2002).

Matthew Paris, *Chronica Majora*, ed. H. R. Luard, 7 vols. (Rolls Ser., London, 1872–83).

——, *Flores Historiarum*, ed. H. R. Luard, 3 vols. (Rolls Ser., London, 1890).

Melville, C. & A. Ubaydli, *Christians and Moors in Spain*, III (Warminster, 1992).

Memorial Histórico Español, I–III (Madrid, 1851–2).

Miquel Rosell, F. (ed.), *Liber Feudorum Maior. Cartulario real que se conserva en el Archivo de la Corona de Aragón*, 2 vols. (Barcelona, 1945–7).

Morgan, M. A. (transl.), *Sepher Ha-Razim. The Book of the Mysteries* (Chico, CA, 1983).

Muntaner: see Goodenough.

Oldradus de Ponte, *Consilia* (Lyons, 1550).

Pereda Llarena, F. J., *Documentación de la catedral de Burgos (1254–1293)* (Burgos, 1984).

Pérez Celada, J. A., *Documentación del monasterio de San Zoilo de Carrión (1047–1300)* (Palencia, 1986).

Pérez Rodríguez, E., *El Verbiginale: una gramática de Castilla del siglo XIII* (Valladolid, c.1990).

[Piccolomini] Aeneae Sylvii episcopi Senensis postea Pii papae II, *Historia rerum Frederici III. imperatoris* (Helmstadt, 1700).

Powers, J. F. (transl.), *The Code of Cuenca. Municipal law on the twelfth-century Castilian frontier* (Philadelphia, 2000).

'Prefatio de Almaria', ed. J. Gil, CCCM 71/1 (1990), 249–67.

(Carlos,) Principe de Viana, *Crónica de los reyes de Navarra*, ed. J. Yanguas y Miranda (Pamplona, 1843; repr. Valencia, 1971).

Ptolemy of Lucca, *Historia ecclesiastica*, ed. L. A. Muratori, RIS, XI (Milan, 1727).

Die Annalen des Tholomeus von Lucca in doppelter Fassung, ed. B. Schmeidler, MGH SS. rer. Germanicarum, n. F., VIII (Berlin, 1930).

Puyol, Julio (ed.), *Crónica de España por Lucas, obispo de Túy* (Madrid, 1926).

Quintana Prieto, A., *Tumbo Viejo de San Pedro de Montes* (León, 1971).

Ralph of Coggeshall, *Chronicon Anglicanum*, ed. J. Stevenson (Rolls Ser., London, 1875).

Les registres d'Alexandre IV, ed. C. Bourel de la Roncière *et al.*, 3 vols. (Paris, 1895–1899).

Les registres de Clément IV, ed. E. Jordan (Paris, 1893–1945).

Les registres de Grégoire IX, ed. L. Auvray *et al.*, 4 vols. (Paris, 1890–1955).

Les registres de Grégoire X, ed. J. Guiraud (Paris, 1892–1906).

Les registres d'Innocent IV, ed. E. Berger, 4 vols. (Paris, 1884–1921).

Les registres d'Urbain IV, ed. J. Guiraud & S. Clémencet, 4 vols. (Paris, 1899–1958).

Riquer, M. de, *Obras completas del trovador Cerverí de Girona* (Barcelona, 1947).

Rodrigo of Toledo, *Historia de rebus Hispanie*, ed. J. Fernández Valverde, CCCM 72 (1987).

——, *Historia arabum*, ed. J. Fernández Valverde, CCCM 72/C (1999), 87–149.

Rodríguez Molina, J., *Colección documental del Archivo Municipal de Úbeda* (Granada, 1990).

Rodríguez R. de Lama, I., *La documentación pontificia de Alejandro IV (1254–1261)* (Rome, 1976).

——, *La documentación pontificia de Urbano IV (1261–1264)* (Rome, 1981).

Roger of Howden, *Chronica*, ed. W. Stubbs, 4 vols. (Rolls Ser., London, 1868–71).

Ruiz Asencio, J. M. & J. A. Martín Fuertes, *Colección documental del Archivo de la Catedral de Leon*, IX *(1269–1300)* (León, 1994).

Rymer, T., *Foedera, conventiones, litterae . . .* [1727], I, 2 vols. (London, 1816).

Sáez, E., *Los fueros de Sepúlveda* (Segovia, 1953).

Salimbene de Adam, *Cronica*, ed. G. Scalia, CCCM 125, 125/A (1998–9).

Sancho IV, *Castigos*, ed. H. O. Bizzarri (Frankfurt am Main, 2001).

Sans i Travé, J. M., 'L'inedito processo dei Templari in Castiglia (Medina del Campo, 27 aprile 1310)', in F. Tomassi (ed.), *Acri 1291. La fine della presenza degli ordini militari in Terra Santa e i nuovi orientamenti nel XIV secolo* (Perugia, 1996), 227–64.

Serrano, L., *Cartulario del Infantado de Covarrubias* (Silos, 1907).

Shepard, W. & F. Chambers, *The Poems of Aimeric de Peguilham* (Illinois, 1950).

Sicardi episcopi Cremonensis Chronica, ed. O. Holder-Egger, MGH, SS., 32 (Hanover-Leipzig, 1905–13).

Simpson, G. G.: see Stones.

Soldevila, F. (ed.), *Les Quatre Grans Cròniques* (Barcelona, 1971).

Stones, E. L. G. & G. G. Simpson, *Edward I and the Throne of Scotland 1290–1296. An edition of the record sources for the Great Cause*, 2 vols. (Oxford, 1978).

Tanner, N. F. (ed.), *Decrees of the Ecumenical Councils*, 1 (London-Washington, DC, 1990).

Udina Martorell, F. (ed.), *El 'Llibre Blanch' de Santes Creus (cartulario del s. XII)* (Barcelona, 1947).

Usatges de Barcelona. El codi a mitjan segle XII, ed. J. Bastardas (Barcelona, 1984).

Villar García, L.-M., *Documentación medieval de la catedral de Segovia (1115–1300)* (Salamanca, 1990).

Vincke, J. (ed.), *Documenta selecta mutuas civitatis Arago-Cathalaunicae et Ecclesiae relationes illustrantia* (Barcelona, 1936).

[Virgil of Córdoba] Virgilii Cordubensis *Philosophia, apud* G. Heine, *Biblioteca anecdotorum seu veterum monumentorum ecclesiasticorum Collectio novissima*, I. *Monumenta regni Gothorum et Arabum in Hispaniis* (Leipzig, 1848), 211–44.

Weiland, L. (ed.), *Constitutiones et acta publica imperatorum et regum inde ab a. MCXCVIII usque ad annum MCCLXXII (1198–1272)* (Hannover, 1896).

William of Newburgh, *Historia rerum anglicarum*, ed. R. Howlett, *Chronicles of the reigns of Stephen, Henry II, and Richard I*, I (Rolls Ser., London, 1884).

Winkelmann, E., *Acta imperii inedita saeculi XIII et XIV. Urkunden und Briefe zur Geschichte des Kaiserreichs und des Königreichs in Sizilien in den Jahren 1198 bis 1400*, 2 vols. (Innsbruck, 1880).

Yellin, D. (ed.), *Gan ha-meshalim we-Hahidoth. Diwan of Don Tadros, son of Yehuda Abu-l-'Afiah*, 2 vols. in 3 parts (Jerusalem, 1932–6).

The Zohar, transl. and comm. D. C. Matt, I (Stanford, 2004).

Secondary

Abulafia, D., *Frederick II. A medieval emperor* (London, 1988).

——, *A Mediterranean Emporium. The Catalan kingdom of Majorca* (Cambridge, 1994).

—— (ed.), *NCMH*, V (Cambridge, 1999).

Aguadé Nieto, S., 'En los orígenes de una coyuntura depresiva: la crisis agraria de 1255 a 1262 en la Corona de Castilla': *De la sociedad arcaica a la sociedad campesina en la Asturias medieval. Estudios de historia agraria* (Alcalá de Henares, 1988), 335–70.

Almagro, M., *Historia de Albarracín y su sierra*, III–IV (Teruel, 1959, 1964).

Almeida, F. de, *História da Igreja em Portugal*, ed. D. Peres, 4 vols. (Porto, 1967–71).

Altisent, A. *Història de Poblet* (Poblet, 1974).

Alvar, C., *La poesía trovadoresca en España y Portugal* (Madrid, 1977).

——, *Textos trovadorescas sobre España y Portugal* (Madrid, 1978).

——, 'Poesía y política en la corte alfonsí', *Cuadernos Hispanoamericanos*, n. 410 (Aug. 1984), 5–20.

Alverny, M. T. d', 'Translations and translators', in R. L. Benson & G. Constable (eds.), *Renaissance and Renewal in the Twelfth Century* (Oxford, 1982), 421–62.
—— & G. Vajda, 'Marc de Tolède, traducteur d'Ibn Tūmart', *al-Andalus*, 16 (1951), 99–140, 259–307.
Alvira Cabrer, M., 'La imagen del Miramolín al-Nasir (1199–1213) en las fuentes cristianas del siglo XIII', *AEM*, 26 (1996), 1003–28.
Amasuno, M. V., *La materia medica de Dioscórides en el Lapidario de Alfonso X el Sabio* (Madrid, 1987).
Argüello, V., 'Memoria sobre el valor de las monedas de D. Alfonso el Sabio . . .', *Memorias de la Real Academia de la Historia*, 8 (1852).
Arié, R., *L'Espagne musulmane au temps des Nasrides (1232–1492)* (Paris, 1973).
Arizaleta, A., *La translation d'Alexandre. Recherches sur les structures et les significations du* Libro de Alexandre (Paris, 1999).
Arjona Castro, A., *Zuheros. Estudio geográfico e histórico de un municipio cordobés* (Córdoba, 1973).
Arranz Guzmán, A., 'Alfonso X y la conservación de la naturaleza', in M. Rodríguez *et al.* (eds.), *Alfonso X el Sabio, vida, obra y época* (Madrid, 1989), 127–35.
Arroyo, F., 'Blasco de Alagón y el comienzo de la reconquista valenciana', *EEMCA*, 9 (1973), 71–99.
Arvizu, F. de: see Estepa Díez.
Asenjo González, M., 'Fiscalidad regia y sociedad en los concejos de la Extremadura castellano-oriental durante el reinado de Alfonso X', *Homenaje al profesor Juan Torres Fontes* (Murcia, 1987), 69–84.
Asín Palacios, M., 'El juicio de P. Mariana sobre Alfonso el Sabio', *al-Andalus*, 7 (1942), 479.
Assis, Yom Tov, 'Sexual behaviour in mediaeval Hispano-Jewish society', in A. Rapoport-Albert & S. J. Zipperstein (eds.), *Jewish History. Essays in honour of Chimen Abramsky* (London, 1988), 25–59.
Aurell, M., *Les Noces du comte. Mariage et pouvoir en Catalogne (785–1213)* (Paris, 1995).
Avalle, S. d'A., *Peire Vidal. Poesie* (Milan-Naples, 1960).
Ayala Martínez, C. de, *Directrices fundamentales de la política peninsular de Alfonso X* (Madrid, 1986).
——, *Las órdenes militares hispánicas en la Edad Media (siglos XII–XV)* (Madrid, 2003).
——, 'Paces castellano-aragonesas de Campillo-Agreda', *EEM*, 5 (1986), 151–68.
——, 'Jaime I y la sublevación mudéjar-granadina de 1264': *Homenaje al profesor Juan Torres Fontes* (Murcia, 1987), 91–107.
——, 'Las relaciones de Alfonso X con la Santa Sede durante el pontificado de Nicolás III (1277–1280)', in C. de Miguel Rodríguez *et al.* (eds.), *Alfonso X el Sabio. Vida, obra y época* (Madrid, 1989), 137–51.
——, 'La monarquía y las ordenes militares durante el reinado de Alfonso X', *Hispania*, 51 (1991), 409–65.

———, 'Alfonso X y sus relaciones políticas con la Corona de Aragón: los decisivos años de la alianza gibelina (1264–1274)'; *XV Congreso de Historia de la Corona de Aragón. Actas*, II (Zaragoza, 1997), 43–71.

———, 'Relaciones de Alfonso X con Aragón y Navarra', *Alcanate*, 4 (2004–5), 101–46.

Baer, Y., *A History of the Jews in Christian Spain*, I. *From the age of the reconquest to the fourteenth century* (Philadephia-Jerusalem, 1992).

Bagby, A. I., 'The Jew in the *Cántigas* of Alfonso X, el Sabio', *Speculum*, 46 (1971), 670–88.

Ballesteros Beretta, A., *Alfonso X el Sabio* (Barcelona, 1963).

———, 'La toma de Salé en tiempos de Alfonso X el Sabio', *al-Andalus*, 8 (1943), 89–128.

———, 'Burgos y la rebellion del Infante D. Sancho', *BRAH*, 119 (1946), 93–194.

Barrero García, A. M., 'Un formulario de cancillería episcopal castellano leonés del siglo XIII', *AHDE*, 46 (1976), 671–711.

Barrios García, A., *Documentación medieval de la catedral de Ávila* (Salamanca, 1981).

———, *Estructuras agrarias y de poder en Castilla. El ejemplo de Ávila (1085–1320)*, I (Salamanca, 1983).

Barton, S., *The Aristocracy in Twelfth-century León and Castile* (Cambridge, 1997).

———, 'Two Catalan magnates in the courts of the kings of León-Castile: the careers of Ponce de Cabrera and Ponce de Minerva re-examined', *Journal of Medieval History* 18 (1992), 233–66.

Bautista, F., *La Estoria de España en época de Sancho IV: sobre los reyes de Asturias* (London, 2006).

———, 'Escritura cronística e ideología histórica: la *Chronica latina regum Castellae*', *e-Spania*, 2 (2007).

Bayley, C. C., 'The diplomatic preliminaries of the Double Election of 1257 in Germany', *EHR*, 62 (1947), 457–83.

Beltrán de Heredia, V., *Cartulario de la Universidad de Salamanca*, 6 vols. (Salamanca, 1970–73).

Benavides, A., *Memorias de Don Fernando IV de Castilla*, 2 vols. (Madrid, 1860).

Benito i Monclús, P., 'Els "clamores" de Sant Cugat contra el fill del Gran Seneschal i altres episodis de terrorisme nobiliari (1161–1162)', *AEM*, 30 (2000), 851–86.

Benito Ruano, E., 'La iglesia española ante la caída del Imperio Latino de Constantinopla', *HS*, 11 (1958), 5–20.

Bensch, S. P., *Barcelona and its Rulers, 1096–1291* (Cambridge, 1995).

Bertolucci Pizzorusso, V., 'La supplica di Guiraut Riquier e la risposta di Alfonso X di Castiglia', *Studi Mediolatini e Volgari*, 14 (1966), 9–135.

———, 'Un trattato di "Ars dictandi" dedicato ad Alfonso X', *Studi Mediolatini e Volgari*, 15–16 (1968), 9–88.

Bisson, T. N., *Fiscal Accounts of Catalonia under the Early Count-kings (1151–1213)*, 2 vols. (Berkeley, 1984).

———, *The Medieval Crown of Aragon. A short history* (Oxford, 1986).

———, *Tormented Voices. Power, crisis and humanity in rural Catalonia 1140–1200* (Cambridge, MA-London, 1998).

——, 'A general court of Aragon (Daroca, February 1228)', *EHR*, 92 (1977), 107–24.

——, 'L'essor de la Catalogne: identité, pouvoir et idéologie dans une société du XIIe siècle', *Annales ESC*, 39 (1984), 459–61.

Bizzarri, H., *'Castigos del rey D. Sancho IV': una reinterpretación* (London, 2004).

——, 'Reflexiones sobre la empresa cultural del rey don Sancho IV de Castilla', *AEM*, 31 (2001), 429–49.

Blöcker-Walter, M., *Alfons I. von Portugal. Studien zu Geschichte und Sage des Begründers der portugiesischen Unabhängigkeit* (Zurich, 1966).

Boni, M., *Sordello, Le poesie* (Bologna, 1954).

Bonnassie, P., *La Catalogne du milieu du Xe à la fin du XIe siècle*, 2 vols. (Toulouse, 1975–6).

Borrás Gualis, G. M., *Arte mudéjar aragonés*, 2 vols. (Zaragoza, 1985).

Boscolo, A., 'L'eredità sveva di Pietro il Grande, re d'Aragona': *La società mediterranea all'epoca del Vespro; XI Congresso di Storia della Corona d'Aragona . . . 1982* (Palermo, 1983), I, 83–99.

Boswell, J., *The Royal Treasure. Muslim Communities under the Crown of Aragon in the Fourteenth Century* (New Haven & London, 1977).

——, *The Marriage of Likeness. Same-sex unions in pre-modern Europe* (London, 1995).

Brancaforte, B., *Alfonso el Sabio. Prosa histórica* (Madrid, 1984).

Branciforti, F., *Le rime di Bonifaci Calvo* (Catania, 1955).

Brett, M., 'The Maghrib' in Abulafia (ed.), *NCMH*, V, 622–35.

Brooke, Christopher, *Europe in the Central Middle Ages. 962–1154*, 2nd edn (London, 1987).

Brundage, J. A., 'Matrimonial politics in thirteenth-century Aragon: Moncada v. Urgel', *JEH*, 31 (1980), 271–82.

Burnett, C., 'Filosofía natural, secretos y magia', in L. García Ballester (ed.), *Historia de la ciencia y de la técnica en la Corona de Castilla*, I, *Edad Media* (Salamanca, 2002), 95–144.

Burns, R. I., *The Crusader Kingdom of Valencia. Reconstruction on a thirteenth-century frontier*, 2 vols. (Cambridge, MA, 1967).

——, *Islam under the Crusaders. Colonial survival in the thirteenth-century kingdom of Valencia* (Princeton, 1973).

——, *Muslims, Christians and Jews in the Crusade Kingdom of Valencia* (Cambridge, 1984).

——. (ed.), *The Emperor of Culture. Alfonso X the Learned of Castile and his thirteenth-century Renaissance* (Philadelphia, 1990).

——, 'The parish as a frontier institution in thirteenth-century Valencia', *Speculum*, 37 (1962), 244–51.

——, 'A medieval earthquake: Jaume I, al-Azrag, and the early history of Onteniente in the kingdom of Valencia', *Jaume I y su época: X Congreso de Historia de la Corona de Aragón*, 1–2 (Zaragoza, 1979–82), 209–44.

——, 'The spiritual life of Jaume the Conqueror king of Arago-Catalonia, 1208–1276. Portrait and self-portrait', *Jaume I y su época: X Congreso de Historia de la Corona de Aragón*, 1–2 (Zaragoza, 1979–82), 323–57.

——, 'Warrior neighbors: Alfonso el Sabio and crusader Valencia', *Viator* 21 (1990), 147–202.

——, 'Muslims in the thirteenth-century realms of Aragon', in Powell, *Muslims*, 57–101.

—— & P. E. Chevedden, *Negotiating Cultures. Bilingual surrender treaties in Muslim-Crusader Spain* (Leiden, 1999).

Cabrera, E., 'The medieval origins of the great landed estates of the Guadalquivir valley', *Economic History Review*, 2nd ser., 42 (1989), 465–83.

Calderón Calderón, M., 'La imagen del rey en la Crónica de Alfonso X', *BRAH*, 197 (2000), 255–66.

Capmany y de Montpalau, A. de, *Memorias historicas sobre la marina, comercio, y artes de la antigua ciudad de Barcelona*, II (Madrid, 1779).

Cárdenas, A. J., 'Toward an understanding of the astronomy of Alfonso X, el Sabio', *Indiana Social Studies Quarterly*, 31/3 (1978–9), 81–90.

——, 'Alfonso el Sabio's "castellano drecho"', *La Corónica*, 9 (1980), p. 3 (summary).

——, 'Alfonso X and *the Studium generale*', *Indiana Social Studies Quarterly*, 33 (1980–81), 65–75.

——, 'Alfonso's scriptorium and chancery', Burns, *Emperor of Culture*, 90–108.

——, 'The myth of Hercules in the works of Alfonso X', *BHS*, Glasgow, 74 (1997), 5–20.

Carpenter, D. E., *Alfonso X and the Jews. An edition of and commentary on Siete Partidas 7.24 'De los judios'* (Berkeley, 1986).

Carreras i Casanovas, A., *El monestir de Santes Creus (1150–1200). Adquisició i formació del domini*, 2 vols. (Valls, 1992).

Cartellieri, O., *Peter von Aragon und die sizilianische Vesper* (Heidelberg, 1904).

Catalán, D., *De Alfonso X al Conde de Barcelos* (Madrid, 1962).

——, *La Estoria de España de Alfonso X* (Madrid, 1992).

——, *De la silva textual al taller historiográfico alfonsí* (Madrid, 1996).

——, *La épica española* (Madrid, 2002).

—— & E. Jerez, *'Rodericus' romanzado en los reinos de Aragón, Castilla y Navarra* (Madrid, 2005).

Catlos, B. A., *The Victors and the Vanquished. Christians and Muslims of Catalonia and Aragon, 1050–1300* (Cambridge, 2004).

Cavero Domínguez, G., C. Álvarez Álvarez & J. A. Martín Fuertes, *Colección documental del Archivo Diocesano de Astorga* (León, 2001).

Cerro Malagón, R. del, *et al.*, *Arquitecturas de Toledo, del Romano al Gótico* (Ciudad Real, 1991).

Chamberlin, C. L., ' "Unless the Pen Writes as it Should": the proto-cult of Saint Fernando III in Seville in the thirteenth and fourteenth centuries', *Sevilla 1248*, 389–417.

Chazan, R., *Barcelona and Beyond. The disputation of 1263 and its aftermath* (Berkeley-Los Angeles, 1992).

Chevedden, P. E. see Burns.

Cobban, A. B., *The Medieval Universities, their Development and Organization* (London, 1975).

Codera, F., 'Catálogo de los libros árabes adquiridos para la Academia en virtud del Viaje á Túnez', *BRAH*, 16 (1890), 377–94.

Cohen, J., *The Friars and the Jews. The evolution of medieval anti-Judaism* (Ithaca, NY & London, 1982).

Coleman, E., 'Infanticide in the early Middle Ages', in S. M. Stuard, *Women in Medieval Society* (Philadelphia, 1976), 47–70.

Coll, J. M., 'Escuelas de lenguas orientales en los siglos XIII y XIV (período Raymundiano)', *Analecta Sacra Tarraconensia*, 17 (1944), 115–35.

Coll i Alentorn, M., 'La historiografia de Catalunya en el període primitiu', *Estudis Romànics,* 3 (1951–2), 139–96.

Collins, R., *The Arab Conquest of Spain, 710–797* (Oxford, 1989).

Cómez Ramos, R., 'El retrato de Alfonso X en la primera *Cantiga de Santa María*', in Katz & Keller, 35–52.

——, 'Tradición e innovación artísticas en Castilla en el siglo XIII', *Alcanate*, 3 (2002–3), 135–63.

Constable, O. R. (ed.), *Medieval Iberia. Readings from Christian, Muslim and Jewish sources* (Philadelphia, 1997).

Cortabarría Beitia, A., 'L'étude des langues au Moyen Âge chez les Dominicains. Espagne, Orient, Raymond Martin', *Mélanges de l'Institut Dominicain d'Études Orientales du Caire*, 10 (1970), 189–248.

Las Cortes de Castilla y León en la Edad Media. Actas de la Primera Etapa del Congreso Científico sobre la Historia de las Cortes de Castilla y León. Burgos, 30 de Septiembre a 3 de Octubre de 1986, 2 vols. (Valladolid, 1988).

Las Cortes de Castilla y León 1188–1988. Actas de la Tercera Etapa del Congreso Científico sobre la Historia de las Cortes de Castilla y León. León, del 26 al 30 de Septiembre de 1988 (Valladolid, 1990).

Cortese, E., 'Il tramonto del mito dell'Impero universale. Un parere di Oldrado e la sua fortuna in Spagna tra Tre e Quattrocento (da Iacobus Ciionis a Petrus Belluga e Rodericus Sancius de Arévalo)', in O. Condorelli (ed.), *"Panta rei". Studi dedicati a Manlio Bellomo* (Rome, 2004), II, 23–67.

Costa, A. D. de Sousa, *Mestre Silvestre e Mestre Vicente, juristas da contenda entre D. Afonso II e suas irmãs* (Braga, 1963).

——, 'Concilio provincial de Compostela realizado em 1292', *Itinerarium*, 32 (1987), 393–470.

Cowdrey, H. E. J., 'The Peace and the Truce of God in the eleventh century', *Past & Present*, no. 46 (1970), 42–67.

Craddock, J. R., 'La cronología de las obras legislativas de Alfonso X el Sabio', *AHDE*, 51 (1981), 365–418.

——, 'Dynasty in dispute: Alfonso X el Sabio and the succession to the throne of Castile in history and legend', *Viator*, 17 (1986), 197–219.

——, 'El *Setenario*: última e inconclusa refundición alfonsina de la primera *Partida*', *AHDE*, 56 (1986), 441–66.

——, 'The legislative works of Alfonso el Sabio', Burns, *Emperor of Culture*, 182–97.

——, 'El texto del *Espéculo*', *Initium*, 3 (1998), 221–74.

Crone, P., *Medieval Islamic Political Thought* (Edinburgh, 2004).

Daumet, G., *Mémoire sur les relations de la France et de la Castille de 1255 à 1320* (Paris, 1913).

——, 'Les testaments d'Alphonse X le Savant, roi de Castille', *BEC*, 67 (1906), 70–99.

Defourneaux, M., *Les Français en Espagne aux XIe et XIIe siècles* (Paris, 1949).

——, 'Louis VII et les souverains espagnols: l'énigme du "pseudo-Alphonse"', *Estudios dedicados a Ramón Menéndez Pidal*, VI (Madrid, 1956), 647–61.

del Giudice, G., *Don Arrigo, infante di Castiglia* (Naples, 1875).

Delgado Roig, J., 'Examen medico-legal de unos restos históricos: los cadaveres de Alfonso X el Sabio y doña Beatriz de Suabia', *Archivo Hispalense*, 9 (1948), 135–53.

Deyermond, A., 'The death and rebirth of Visigothic Spain in the *Estoria de España*', *Revista Canadiense de Estudios Hispánicos*, 9 (1984–5), 345–67.

——, D. G. Pattison & E. Southworth, Mio Cid *Studies. Some problems of diplomatic fifty years on* (London, 2002).

Díaz Bodegas, P., 'Aproximación a la figura de D. Aznar López de Cadreita, obispo de Calahorra y La Calzada (1238–1263)', *Anthologica Annua*, 39 (1992), 11–101.

Díaz y Díaz, M. C., *El Códice Calixtino de la catedral de Santiago* (Santiago de Compostela, 1988).

Diego Lobejón, M. W. de, *El Salterio de Hermann el Alemán (Ms. Escurialense I-j-8)* (Valladolid, 1993).

Dillard, H., *Daughters of the Reconquest. Women in Castilian town society, 1100–1300* (Cambridge, 1984).

Domínguez Rodríguez, A., *Astrología y arte en el Lapidario de Alfonso X el Sabio* (Madrid, 1984).

——, '"Compassio" y "co-redemptio" en las Cantigas de Santa María. Crucifixión y Juicio Final', *Archivo Español de Arte*, 71 (1998), 17–35.

See also Montoya Martínez.

Dossat, Y., 'De singuliers pèlerins sur le chemin de Saint-Jacques en 1272', *Annales du Midi*, 82 (1970), 209–20.

Doubleday, S. R., *The Lara Family. Crown and nobility in medieval Spain* (Cambridge, MA, 2001).

Duby, G., *Medieval Marriage* (Baltimore, 1978).

——, 'Les "jeunes" dans la société aristocratique dans la France du Nord-Ouest au XII siècle': Duby, *Hommes et structures du Moyen Âge* (Paris, 1973), 213–25.

Dufourcq, C.-E., *L'Espagne catalane et le Maghrib aux XIIIe et XIVe siècles. De la bataille de Las Navas de Tolosa (1212) à l'avènement du sultan mérinide Aboul-Hasan (1331)* (Paris, 1966).

——, 'Un projet castillan du XIIIe siècle: la "croisade d'Afrique"', *Revue d'Histoire et de Civilisation du Maghreb*, 1 (1966), 27–51.

Dunbabin, J., *Charles I of Anjou. Power, kingship and state-making in thirteenth-century Europe* (London, 1998).

Ecker, H. L., 'Administradores mozárabes en Sevilla después de la conquista', *Sevilla 1248*, 821–38.

See also Marín.

Engels, O., 'La idea imperial de Alfonso X y Sevilla', in P. M. Piñero Ramírez & C. Wentzlaff-Eggehert (eds.), *Sevilla en el Imperio de Carlos V: encrucijada entre dos mundos y dos épocas. Actas del Simposio Internacional celebrado en la Facultad de Filosofía y Letras de la Universidad de Colonia (23–25 de junio de 1988)* (Seville, 1991), 31–6.

Epalza, M. de, *Jésus otage. Juifs, chrétiens et musulmans en Espagne (VIe–XVIIe siècles)* (Paris, 1987).

——, 'Mutaciones urbanísticas debidas a la transformación de mezquitas en iglesias', *VI Simposio Internacional de Mudejarismo. Actas. Teruel, 16–18 de septiembre de 1993* (Teruel, 1995), 501–18.

Erdmann, C., *Das Papsttum und Portugal im ersten Jahrhundert der portugiesischen Geschichte*; Abhandlungen der Preuss. Akad. der Wissenschaften, Phil.-hist. Kl., 5 (Berlin, 1928).

Ernst, W., 'Die Lieder des provenzalischen Trobadors Guiraut von Calanso', *Romanische Forschungen*, 44 (1930), 255–406.

Escalona, R. (ed. J. Pérez), *Historia de la real monasterio de Sahagún* (Madrid, 1782; repr. Madrid, 1982).

E[scudero de la] P[eña], J. M., 'Variedades', *RABM*, 2 (1872), 59–60.

España Sagrada: see Flórez.

Estepa Díez, C., 'El "fecho de Imperio" y la política internacional en la época de Alfonso X', Mondéjar & Montoya, *Estudios Alfonsíes*, 189–205.

——, 'La política imperial de Alfonso X. Esbozo de una possible ideología política alfonsina', in M. J. Hidalgo de la Vega (ed.), *La historia en el contexto de las ciencias humanas y sociales. Homenaje a Marcelo Vigil Pascual* (Salamanca, 1989), 205–15.

—— & F. de Arvizu, 'Notas críticas a la bibliografía reciente sobre las Cortes de León de 1188', *Las Cortes de Castilla y León 1188–1988*, 59–74.

Fanta, A., 'Ein Bericht über die Ansprüche des Königs Alfons auf den deutschen Thron', *MIöG*, 6 (1885), 94–104.

Fawtier, R., *The Capetian Kings of France* (London, 1965).

Feige, P., 'Die Anfänge des portugieschichen Königtums und seiner Landeskirche', *Spanische Forschungen der Görresgesellschaft*, Reihe 1, 29 (1978).

Fernández-Armesto, F., *Before Columbus. Exploration and colonisation from the Mediterranean to the Atlantic, 1229–1492* (London, 1987).

Fernández-Catón, J. M., 'La Curia Regia de León de 1188 y sus "decreta" y constitución', *El Reino de León en la Alta Edad Media, IV. La monarquía (1109–1230)* (León, 1993), 351–532.

Fernández Martín, L., 'La participación de los monasterios en la "hermandad" de los reinos de Castilla, León y Galicia (1282–1284)', *HS*, 25 (1972), 5–31.

Fernández-Ordóñez, I., *Las Estorias de Alfonso el Sabio* (Madrid, 1992).

—— *Versión crítica de la Estoria de Espana* (Madrid, 1993).

—— (ed.), *Alfonso X el Sabio y las Crónicas de España* (Valladolid, 2000).

——, 'El taller historiográfico alfonsí. La *Estoria de España* y la *General estoria* en el marco de las obras promovidas por Alfonso el Sabio', in Montoya Martínez & Domínguez Rodríguez, 105–26.

——, 'El taller de las "Estorias" ', in Fernández-Ordóñez, *Alfonso X el Sabio y las Crónicas de España*, 61–82.

——, 'Variación en el modelo historiográfico alfonsí en el siglo XIII. Las versiones de la *Estoria de España*, in G. Martin (ed.), *La historia alfonsí: el modelo y sis destinos (siglos XIII–XV). Seminario organizado por la Casa de Velázquez (30 de enero de 1995)* (Madrid, 2000), 41–74.

——, 'De la historiografía fernandina a la alfonsí', *Alcanate* 3 (2002–3), 93–133.

——, 'La técnica historiográfica del Toledano', *CLCHM* 26 (2003), 187–221.

Fernández-Xesta y Vázquez, E., ' "El Motín de la trucha" y sus consecuencias sobre don Ponce Giraldo de Cabrera", *Primer Congreso de la Historia de Zamora*, III (Zamora, 1991), 261–83.

Fernando III y su tiempo (1201–1252), VIII Congreso de Estudios Medievales (León, 2003).

Ferreiro Alemparte, J., 'Hermann el Alemán, traductor del siglo XIII en Toledo', *HS*, 35 (1983), 9–56.

Ferrer Mallol, M. T., 'A propósito de un libro de David Abulafia', *AEM*, 31 (2001), 453–61.

Filgueira Valverde, J., *Sobre lírica medieval gallega y sus perduraciones* (Valencia, 1977).

Fita, F., 'Igualación de pesos y medidas por D. Alfonso el Sabio', *BRAH*, 38 (1901), 137–44.

——, 'Santiago de Galicia. Nuevas impugnaciones y nueva defensa, IV, V', *Razón y Fe*, 2 (1902), 35–45, 178–95.

Flahiff, G. B., '*Deus non vult*. A critic of the Third Crusade', *Mediaeval Studies*, 9 (1947), 162–88.

Fleisch, I., *Sacerdotium – Regnum – Studium. Der westiberische Raum und die europäische Universitätskultur im Hochmittelalter* (Berlin, 2006).

Fletcher, R. A., *The Quest for El Cid* (London, 1989).

——, 'Reconquest and crusade in Spain *c.*1050–1150', *Transactions of the Royal Historical Society*, 5th ser. 37 (1987), 31–47.

Flórez, E., *Memorias de las reynas cathólicas, historia genealógica de la casa real de Castilla, y de León*, 2 vols. (Madrid, 1761).

——, M. Risco *et al.*, *España Sagrada*, 51 vols. (Madrid, 1747–1879).

Forey, A., *The Military Orders from the Twelfth to the early Fourteenth Centuries* (Basingstoke, 1992).

Fradejas Lebrero, J., *Estudios épicos* (Ceuta, 1962).

Fraker, C. F., 'Alfonso X, the Empire and the *Primera* crónica', *BHS*, 55 (1978), 95–102.

Fransen, G. & A. García y García, 'Nuevas decretales de Gregorio IX en la Biblioteca del Cabildo de Córdoba', *REDC*, 15 (1960), 147–51.

Freedman, P. H., *The Diocese of Vic. Tradition and regeneration in medieval Catalonia* (New Brunswick, NJ, 1983).

——, 'Another look at the uprising of the townsmen of Vic (1181–1183)', *Acta Historica et Archaeologica Mediaevalia*, 20–21 (1999–2000) [*Homenatge al dr. Manuel Riu i Riu*, I], 177–86.

Fried, J., *Der päpstliche Schutz für Laienfürsten. Die politische Geschichte des päpstlichen Schutzprivilegs für Laien (11.–13. Jh.)* (Heidelberg, 1980).

Funes, L., *El modelo historiográfico alfonsí: una caracterización* (London, 1997).

Gaibrois de Ballesteros, M., *Historia del reinado de Sancho IV de Castilla*, 3 vols. (Madrid, 1922–8).

——, 'Tarifa, y la política de Sancho IV de Castilla', *BRAH*, 74 (1919), 418–36, 521–9; 75 (1919), 349–55; 76 (1920), 53–77, 123–60.

Gallagher, J. & R. E. Robinson, 'The imperialism of free trade', *Economic Hist. Rev.*, 2nd ser., 6 (1953), 1–15.

García Avilés, A., 'Alfonso X y la tradición de la magia astral', in Montoya Martínez & Domínguez Rodríguez, 83–103.

——, 'Alfonso X y el *Liber Razielis*: imágines de la magia astral judía en el *scriptorium* alfonsí', *BHS* [Glasgow], 74 (1997), 21–39.

García-Ballester, L., *Historia social de la medicina en la España de los siglos XIII al XVI* (Madrid, 1976).

——, 'Nature and science in thirteenth-century Castile. The origins of a tradition: the Franciscan and Dominican *studia* at Santiago de Compostela (1222–1230)', in *Medicine in a Multicultural Society: Christian, Jewish and Muslim practitioners in the Spanish Kingdoms, 1222–1610* (Aldershot, 2001), item II (1–44).

García de Cortázar, J. A., *La sociedad rural en la España medieval*, 2nd edn (Madrid, 1990).

García Fitz, F., 'El cerco de Sevilla: reflexiones sobre la guerra de asedio en la Edad Media', *Sevilla 1248*, 115–54.

García Gallo, A., 'El "Libro de las leyes" de Alfonso el Sabio: del Espéculo a las Partidas', *AHDE*, 21–22 (1951–2), 345–528.

——, 'Los fueros de Toledo', *AHDE*, 45 (1975), 341–488.

García y García. A.: see Fransen.

García Gómez, E., 'Traducciones alfonsíes de agricultura árabe', *BRAH*, 181 (1984), 387–97.

Garnett, G., *Conquered England. Kingship, succession, and tenure 1066–1166* (Oxford, 2007).

Gautier Dalché, J., *Historia urbana de León y Castilla en la Edad Media (siglos IX–XIII)* (Madrid, 1979).

——, 'L'histore castillane dans la première moitié de XIVe siècle', *AEM*, 7 (1970–71), 239–52.

Geanakoplos, D. J., *The Emperor Michael Palaeologus and the West, 1258–1282* (Cambridge, MA, 1959).

Gelsinger, B., 'A thirteenth-century Norwegian-Castilian alliance', *Medievalia et Humanistica*, n. s. 10 (1981), 55–80.

Gibert, R., 'El derecho municipal de León y Castille', *AHDE*, 31 (1961), 695–753.

Giesey, R. A., *If Not, Not. The oath of the Aragonese and the legendary laws of Sobrarbe* (Princeton, 1968).

Gil, J., 'A apropriação da ideia de império pelos reinos da península ibérica: Castela', *Penélope*, no. 15 (1995), 11–30.

——, 'La historiografía': *La cultura del románico, siglos XI al XIII* [*Historia de España Menéndez Pidal*, XI], ed. F. López Estrada (Madrid, 1995), 1–109.

Gil, J. S., *La escuela de traductores de Toledo y los colaboradores judíos* (Toledo, 1985).

Giménez Soler, A., *Don Juan Manuel. Biografía y estudio crítico* (Zaragoza, 1932).

Gingerich, O., 'Alfonso the Tenth as a patron of astronomy', in Márquez Villanueva & Vega, 30–45.

Glick, T. F., *From Muslim Fortress to Christian Castle. Social and cultural change in medieval Spain* (Manchester, 1995).

——,'Science in medieval Spain: the Jewish contribution in the context of *convivencia*', in V. B. Mann et al. (eds.), Convivencia. *Jews, Muslims, and Christians in Medieval Spain* (New York, 1992), 82–111.

Gómez Redondo, F., *Historia de la prosa medieval castellana*, I, *La creación del discurso prosístico: el entramado cortesano* (Madrid, 1998).

Goñi Gaztambide, J., *Historia de los obispos de Pamplona, s. IV–XIII*, I (Pamplona, 1979).

González, Julio, *Regesta de Fernando II* (Madrid, 1943).

——, *El reino de Castilla en la época de Alfonso VIII*, 3 vols. (Madrid, 1960).

——, *Reinado y diplomas de Fernando III*, 3 vols. (Córdoba, 1980–86).

González Alonso, B., *El Fuero Viejo de Castilla. Consideraciones sobre la historia del derecho de Castilla (c.800–1356)* (Salamanca, 1996).

González Antón, L., *Las Uniones aragonesas y las cortes del reino (1283–1301)*, 2 vols. (Zaragoza, 1975).

——, 'La revuelta de la nobleza aragonesa contra Jaime I en 1224–1227', *Homenage a J. M. Lacarra*, II (Zaragoza, 1977), 143–63.

González Díez, G., *El regimen foral vallisoletano* (Valladolid, 1986).

——, 'Curia y cortes en el reino de Castilla', *Las Cortes de Castilla y León . . . Primera etapa*, I, 107–51.

González Jiménez, M., *En torno a los orígenes de Andalucía: la repoblación del siglo XIII*, 2nd edn (Seville, 1988).

——, *Alfonso X el Sabio* (Palencia, 1993).

——, *Andalucía a debate y otros estudios* (Seville, 1994).

——, *Alfonso X el Sabio* (Barcelona, 2004).

——, *Fernando III el Santo* (Seville, 2006).

——, 'Población y repartimiento de Écija': *Homenaje al prof. Juan Torres Fontes* (Murcia, 1987), 691–711.

——, 'Alfonso X y las oligarquías urbanas de caballeros', *Glossae*, 5–6 (1993–4), 195–214.

——, 'Cortes de Sevilla de 1261', *HID*, 25 (1998), 295–311.

——, '¿Re-conquista? Un estado de la cuestión', in E. Benito Ruano (ed.), *Tópicos y realidades de la Edad Media*, I (Madrid, 2000), 155–78.

——, 'Fernando III el Santo, legislador', *Boletín de la Real Academia Sevillana de Buenas Letras* (Seville, 2001), 111–31.

——, 'El Infante don Fernando de la Cerda. Biografía e itinerario', in M. J. Alonso García *et al.*, *Literatura y cristianidad. Homenaje al prof. J. Montoya Martínez* (Granada, 2001), 531–55.

——, 'Sancho IV, Infante', *HID*, 28 (2001), 151–216.

——, 'Alfonso X y Portugal', *Alcanate*, 4 (2004–5), 19–34.

See also *Sevilla 1248*.

González Mínguez, C., *Fernando IV de Castilla (1295–1312). La guerra civil y el predominio de la nobleza* (Vitoria, 1976).

Gonzálvez, R., *Hombres y libros de Toledo* (Madrid, 1997).

——, 'El traductor Maestro Juan de Toledo. Una propuesta de identificación', *Toletum*, 11 (1981), 177–89.

——, 'La escuela de Toledo durante el reinado de Alfonso VIII', in R. Izquierdo Benito & F. Ruiz-Gómez (eds.), *Alarcos 1195. Actas del Congreso Internacional Conmemorativo del VIII Centenario de la Batalla de Alarcos (1995. Ciudad Real)* (Cuenca, 1996), 171–209.

——, 'The "Bible of St Louis" of Toledo cathedral', in R. Gonzálvez (ed.), *The Bible of St Louis*, II, *Commenatary volume* (Barcelona, 2002), 59–117.

Gouron, A., 'Aux origines médiévales de la maxime "Quod omnes tangit"', *Histoire du droit social. Mélanges en hommage à Jean Imbert* (Paris, 1989), 277–86.

Grabmann, M., *Forschungen über die lateinischen Aristotelesübersetzungen des XIII. Jahrhunderts* (Münster-in-W., 1916).

Granja, F. de la, 'Relato [de la disputa] de Ibn Rašīq con los monjes a propósito de la inimitabilidad del Corán', *al-Andalus*, 31 (1966), 67–72.

Grassotti, H., 'Don Rodrigo Ximénez de Rada, gran señor y hombre de negocios en la Castilla del siglo XIII', *CHE*, 55–6 (1972), 1–302.

Guichard, P., *Les musulmans de Valence et la reconquête (XIe–XIIIe siècles)*, II (Damascus, 1991).

Guijarro, S., 'Libraries and books used by cathedral clergy in Castile during the thirteenth century', *Hispanic Research Jouirnal*, 2 (2001), 191–210.

Guinard, P.: see Petit-Dutaillis.

Gutiérrez Baños, F., *Las empresas artísticas de Sancho IV el Bravo* (Valladolid, 1997).

Guzmán y Gallo, J. P., 'La princesa Cristina de Norvega y el Infante don Felipe', *BRAH*, 74 (1919), 39–65.

Harvey, L. P., *Islamic Spain, 1250 to 1500* (Chicago-London, 1990).

——, The Alfonsine school of translators: translations from Arabic into Castilian produced under the patronage of Alfonso the Wise of Castile (1221–1252–1284)', *Journal of the Royal Asiatic Society of Great Britain & Ireland*, 1977, 109–17.

Harvey, S., 'The knight and the knight's fee in England', *Past & Present*, 49 (1970), 1–43.

Hernández, F, J., *Los cartularios de Toledo. Catálogo documental* (Madrid, 1985).

——, 'Los mozárabes del siglo XII en la ciudad y la iglesia de Toledo', *Toletum*, 16 (1985), 57–124.

——, 'Las Cortes de Toledo de 1207', *Las Cortes de Castilla y León ... Primera etapa*, I, 219–63.

——, 'Alfonso X in Andalucía', *HID*, 22 (1995), 293–306.

——, 'La fundación del Estudio de Alcalá de Henares', *EEM*, 18 (1995), 61–83.

——, 'Sobre los orígenes del español escrito', *Voz y Letra*, 10 (1999), 133–66.

——, 'La corte de Fernando III y la casa real de Francia', *Fernando III y su tiempo*, 103–55.

——, 'Relaciones de Alfonso X con Inglaterra y Francia', *Alcanate*, 4 (2004–5), 167–242.

——, 'El testamento de Benvenist de Saporta (1268)', *Hispania Judaica Bulletin*, 5 (5767/2007), 115–51.

—— and Peter Linehan, *The Mozarabic Cardinal. The life and times of Gonzalo Pérez Gudiel* (Florence, 2004).

Hernando Pérez, J., *Hispano Diego García, escritor y poeta medieval, y el Libro de Alexandre* (Burgos, 1992).

Hijano Villegas, 'Continuaciones del Toledano: el caso de la *Historia hasta 1288 dialogada*', in F. Bautista (ed.), *El relato historiográfico: textos y tradiciones en la España medieval* (London. 2006), 123–48.

Hillgarth, J. N., *The Spanish Kingdoms 1250–1516*, I. *1250–1410*. (Oxford, 1976).

——, 'The problem of a Catalan Mediterranean empire 1229–1327', *English Historical Review Supplement*, 8 (London, 1975).

——, 'The Disputation of Majorca (1286): two new editions', *Euphrosyne*, n. s. 22 (1994), 403–13.

Hilty, G., 'El Libro Conplido en los Iudizios de las Estrellas', *al-Andalus*, 20 (1955), 1–74.

Hinojosa, E. de, 'La fraternidad artificial en España', *RABM*, 3a época 13 (1905), 1–18.

Hohler, C., 'A Note on Jacobus', *Journal of the Warburg and Courtauld Institutes* 35 (1972), 31–80.

Holloway, J. B., 'The road through Roncesvalles. Alfonsine formation of Brunetto Latini and Dante – diplomacy and literature', in Burns, *Emperor of Culture*, 109–25.

Hook, D., *The Earliest Arthurian Names in Spain and Portugal* (St Albans, 1991).

Hourani, G., *Averroës on the Harmony of Religion and Philosophy* (London, 1961).

Huici Miranda, A., *Las grandes batallas de la Reconquista durante las invasiones africanas (almorávides, almohades y benimerínes)* (Madrid, 1956).

——, 'La toma de Salé por la escuadra de Alfonso X', *Hespéris*, 39 (1952), 41–74.

Iglesia Ferreirós, A., 'Las Cortes de Zamora de 1274 y los casos de corte', *AHDE*, 41 (1971), 945–71.

——, 'Alfonso X, su labor legislativa y los historiadores', *HID*, 9 (1982), 9–112.

——, 'Fuero Real y Espéculo', *AHDE*, 52 (1982), 111–191.

——, 'El privilegio general concedido a las Extremaduras en 1264 por Alfonso X. Edición del ejemplar enviado a Peñafiel el 15 de abril de 1264', *AHDE*, 53 (1983), 455–521.

——, 'La labor legislativa de Alfonso X el Sabio', in Pérez Martín, *España y Europa*, 275–599.

Insoll, T., 'Timbuktu and Europe', in Linehan & Nelson, 469–84.

Iturmendi Morales, J., 'En torno a la idea de imperio en Alfonso X el Sabio', *Revista de Estudios Políticos*, no. 182 (marzo–abril 1972), 83–157.

Jerez: see Catalán.

Jordan, E., *Les Origines de la domination angevine en Italie* (Paris, 1909).

——, *L'Allemagne et l'Italie aux XIIe et XIIIe siècles* (Paris, 1939).

Josserand, P., *Église et pouvoir dans la péninsule ibérique, Les ordres militaires dans le royaume de Castille (1252–1369)* (Madrid, 2004).

Kasten, L. [A.], 'The utilization of the *Historia Regum Britanniae* by Alfonso X', *Hispanic Review*, 38 (1970; Extraordinary Number), 97–114.

Katz, I. J. & J. E. Keller (eds.), *Studies on the Cantigas de Santa María. Proceedings of the International Symposium on the Cantigas de Santa María of Alfonso X, el Sabio (1221–1284) in Commemoration of its 700th Anniversary Year – 1981 (New York, November 19–21)* (Madison, WI, 1987).

Kedar, B. Z., *Crusade and Mission. European approaches toward the Muslims* (Princeton, 1984).

——, 'Canon law and the burning of the Talmud', *Bulletin of Medieval Canon Law*, n. s. 9 (1979), 79–82.

Kehr, P., *Das Papsttum und die Königreiche Navarra und Aragon bis zur Mitte des XII Jahrhunderts* (Abhandlungen der Preussischen Akademie der Wissenschaften, Phil.-hist. Kl.; Berlin, 1928).

Keller, J. E.: see Kinkade.

Kennedy, H., *Muslim Spain and Portugal. A political history of al-Andalus* (London, 1996).

Kennedy, K., 'The *sabio*-topos: prologues of Alfonso X in the context of his thirteenth-century royal contemporaries', in A. M. Beresford and A. Deyermond (eds.), *Proceedings of the Ninth Colloquium of the Medieval Hispanic Research Seminar* (London, 2000), 175–90.

Kinkade, R. P., 'Sancho IV: puente literario entre Alfonso el Sabio y Juan Manuel', *Publications of the Modern Languages Association of America*, 87 (1972), 1039–51.

——, 'Alfonso X, *Cantiga* 235, and the events of 1269–1278', *Speculum*, 67 (1992), 284–323.

——, 'Violante of Aragon (1236?-1300?): an historical overview', *Exemplaria Hispanica*, 2 (1992–3), 1–37.

——, 'A royal scandal and the rebellion of 1255', in F. M. Toscano (ed.), *Homage to Bruno Damiani from his Loving Students and Various Friends. A Festschrift* (Lanham, MD & London, 1994), 185–98.

—— & J. E. Keller, 'An orphaned miniature of *Cantiga* 235 from the Florentine codex', *Cantigueiros*, 10 (1998), 27–50.

Kosto, A. J., *Making Agreements in Medieval Catalonia. Power, order, and the written word, 1000–1200* (Cambridge, 2001).

Lacarra, J. M., *Historia política del reino de Navarra desde sus orígenes hasta su incorporación a Castilla*, I (Pamplona, 1972).

——, 'El lento predominio de Castilla', *Revista Portuguesa de Historia* 16 (1976), 63–81.

Lacarra, M. E., *El poema de mio Cid. Realidad histórica e ideología* (Madrid, 1980).

Ladero Quesada, M. A., 'Los mudéjares de Castille en la baja Edad Media', *HID*, 5 (1978), 257–304.

——, 'Las transformaciones de la fiscalidad regia castellano-leonesa en la segunda mitad del siglo XIII (1252–1313)', *Historia de la hacienda española (épocas antigua y medieval). Homenaje al Prof. García de Valdeavellano* (Madrid, 1983), 322–405.

——, 'Aspectos de la política económica de Alfonso X', *Alfonso X el Sabio. VII Centenario (Revista de la Facultad de Derecho Universidad Complutense)* (Madrid, 1985), 69–82.

Lafuente, V. de, *Historia de las universidades, colegios y demás establecimientos de enseñanza en España*, 4 vols. (Madrid, 1884).

Lapesa, R., *Historia de la lengua española* (Madrid, 1980).

Lapesa, R., *Estudios de historia lingüística española* (Madrid, 1985).

Le Bras, G., 'Boniface VIII, symphoniste et modérateur', *Mélanges Louis Halphen* (Paris, 1951), 383–94.

Le Goff, J., *Saint Louis* (Paris, 1996).

Le Tourneau, R., *The Almohad Movement in North Africa in the Twelfth and Thirteenth Centuries* (Princeton, 1969).

Lecuona, M., 'Los sucesos calceatenses de 1224–1234', *Scriptorium Victoriense*, 1 (1954), 134–46.

Lera Maíllo, J. C. de, *Catálogo de los documentos medievales de la Catedral de Zamora* (Zamora, 1999).

Levy, E., 'Le troubadour Paulet de Marseille', *Revue des langues romaines*, 21 (1882), 261–89.

Lida de Malkiel, M. R., 'La *General estoria*: notas literarias y filológicas', *Romance Philology*, 12 (1958–59), 111–42; 13 (1959–60), 1–30.

Linehan, Peter, *The Spanish Church and the Papacy in the Thirteenth Century* (Cambridge, 1971).

——, *Spanish Church and Society 1150–1300* (London, 1983).

——, *Past and Present in Medieval Spain* (Aldershot, 1992).

——, *History and the Historians of Medieval Spain* (Oxford, 1993).

——, *The Ladies of Zamora* (Manchester, 1997).

——, *The Processes of Politics and the Rule of Law. Studies on the Iberian kingdoms and papal Rome in the Middle Ages* (Aldershot, 2002).

—— & J. L. Nelson (eds.), *The Medieval World* (London, 2001).

——, 'The *gravamina* of the Castilian Church in 1262–3', *EHR*, 85 (1970), 730–54 [repr. *Spanish Church and Society*].

——, 'The Spanish Church revisited: the episcopal *gravamina* of 1279', in B. Tierney & P. Linehan (eds.), *Authority and Power. Studies on medieval law and government presented to Walter Ullmann on his seventieth birthday* (Cambridge, 1980), 127–147 [repr. *Spanish Church and Society*].

——, 'The Synod of Segovia (1166)', *Bulletin of Medieval Canon Law*, n.s. 10 (1980), 31–44 [repr. *Spanish Church and Society*].

——, 'Segovia: a "frontier" diocese in the thirteenth century', *EHR*, 96 (1981), 481–508 [repr. *Spanish Church and Society*].

——, 'The politics of piety: aspects of the Castilian monarchy from Alfonso X to Alfonso XI', *Rev. Canadiense de Estudios Hispánicos*, 9 (1985) 385–404.

——, 'The beginnings of Santa María de Guadalupe and the direction of fourteenth-century Castile', *JEH*, 36 (1985), 284–304 [repr. *Past and Present in Medieval Spain*].

——, 'Pseudo-historia y pseudo-liturgia en la obra alfonsina', in Pérez Martín, *España y Europa*, 259–74.

——, 'The Cid of history and the History of the Cid', *History Today* (Sept. 1987), 26–32.

——, 'Ecclesiastics and the Cortes of Castile and León', *Las Cortes de Castilla y León . . . Primera etapa*, II, 99–141.

——, 'The Toledo forgeries c.1150 – c.1300', *Fälschungen im Mittelalter*, I (MGH Schriften, 33/1) (Hannover, 1988), 643–74 [repr. *Past and Present in Medieval Spain*].

——, 'The accession of Alfonso X (1252) and the origins of the War of the Spanish Succession', in D. W. Lomax & D. Mackenzie (eds.), *God and Man in Medieval Spain* (Warminster, 1989), 59–79 [repr. *Past and Present in Medieval Spain*].

——, 'Royal influence and papal authority in the diocese of Osma: a note on "Quia requisistis" ', *Bulletin of Medieval Canon Law*, n. s. 20 (1990), 31–41 [repr. *The Processes of Politics*].

——, 'A Tale of Two Cities: capitular Burgos and mendicant Burgos in the Thirteenth Century', in D. Abulafia *et al.* (eds.), *Church and City 1000–1500. Essays in Honour of Christopher Brooke* (Cambridge, 1992), 81–110 [*repr. Processes of Politics*].

——, 'History in a changing world: the case of medieval Spain', *Past and Present in Medieval Spain*, item I (1–22).

——, 'Alfonso XI of Castile and the Arm of Santiago (with a Note on the Pope's Foot)', in A. García y García & P. Weimar (eds.), *Miscellanea D. Maffei dicata* (Frankfurt, 1995), 121–46 [*repr. Processes of Politics*].

——, 'The king's touch and the dean's ministrations', in M. Rubin (ed.), *The Work of Jacques Le Goff and the Challenges of Medieval History* (Woodbridge, 1997), 189–206.

——, 'Utrum reges Portugalie coronabantur annon', 2° Congresso Histórico de Guimarães (Guimarães, 1997), II, 389–410 [repr., with additional material, *Processes of Politics*].

——, 'On further thought: Lucas of Tuy, Rodrigo of Toledo and the Alfonsine histories', *AEM*, 27 (1998), 415–36 [repr. *Processes of Politics*].

——, 'Castile, Portugal and Navarre', in Abulafia, *NCMH*, V, 668–99.

——, 'Lucas de Tuy, Rodrigo Jiménez de Rada y las historias alfonsíes', in Fernández-Ordóñez, *Alfonso X el Sabio y las Crónicas de España*, 19–36.

——, 'La conquista de Sevilla y los historiadores', *Sevilla 1248*, 229–44.

——, ' "Quedam de quibus dubitans": on preaching the crusade in Alfonso X's Castile', *HID* 27 (2000), 129–54.

——, 'A papal legation and its aftermath: Cardinal John of Abbeville in Spain and Portugal, 1228–1229', in I. Birocchi *et al.* (eds.), *A Ennio Cortese* (Rome, 2001), II, 36–56.

——, 'At the Spanish frontier', in Linehan & Nelson, 37–59.

——, 'The economics of episcopal politics: the cautionary tale of Bishop Suero Pérez of Zamora', *Processes of Politics*, item V (1–52).

——, 'Don Rodrigo and the government of the kingdom', *CLCHM*, 26 (2003), 87–99.

——, 'Juan de Soria: *unas apostillas*', *Fernando III y su tiempo*, 375–93.

——, 'Spain in the twelfth century', in D. Luscombe and J. Riley-Smith (eds.), *NCMH*, IV/2 (Cambridge, 2004), 475–509.

——, 'El cuatro de mayo de 1282', *Alcanate*, 4 (2004–5), 147–65.

——, 'Juan de Soria: the chancellor as chronicler', *e-Spania*, 2 (2007).

——, 'The case of the impugned chirograph, and the juristic culture of early thirteenth-century Zamora', in G. Colli (ed.), *Manoscritti, editoria e biblioteche tra medioevo ed età moderna. Studi offerti a Domenico Maffei* (Rome, 2006), 461–513.

——, 'The invention of Toledo' (forthcoming).

—— & M. Torre Sevilla, 'A misattributed tomb and its implications: Cardinal Ordoño Álvarez and his friends and relations', *Rivista di Storia della Chiesa in Italia*, 57 (2003), 53–63.

See also Hernández, F. J.

Lizabe de Savastano, G. I., 'El título XXI de la *Segunda partida* y la frustración política de Alfonso X', *BHS*, Liverpool (1993), 393–402.

Lomax, D. W., *The Reconquest of Spain* (London, 1978).

——, 'El arzobispo D. Rodrigo Jiménez de Rada y la Orden de Santiago', *Hispania*, 19 (1959), 323–365.

——, 'Don Ramón, bishop of Palencia (1148–84)', *Homenaje a Jaime Vicens Vices* (Barcelona, 1965), I, 279–91.

——, 'La conquista de Andalucía a través de la historiografía europea de la época', in E. Cabrera (ed.), *Andalucía entre Oriente y Occidente (1236–1492). Actas del V Coloquio Internacional de historia medieval de Andalucía* (Córdoba, 1988), 37–49.

Lopez, R. S., *Genova marinara nel Duecento. Benedetto Zaccaria* (Messina-Milan, 1933).

——, 'Ugo Vento primo genovese ammiraglio di Castiglia' [1951]: repr. Lopez, *Su e giù per la storia di Genova* (Genoa, 1975), 241–52.

——, 'Back to gold, 1252', *Economic History Review*, 2nd ser., 9 (1956–7), 219–40.

López Ferreiro, A., *Fueros municipales de Santiago y de su tierra* (Santiago de Compostela, 1895).

——, *Historia de la santa iglesia de Santiago de Compostela*, V (Santiago de Compostela, 1902).

López Gutiérrez, A. J., 'Sevilla, Alfonso X y el "sigillum aureum" ', *Archivo Hispalense*, 2a época, 72, no. 220 (1989), 309–20.

Lorenzo Gradín, P., 'Gomez Garcia, abade de Valadolide', in C. Alvar & J. M. Lucía Megías (eds.), *La literatura en la época de Sancho IV (Actas del Congreso Internacional 'La literatura en la época de Sancho IV', Alcalá de Henares, 21–24 de febrero de 1994)* (Alcalá de Henares, 1996), 213–26.

Lourie, E., 'A society organised for war: medieval Spain', *Past & Present*, 35 (1966), 54–76.

MacDonald, R. A., 'Alfonso the Learned and succession: a father's dilemma', *Speculum*, 40 (1965), 647–53.

——, 'El Espéculo atribuido a Alfonso X, su edición y problemas que plantea', in Pérez Martín, *España y Europa*, 611–53.

——, 'Law and politics: Alfonso's program of political reform', in R. I. Burns (ed.), *The Worlds of Alfonso the Learned and James the Conqueror. Intellect and force in the Middle Ages* (Princeton, 1985), 150–202.

Maddicott, J., '"1258" and "1297": some comparisons and contrasts', *Thirteenth Century England*, IX (Woodbridge, 2003), 1–14.

Maffei, D., 'Fra Cremona, Montpellier e Palencia nel secolo XII. Ricerche su Ugolino da Sesso', *Rivista Internazionale di Diritto Comune*, 1 (1990), 9–30.

Mahn, C. A. F., *Die Werke des Troubadours in provenzalischer Sprache*, I (Berlin, 1846).

Maldonado y Fernández del Torco, J., 'En torno a un texto modificado de una ley de Partidas', *Revista de la Universidad de Madrid. Derecho*, 2 (1942), 79–106.

Mandianes Castro, M., 'Personalidad del judío en la obra de Martino de León', *Santo Martino de León. Ponencias del I Congreso Internacional sobre Santo Martino en el VIII Centenario de su obra literaria 1195–1985* (Isidoriana, 1; León, 1987), 89–95.

Manning, W. F., *The Life of St Dominic in Old French Verse* (Cambridge, MA, 1944).

Maravall, J. A., *El concepto de España en la Edad Media*, 2nd edn (Madrid, 1964).

——, 'El pensamiento político de la alta Edad Media', *Estudios de historia del pensamiento español*, 2nd edn (Madrid, 1973), 33–66.

Marcos Pous, A., 'Los dos matrimonios de Sancho IV de Castilla', *Escuela Española de Arqueología e Historia en Roma: Cuadernos de Trabajo*, 8 (1956), 7–108.

Mariana, J. de, *Historia de rebus Hispaniæ* (Madrid, 1608).

Marín, M, & H. Ecker, 'Archaeology, Arabic sources and Christian documents', *British Journal of Middle Eastern Studies*, 25 (1998), 335–48.

Márquez Villanueva, F., *El concepto cultural alfonsí*, 2nd edn (Barcelona, 2004).

——, 'Las lecturas del dean de Cádiz en una *cantiga de mal dizer*', in Katz & Keller, 329–54.

——, 'The Alfonsine cultural concept', Márquez Villanueva & Vega, 75–109.

—— & C. A. Vega (eds.), *Alfonso X of Castile, the Learned King (1221–1284). An international symposium: Harvard University, 17 November 1984* (Cambridge, MA, 1990),

Marti, B. M., *The Spanish College at Bologna in the Fourteenth Century* (Philadelphia, 1966).

Martin, G., *Les Juges de Castille. Mentalités et discours historique dans l'Espagne médiévale* (Paris, 1992).

——, 'Alphonse X ou la science politique (*Septénaire*, 1–11)', *CLHM*, 18–19 (1993–4), 79–100; 20 (1995), 7–33.

——,'Alphonse X maudit son fils', *Atalaya*, 5 (1994), 153–78.

——, 'Alphonse X, roi et empereur. Commentaire du premier titre de la *Deuxième partie*', *Imprévue* (1998), 23–54.

——, 'L'escarboucle de Saint-Denis, le roi de France et l'empereur des Espagnes', in F. Autrand, C. Gauvard & J.-M. Moeglin (eds.), *Saint-Denis et la royauté. Études offertes à Bernard Guenée* (Paris, 1999), 439–62.

——, 'El modelo historiográfico alfonsí y sus antecedentes', in Fernández-Ordóñez, *Alfonso X el Sabio y las Crónicas de España*, 37–59.

——, 'Régner sans régner. Bérengère de Castille (1214–1246) au miroir de l'his-toriographie de son temps', *e-Spania*, 1 (2006).

——, 'La contribution de Jean d'Osma à la pensée politique castillane sous le règne de Ferdinand III', *e-Spania*, 2 (2006).

——, 'De nuevo sobre la fecha del *Setenario*', *e-Spania*, 2 (2006).

Martín Fuertes, J. A.: see Ruiz Asencio.

Martín López, M. E., *Patrimonio cultural de San Isidro de León. Documentos de los siglos X-XIII* (León, 1995).

Martínez Gázquez, J., 'La Summa de Astronomía de Pedro Gallego y el Liber de aggregationibus scientie stellarum de Al-Fargānī', in M. Comes, R. Puig & J. Samsó (eds.), *De Astronomia Alphonsi regis. Actas del Simposio sobre Astronomía Alfonsí celebrado en Berkeley (Agosto 1985) y otros trabajos sobre el mismo tema* (Barcelona, 1987), 153–79.

Martínez Montávez, P., 'Relaciones de Alfonso X de Castilla con el sultan Baybars y sus sucesores', *al-Andalus*, 27 (1962), 343–76.

Martínez Ripoll, A., 'Aportaciones a la vida cultural de Murcia en el siglo XIII. La «madrissa» de M. al-Ricotí y el «studium solemne» de los dominicos', *Murgetana*, 28 (1968), 33–46.

McCrank, L. J., *Medieval Frontier History in New Catalonia* (Aldershot, 1996).

Menéndez Pidal, G., 'Cómo trabajaron las escuelas alfonsíes', *Nueva Revista de Filología Hispánica*, 5 (1951), 363–80.

Menéndez Pidal, R., *Poesía juglaresca y orígenes de las literaturas románicas*, 6th edn (Madrid, 1957).

——, 'Relatos poéticos en las crónicas generales: nuevas indicaciones', *RFE*, 10 (1923), 329–72.

Menéndez Pidal de Navascues, F., *Heráldica medieval española. I. La casa real de León y Castilla* (Madrid, 1982).

Menjot, D., *Murcie castillane. Une ville au temps de la frontière (1243–milieu du XVe siècle)*, 2 vols. (Madrid, 2002).

Milhou, A., 'De Rodrigue le pécheur à Ferdinand le restaurateur', in J. Fontaine and C. Pellistrandi (eds.), *L'Europe héritière de l'Espagne wisigothique* (Madrid, 1992), 365–82.

Millás Vallicrosa, J. M., *Las traducciones orientales en los manuscritos de la Biblioteca Catedral de Toledo* (Madrid, 1942).

Minguella y Arnedo, T., *Historia de la diócesis de Sigüenza y de sus obispos*, 3 vols. (Madrid, 1910–13).

Miret i Sans, J., 'Le roi Louis VII et le comte de Barcelone à Jaca en 1155', *Le Moyen Age*, 2e ser., 16 (1912), 289–300.

Molénat, J. P., *Campagnes et monts de Tolède du XIIe au XV siècle* (Madrid, 1997).

——, 'Des musulmans aux mudéjars', *Actas Simposio Internacional de Mudejarismo [Mudéjares y moriscos. Cambios sociales y culturales]. Teruel, 12–14 de septiembre de 2002* (Teruel, 2004), 5–17.

Mondéjar, J. & J. Montoya, *Estudios Alfonsíes. Lexicografía, lírica, estética y política de Alfonso el Sabio* (Granada, 1985).

Mondéjar, Marqués de (Gaspar Ibáñez de Segovia, Peralta y Mendoza), *Memorias históricas del rei D. Alonso el Sabio*, ed. F. Cerdá y Rico (Madrid, 1777).

Monneret de Villard, U., *Lo studio dell'Islām in Europa nel XII e nel XIII secolo* (Vatican City, 1944).

Montes Romero-Camacho, I., 'Mudéjares y judíos en la Sevilla del siglo XIII', *Sevilla 1248*, 467–98.

Montoya Martínez, J., 'El concepto de "autor" en Alfonso X', in A. Gallego Morell *et al.* (eds.), *Estudios sobre literatura y arte dedicados al profesor Emilio Orozco Díaz*, I (Granada, 1979), 455–62.

——, 'Algunas precisiones acerca de los *Cantigas de Santa María*', in Katz & Keller, 367–85.

——, 'La "gran vingança" de Dios y de Alfonso X', *Cantigueiros*, 3 (1990), pp. 53–9.

——, 'O cancioneiro marial de Alfonso X. El primer cancionero cortesano español', *O Cantar dos Trobadores. Actas do Congreso celebrado en Santiago de Compostela entre os dias 26 a 29 de abril de 1993*, ed. M. Brea (Santiago de Compostela, 1993), 199–219.

—— & A. Domínguez Rodríguez (eds.), *El scriptorium alfonsí: de los libros de astrología a las «Cantigas de Santa Maria»* (Madrid, 1999).

See also Mondéjar, J.

Moore, R. I., *The Formation of a Persecuting Society* (Oxford, 1987).

Morreale, M., 'Vernacular scriptures in Spain', in G. W. H. Lampe (ed.), *The Cambridge History of the Bible*, II, *The West from the Fathers to the Reformation* (Cambridge, 1969), 465–91.

Morris, C., *The Papal Monarchy. The Western Church from 1050 to 1250* (Oxford, 1989).

Moxó, S. de, *Repoblación y sociedad en la España cristiana medieval* (Madrid, 1979).

——, 'De la nobleza vieja a la nobleza nueva. La transformación nobiliaria castellana en la baja Edad Media', *Cuadernos de Historia*, 3 (1969), 1–270.

——, 'La descendencia deconocida de un infante de Castilla', *Hidalguía*, 27 (1979), 77–86.

Muldoon, J., *Popes, Lawyers, and Infidels* (Liverpool, 1979).

Mundó, A. M., 'La datación de los códices litúrgicos visigóticos toledanos', *HS*, 17 (1965), 1–25.

Needham, J., *Clerks and Craftsmen in China and the West* (Cambridge, 1970).

Nelson, J. L.: see Linehan.

Nieto Soria, J. M., *Fundamentos ideológicos del poder real en Castilla (siglos XIII–XVI)* (Madrid, 1988).

——, 'Origen divino, espíritu laico y poder real en la Castilla del siglo XIII', *AEM*, 27 (1997), 43–101.

Nirenberg, D., *Communities of Violence. Persecution of minorities in the Middle Ages* (Princeton, 1996).

Nowell, C. E., 'The Old Man of the Mountains', *Speculum*, 22 (1947), 497–519.

Nykl, A. R., *Hispano-Arabic Poetry and its Relations with the Old Provençal Troubadours* (Baltimore, 1946).

Oakeshott, W., *Sigena. Romanesque paintings in Spain and the artists of the Winchester Bible* (London, 1972).

O'Callaghan, J. F., *The Cortes of Castile-León 1188–1350* (Philadelphia, 1989).

——, *The Learned King. The reign of Alfonso X of Castile* (Philadelphia, 1993).

——, *Alfonso X, the Cortes, and Government in Medieval Spain* (Aldershot, 1998).

——, *Alfonso X and the* Cantigas de Santa María. *A poetic biography* (Leiden, 1998).

——, *Reconquest and Crusade in Medieval Spain* (Philadephia, 2003).

——, 'Sobre la promulgación del *Espéculo* y del *Fuero real*', in *Estudios en homenaje a don Claudio Sánchez Albornoz en sus 90 años*, III (Buenos Aires, 1985), 167–79.

——, 'The Mudejars of Castile and Portugal in the twelfth and thirteenth centuries', in Powell, *Muslims*, 11–56.

Olstein, D. A., *La era mozárabe. Los mozárabes de Toledo (siglos XII y XIII) en la historiografía, las fuentes y la historia* (Salamanca, 2006).

Ortiz de Zúñiga, D., *Anales eclésiasticos y seculares de la muy noble y muy leal ciudad de Sevilla* [1677], 2 vols. (Sevilla, 1985).

Palacios Martín, B., *La coronación de los reyes de Aragón 1204–1410. Aportación de las estructuras medievales* (Valencia, 1975).

——, 'Investidura de armas de los reyes españoles en los siglos XII y XIII', *Gladius*, special issue (1988), 153–92.

Pastor de Togneri, R., *Resistencias y luchas campesinas en la época del crecimiento y consolidación de la formación feudal, Castilla y León, siglos X-XIII* (Madrid, 1980).

Pattison, D. G.: see Deyermond.

Pereira, I. da Rosa, 'O canonista Petrus Hispanus Portugalensis', *Arquivos de História da Cultura Portuguesa*, 2/4 (1968), 3–18.

Pérez Martín, A. (ed.), *España y Europa. Un pasado jurídico común. Actas del I Simposio Internacional del Instituto de Derecho Común (Murcia, 26/28 de marzo de 1985)* (Murcia, 1986).

——, 'El Fuero real y Murcia', *AHDE*, 54 (1984), 55–96.

Peters E., *The Shadow King* Rex inutilis *in medieval law and literature, 751–1327* (New Haven-London, 1970).

Petit, C., *AHDE*, 56 (1986), 1087–93 (review).

Petit-Dutaillis, Ch. & P. Guinard, *Histoire du Moyen Âge*, 4/2, *L'essor des états d'Occident* (Paris, 1937).

Pick, L. K., *Conflict and Coexistence. Archbishop Rodrigo and the Muslims and Jews on Medieval Spain* (Ann Arbor, MI., 2004).
——, 'Rodrigo Jiménez de Rada and the Jews. Pragmatism and patronage in thirteenth-century Toledo', *Viator*, 28 (1997), 203–22.
Portela, E., 'Del Duero al Tajo', in J. M. García de Cortázar *et al.* (eds.), *Organización social del espacio en la España medieval: la corona de Castilla en los siglos VIII a XV* (Barcelona, 1985), 86–122.
Post, G., *Studies in Medieval Legal Thought* (Princeton, 1964).
Powell, J. M. (ed.), *Muslims under Latin Rule, 1100–1300* (Princeton, 1990).
Powers, J. F., *A Society Organized for War. The Iberian municipal militias in the central Middle Ages, 1000–1284* (Berkeley, 1988).
——, 'Frontier municipal baths and social interaction in thirteenth-century Spain', *American Historical Review*, 84 (1979), 649–67.
Presilla, M., 'The image of death and political ideology in the *Cantigas de Santa María*', in Katz & Keller, 403–59.
Prieto Prieto, A., 'La autenticidad de los "decreta" de la Curia Leonesa de 1188 (Notas de urgencia)', *Las Cortes de Castilla y León 1188–1988*, 41–58.
Procter, E. S., *Alfonso X of Castile, Patron of Literature and Learning* (Oxford, 1951).
——, *Curia and Cortes in León and Castile 1072–1295* (Cambridge, 1980).
——, 'The scientific works of the court of Alfonso X of Castile: the king and his collaborators', *Modern Language Review*, 40 (1945), 12–29.
Pryor, J. H., *Geography, Technology and War. Studies in the maritime history of the Mediterranean, 649–1571* (Cambridge, 1988).
Pujol y Tubau, P., 'Mudança en la elecció de sepultura per lo rey Alfons I', *BRABL*, 7 (1913–14), 86–9.
Rashdall, H., *The Universities of Europe in the Middle Ages*, ed. F. M. Powicke & A. B. Emden, 3 vols. (Oxford, 1936).
Rassow, P., *Der Prinzgemahl: ein Pactum matrimoniale aus dem Jahre 1188* (Weimar, 1950).
Redlich, O., 'Zur Wahl des römischen Königs Alfons von Castilien (1257)', *MIöG*, 16 (1895), 659–62.
Régné, J., *History of the Jews in Aragon. Regesta and documents 1213–1327* (Jerusalem, 1978).
Reilly, B. F., *The Contest of Christian and Muslim Spain 1031–1157* (Oxford, 1992).
Rembaum, J., 'The Talmud and the popes: reflections on the Talmud trials of the 1240s', *Viator*, 13 (1982), 203–23.
Retana, L. F. de, *San Fernando III y su época* (Madrid, 1941).
Ricketts, P. T., *Les poésies de Guilhem de Montanhagol* (Toronto, 1964).
Rico, F., *Alfonso el Sabio y la 'General estoria'*, 2nd edn (Barcelona, 1984).
——, 'Aristotles Hispanus: en torno a Gil de Zamora, Petrarca y Juan de Mena', *Italia Medioevale e Umanistica*, 10 (1967), 143–64.
——, 'La clerecía del mester', *Hispanic Review*, 53 (1985), 1–23, 127–50.
Riera i Sans, J., 'La invenció literària de Sant Pere Pasqual', *Caplletra*, 1 (1986), 45–60.
Riquer, M. de, *Los trovadores. Historia literaria y textos*, 3 vols. (Barcelona, 1975).
——, *Història de la literatura catalana. Part antiga*, I (Barcelona, 1980).

———, 'El trovador Giraut del Luc y sus poesías contra Alfonso II de Aragón', *BRABL*, 23 (1950), 209–48.

Rivera, J. F., *La iglesia de Toledo en el siglo XII*, I (Rome, 1966).

Robinson, R. E.: see Gallagher.

Roca Traver, F. A., 'Un siglo de vida mudéjar en la Valencia medieval (1239–1338)', *EEMCA*, 5 (1952), 115–208.

Rodgers, P., 'Alfonso X writes to his son: reflections on the *Crónica de Alfonso X*', *Exemplaria Hispanica*, 1 (1991–2), 58–79.

Rodríguez Díez, M., *Historia de la ciudad de Astorga* 2nd edn (Astorga, 1909).

Rodríguez López, A. *La consolidación territorial de la monarquía feudal castellana. Expansión y fronteras durante el reinado de Fernando III* (Madrid, 1994).

———, La política eclesiástica de la monarquía castellano-leonesa durante el reinado de Fernando III (1217–1252)', *Hispania*, 48 (1988), 7–48.

———, 'El reino de Castilla y el imperio germánico en la primera mitad del siglo XIII. Fernando III y Federico II', in M. A. Loring García (ed.), *Historia social, pensamiento historiográfico y Edad Media. Homenaje al Prof. Abilio Barbero de Aguilera* (Madrid, 1997), 613–30.

———, '*Quod alienus regnet et heredes expellatur*. L'offre du trône de Castille au roi Louis VIII de France', *Le Moyen Âge*, 105 (1999), 109–28.

Rodríguez Velasco, J. D., 'De oficio a estado. La caballería entre el *Espéculo* y las *Siete Partidas*', *CLHM*, 18–19 (1993–4), 49–77.

Rojinsky, D., 'The rule of law and the written word in Alfonsine Castile: demystifying a consecrated vernacular', *BHS* [Liverpool], 80 (2003), 287–305.

Romano, D., 'Le opere scientifiche di Alfonso X e l'intervento degli ebrei', *Accademia Nazionale dei Lincei. Atti dei Convegni*, 13 (Rome, 1971), 677–711.

———, 'Los judíos y Alfonso X', *Alfonso X y su época* (*Revista de Occidente*, 43 [1984]), 203–17.

Roth, N., 'Jewish collaborators in Alfonso's scientific work', in Burns, *The Emperor of Culture*, 59–71.

Rousset de Missy, J., *Supplement au corps universel diplomatique du droit des gens*, V (Amsterdam-The Hague, 1739).

Rubio García, L., 'En torno a la biblioteca de Alfonso X el Sabio', *La lengua y la literatura en tiempos de Alfonso X. Actas del Congreso Internacional, Murcia, 5–10 marzo 1984* (Murcia, 1985), 531–51.

Rucquoi, A., *Valladolid en la Edad Media. Génesis de un poder (1085–1367)*, 2nd edn, 2 vols. (Valladolid, 1997).

Ruiz, T. F., *Crisis and Continuity. Land and town in late medieval Castile* (Philadelphia, 1994).

———, *From Heaven to Earth. The reordering of Castilian society, 1150–1350* (Princeton, 2004).

———, 'Festivités, couleurs et symboles du pouvoir au XVe siècle. Les célébrations de mai 1438'. *Annales-Économies-Civilisations-Sociétés*, 46 (1991), 521–46.

Ruiz de la Peña, J. I., 'Los procesos tardíos de repoblación urbana en las tierras del norte del Duero (siglos XII–XIV)', *Boletín del Instituto de Estudios Asturianos*, 30 (1976), 735–77.

——, 'Aportación al estudio de las Hermandades concejiles en León y Castilla durante la Edad Media', *Homenaje al prof. Juan Torres Fontes* (Murcia, 1987), II, 1505–13.

Runciman, S., *A History of the Crusades*, 3 vols. [1951–4] (Harmondsworth, 1965).

——, *The Sicilian Vespers* (Cambridge, 1958).

Russell, Peter, *Prince Henry 'the Navigator'. A life* (New Haven & London, 2000).

——, 'Some problems of diplomatic in the "Cantar de Mio Cid" and their implications', *Modern Languages Review*, 47 (1952), 340–9.

Sagarra, F. de, 'Noticias y documentos inéditos referentes al Infante Don Alfonso, primogénito de Don Jaime I y de Doña Leonor de Castilla', *BRABL* 9 (1917), 285–301.

Salavert y Roca, V., 'El Tratado de Anagni y la expansión mediterranea de la Corona de Aragón', *EEMCA*, 5 (1952), 209–360.

Salvador Martínez, H., *Alfonso X. Una biografía* (Madrid, 2003).

——, 'La locura alfonsí y el Setenario', *Historia*, no. 325 (mayo 2003), 36–49.

Samsó, J., 'Sevilla y la obra científica de Alfonso X', *Sevilla 1248*, 567–77.

Sánchez Albornoz, C., *La España musulmana según los autores islamitas y cristianos medievales*, 3rd edn (Madrid, 1973).

Sánchez Ameijeiras, R., 'Imagery and interactivity: ritual transaction at the saint's tomb', in S. Lamia & E. Valdez del Álamo (eds.), *Decorations for the Holy Dead. Visual embellishment on tombs and shrines of saints* (Turnhout, 2002), 21–38.

——, '*Mui de coraçon rogava* a Santa María: culpas irredentas y reivindicación política en Villasirga', in A. Franco Mata *et al.* (eds.), *Patrimonio artístico de Galicia y otros estudios. Homenaje al Prof. Dr. Serafín Moralejo Álvarez*, III (Santiago de Compostela, 2004), 241–52.

Sánchez Pérez, J. A., ' "Libro del tesoro", falsamente atribuido a Alfonso el Sabio', *RFE*, 19 (1932), 158–80.

Sancho de Sopranis, H., 'La incorporación de Cádiz a la Corona de Castilla bajo Alfonso X', *Hispania*, 9 (1949), 355–86.

Santacana Tort, J., *El monasterio de Poblet (1151–81)* (Barcelona, 1974).

Sanz Fuentes, M. J., 'Repartimiento de Éjica', *HID*, 3 (1976), 533–51.

Sayili, A., *The Observatory in Islam and its Place in the General History of the Observatory* (Ankara, 1960).

Scheffer-Boichorst, P., 'Zur Geschichte Alfons' X. von Castilien', *MIöG*, 9 (1888), 226–48.

Scholberg, K. R., *Sátira e invectica en la España medieval* (Madrid, 1971).

Schwab, I., 'Kanzlei und Urkundenwesen König Alfons' X. von Kastilien für das Reich', *Archiv für Diplomatik*, 32 (1986), 569–616.

Seemann, H. J., 'Die Instrumente der Sternwarte zu Marāgha nach den Mitteilungen von al 'Urḍī', *Sitzungsberichte der Physikalisch-medizinischen Sozietät zu Erlangen*, 60 (1928), 15–126.

Sénac, P., *La frontière et les hommes (VIIIe-XIIe siècle), Le peuplement musulman au nord de l'Ebre et les débuts de la reconquête aragonaise* (Paris, 2000).

Septimus, B., *Hispano-Jewish Culture in Transition. The career and controversies of Ramah* (Cambridge, MA, 1982).

Sevilla 1248. Congreso Internacional conmemorativo del 750 aniversario de la conquista de la ciudad de Sevilla por Fernando III, rey de Castilla y León. Sevilla, Real Alcázar, 23–27 de noviembre de 1998, ed. M. González Jiménez (Madrid, 2000).

Shadis, M., 'Berenguela of Castile's political motherhood: the management of sexuality, marriage, and succession': *Medieval Mothering*, ed. J. C. Parsons & B. Wheeler (New York & London, 1996), 335–58.

Shideler, J. C., *A Medieval Catalan Noble Family. The Montcadas 1000–1230* (Berkeley-Los Angeles, 1983).

——, 'Les tactiques politiques des Montcada seigneurs de Vic du début du XIIIe siècle', *Ausa*, 9 (1981), 329–42.

Smalley, B., *The Study of the Bible in the Middle Ages*, 3rd edn (Oxford, 1982).

Smith, D. J., *Innocent III and the Crown of Aragon. The limits of papal authority* (Aldershot, 2004).

Snow, J. T., 'A chapter in Alfonso's personal narrative: the Puerto de Santa María poems in the *CSM*', *La Corónica*, 3 (1979–80), 10–21.

——, 'The satirical poetry of Alfonso X: a look at its relationship to the "Cantigas de Santa Maria"', in Márquez Villanueva & Vega, 110–27.

Socarras, C., *Alfonso X of Castile. A study on imperialistic frustration* (Barcelona, 1976).

Solalinde, A. G., *Antología de Alfonso X el Sabio*, 6th edn (Madrid, 1977).

——, 'Intervención de Alfonso X en la redacción de sus obras', *RFE*, 2 (1915), 283–8.

——, 'Alfonso X astrólogo. Noticia del MS Vat. Reg. Lat. 1283', *RFE*, 13 (1926), 350–6.

Soldevila, F., *Pere el Gran. Primera part: L'Infant*, I, 3 parts (Barcelona, 1950–56).

——, *Història de Catalunya*, 2nd edn, I (Barcelona, 1962).

——, *Els primers temps de Jaume I* (Barcelona, 1968).

Southern, R. W., *The Making of the Middle Ages* (London, 1953).

——, *Western Views of Islam in the Middle Ages* (Cambridge, MA & London, 1962).

——, *Western Society and the Church in the Middle Ages* (Harmondsworth, 1970).

Southworth, E.: see Deyermond.

Suárez Fernández, L., 'Evolución histórica de las hermandades castellanas', *CHE*, 16 (1951), 5–78.

Swift, F. D., *The Life and Times of James the First the Conqueror* (Oxford, 1894).

Targarona, J., 'Todros ben Yehudah ha-Leví Abulafia, un poeta hebreo en la corte de Alfonso X el Sabio', *Helmantica*, 36 (1985), 195–209.

Teetaert, A., 'La doctrine pénitentielle de St Raymond de Penyafort', *Analecta Sacra Tarraconensia*, 4 (1928), 121–82.

Todesca, J. J., 'The monetary history of Castile-Leon (ca.1100–1300) in light of the Bourgey hoard', *American Numismatic Society Museum Notes*, 33 (1988), 129–203.

Tolan, J. V., *Saracens. Islam in the medieval European imagination* (New York, 2002).

Torre Sevilla, M.: see Linehan.

Torres Fontes, J., *La cultura murciana en el reinado de Alfonso X* (Murcia 1960).

——, *La reconquista de Murcia en 1266 por Jaime I de Aragón*, 2nd edn (Murcia, 1987).

——, 'El monasterio de S. Ginés de la Jara en la Edad Media', *Murgetana*, 25 (1965), 39–90.

——, 'La Orden de Santa María de España', *Miscelánea medieval murciana*, 3 (1977), 75–118.

—— & F. de A. Veas Arteseros, 'La procedencia de los repobladores en el repartimiento de Orihuela', *Miscelánea medieval murciana*, 13 (1986), 9–27.

Torres González, F., 'Rasgos medico-psicológicos de Alfonso, el Sabio', *Alfonso X y Ciudad Real. Conferencias pronunciadas con motivo del VII centenario de la muerte del Rey Sabio (1284–1984)*, ed. M. Espadas Burgos (Ciudad Real, 1986), 107–40.

Torró, J., 'Jérusalem ou Valence: la première colonie d'Occident', *Annales*, 55 (2000), 983–1008.

Tourtoulon, C. de, *Études sur la maison de Barcelone: Jacme Ier le Conquérant, roi d'Aragon . . .* , 2 vols. (Montpellier, 1863–7).

Ubieto Arteta, A., *Historia de Aragón. Creación y desarrollo de la Corona de Aragón* (Zaragoza, 1987).

——, 'La aparición del falso Alfonso I el Batallador', *Argensola*, 9 (1958), 29–38.

——, 'Un frustrado matrimonio de Alfonso II de Aragón', *VII Congreso de la Corona de Aragón*, II (Barcelona, 1962), 263–7.

Ullmann, W., *Principles of Government and Politics in the Middle Ages* (London, 1961).

——, *A Short History of the Papacy in the Middle Ages* (London, 1972).

——, 'The medieval interpretation of Frederick I's authentic "Habita" ', *L'Europa e il diritto romano. Studi in memoria di Paolo Koschaker*, 1 (Milan, 1954), 99–136.

Urvoy, D., 'Une étude sociologique des mouvements religieux dans l'Espagne musulmane de la chute du califat au milieu du XIIIe siècle', *Mélanges de la Casa de Velázquez*, 8 (1972), 223–93.

Vajay, S. de, 'Ramiro II le Moine, roi d'Aragon, et Agnès de Poitou dans l'histoire et dans la légende', in P. Gallais & Y.-J. Rion (eds.), *Mélanges offerts à René Crozet à l'occasion de son soixante-dixième anniversaire* (Poitiers, 1966), II, 727–50.

Valbonnais, J. P. M. de B., *Histoire de Dauphiné et des princes qui ont porté le nom de Dauphin*, 2 vols. (Geneva, 1722).

Valls Taberner, F., 'Relacions familiars i politiques entre Jaume el Conqueridor i Anfós el Savi', *Bulletin Hispanique*, 21 (1919), 9–52.

van Kleffens, E. N., *Hispanic Law until the End of the Middle Ages* (Edinburgh, 1968).

van Koningsveld, P. S. & G. A. Wiegers, 'The polemical works of Muḥammad al-Qaysī (fl. 1309) and their circulation in Arabic and Aljamiado among the Mudejars in the fourteenth century', *al-Qanṭara*, 15 (1994), 163–99.

Vauchez, A., 'Les stigmates de S. François et leurs détracteurs dans les derniers siècles du Moyen Âge', *École Française de Rome: Mélanges d'archéologie et d'histoire*, 80 (1968), 595–625.

Veas Arteseros, F. de A.: see Torres Fontes.

Vega, C. A.: see Márquez Villanueva.

Ventura, J., *Alfons 'el Cast' el primer comte-rei* (Barcelona, 1964).

——, 'El catarismo en Cataluña', *BRABL*, 28 (1959–60), 75–168.

Verlinden, C., *L'Esclavage dans l'Europe médiévale*, I, *Péninsule Ibérique – France* (Bruges, 1955).

Vernet, J., 'Un texto árabe de la corte de Alfonso X el Sabio. Un tratado de autómatas', *al-Andalus*, 43 (1978), 405–21.

——, 'Alfonso X el Sabio: mecánica y astronomía', *Real Academia de Ciencias exactas, físicas y naturales. Conmemoración del centenario de Alfonso X el Sabio. Sesión celebrada el día 4 de Abril de 1984* (Madrid, 1984), 23–32.

Vestiduras pontificales del arzobispo Rodrigo Ximénez de Rada, s. XIII. Su estudio y restauración (Madrid, 1995).

Vestiduras ricas. El monasterio de Las Huelgas y su época (Madrid, 2005).

Vicens Vives, J., *Manual de historia económica de España*, 5th edn (Barcelona, 1967).

——, transl. J. C. Ullman, *Approaches to the History of Spain* (Berkeley & London, 1970).

Vilar, H. Vasconcelos, *Afonso II* (n. p., n. d. ?2005).

Villanueva, Jaime, *Viage literario a las iglesias de España*, 22 vols. (Madrid, 1803–52).

Weiler, B., 'Image and reality in Richard of Cornwall's German career', *EHR*, 113 (1998), 1111–42.

Wieruszowski, H., *Politics and Culture in Medieval Spain and Italy* (Rome, 1971).

Wolff, R. L., 'Mortgage and redemption of an emperor's son: Castile and the Latin Empire of Constantinople', *Speculum*, 29 (1954), 45–84.

Wright, R., *El tratado de Cabreros (1206): estudio sociofilológico de una reforma ortográfica* (London, 2000).

——, 'Latin and Romance in the Castilian chancery (1180–1230)', *BHS* (Liverpool) 73 (1996), 115–28.

Zacour, N., *Jews and Saracens in the Consilia of Oldradus de Ponte* (Toronto, 1990).

Zurita, J. de, *Anales de la Corona de Aragón* [1561–1580], ed. A. Canellas López, I–IV (Zaragoza, 1967–73).

——, *Indices rerum ab Aragoniae regibus gestarum ab initiis regni ad annum MCDX* (Zaragoza, 1578).

Glossary

adelantamiento	frontier official; territory of his jurisdiction
alcalde (mayor)	(senior) municipal judge
alférez real	royal standard-bearer
aljama	community of Jews or Muslims; their governing body
almoxarife mayor	chief tax collector
alvedrio	arbitrary decision
bovatge	an accession tax (in Aragón)
campesino	agricultural worker
cofradía	brotherhood, guild
compadrazgo	relationship between natural parents and god-parents of a child
concejo	municipal council
convivencia	coexistence
dār al-'ahd	area between Islam's homeland and the territory of the infidel
fazanna	oral precedent
fijodalgo **and variants**	member of hereditary nobility
fuero (**Catalan** *fur*)	law code
gonfalonier	standard bearer
hermandad	confraternity having either charitable or political purposes
latifundio	great estate
madrasa	academy of higher learning in which teachers lived as well as taught
mayordomo mayor	official in charge of royal household
mesnad	mounted, armed following
mesnadero	member of *mesnada*

Mozarab	Christian living under Muslim rule
Mudéjar	Muslim living under Christian rule
parias	protection money
privado	favourite
qā'id	military administrator
regidor	royal governor of city
repartidor	official charged with *repartimiento* of territory
repartimiento	process of dividing and distributing lands
ricos hombres; ricos homes	and variants 'according to the custom of Spain [. . .] those who in other lands are called counts or barons' (*Part.* 4.25.10)
sayyid	Almohad prince of the blood
señorío	dominion, lordship
serranos	mountain people
sharī'ah	Islamic religious law
soldadeira	loose woman about court
tercias (reales)	the proportion (two-ninths) of the ecclesiastical tithe appropriated by the Castilian crown
usos	customs
usos desaguisados	unjustifiable customs
vistas	diplomatic gathering
wālī	governor

Index

Abbreviations and contractions: a[rch]b[isho]p; br[other]; ch[urch]; c[oun]tess; c[oun]ty; d[aughter]; dioc[ese]; el[ect]; inf[anta/e]; k[in]gdom; v[is]c[oun]t; q[ueen]; s[on]

Printed and bound by CPI Group (UK) Ltd, Croydon, CR0 4YY
24/09/2021
03084267-0001